The New Era

AMERICAN THOUGHT AND CULTURE

Lewis Perry and Howard Brick, Series Editors

The New Era

American Thought and Culture in the 1920s

Paul V. Murphy

ROWMAN & LITTLEFIELD
Lanham • Boulder • New York • London

Published by Rowman & Littlefield Publishers, Inc.
A wholly owned subsidiary of The Rowman & Littlefield Publishing Group, Inc.
4501 Forbes Boulevard, Suite 200, Lanham, Maryland 20706
www.rowmanlittlefield.com

Unit A, Whitacre Mews, 26-34 Stannary Street, London SE11 4AB

British Library Cataloguing in Publication Information Available

Library of Congress Cataloging-in-Publication Data

The hardback edition of this book was previously cataloged by the Library of Congress
as follows:

Murphy, Paul V. (Paul Vincent), 1966–
  The new era : American thought and culture in the 1920s / Paul V. Murphy.
    p. cm. — (American thought and culture)
  Includes bibliographical references and index.
  1. United States—Civilization—1918–1945. 2. United States—Intellectual life—20th
century. 3. Popular culture—United States—History—20th century. 4. Political
culture—United States—History—20th century. 5. Social change—United States—
History—20th century. I. Title.
  E169.1.M958 2012
  973.91—dc23

                                                                        2011039083

ISBN 978-0-7425-4925-8 (cloth : alk. paper)
ISBN 978-0-7425-4926-5 (pbk. : alk. paper)
ISBN 978-1-4422-1540-5 (electronic)

∞™ The paper used in this publication meets the minimum requirements of
American National Standard for Information Sciences—Permanence of Paper
for Printed Library Materials, ANSI/NISO Z39.48-1992.

Printed in the United States of America

To LAE

Contents

~

Foreword

Over twenty years ago, this series on American Thought and Culture began with the aim of offering concise, provocative volumes that, taken together, would survey the long span of American intellectual and cultural life from the sixteenth century to the present. Since then, the output of richly documented monographs in the field has continued to grow, sustaining the demand for inventive historical syntheses. The goal of the series has always been to bring together readable, well-informed books that stand on their own as introductions to significant periods in American thought and culture. There is no attempt to establish a single interpretation of all of America's past, for the range of American experiences and their change over time would frustrate any such attempt. All the authors in the series, innovative practitioners in the field in their own right, bring their own independent research to bear as they strive for a broad reach in interpretation. They aim to explore issues that are of critical importance to the particular period under discussion and, on that basis, to cast new light on the whole of American experience as it both shaped and was transformed by that time.

The series now nears completion with the publication of this and one additional forthcoming volume treating discrete periods of the twentieth century. The culture and intellectual life of the United States remain subjects of heated debate. Scholars of the mid-twentieth century often assumed that the country bore a common culture that could be summed up in a few basic themes or characteristic dilemmas. By the 1980s, historians were more likely to recognize a plurality of thoughts and traditions in the American past. Variation and contention among the multiple strands of American consciousness made it difficult to achieve a synthetic view of the culture in times past. Nonetheless, the relation between the many and the one continues to preoccupy historical observers. Few historians today are likely to challenge a strong emphasis on diversity among subcultures in American life. At the same time, the international primacy this country has attained—for example, as a purveyor of mass culture, a shaper of world economy, or the superpower whose continued hegemony is now debated—poses still the question of what collective identity or cultural wholeness Americans share. As the United States looks out on the world at large, and the world looks back, who are "we"?

Paul Murphy's book does something entirely new with "The New Era." That phrase has been most often identified with Herbert Hoover and a view that American capitalism had now achieved an unprecedented form. In the 1920s, the American model of capitalism was remarkable in its capacity for growth, for distributing widely the many goods that industry invented daily, for ending the destructive "boom-bust" cycle that proved so costly and humanly destructive through the nineteenth century, and indeed for wiping out poverty in a land of wealth. The inception of the Great Depression made a mockery of such claims. Yet, as Murphy shows, Hoover did not invent the idea. "The New Era" was on almost everyone's lips, here and abroad, meaning simply that whatever came out of the wreckage of the Great War (even if the United States had been able to escape the mass physical destruction of war) would be something vastly different from the past. The decade after World War I was the first time that American intellectuals—who had troubled over the meaning of *modernity* for several decades already—encountered "the new" as the *unquestioned* hallmark of the age. In Murphy's analysis, the idea of cultural lag, coined by sociologist William Ogburn, was overtly or tacitly the common assumption of cultural observers: something was amiss in a land where the new outstripped nearly all inherited religious, cultural, social, and political traditions that had given American life its ballast for generations.

And this very condition put "intellectuals" in a special quandary. While the term *intellectual* was relatively new, men and women of letters had often played a role as moral guardians, the voices of orthodoxy and of all that was morally normative—a key role, that is, as gatekeepers of "culture." The new intellectuals of the 1920s disdained that role, but they also missed it. They were suspected by many conservative Americans of holding disruptive ideas of life as a field of experiment, innovation, and unloosed individualism. Yet the intellectuals, even as they freely voiced their estrangement from the "Babbitts" or the anti-Darwinian "fundamentalists" of the age, still sought a central, recognized social role for themselves. For many, that role amounted to the "reconstruction of the culture"—creating or restoring something to be held in common by Americans at large. But culture itself was now understood in new terms: the anthropological notion of culture, just one way of life governing a group of humans in a world of many cultures, had taken hold, and it consisted of ideas, practices, techniques, values, and attitudes, as well as "symbols," "myths" (not necessarily a pejorative), and "images" (like those of the movies) that made one people distinct among others. However difficult it was for many Americans to accept that notion of cultural relativism—*ways* of life that differed, validly, from one group to another—it was the "intellectuals" whose job it was to make sense of this sphere. Their expertise as observers, analysts, and critics—even creators?—of symbols, myths, and images that structured the common field of social experience gave intellectuals a vocation. This is what made *their* "new era."

Within this framework, Paul Murphy synthesizes an enormous range of intellectual and cultural experience of the 1920s, from popular culture (Buster Keaton's "slapstick," the blues, and the new jazz music) and changing sexual mores and morals to the distinct strains of modern art, including American importers of Europe's transgressive Dada movement, and the sober debates in political philosophy between Walter Lippmann and John Dewey over the prospects of real democracy amid a modern, fractured "public." The ways in which the Harlem Renaissance shouldered the general intellectuals' project of "reconstructing culture" amid overwhelming "newness" receive a wholly original analysis here. Murphy concludes with a careful examination of the tension between "liberal modernism," on the one hand, and traditionalism and conservatism, on the popular level of anti-Darwinianism or the erudite level of the classics-minded "New Humanist" group. The former—the modernist intellectuals imbued with their self-defined vocation as "critics" (and makers and shapers) of symbols, myths, and images—occupied the dominant position in that debate. Thus they were able to define the terms of American intellectual and cultural life for much of the remaining twentieth century.

—Howard Brick and Lewis Perry, Series Editors

~

Acknowledgments

I depended on four libraries in doing the research for this book and am greatly indebted to the staffs of Zumberge Library at Grand Valley State University (including the document delivery staff), Hekman Library at Calvin College, the Grand Rapids Public Library, and the Michigan State University Library. Of the many forms of assistance provided by Grand Valley State University, one of the most important was a sabbatical leave provided early in the course of my research. I wish to thank Howard Brick and Lewis Perry for offering me the opportunity to write this volume, particularly Howard, who has been a thoughtful, generous, and exceedingly patient editor. My thanks, too, to Carrie Broadwell-Tkach and the staff of Rowman & Littlefield, particularly Jehanne Schweitzer and Elizabeth Lund. Sarah Sweers proved an excellent research assistant. Many individuals have provided encouragement and assistance in ways large and small, but I would like especially to thank the following who read the manuscript, in whole and in part; provided a venue for the airing of ideas; or simply offered friendly encouragement: Daniel Borus, George Cotkin, Jason Crouthamel, Lisa Feurzeig, Eugene McCarraher, Doug Montagna, Andy Shankman, John Sienicki, and Steven Rosales. I am most indebted, and most thankful, to those who lived with this project as closely as I have: George, an excellent silent movie companion; John, who arrived in time to provide much good cheer; and Leigh, who allowed me the time needed to complete the book as well as providing support, encouragement, more good cheer, and much else in the bargain.

Introduction

The New Era

In the 1920s, Americans talked of their times as "modern," which is to say, fundamentally different, in pace and texture, from what went before—a new era. "It is a platitude to say that we are at the beginning of a new era facing a wholly altered world," observed James Truslow Adams in 1929. Businessmen heralded a "new economy" resulting from both technological change and managerial innovation. Technology transformed the workplace, allowing greater efficiency and higher profits. Rationalized, expert-run bureaucracies promised a more effectively managed capitalist nation. Social scientists felt social intelligence the new national lodestone. The promise was prosperity for all: As Frederick Lewis Allen observed of the great bull market in his instant history of the 1920s, *Only Yesterday* (1931), "This was a new era. Prosperity was coming into full and perfect flower."[1]

The realization that what had seemed progress was instead a relentless and invariable force that was predictable only in that it would produce profound change, whether for good or ill, wanted or not, was a startling and profound insight of the era and one productive of deep ambivalence. "Never before in the history of mankind have so many and so frequent changes occurred," observed the sociologist William F. Ogburn in *Social Change* (1922). As the flawed hero of Booth Tarkington's fable of change, *The Magnificent Ambersons* (1918), realizes, "nothing stays or holds or keeps where there is growth." The magnificent Amberson family lost their grip on power and wealth, but so, inevitably, will all great families: "The Ambersons had passed, and the new people would pass, and the new people that came after them, and then the next new ones, and the next—and the next," Tarkington wrote. Or as John Dewey observed "nothing stays long put."[2]

The disruptions of the new era were profound. Rural Americans, many from the South, flooded into the cities, which, already reshaped by generations of immigrants, were further transformed as a consequence. Improved machinery displaced industrial workers. A new warp-tying device in the textile industry eliminated ten to fifteen workers per machine, while in automobile manufacturing, one machine that painted stripes on a body eliminated ten workers. Telephones, automobiles, records, and movies invaded America's "rural islands" (William Leuchtenburg's phrase). Small-town and rural Americans no longer lived in relative isolation and sleepy autonomy, connected only tenuously to the poles of American financial, political, and cultural power. New, high-speed connections proliferated, each bringing new items and new data, bits of a new American culture. "Modern inventions and the industrialism that has been built upon them have given us in many respects a new world to live in; we can no more remove ourselves from that world than we can escape from the atmosphere that we breathe," noted the Princeton biblical scholar J. Gresham Machen.[3]

The overwhelming force of this new national culture simultaneously integrated the vast country and disintegrated much previously unquestioned social custom and cultural habit. The narrator of Sherwood Anderson's *Winesburg, Ohio* (1919) commented on the "vast change" that had taken place in the nation since the Civil War: "The coming of industrialism, attended by all the roar and rattle of affairs, the shrill cries of millions of new voices that have come among us from over seas, the going and coming of trains, the growth of cities, the building of the interurban car lines that weave in and out of towns and past farmhouses, and now in these later days the coming of the automobiles has worked a tremendous change in the lives and in the habits of thought of our people of Mid-America." The "farmer by the stove," previously ignorant but also innocent, is now as glib and senseless as the city man. No part of the nation was out of touch of the metropolis, for good or ill. In *Main Street* (1920), Sinclair Lewis dismissed stereotyped images of the small town as hopelessly out-of-date or sturdily virtuous. The modern town was more complex. Gopher Prairie, he declared, "thinks not in hoss-swapping but in cheap motor cars, telephones, ready-made clothes, silos, alfalfa, Kodaks, phonographs, leather-upholstered Morris chairs, bridge-prices, oil-stocks, motion-pictures, land-deals, unread sets of Mark Twain, and a chaste version of national politics."[4]

Disruptions in the social and cultural order redistributed power and authority. Old customs of family, community, and religion withered, and new ways of independent living proliferated. Metropolitan values displaced small-town mores. Numerous American intellectuals had hailed the trends toward consolidation and social unification since the Civil War, even advocating a more powerful, expert-driven state. In the 1920s, what many progressive-minded reformers had wanted was, seemingly, achieved, only to yield second thoughts, an awareness of the costs and dangers of consolidation: a commercialized culture, a single national mind, a conforming people. Moreover, the precise role of intellectuals in such a society was not clear.[5]

For literary intellectuals, Harvard philosopher George Santayana's put-down of American Calvinism and transcendentalism as the "genteel tradition" marks an important point of transition in American intellectual life. As Wilfred M. McClay observed, the "rebellion against Victorianism" derived from Santayana's critique became "one of the organizing principles of 20th-century intellectual activity." Santayana's 1911 lecture shut a door on certain preoccupations of the literary intelligentsia and announced a "new philosophical vista." America was "a young country with an old mentality," Santayana declared. To Santayana, himself an atheist and a pessimist, the Calvinist and transcendentalist traditions, one God-haunted and apocalyptic, the other yea-saying and near pantheistic, evoked the declining Victorian lady of gentility. The genteel tradition was old, "stale," false, retreating before the truths of modern life and incapable of equipping American artists and intellectuals for creative response to a dynamic world. As a result American intellectualism was a becalmed backwater, while industrial, commercial America leaped forward like the Niagara Falls; American life was split between a reproduction colonial mansion and a skyscraper. Intellectuals lived within the feminine mansion.[6]

By the 1920s, then, intellectuals had witnessed a societywide crisis of authority and become acutely aware of a bifurcation between themselves and the rest of society. The inevitable pressure of industrial and technological progress compelled these realizations. Progress—what an older generation assumed to be divinely planned—now seemed more prosaic in its human origins, relentless in its application, and impervious in its independence of any individual or collective intention. It was a force that ran on its own accord. Intellectuals responded in two ways. First, a large number gravitated toward modernist beliefs that were concerned, above all, with the autonomy and independence of writers and artists. These values reinforced a deepening split with many Americans who preserved traditional faiths and expectations. Second, intellectuals redefined and reconceptualized culture in fundamentally new ways that allowed them to style a new kind of cultural politics that could potentially allow them to shape and direct the American response to change.

In the space opened by Santayana's essay, intellectuals championed an insistent, ultimately Romantic imperative for individual autonomy and self-rule. They renounced their older role as moral guardians, one that had given them great influence, in favor of a new role as tribunes of openness, experimentation, and tolerance. In self-consciously repudiating their traditional social responsibility, they were embracing modernism. Even while placing themselves at odds with the broader public, however, intellectuals defined a new and potentially vital public role as cultural critics. They did this in part by reimagining the very meaning of culture. In the nineteenth century, culture had been bound up with individual moral self-development and personal refinement; intellectuals now saw it as something broader and all-inclusive, and they gave themselves the role of interpreting it.

Van Wyck Brooks exemplified the hankering for a cultural politics of a younger generation of intellectuals. In *America's Coming-of-Age* (1915), he envisioned intellectuals creating a new national art and literature that would ameliorate what he saw as the destructive effects of industrialism and would instead foster an organic community in America. He divided American intellectual life between highbrow and lowbrow, meaning by this not just the coexistence of separate literatures, one high and dry, the other popular and best-selling, but in a more general sense, the separation of culture itself from the everyday, "catchpenny realities" of American life. He blamed the long-term effects of the Puritan impulse to otherworldliness for this unhealthy disjunction. What modern Americans needed, Brooks averred, was a middle ground of discourse, the level of artistic and literary work that would be intellectual and broadly appealing. Isolated and abstracted, culture was unable to accomplish its rightful task, which was to modify competitive individualism and make people whole. Brooks aspired to foster a new relationship between intellectuals and the broader public founded on a program of cultural renewal.[7]

The fruits of this intellectual ferment were contradictory: Modernism accentuated intellectuals' distance from the mainstream of society, yet the embrace of cultural criticism—the expert analysis of culture but often, too, the advocacy of cultural reconstruction exemplified by Brooks—suggested a desire for intimate connection. The resulting pattern of self-contradiction and ambivalence defined American thought and culture in the 1920s and for a significant period thereafter. American intellectuals tended to think the American public needed to adjust its values and beliefs to match realities of modern life; Americans needed to catch up. Intellectuals also expressed an intense desire to immerse themselves in the quotidian realities of American life, to root themselves in a national or ethnic past, and to provide new sym-

bols, myths, or images that would foster moral progress and the full achievement of personality.

Used loosely and retrospectively, _modernism_ evokes a mélange of intellectual positions and tendencies growing out of conflicting European intellectual traditions.[8] In each instance, modernists responded to new scientific
and philosophical claims—evolution, Freudian psychoanalysis, the Higher
Criticism, theories of relativity, new principles of uncertainty. However,
first and foremost, modernism was an internal discussion among artists and
writers about their own precarious social status, which resulted from a loss
of a vital connection between themselves and the masses. Modernists posed
key questions about art: Should it represent a recognizable figure? Need it be
broadly appealing or readily understood? The answers produced the distinctive features of modernism: movements toward abstraction in visual art; ato-
nality in music; and stream of consciousness, free association, and fractured
narrative lines in literature. Modernism redefined aesthetic criteria in terms
of the values and intentions of the artist. The art object would be judged on
its own terms, free and independent of the audience's response. Individual
autonomy and integrity, not tradition or communal responsibility, were
the essential values. Modernist intellectuals crafted a highly individualistic
credo, one that embraced the emerging bifurcation between the intellectuals
and the public.

Prior to the twentieth century, "culture" had been a marker of native-
born, middle-class elite gentility.[9] The term derived from horticultural usage
(tending to the growth of a plant). Insofar as culture fostered moral and
aesthetic refinement and implied an individual process of self-culture, it had
been a powerful and prevalent discourse of self-rule (both collective and
individual) since before the nation's founding.[10] As a process of moral and
aesthetic refinement, culture distinguished the refined sensibility from the
money-conscious commercial mind. For the American middle classes in the
nineteenth century, culture amounted to the "key term in an ideology that
honored good manners," an essential part of what made a family respectable.
All could avail themselves of culture but not through simple purchase; as
an "inward virtue" of taste and character, genuine culture was only created
through extended self-development.[11] In the nineteenth century, culture had
constituted the gap between the refined and the masses. Twentieth-century
critics understood that this was true no longer. In a consumer society, fine
clothing or furniture could be purchased; cheap facsimiles proliferated. Distinctions of taste lost force, and high art (another meaning of _culture_) was increasingly relegated to the symphony hall, museum, and library, cut off from
the vibrant thoroughfares of modern life. By the 1920s, the great Niagara of

American industrial growth seemed more imposing than ever and threatened to supplant culture entirely.

Culture, reimagined in dramatically different ways, allowed younger intellectuals to remain loyal to modernist values and at the same time assume a broader influence. Anthropologists played the key role in this project by promoting a concept of culture as the holistic account of a people's distinctive way of living—their values, beliefs, practices, worldview, and technologies. In the anthropologists' conception, culture was less about choice, either on the individual or social level, than an explanation of how choices were limited, how an outlook was determined by centuries of evolutionary development. They dispensed with distinctions between highbrow and lowbrow, civilized and primitive. Culture simply was. The anthropological perspective was pluralist and relativist: All peoples possessed a general pattern of belief and values, which resulted from a historical and contingent evolutionary process and reflected unique environmental and sociological conditions.

The career of one of the most important younger critics of the 1920s, Edmund Wilson, illuminates the transformations experienced by this generation of intellectuals. Raised in a comfortable bourgeois household in New Jersey (his father was a Republican state attorney general who served under Woodrow Wilson), Wilson imbibed the ideology of culture at boarding school and eventually Princeton University, where he studied British literature and Latin and Greek. (He remembered his collegiate delight upon acquiring the imposing Liddell and Scott Greek-English lexicon, swinging it with one hand as he bicycled from the bookstore.) While his training allowed Wilson to dispute with traditionalist critics on matters of Greek translation as a mature critic, his outlook was essentially modernist. Wilson was a religious skeptic from the time he was in boarding school, and his Princeton mentor, the German émigré Christian Gauss, communicated a *fin de siècle* aestheticism to Wilson, upholding the special morality of the artist, which was centered above all on "fidelity to a kind of truth that is rendered by the discipline of aesthetic form." Modern Americans must make their own ideals of beauty, righteousness, and justice.[12]

In the 1920s, Wilson became a model of the new, wide-ranging cultural critic. Intellectuals were recognizing that they constituted a new social class defined by intellect and not wealth. (In the years between the world wars, New York City became "the home for intellectuals who coalesced in the first significant intelligentsia in the country's history.") They were in a position to break free of the obligations of moral uplift that were part and parcel of the nineteenth-century ideology of culture.[13] At the same time, Wilson and other modernist critics possessed a strong desire to bridge the gap between intellectuals and the public. For all of his aestheticism, Wilson chose literary journalism as a career and reveled in the hedonistic pleasures of New York in the 1920s. After service in the hospital corps and military intelligence during the Great War, Wilson made his career in New York City as a writer, editor, and, above all, critic, reviewing writers high and low. He would assess Alexander Pope and Alfred Lord Tennyson and also comment appreciatively on the character of the magician and escape artist Harry Houdini. He initiated a groundbreaking study of the Symbolist poets and also expressed his delight in the vulgarities of the National Winter Garden's burlesque show. Wilson's commitment to the truth of aesthetic form led to an experimental novel; his devotion to plebeian pleasures took the form of an acute attention to popular entertainments; and his adoption of a modern sexual morality led to numerous sexual liaisons (minutely detailed in journals) and a long-term affair with Frances Minihan, a waitress and taxi dancer.[14]

While modernist impulses set many American intellectuals and artists in the 1920s apart from society, the aspiration to become arbiters of cultural change promoted connection. The critic and cultural theorist Lewis Mumford typified modernist dismay at American society when he scorned the "soporific" rather than stimulating urban lyceum lectures of the cities. The lectures were a substitute for thought in the same way church attendance was a substitute for religion, he declared, the "prayer wheels of a preoccupied commercialism."[15] His response was to craft a cultural theory centered on fashioning symbols that would foster organic community and reintegrate America. When thinking of cultural power, intellectuals sometimes spoke in terms of symbols, images, and myths, terms that evoked for them the forms in which great, overarching ideas were embodied—the ways in which culture worked. Modernist poets replaced things with symbols, Wilson observed in a review of the work of Wallace Stevens and E. E. Cummings. In another review, he claimed that influential critics addressed modern discontents through the promulgation of powerful myths. The radical novelist John Dos Passos, for example, indulged in the "myth of a serious-minded and clear-eyed proletariat"; the conservative T. S. Eliot favored the "aristocratic myth" of English royalism and high-church Anglicism. "The task of the intellectual is not merely to study the common life but to make his thoughts and symbols *seem* relevant to it—that is, to express them in terms of the actual American world without either cheapening them or rendering them vapid," Wilson declared. The notion that symbols and images were immensely powerful and the constitutive elements of a new cultural politics was becoming a critical commonplace.[16]

American intellectuals committed to both modernism and culture generated a profoundly ambivalent body of criticism. The bifurcation between a new class of intellectuals and the larger society mirrored their own self-division. Increasingly self-conscious of their distinct status in America, many often felt set apart—irrelevant, scorned, out of step with the larger society, or alienated from it. The story of American thought and culture in the 1920s is one of an emerging generation of modernist and liberal-minded intellectuals trying to identify their role in a complex and evolving America. They betrayed many contradictory impulses and much ambivalence: Intellectuals embraced modernist values that they perceived the public to resist, attributing this disparity to "cultural lag." Critical of the commercialized culture of the masses, they consistently missed the ways in which popular culture served popular desires and was often responsive to popular tastes. Desiring to root themselves in the culture of the folk or to identify themselves with the artifacts of machine-age America, their ambitious agendas to reconstruct American culture frequently fell short. The impulse to tap into a root identity often failed to satisfy in personal ways. Prone to the assumption of a single American mind, they missed the ethnic and racial hybridity occurring all around them. Aiming to vindicate democracy, they inevitably were drawn to theories of elite control. Only at the end of the decade did the new generation of cultural critics, now self-consciously modernist, begin to come to terms with their unalterable ambivalence toward modern American life.

The popular perception of the 1920s long derived from Frederick Lewis Allen's bemused panorama of American consumerism, "ballyhoo," and faddishness in *Only Yesterday*. As early as the 1950s, historians began to discard this image of a carefree and hedonistic 1920s as well as the mythology of the "Lost Generation" expatriate writers generated by Ernest Hemingway, F. Scott Fitzgerald, and other writers of the time and focus consistently on the profound conflict generated by social and cultural change. Emphases have shifted to racial antagonisms, anti-immigrant legislation, and the brief ascendancy of the Ku Klux Klan since that time, yet the story of the 1920s has remained one of social, political, and cultural turmoil.[17] The history of American intellectual life in the decade likewise has been defined by change. Henry May stressed the shift from a common culture to the social-scientific faith in "social intelligence" as the means to effective social management. He found *Recent Social Trends* (1933), the two-volume report of the President's Committee on Social Trends, a text illustrative of the decade—a "work of art as well as of social science" and "one of the few books about the twenties that point the way toward a comprehensive understanding of the period." May and later Warren Susman linked the decade to the long-term reconceptualization of culture and the role of intellectuals. Susman found 1920s intellectuals obsessively focused on the instrumentalities of mass communication and fretful about the viability of communities; he premised his interpretation of the decade on the communications revolution and the organizational imperatives of the new national professional class, emphasizing the way in which mass communications and modern transportation created a world more individualistic, consumerist, and permissive than that which existed before. Communications displaced an older order based on place and community; contemporaries noted ironically and perhaps regretfully that "in a new era of advanced and easy communications men had increasingly little they wanted to, or were able to, communicate with each other." Susman cited the poet Vachel Lindsay who suggested that American civilization becomes "more hieroglyphic every day."[18]

We live in a "new world of new knowledge," Susman declared, a "new age of criticism," premised on the hope that knowledge and criticism themselves will bridge the discomfiting gap between old and new, between community and the system of mass communications that erodes it. Modernism and the new conception of culture, both crucial to a generation of intellectuals, posed dilemmas intellectuals needed to resolve: Can intellectuals and artists be a part of modern American culture, *join in it*, and still maintain their standards and integrity? Given the atomized nature of American culture, can Americans escape the pressures of conformity conveyed in increasingly standardized and nationalized cultural products? As Warren Susman noted, due to the specialization of intellectual inquiry and knowledge in the 1920s, "the great fear that runs through much of the writing of the 1920s and 1930s is whether any great industrial and democratic mass society can maintain a significant level of civilization, and whether mass education and mass communication will allow any civilization to survive."[19]

In the 1920s writers, artists, and social scientists took art and culture—and themselves—very seriously, bequeathing to succeeding generations of critics a way of thinking, speaking, and writing in images, symbols, and myths—the constitutive elements, they thought, of a national culture and popular mind and the basis, ultimately, of a new and powerful cultural politics. In the wake of the Great War, Alfred Kazin observed, liberal critics "enjoyed a public prestige and position which afforded them unusual cultural influence and an intoxicating sense of their own power."[20] They had created new critical vocabularies and promoted a vocational self-identity as broad-ranging, erudite, and self-confident experts in the many modes of cultural production. This was an outlook most ably represented by self-consciously modernist men and women, notably the New York Intellectuals: Lionel Trilling, Dwight Macdonald, and the *Partisan Review* circle as well as a network of other ambitious, brilliant, and polymathic thinkers. There was a political valence to their modernism, and it was liberal, and there was a historical root, which lay in the 1920s.

After the 1920s, culture became the essential terrain of social and political action. Modernist liberals valued freedom of thought and expression, an open and critical spirit, tolerance and cosmopolitanism. They assumed that a national culture was subject to competition and control. It was worth fighting for: whoever could shape public perceptions could redirect the course of the national mind. The progressive-minded, the partisans of youth, and the experimental and avant-garde fought their conservative opponents for the right to control culture, but, in a larger sense, the battle was over what force would shape change—industrial and technological progress or culture. Would the nation be defined by purely industrial and commercial imperatives or humanistic ones? Whether modern culture would keep up with the forces of social, technological, and political transformation (with "growth" broadly defined) remained, as it had in Santayana's lecture, very much an open question.

CHAPTER ONE

∼

The Gay Table

The old and new were often in stark juxtaposition in the 1910s and 1920s. Ernest Hemingway remembered that a goatherder would bring a flock through the streets of his Paris neighborhood, alerting customers by playing pipes and providing fresh milk on the spot. On an adventurous 1916 cross-country automobile western tour along sometimes rutted roads, Sinclair Lewis and his wife, Grace, encountered homesteaders driving a prairie schooner. Such incidents reinforced the sense of life lived amidst intense change, a mode conducive to nostalgia and intimations of rebirth. Looking back, the southern poet Allen Tate felt that the South, as it "reentered" the world after the Great War, "gave a backward glance as it stepped over the border: that backward glance gave us the Southern renascence, a literature conscious of the past in the present." The same might be said for African American literature, as black intellectual and artistic life blossomed in Harlem and American letters more generally. Historic preservation and public commemoration of the past accelerated in the 1920s: the nation dedicated the Lincoln Memorial in 1922; the Thomas Jefferson Memorial Society purchased Monticello in 1925; the Rockefeller-funded restoration of colonial Williamsburg began in 1926 and, in the same year, Henry Ford began construction of Greenfield Village, his idiosyncratic collection of restored chunks of the American past; Henry Francis du Pont began the collection of antique American furnishings that would become the heart of the Winterthur Museum in 1927.[1]

This consciousness of the past was perhaps a function of so much that was novel in Americans' lives. "By the 1920s the sense of change had penetrated to the roots of popular thought," Roderick Nash asserted.[2] The first crushing wave of mass culture entranced millions: the mass-produced automobiles, the black-white hybrid of jazz music, the jabbing cynicism of the "smart set" wits and the fashionable pessimism of the "lost generation" modernists, the charismatic Greenwich Village bohemians like the poet Edna St. Vincent Millay espousing passion and free love, the awe-inspiring sports heroes and glamorous movie icons who now became mass-marketed "celebrities," and the passing fads and fancies of a prosperous white middle class, led first and foremost by its insouciant sons and daughters, the pioneers of "youth." The new era brought a new morality—a "fun morality" of pleasure-seeking and recreation, perhaps in Florida, the carefree land of sun and leisure that boomed in the mid-1920s—and a new promise of democratized consumption, driven by machine-age gains in productivity that could ensure plenty for everyone. In short, the new era of the 1920s defined a modern American mass culture founded upon optimism, joy in the goods of life, and a commitment to personal fulfillment (or, to those of a more critical bent, complacency, greed, and license). One might find hedonism in this hypercharged thirst for pleasure, recreation, and plenty, or perhaps greed, but it was a greediness of spirit, and it was aimed at a kind of fulfillment deeper than material.

It was this hearty embrace of a commercialized mass culture, with its often cheap character and the seemingly crude and superficial pleasures it provided, that troubled intellectuals and widened the gap between them and the mass public. Conservative or liberal, traditionalist or modernist, critics stood aghast before the perceived meretricious pleasures of American society at the peak of its pre-Depression, consumer-driven boom. Lacking the inclination to uphold genteel standards and the authority to do so, intellectuals needed new methods even to conceptualize and analyze what they were seeing, and the emerging discipline of cultural anthropology provided them. A new form of criticism and set of values were implicit in the new cultural analysis. Even as liberal intellectuals articulated critical tools for analyzing culture, they repeatedly put themselves at variance with popular assumptions. This was evident in the popularity of William F. Ogburn's notion of "cultural lag."

A sociologist at Columbia University and later the University of Chicago, Ogburn believed there are distinct components of culture: material culture (the tools, instruments, and technologies that humans create) and folkways and social institutions (social mores, customs, habits, philosophy, law, government). "Cultural inertia" may result in a faltering adaptation of folkways and social institutions to the changes wrought by industry and technology.

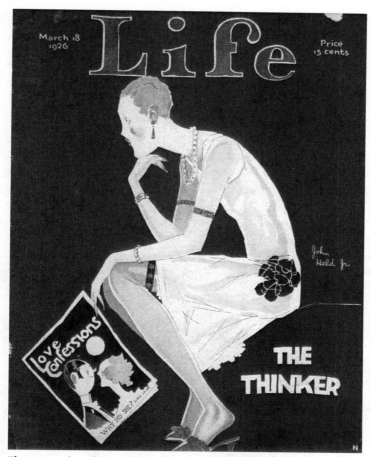

The cartoonist John Held Jr., a Mormon from Salt Lake City who made his reputation with witty illustrations and cartoons for magazines such as *Life* and the *New Yorker*, reflects a popular stereotype of young women in the 1920s: sexually bold, deeply informed on romance, but intellectually shallow.

"The Thinker," cover of *Life*, March 18, 1926. Courtesy Prints and Photographs Division, Library of Congress, LC-USZC4-5627.

Because "the various parts of modern culture are not changing at the same rate," folkways and social institutions (the "adaptive culture") may fail to keep up with the material fruits of industrial and technological change, resulting in cultural lag, a problem of "maladjustment." So, for example, the belief that women belonged in the home was an example of cultural lag, as it persisted despite the fact that so many functions of housekeeping previously composing a woman's labor, such as weaving or soapmaking, were now done in factories. In various and sundry ways, liberal intellectuals considered themselves to be advancing healthy adaptations to the modern age and were frustrated at the inability of all Americans to adjust to new values.[3]

⁓

The Great War signaled an end to the nineteenth-century social and international order in Europe and to complacent assumptions that progress in human affairs was a natural and beneficent process. The epochal slaughter led many artists and intellectuals to conclude that the moral nature of modern humanity was, in T. S. Eliot's conceit, a "waste land." American involvement in the war had been sharp, massive, and unprecedented, not only in the domestic divisions that marked the home front (the progressive administration of President Woodrow Wilson pursued unity of opinion with alacrity) and the outfitting and dispatch of a large military expeditionary force to Europe but also in the scope of federal power required for economic mobilization. The end of the war introduced several years of tumult: President Wilson negotiated a peace treaty committing the United States to membership in a new League of Nations, which the Republican-controlled Senate refused to ratify; labor strife broke out across the country, with over four million workers participating in strikes at some point, a peak of labor mobilization in a decade marked by strife between capital and labor; business interests and the newly founded American Legion joined Attorney General A. Mitchell Palmer in launching a "red scare," a fierce campaign against socialists, anarchists, and other radicals, which was punctuated by a wave of anarchist bombings in 1919 targeting public officials, including Palmer; and racial violence, including a devastating two-week riot in Chicago, broke out across the country in 1919. Republican Warren Harding won the 1920 presidential election promising conservative leadership, and Republicans succeeded with a highly nationalistic platform. Within four years, Congress passed the most restrictive immigration law in its history.[4]

Progressives initially looked forward to a postwar "reconstruction," a projected burst of social reform. They envisioned public ownership of the railroads, utilities, and natural resources; national welfare and social insurance programs; new federal conservation, public works, and home-building programs; civil rights protections; and labor regulations that would help realize the dream of "industrial democracy," a term which implied better pay and work conditions for industrial laborers but also the sharing of power with workers in the workplace. Such a reconstruction was not to happen, as the Wilsonian coalition of labor, western and southern farmers, social justice activists, and independent radicals collapsed, yet for many social scientists the war years were remembered fondly as a moment when their skills were in demand by the federal government and visions of a technocratic state seemed possible.[5]

American novelists, speaking for the younger generation, voiced bitter disillusionment and evoked a tragic sensibility, typified in the heroes of Ernest Hemingway's novels and stories—broken war veterans living by a demanding credo of their own design. John Dos Passos's protagonist in *Three Soldiers* (1921), John Andrews, a self-loathing composer, provides another example. Andrews initially welcomed the erasure of his personality by his military training, as he became an indistinguishable part of a larger unit. ("This is what he had sought when he had enlisted. . . . He was sick of revolt, of thought, of carrying his individuality like a banner above the turmoil.") Andrews eventually rebels against the regimentation of mind and body as well as the glib pieties of the spokesmen of war. He sees that combat is inglorious and marked by casual barbarities. His artistic temperament revives as he becomes a disillusioned protester. Andrews contrasts the "pitifully arid" modern world with Renaissance Italy. "Men seemed to have shrunk in stature before the vastness of the mechanical contrivances they had invented," he feels. In love with a French woman, he eventually deserts the army in a futile but authentic act of nonconformity. In *This Side of Paradise* (1920), F. Scott Fitzgerald generalized the sentiment to all young men, the romantic victims, generation after generation, of the "old cries" and "old creeds" of "dead statesmen and poets," doomed ever and again to find these beliefs hollow, and "all Gods dead, all wars fought, all faiths in men shaken."[6]

E. E. Cummings, in *The Enormous Room* (1922), a memoir of his misadventures while a member of the French Norton-Harjes Ambulance Corps during the war, provided an epitome of the attitude. Unhappy in the ambulance corps once in France, Cummings found himself imprisoned by French authorities in a detention center for suspected traitors and prostitutes with his friend William Slater Brown due to Brown's ill-considered remarks on the war in letters home. In the book, Cummings celebrated the impudent rebellions of the center's inmates as acts of romantic defiance of rationalized authority. He hated the director of the center, whom he considered a petty tyrant. In war "any little annoying habits of independent thought or action" become treason. He drew strength from the simple, decent, even primitive French commoners imprisoned alongside him. In his upside-down telling of the war, the tough, defiant, and in his view beautiful prostitutes were heroes (or antiheroes) deserving honor; the authorities were obscene and justly objects of scorn. He recalled one prostitute who showed no "Fear" in the face of the officials; she was "someone finally completely and unutterably Alive," whom the director's "slavering tongue . . . could not kill."[7]

Not all veterans were traumatized; Hemingway returned from his experience as an ambulance driver in Italy eager to bask in the glory of his exploits. Despite the inauspicious beginnings of the decade, which included an economic recession, Americans were primed for the consumption of goods and entertainment on a large scale. In the new economy of the 1920s, Americans experienced—and embraced—a typical twentieth-century, and now twenty-first-century, pattern of growth: technological innovation and improved efficiency yielded more, better, and less expensive consumer goods; more Americans experienced affluence as the middle class expanded, and many reaped enormous profits; however, the bottom segment of the labor market shared to a lesser degree in prosperity, as wages increased more slowly and, in some cases, stagnated and as, at the same time, consumer debt ballooned. In other words, Americans enjoyed a bubble economy. Finding no productive outlet, business profits and the wealthy's earnings went into speculative investment.[8]

The American economy of the 1920s grew remarkably: industrial production rose 64 percent over the decade and the gross national product increased almost 40 percent between 1919 and 1929. Car production alone shot up from 1.5 million in 1919 to 4.8 million in 1929; by the latter year, 26 million cars and trucks were on the road. Mechanization and the increased use of electricity increased productivity gains. Output per worker increased over 70 percent, with labor productivity in manufacturing increasing 43 percent between 1919 and 1929. New industries such as aluminum, food canning, chemicals, and synthetics advanced quickly from 1914 onward; the production of Bakelite, lacquers, and cellophane boomed.

Per capita income rose and real wages of some workers advanced, but in general corporate profits were not passed along as higher wages, a fact which contributed to the consumer economy's stall later in the decade. Wages varied significantly, depending on skill level, race, ethnicity, and gender; for example, wages in manufacturing rose at only a modest rate. The wages of workers in "sick" industries like cotton mills, bituminous coal mining, railroads, and shipping, as well as the wages of common laborers and women workers, stagnated. Unemployment rates were low but noticeable, ranging from an estimated 3.3 to 5.1 percent and perhaps as much as 7 percent for nonfarm workers. Due to increased mechanization and productivity, the large increase in production did not result in new capital investment and therefore large numbers of new industrial jobs. Layoffs and underemployment were chronic problems for workers; many workers were displaced and many farmers were also in chronic distress. There was little margin of security for working families; one-third to two-fifths of all nonfarm family incomes fell at or below the poverty line in 1929, and perhaps 40 percent had incomes insufficient for an adequate diet.

The increased profits of manufacturing corporations, which derived from the rapid gains in output and productivity (corporate profits rose 63 percent and dividends doubled as the share of corporate revenue going to wages declined), did not result in a proportional increase in productive domestic capital investment (and after 1927 foreign capital investment). Rather, some of the profits were deposited in commercial banks, which fed speculative investment. Consumers' outlay rose 37 percent from 1922 to 1929, which drove a large increase in production of consumer durable goods. Debt grew. The personal savings rate dropped by almost half in the 1920s, debt as share of income doubled, and installment debt on consumer durable goods tripled. Consumer debt for the purchase of cars alone increased 500 percent between 1922 and 1929. By 1929, 90 percent of taxpayers had less disposable income than in 1922. Nevertheless, despite the exceedingly variegated economic reality of the "roaring" 1920s (continued economic insecurity, variable gains in wages, and persisting long work hours for many), the relative changes for many were immense and advantageous. Consumer goods proliferated and the length of the average workweek declined, even if many were increasingly in debt. The nation was wealthy, even if the wealth was not evenly distributed. For much of the decade, the promise of future gains seemed great.

Economic growth fed social transformation, and the scale of both was matched by cultural change. The scope and content of change were conveyed by the mass media, the symbols of the new were women's emancipation and a broader sexual freedom for both sexes, and the agents of change were youth. Contemporary critics of American culture drew inspiration from the dynamism of American life, the eagerness with which youth shed the ideology of culture and refashioned its rules. Young people embodied the optimism of the 1920s and became—particularly young adults in college—the subject of popular fascination.

The emblem of modernity was the city. The 1920 census was the historical marker of the national shift from rural to urban (something of a statistical exaggeration, "urban" being towns with over 2500 inhabitants; the percentage of Americans living in villages below this line fell to 48.6 percent in 1920 from 54.2 percent in 1910). Over the decade, approximately six million Americans moved to a city, and urban population grew 27 percent.[9] The impact was visual: in the comedy silents of the period, the navigation of crowded streets or the attempt to jump on a packed streetcar became setups for gags, as did reckless and haphazard automobile driving. Youth and urban life converged: in his hugely popular screen comedies, Harold Lloyd's screen persona of the innocent but ambitious young man on the make often was negotiating the move from the sleepy village to the bustling city. Allen Tate moved to New York in 1924 and thrilled at the "mere *physique*" of the city and marveled at the subway system: "Fancy going under a huge river at the rate of 40 miles an hour!" What New York offered a young southerner like Tate was freedom from strict moral codes and the censoriousness of his native region. He longed, he wrote, "merely to live as a civilized being in a place where it isn't important whether you drink liquor or are a virgin." Tate was not the first provincial artist to find his home in the city, nor the only one in the 1920s.[10]

Sexuality lay at the center of a new imagery of youth-driven freedom. To the astute mythologizer of American culture, F. Scott Fitzgerald, the unleashing of sexual energies constituted the main innovation of the era. In "Echoes of the Jazz Age," he chronicled the popular embrace of hedonism and pleasure-seeking; the 1920s was a decade-long dinner party, with Americans choosing a seat at either the "gay table" or "sober table." In matters of sex, petting, prewar "social revelation" to some, went mainstream. "Only in 1920 did the veil finally fall—the Jazz Age was in flower." This meant dropping inhibitions, embracing pleasure, *being honest*. Attitudes toward sex revealed an entirely new attitude of openness, rebellion, and shamelessness. Youth took the lead, but not for long. "The sequel was like a children's party taken over by the elders. . . . " It was a "whole race going hedonistic, deciding on pleasure."[11]

Middle-class Americans adopted sexual norms previously more characteristic of the working class and bohemians, reflecting trends in place since the turn of the century. Limited evidence suggests that the percentage of women coming of age in the 1920s who engaged in premarital sex increased to about 50 percent of the cohort, although this usually meant intercourse with the man whom they planned to marry. Rituals of courtship among young people changed: by the mid-1920s dating almost completely replaced older customs of courtship, in which a young man paid a call at a young woman's home under the supervision of her parents. When dating, men and women went out unchaperoned, pursuing pleasure in public, commercial venues in which mixed-sex mingling was the norm. Hollywood films often featured Coney Island–style amusement parks; Coney Island was the scene of first dates in *The Crowd* (1928) and the Clara Bow vehicle *It* (1927). In Muncie, Indiana, in the 1920s, even as premarital sex remained taboo, the rules governing the behavior of adolescent boys and girls relaxed. As dating replaced group parties, "lovemaking in public" became more acceptable among groups of youth viewing movies together, and schools provided more education on sexual hygiene. Dating and privacy, whether attained in the darkened movie theater or the auto, resulted in an increase in sexual play, or "petting"; one 1924 study found that 92 percent of college women admitted to petting at some point.[12]

Movies reflected this loosening of mores: despite a very public display of moral self-policing by Hollywood studios in the 1920s, films still featured a significant amount of flesh and sexual promiscuity. Most every female star did a lingerie scene, according to the historian Mary P. Ryan. Muncie film-goers could enjoy "sensational society films," which proved quite popular, including *Alimony, Married Flirts, The Daring Years, Sinners in Silk, Women Who Give, The Price She Paid, Rouged Lips,* and *The Queen of Sin.* (Sensationalistic romance magazines like *True Confessions, Telling Tales,* and *True Stories* were rampant.)[13] Even mainstream films featured glimpses of women's breasts and male buttocks. Gloria Swanson entered the bath shielded only by a diaphanous wrap in *Male and Female* (1919); Clara Bow displayed her cleavage bending low in *Wings* (1927). Sexual heat featured prominently in Hollywood melodrama, with the vampish Nita Noldi declaring to a young bullfighter played by Rudolph Valentino in *Blood and Sand* (1922), "Some day you will beat me with those strong hands! I should like to know what it feels like." Gloria Swanson's title character in *Sadie Thompson* (1928), based on a W. Somerset Maugham story subsequently turned into the Broadway play *Rain*, was a stunningly alluring fallen women, triumphing over a would-be reforming minister by the end of the film, who commits suicide after seduction by the falsely penitent Thompson. In *Flesh and the Devil* (1927), Greta Garbo demands a cigarette in the dark outdoors from her future lover, played by John Gilbert, a prop that, over the course of the scene, holds ever greater phallic significance. In *The Mysterious Lady* (1928), the seductress places the right hand of her lover over her own left hand, which in turn is placed over one of her breasts. Douglas Fairbanks's lavish fantasy *The Thief of Bagdad* (1924) featured cadres of bare-chested men and midriff-baring women attendants, the preening Fairbanks taking pride of place among them.

Gay men created a distinctive, somewhat autonomous, and relatively open gay culture in early twentieth-century America, comprised of a variety of social networks that developed around particular neighborhoods (such as Greenwich Village, Harlem, and Times Square in New York City), institutions (the YMCA, cafés, cafeterias, and bathhouses), and customs (for example, extravagant drag balls). Although most gay men hid their identities, they do not seem to have felt isolated, ashamed, or "closeted." The image of the closet did not develop in the gay community until the 1960s. (The self-designation "gay" was not frequently used until later, as well; in the 1920s, homosexual men considered themselves "queer" or, if gender-identifying themselves as female, used the identifier "fairy.") When gay men talked of "coming out" at this time, they were burlesquing the culture of debutantes and their formal presentation at annual society balls. "Gay people in the pre-war years, then, did not speak of *coming out of* what we call the 'gay closet,'" observed the historian George Chauncey, "but rather of *coming out into* what they called 'homosexual society' or the 'gay world,' a world neither so small, nor so isolated, nor, often, so hidden as 'closet' implies."[14]

Large-scale drag balls became important institutions of community building among gays while simultaneously allowing both gays and straights to transgress social boundaries. They first began to occur regularly in the 1890s, patterned on popular masquerade balls. The Hamilton Lodge Ball held in Harlem, at which the gay element was predominant in the 1920s, when it became known as the "Faggots Ball," had been organized by the Odd Fellows since 1867. By the late 1920s, several major drag balls were held in New York City every year (drag balls were held in other cities as well), in venues as prominent as Madison Square Garden, and were enormously popular. In 1920s New York, there was a veritable "pansy craze," as broad public interest in gay life led to gay novels, films, and dramas as well as the popularity of gay performers in nightclubs.[15]

"Men and women are ignoring old laws," observed Freda Kirchwey, introducing a symposium on "Our Changing Morality" based on a series of articles from the *Nation*. The bulk of the contributors welcomed changing moral standards, particularly the end of the double standard by which women were judged more harshly than men. The English philosopher and critic Bertrand Russell advocated legal divorce and free and consensual sexual intercourse. "The cramping of love by institutions is one of the major evils of the world," he declared. "The sex relations of an individual should no more be subjected to social legislation than his friendships," argued Barnard philosophy professor Isabel Leavenworth. Rather, sexual experiences, she suggested, "like other experiences, can be judged of only on the basis of the part which they play in the creative drama of the individual soul." The veteran bohemian Floyd Dell argued that changing sexual standards gave men and women an equality of choice, which, for the first time, allowed genuine friendships between men and women, succored (as friendships must be) by long talks, perhaps at a restaurant, even until past midnight. (Sexual attraction would be inevitable in such friendships, and married partners must expect occasional "exuberances," which should be less disruptive given the new sexual ethics.)[16]

In *Love in the Machine Age*, published in 1930, Dell strongly advocated monogamous relationships and marriage, however, he was among a number of advocates of a new, more modern, conception of marriage, rooted above all in a revised perspective on sexuality. Judge Ben Lindsey, a noted Progressive Era proponent of juvenile courts, sparked a passionate debate in the summer of 1927 with his proposal for "companionate marriage," a term first used by a historian in 1924 to describe marriages entered into for companionship and not children. In *The Companionate Marriage* (1927), coauthored with journalist Wainwright Evans, Lindsey imagined young people marrying with the intention of delaying a family. The woman could work and the couple would have access to birth control and educational materials on sex; as long as they had no children, they should be allowed to divorce by mutual consent. Lindsey believed passionately that young people, even if defying social norms by engaging in premarital sex, were essentially good and, in fact, were abiding by their own moral code, one less hypocritical than that of their elders. The proposal for companionate marriage recognized their need for fulfilling sexual relationships. While conservatives were appalled at what they considered "trial marriage" (a characterization Lindsey vigorously denied), the broader effort to modernize marriage stressed the value and desirability of sexual expression and the vital role of a healthy sexual relationship in a good marriage; the right of couples to privacy and to be free of the intrusion of others, particularly authorities, into their marriage; and the importance of greater equality between men and women. There were limits to this vision of equality and sexual freedom: few argued, as did Crystal Eastman, that both boys and girls should be trained for careers and housework or, as did free love advocates, that marriage should be nonmonogamous (although Lindsey considered open marriages fine for couples without children). Indeed, most marriage revisionists assumed that women would leave the workforce after the arrival of children and assume primary responsibility for childcare.[17]

The cultural prominence of the "new psychology," particularly the vogue for Freudian psychoanalysis, reflected changed attitudes toward sex. Sigmund Freud placed the sexual drives at the heart of healthy social development and stressed the importance of sexual satisfaction for women as well as men, the release of repressions, and the gratification of sexual desires. Like contemporary theories of culture, the new psychology of the 1920s was a body of scientific knowledge that displaced authority, this time the presumed authority of the conscious human being. Aside from psychoanalysis, the new psychology included glandular theories of personality, which linked personality to the balance of chemicals secreted from glands, and behaviorism, the distinctively American and radically environmentalist emphasis on stimulus and response first broached by psychologist John B. Watson in 1913 and popularized by him in the 1920s. Watson believed that the study of consciousness did not properly belong to psychology; he instead analyzed only behavior, and that on the basis of conditioned responses rooted in three basic instincts: fear, rage, and joy (or love). Behaviorism was a theory of control, as it promised new tools to manage both society and the individual based on the mastery of techniques of stimulus and response. "Give me a dozen healthy infants," Watson wrote in *Behaviorism* (1924), "well-formed, and my own specified world to bring them up in and I'll guarantee to take any one at random and train him to become any type of specialist I might select—doctor, lawyer, artist, merchant-chief, and, yes, even beggar-man and thief, regardless of his talents, penchants, tendencies, abilities, vocations, and race of his ancestors."[18]

First introduced in the United States in 1906, psychoanalysis became a subject of popular discussion after 1915. Taken up with especial vigor by rebellious writers and intellectuals, psychoanalysis caught on amongst the professional upper middle class. By the 1920s, it was a subject of broad public interest and humorous commentary. While Freud's therapeutic techniques and theories were most influential, American physicians, neurologists, and psychoanalysts often fashioned an eclectic psychoanalytical therapy drawing on Carl Jung, Alfred Adler, and others. Freudian psychotherapists professionalized their movement and codified it as theory and therapy in the 1920s, establishing psychoanalytic institutes for the training of therapists in Europe and the United States. Important Freudian analysts, such as Otto Rank and Sandor Ferenczi, made short, hectic visits to America to spread his theory. Alfred Booth Kuttner translated Freud's works; Floyd Dell wrote on Freud and Jung; James Oppenheim, the author of *Your Hidden Powers* (1923), and the physician and psychoanalyst Beatrice M. Hinkle popularized Jung; and André Tridon published a series of best-selling volumes on psychoanalysis reflecting his own idiosyncratic, somewhat anarchistic, self-consciously radical, and eclectic approach, which drew the disdain of medical practitioners.[19]

Undergoing therapy, or getting "psyched," which was somewhat expensive, became for intellectuals and the upper middle class a mark of their status, a sign of open-mindedness, and an illustration of the ways in which expertise and novel theories of human behavior promised personal transformation through knowledge of a hitherto hidden self. The classic Freudian therapeutic model of catharsis and cure was a talking therapy, undertaken between a patient, instructed to say whatever comes to mind, no matter what, and an analyst, usually seated behind the patient, who enforces the rule of complete honesty and assists the patient in breaking down resistances. The adult patient is to recall childhood experiences, perhaps remembering and working through childhood traumas; the analyst identifies and analyzes the patient's resistances, breaking down barriers to free association constructed by the conscious self in order to gain knowledge of the instinctive drives and repressed traumas in the unconscious. Freud appealed to intellectuals because he embraced cultural criticism through his analysis of the psychic costs of "civilized" morality. While Victorian morality was necessary, in Freud's view, it also repressed the essentially human. The monitory "superego" fashioned by Western civilization had become overweening, excessively harsh, and productive of neurotic behavior in many cases. For male intellectuals, Freudian theory had the added advantage of being based on the purported psychosexual development of men, beginning with the need to overcome an initial desire for one's mother.[20]

Public debates about obscenity, sexuality, and art signaled the profound alteration in attitudes to public life and the civil sphere countenanced by twentieth-century intellectuals. In the nineteenth century, to speak of private things in public was morally deleterious. Critics judged art and literature in moral terms. Obscenity meant the stripping away of a person's dignity, the reducing of a person to the status of a thing or an object of gratification. Obscenity and topics suitable only for private discussion were off-limits because they were too damaging to civil life. Despite Randolph Bourne's judgment that Victorian reticence was already a "little stale" in the 1910s and the general retreat of vice societies in the 1920s, taste, judgment, and morality were matters of public judgment and enforcement into the 1920s. Censors, public and private, continued to wield authority: the postmaster banned an issue of H. L. Mencken's *American Mercury* from the mails for a relatively tame story about a prostitute (although a court later overturned the decision); the English professor and critic George Shuster had to leave Notre Dame for assigning a work by D. H. Lawrence. Advocates for free speech maintained a withering campaign on censors, Victorian moralists, and genteel critics—the "party of reticence"—as evasive, hypocritical, prudish, smug, complacent, timid, secretly driven by lusts, and engaged in a damaging "conspiracy of silence" to repress needed knowledge about sex and human life. Mencken derided modern "puritanism" as an offense to the sensibilities of sophisticated urbanites.[21]

In 1920, the New York Society for the Suppression of Vice prosecuted Margaret Anderson and Jane Heap, editors of the *Little Review*, on obscenity charges for publishing excerpts from James Joyce's unpublished novel *Ulysses*, and publication of the novel was effectively banned the following year, resulting in a series of court cases ending in 1933, when Judge John M. Woolsey of the United States District Court for the Southern District of New York lifted the ban. In 1928, Mary Ware Dennett was indicted for sending obscene material through the mails for distributing an advice pamphlet for adolescents, *The Sex Side of Life: An Explanation for Young People*, which she had prepared for her sons. "In not a single one of all the books for young people that I have thus far read," Dennett declared, "has there been the frank unashamed declaration that the climax of sex emotion is an unsurpassed joy, something which rightly belongs to every normal human being, a joy to be proudly and serenely experienced." Both Dennett and Joyce were vindicated in the courts in landmark decisions. Liberals eroded Victorian reticence and articulated new assumptions about obscenity—that the definition of obscenity changed with the times and depended on whether the author intended to exploit obscenity (whether the intention was "pornographic"). In the Dennett case, Judge August Hand ruled that her pamphlet displayed no intention to "arouse lust": "We hold that an accurate exposition of the relevant facts of the sex side of life in decent language and in manifestly serious and disinterested spirit cannot ordinarily be regarded as obscene." In moving to a modernist assertion that art must be judged by aesthetic and not moral criteria, artists and intellectuals were implicitly denying that art had the power to damage either individuals or the public as a whole in moral terms, or, alternatively, that it did not matter, that the public had no right to protect a civic sphere free of obscenity. Liberal intellectuals made taste a purely private matter, reduced obscenity to individual judgments, cordoned off art as a matter of elite aesthetic judgment, and ratified a conception of civic life as an arena for self-interested and unregulated public performance rather than virtuous action.[22]

Those who objected to the *Nation* symposium "Our Changing Morality" were, Freda Kirchwey declared, objecting to the "sin of intelligence." In making this claim, Kirchwey aligned with the forces of change as well as intellectual classes and their preferred values of fearless inquiry, scientific rationality, and an open mind. Kirchwey linked changing sexual standards to increased freedom for women, an assumption that informed many contributions to the symposium, which often focused on the current status of women in society. As Beatrice Hinkle, who argued in the 1920s that the standard definitions of male and female were "purely conventional," observed, women were in the lead in changing sexual morality. With the 1920 ratification of the Nineteenth Amendment, which barred federal and state governments from denying the vote to women on account of their sex, women were at a peak of political strength, poised for a new era of social and political power. Women political activists had achieved great success in the Progressive Era in part through a politics of domesticity, or public motherhood, asserting a public role on the basis of women's domestic responsibilities and the traits of character supposedly derived from their sex, particularly their maternal instincts. On such premises, women had built a distinct political culture and a potent lobbying apparatus on the national and local level and achieved an impressive range of social legislation.[23]

With success came new challenges and new questions: in the 1920s, activist women divided on whether to mobilize within the established political parties or without and, more deeply, whether to continue to pursue the types of sex-specific protective measures for which progressive reformers had fought or move to a politics of full equality with men. The results were paradoxical: most women reformers and activists continued to work through the network of clubs and voluntary organizations that had long pushed for reform outside the partisan system (the Women's Joint Congressional Committee, an umbrella lobbying organization for women's advocacy groups, was briefly the most powerful lobby in Washington) and yet, by the end of the decade, gender solidarity had eroded. As the historian Nancy F. Cott observed, "no palpable form of social or civic identification classed all women together."[24]

With suffrage achieved, women turned their focus to a variety of legal disabilities they faced on the federal and state levels. For example, according to federal law, married women did not have independent citizenship—a woman marrying a foreign national lost her citizenship (a quirk in the law partially remedied by the Cable Act, passed in 1922). In many states, fathers were still recognized as the sole guardians of their children, alone entitled to their earnings and services. In Maryland and Georgia, the father could will away custody of children, regardless of the mother's wishes. In forty states, the husband had a legal right to the services of his wife, often meaning he could collect for the loss of her services. In one case, a woman suing her employer for ten thousand dollars in compensation due to the loss of a leg in an industrial accident was left with no legal remedy when her husband settled out of court for three hundred dollars and disappeared with the award money. More than half of the states barred women from jury service, divorce laws often favored men, and women's property rights were often curtailed.[25]

While a common agenda remained, women disagreed on the postsuffrage direction of the movement. In 1919 and 1920, the prominent leaders Carrie Chapman Catt, who led the final push for suffrage, and Jane Addams, the venerable founder of Hull House, divided on whether women should focus on reconstructing their communities (Addams) or move into politics (Catt). At the dissolution of the National American Woman Suffrage Association (NAWSA), its members organized a successor organization, the League of Women Voters, as a political group, and yet the political parties opposed the

League as unnecessary, as did some local clubs in the General Federation of Women's Clubs. A minority in NAWSA opposed the nonpartisan organization of women voters, arguing that women should join the mainstream party system or do nothing. In 1925, feminist activist Anne Martin, a candidate for the U.S. Senate in Nevada, pressed the argument against this position, noting from experience that women who attempt to work in the regular parties are "bound, gagged, divided" and need rather to be a "separate political force."[26]

The more striking political battle flared over the National Women's Party's proposal for an Equal Rights Amendment (ERA) ("Men and women shall have equal rights throughout the United States and every place subject to its jurisdiction"), which revealed a fundamental division within the women's movement. The term "feminism" only came into common usage in the United States around 1913–1914, connoting opposition to sex hierarchy above all, but more than this, a new radicalism among women activists. It was a "semantic claim to female modernism," Cott observed, the theory behind "female avant-garde self-assertion" in the 1920s. The conflicting impulses to female difference—the assertion of special feminine or maternalist moral natures—and claims of equality were blended in nineteenth-century women's rights thought and activism, but the ERA debate sharpened this tension, as opponents of the amendment and similar proposed "blanket" laws at the state level feared the loss of hard-won legislative victories for sex-specific protective legislation—laws that mandated minimum wages, maximum hours, and prescribed rest periods for women workers and prohibited night labor.[27]

The more radical feminists of the 1910s generated a set of aspirations that challenged prevailing social and cultural norms more than suffrage did: they demanded economic independence, including equal chances for the kind of positions men held, full freedom of expression as well as full independence as citizens, and even sexual rights, including an end to the double standard on extramarital sexuality and the right to birth control. In 1920, Crystal Eastman proposed a broad program for economic independence, education, planned parenthood, and the "endowment for motherhood," a proposal for a government-sponsored program of stipends for mothers. Eastman believed that women should be able to work in any field and should receive remuneration for housework and child-rearing. It was the kind of appeal embedded in Suzanne La Follette's egalitarian feminist tract, *Understanding Women* (1926). Women were subjugated in the home, La Follette believed. Institutionalized marriage was a bulwark of the "exploiting State"; women were defined by their "biological function." The institution of marriage remained sacrosanct to many; veteran women reformers had long recognized the necessity of couching their claims for change in socially acceptable language that recognized this. La Follette disdained this "sickly pawing and adulation" of the married mother; marriage was merely legalized prostitution as it involved an exchange of economic security for sexual favors. (Most feminists, it should be noted, assumed that women would choose conventional marriages.) The question of married women working outside the home most excited popular sensitivities; it was the most-asked question of the popular advice columnist Dorothy Dix. By 1930 married women made up almost 30 percent of all employed women, although less than 12 percent of married women were in the paid labor force.[28]

The heated debate over the ERA pitted feminists against one another, particularly the National Women's Party led by Alice Paul, which challenged the social and labor reformers deeply committed to protectionist legislation. The National Women's Party (NWP) probably never numbered over ten thousand members and clearly tilted toward the aspirations of professional women and the sensibilities of wealthy female donors. (The party was "composed mostly of women who never knew what it meant to work a day in their lives," charged Sara Conway of the American Federation of Labor.) The dispute aroused great passions. In a letter to an equal rights supporter drafted in January 1922 (and perhaps never mailed), protectionist Alice Hamilton clearly struggled to contain her contempt: "I could not help comparing you as you sat there, sheltered, safe, beautifully guarded against even the ugliness of life, with the women for whom you demand 'freedom of contract,'" she wrote, thinking of the struggles of laundresses, textile workers, hotel chambermaids, and waitresses. Ethel Smith, a longtime activist for equal pay and improved working conditions for women, opposed the ERA on the basis of a notion of equality that took "account of difference." Women ought not simply copy male standards, she declared: "We have seen the imitative feminist—she was a manifestation of the immature years of the woman movement, which produced the mannish 'new' woman, and even the trousered woman long before her time. It appears in other forms, where women, in order to be equal to men, have tried to be like men, and do the things men do."[29]

The asperity of opponents of the ERA was matched by the proponents, who eventually came to oppose protective legislation for women on principle, claiming it thwarted women's advance (although the jobs most wage-earning women had did not provide much economic independence or opportunity to challenge sex hierarchy). Anti-ERA activists saw the amendment's supporters as naive and in need of social, political, and scientific education, but Doris Stevens of the NWP belittled the intelligence of her opponents and accused them of assuming female weakness. (Similarly, Suzanne La Follette felt the supporters of protective legislation were well-meaning but unintelligent, victims of "misplaced zeal.") Protective legislation, Stevens argued, penalizes the strong woman: "It asks women to set their pace with the weakest member of their sex. All men are not strong. Happily it has not occurred to society to limit the development of all men because some are weak." Alice Paul, who had made her name importing English-style tactics of civil disobedience to the American suffrage movement in the 1910s, was uncompromising: "The disgraceful situation in which women find themselves today is their own fault," she declared in 1922. "They remain a subject class because they have no sense of solidarity." She evinced contempt for women's passivity in the face of discrimination: "Feminine opponents of the equal rights amendment promulgated by the National Woman's Party are in the same intellectual conditions of women in the harem or the negro before the abolition of slavery—too apathetic of their conditions to want to get out of it."[30]

In the end, Congress never submitted the ERA to the states (the NWP was the sole women's group advocating it before the House Judiciary Committee). Behind the debate was a larger one about the nature of sex equality, an incipient struggle over whether gender distinctions should be simply eliminated or understood as a recognition of women's essential difference from men.[31] In 1921, women activists agreed that women's next objective must be equality, but the meaning of equality was assumed and not articulated in detail. By the end of the decade, equality had split the movement, and women activists outside the National Women's Party largely abandoned the term "feminism."[32]

Changes in sexual morality and gender roles represented the most salient front in social and cultural change in the 1920s, but they were accompanied by a dramatic intellectual shift in the basic assumptions about what culture is and how it functioned. Franz Boas and his students led this movement. A German-born professor of anthropology who was entering the last stages of his career at Columbia University in the 1920s, Boas had challenged the dominant anthropological theory of the nineteenth century, which posited a single, natural process of evolutionary development that culminated in "civilization," the highest form of human enterprise. In this older scheme, anthropologists associated "culture" with art and refinement, with the creative achievements that allowed humans to dominate nature and the environment. Boas and his students, and soon most intellectuals, emphasized another tradition of cultural analysis, seeing the existence of many cultures across geography and time, not a singular pattern of human progress; speaking of almost all human endeavor—high art as well as inherited traditions—as cultural in nature; and espousing a relativism that refused to make invidious distinctions between the cultures of different social groups, even if they evidenced vastly different levels of technological achievement. The Boasian theory of culture spread rapidly to other disciplines in the early twentieth century (for example, it was adopted by many sociologists prior to the Great War) and effectively vanquished earlier hierarchical theories and previously dominant biological explanations of human behavior, which placed great explanatory significance on race and heredity.[33]

Boas had long been in the United States by 1920 and had developed this outlook on culture, which included a challenge to the racism that undergirded dominant assumptions about Western superiority, in the 1880s.[34] Boas rejected the assumption that humans followed a uniform path of civilizational development about which anthropologists could safely generalize on the basis of existing knowledge and theory. He challenged the museum practice of displaying artifacts of widely varying provenance in single comparative displays, which implied that the fabrication of particular types of tools and artifacts follows a universal pattern of evolutionary development and thus occurs at same point in the developmental process of all peoples. Boas argued that similar things (tools, practices, techniques) could have complex and differentiated causes; moreover, the diffusion of knowledge and cultural practices across racial groups and throughout cultural regions, which occurs when isolated peoples come into contact and intermingle, complicates the historical reconstruction of patterns of cultural development. Culture meant more than advanced forms of art, science, technology, and knowledge. Rather, the term *culture* describes all those forms of collective human endeavor that enable a people to exert control of their destiny in the face of natural, environmental, and instinctual forces. A culture is an integrated way of life, entailing tradition, folklore, and custom—things deemed characteristic of primitive societies in previous anthropological theory—as well as language, religion, knowledge, and art. There was no one path of forward development and, by implication, no people's culture should be judged inferior to another's.

Boas did not intend to deny patterns of human progress or even rule out the discovery of laws that would govern that progress. He refused to believe that human culture develops in regular and identical patterns throughout all populations, and he did not distinguish between civilized and savage minds. Humans act from reasoned and unreasoned motives; they then rationalize the customs and categories that govern their automatic behaviors. "If he was still enough of a Victorian liberal-positivist to retain a limited belief in the progress of civilization," George W. Stocking Jr. observed, "the general effect of Boas's argument was to show that the behavior of all men, regardless of race or cultural stage, was determined by a traditional body of habitual behavior patterns passed on through what we would now call the enculturative process and buttressed by ethnically tainted secondary rationalizations—in other words, by the particular 'cultures' in which they lived."[35] The research program Boas developed from this culture concept entailed a kind of "salvage ethnology," often focused on broad, geographically defined culture areas, in which researchers undertook intensive studies of particular peoples and the factors that shaped their cultural practices.

Between the 1890s and mid-1920s, Boas trained nearly half of the scholars who earned PhDs in anthropology in the United States. Many of his students were recent immigrants, usually of Jewish background, and some were mildly radical. Boas trained several women as anthropologists as well, most notably Ruth Benedict and Margaret Mead, both of whom studied with him in the 1920s. By then, the Boasians were established scholars, and a few had begun to systematize his ideas, a project Boas resisted. Moreover, they began to move away from his historically oriented research program and were more concerned with studying how integrated patterns of a culture functioned in a given time, without reference to historical antecedents, using the method of ethnographic observation and extended participant observation, which became dominant in the decade.[36]

The Boasians developed connections to literary intellectuals, linking in various ways to the broader bohemian ferment of the time. For example, one of Boas's students, Edward Sapir, published poetry, reviews, and critical essays on cultural and literary topics throughout the 1910s and 1920s in addition to inventing the field of structural linguistics with Leonard Bloomfield. A German immigrant, Sapir earned his doctorate in 1909 and from 1910 to 1925 was chief of the division of anthropology at the Geological Survey in Canada before taking a position at the University of Chicago. Though situated in Ottawa, Sapir had an affinity for the romantic cultural criticism of prewar radicals such as Randolph Bourne, whom he knew and admired. Likewise, both Mead and Benedict were members of a circle of poets in New York City. Growing up in New York and various locations in the Midwest, Benedict was shy and somewhat neurotic as a child. Given to depressions and partially deaf in one ear, she was emotionally aloof as an adult. After graduation from Vassar College in 1909, she spent much of the ensuing decade searching for a vocation, traveling, writing, doing social work, and teaching, before taking courses at Columbia University with John Dewey and at the New School with anthropologists Elsie Clews Parsons and Alexander Goldenweiser. A bisexual, she married Stanley Benedict, a somewhat rigid and austere scientist with whom she developed a marriage marked by an unusual degree of distance; she quickly rented a separate apartment in which she stayed during the week. She entered the doctoral program in anthropology at Columbia in 1921, completing a dissertation on the vision quest among North American Indians with Boas. It was while working for Boas that she

Margaret Mead as an undergraduate at Barnard University with the Ash Can Cats, a group of friends who shared a passion for literature, politics, and the new freedoms available to young women in the 1920s. From left to right: Mead, Léonie Adams, Deborah Kaplan, Pelham Kortheuer, and Viola Corrigan.
Courtesy Margaret Mead Papers, Library of Congress, folder 8, container Q44.

met Mead, who was enrolled as an undergraduate in Boas's two-semester anthropology course.[37]

Margaret Mead's parents—Edward Mead, a professor of economics at the Wharton School of the University of Pennsylvania, and Emily Fogg Mead, a teacher pursuing doctoral work during Mead's childhood—were freethinkers and atheists who employed progressive child-rearing techniques on Margaret (born in 1901) and her siblings and inculcated liberal values. Mead joined the Episcopalian church at age eleven, which in her family marked her as a rebel. Gifted with a photographic memory, Mead combined a childhood career of intellectual accomplishment with a taste for optimistic bromides; during the war, she was a "four-minute man," making short, patriotic speeches to rally Americans to the cause. She became engaged to Luther Cressman, four years her senior, in her final year of high school; by the time of their marriage in 1923, both had agreed to an open marriage and divorce on demand. After a somewhat unsatisfying year at DePauw University in Indiana, the short, slim, and charismatic Mead enrolled at Barnard University as an English major (Cressman pursued studies at Union Theological Seminary, a center of liberal theology, and later studied sociology at Columbia). There she fell in with a high-spirited and literary gang of friends, which included the poet Léonie Adams. They shared an apartment building, dubbed themselves the Ash Can Cats, and embraced the freedoms offered young women in the decade, bobbing their hair and smoking, dabbling in socialist politics, and delving into academic studies. Mead studied sociology with William Ogburn as well as anthropology with Boas. She and her classmates were enamored with the enigmatic Benedict, with whom she soon established what would become a lifelong friendship. Benedict encouraged Mead to join the anthropology program at Columbia. Mead decided to obtain a master's degree in both psychology and anthropology, before earning the doctorate under Boas.[38]

Freethinking and unconventional in many ways, Mead's personal decisions were complex and somewhat fraught throughout the decade. Bisexual like Benedict, she maintained a lesbian relationship throughout college. Benedict and Mead were for a time lovers as well, beginning in late 1924. Mead's husband, Luther Cressman, embraced free-love ideals as well, and the couple lent their apartment to friends in need of a place for romantic trysts. Mead began an affair with the unhappily married Sapir, who was also a friend of Benedict, in the spring of 1925. Enthralled by Mead, although appalled at her free-love views, Sapir pressed her to marry him, up to and through the period in which she made the decision to pursue ethnographic research in the South Sea Islands. At Boas's insistence, Mead chose American Samoa for her fieldwork on the nature of female adolescence. Mead managed to become disentangled from Sapir at a distance; he moved on to another relationship while she was in Samoa. (Mead would ultimately fall in love with Reo Fortune, a New Zealand anthropologist, upon her return from Samoa, marrying him in 1928 after divorcing Cressman.) Entangled in a series of intense, conflicting, and interconnected emotional commitments (the bad ending of her affair with Sapir left a legacy of sour relations between the male Boasians and Mead and Benedict), Mead did not waver from a commitment to free love and personal autonomy. Upon receiving a fellowship to travel to Samoa in April 1925, Mead and her Ash Can Cats celebrated by paying a midnight visit to the poet Edna St. Vincent Millay, ceremonially presenting a basket of flowers to the Village's reigning poet of defiant passion.[39]

In the 1920s, Boas, who had been aghast at the actions of professional anthropologists in spying for the American government during the war and publicly at odds with the profession over the issue, became interested in cultural interdependence and the relation of the individual to society, particularly the ways in which conformity functioned. Boasian anthropologists began to focus on the ways in which culture represents patterns of values that humans have created but that function largely unconsciously. Boas believed that culture is the result of the slow accretion of knowledge and beliefs over time, subject to the contingencies of history and not to laws of civilizational development, but he also felt that a people's culture defined an organizing "genius" peculiar to themselves, a notion somewhat at odds with his larger culture concept, as it suggests a potentially organic, even racial, imperative at work, beyond the arbitrary details of historical development.[40]

In 1924, Sapir published an important statement on culture in the *American Journal of Sociology* (the essay had appeared earlier in different form) that articulated the Boasian culture concept but also reflected the new predilection for cultural criticism and speculation on national genius. While repeating the ethnological definition of culture as the accumulation of knowledge, beliefs, values, and skills developed over time, Sapir ventured a second, normative definition of culture. Genuine culture, he argued, expresses the spirit of a people and is "inherently harmonious, balanced, self-satisfactory," with the aim of fostering the "growth of personality" in the individual. "It is the expression of a richly varied and yet somehow unified and consistent attitude toward life, an attitude which sees the significance of any one element of civilization in its relation to all others," Sapir wrote. The "genius" or "spirit" of a people does exist, although he cautioned against seeing this as anything more than a historical development. Humans create culture, which becomes the "characteristic mold of a national civilization." Civilization may advance, as a people gain more technological and organizational mastery over the environment, but the people's genuine culture may or may not keep up with progress (a formulation not unlike Ogburn's notion of "cultural lag"). If it does not, as Sapir believed was true in the United States of his time, "cultural maladjustment" proliferates and people fall out of harmony with nature.[41]

A genuine culture, Sapir declared, "refuses to consider the individual as a mere cog, as an entity whose sole *raison d'être* lies in his subservience to a collective purpose that he is not conscious of or that has only a remote relevancy to his interests and strivings." Sounding a Thoreauvian note, Sapir indicted the culture of industrialism for "harnessing" humans to machines. "The telephone girl who lends her capacities, during the greater part of the living day, to the manipulation of a technical routine that has an eventually high efficiency value but that answers to no spiritual needs of her own is an appalling sacrifice to civilization." He contrasted modern American culture unfavorably to that of American Indians, who have hunting techniques that, though on a "relatively low level of civilization," operate on a culturally higher level since they do not produce "spiritual frustration" or a "feeling of subservience to tyrannous yet largely inchoate demands." "A genuine culture cannot be defined as the sum of abstractly desirable ends, as a mechanism," Sapir concluded. "It must be looked upon as a sturdy plant growth, each remotest leaf and twig of which is organically fed by the sap at the core. And this growth is not here meant as a metaphor for the group only; it is meant to apply as well to the individual." Echoing both Van Wyck Brooks and the English critic Matthew Arnold, Sapir articulated an organic conception of culture, which is necessarily internal, building out from the individual, versus civilization (the culture of machines and institutions), which is external.[42]

Sapir struggled with the question of how to retain the wholeness exhibited in primitive Indian society, the harmony of the individual with a society's economic organization, in a modern, complex, and differentiated civilization. Modern Americans seek the fulfillment lacking in the economic sphere in art, religion, science, and social life, but even there become "listless consumers of goods which have received no least impress of our personality." In the end, Sapir called for a program of cultural decentralization, suggesting the possibility of retaining a national, even international, political organization while preserving smaller cultural units, thus recreating the nation as a "series of linked autonomous cultures." He also warned against standardization, inverting the typical warning of conformity by urging a conformity to "the essential nature of one's personality." Such conformity "needs to be urged as a possible counter-irritant to the flat and tedious sameness of spiritual outlook, the anemic make-believe, the smug intolerance of the challenging, that so imprison our American souls."[43]

The product of Mead's ethnographic research in Samoa echoed Sapir's concerns. Published in 1928, *Coming of Age in Samoa* featured cover art of a woman and man, she in grass skirt and nothing else, running from palm trees onto a beach beneath a full moon; it sold well and generated much media commentary on Mead's depiction of Samoan attitudes toward sex. Even before publication, Mead's adventure as a lone, young woman working as a field researcher in the South Seas received attention from the press; in one report from Honolulu, where Mead stopped on her way to Samoa, she suggested that her work on problems of adolescence bore significance for issues of delinquency among single women, or "flappers," in the 1920s. The image of a young American woman studying flappers in their primitive state generated interest.[44] Mead worked in Samoa from September 1925 through May 1926, first making observations and learning the language in Pago Pago on the island of Tutuila (where she stayed at the hotel that was the setting for the story that inspired *Sadie Thompson*) and, in November, moving to Ta'u, the easternmost island in the Manu'a district, where she lived for five months. With little methodological training, no translator, and some difficulty with the language, Mead's data and interpretations, particularly relating to sexual activity, became the subject of fierce debate much later. She relied on interviews with fifty girls, half of whom were past puberty, and many of whom, enjoying her presence, would crowd into her place from early in the morning until late at night. She also had one adult informant who gave a long and detailed interview on Samoan sexual practices, including techniques for masturbation and foreplay, sexual positions, frequency of intercourse, and female behavior in orgasm. Mead also may have snooped around a bit herself at night, looking for evidence of reported outdoor sexual behavior.[45]

Mead portrayed Samoa as something of a South Seas free-love idyll, using the term "love affairs" when describing sexual relations among adolescents and generally portraying a culture preoccupied by, and very open about, sex: couples had intercourse under the palm trees, adolescents were generally uninhibited about sexuality, the techniques of lovemaking were varied, divorce was simple and informal, homosexual practices were accepted casually, and masturbation was common (with boys even masturbating in groups). For Samoans, Mead argued, sex "is a natural, pleasurable thing," limited only by considerations of social status. "Familiarity with sex, and the recognition of a need of a technique to deal with sex as an art," she declared, "have produced a scheme of personal relations in which there are no neurotic pictures, no frigidity, no impotence, except as the temporary result of severe illness, and the capacity for intercourse only once in a night is counted as senility."[46]

Mead's analysis converged with that of Sapir as she used her cultural analysis of primitive Samoa to critique the maladjustments in America's complex society. Her depiction of a casual Samoan attitude toward sex, an issue so wrought with conflicting standards and moral judgments in America, reflected her conclusion that Samoan society was more casual in general, which resulted in lower levels of neurosis and greater levels of happiness—although admittedly at the price of less individuation and emotional depth. Adolescence for girls, she concluded, was devoid of crisis and stress: "The girls' minds were perplexed by no conflicts, troubled by no philosophical queries, beset by no remote ambitions. To live as a girl with many lovers as long as possible and then to marry in one's own village, near one's own relatives and to have many children, these were uniform and satisfying ambitions." Conflict was minimal in Samoan society, she suggested, because of a purported deficit in emotional commitment. "For Samoa is a place where no one plays for very high stakes, no one pays very heavy prices, no one suffers for his convictions or fights to the death for special ends," Mead claimed. Moreover, all children are encouraged to develop at the same rate, the most talented at the same rate as the slowest. Compared to Westerners, the Samoans in Mead's portrait had rather tepid emotional lives, with love, hate, jealousy, and sorrow passing relatively quickly. "From the first months of its life, when the child is handed carelessly from one woman's hands to another's, the lesson is learned of not caring for one person greatly, not setting high hopes on any one relationship."[47]

Encouraged by her publisher to pursue cross-cultural speculations, Mead happily embraced the role of cultural critic in her final chapters, attributing the angst of American adolescent girls both to the multitude of choices they faced, which allowed for greater development of personality but also provoked conflict, and the conflicting moral standards they learned, which were often applied inconsistently in practice. Society, she argued, "presents too many problems to her adolescents, demands too many momentous decisions on a few months' notice." The possibility of choice was the signal advantage of American society, allowing persons of a wide range of temperaments to find "satisfactory adjustment" and fulfillment. Nevertheless, choices were too fraught with pressure and moral judgments too freighted with anguish and guilt. Mead preached tolerance and openness, a conscious reduction in the moral intensity of home life. "The home must cease to plead an ethical cause or a religious belief with smiles or frowns, caresses or threats," she concluded. "The children must be taught how to think, not what to think. . . . They must be taught that many ways are open to them, no one sanctioned above its alternative, and that upon them and upon them alone lies the burden of choice."[48]

⌣

Anthropologists developed the concept of culture in the context of social criticism. Mead's critical perspective on modern American attitudes toward sex and moral values shaped her analysis of Samoan culture. At the same time, she showed powerfully how knowledge and intellect, rooted not in the social authority of a bourgeois elite but ostensibly in objective observation and scientific rigor, could affect the American debate. Over the 1920s, intellectuals as critics, whether scientific or literary, transformed their complaints about American life and their liberal values into potent works of social criticism, which appealed to a broad audience and accrued great authority. They considered the forces of change in America, ostensibly with scientific rigor and detachment, in order to suggest directions for the future.

The Boasians' commitment to cultural relativism and Mead's particular sympathy for sexual freedom and freethinking were part of an emerging modernist mentality. The social and cultural choices made by Americans seated at the "gay table" informed the ideas of intellectuals and cultural critics and were in turn shaped by them. This phenomenon notably shaped the most significant effort to apply "social anthropology" and use the technique of detached observation to American life, Robert S. and Helen Merrell Lynd's study of a supposedly typical American community, Muncie, Indiana, in *Middletown: A Study in Modern American Culture* (1929).[49] The Lynds consciously chose to make the study one of change, contrasting the life of their chosen city in the 1890s to that of their own day and finding ample evidence of problems that had developed because of the effects of modernity: a deeper cleavage between social classes, resulting in individual isolation and consumer passivity; a widespread impulse to conformity in thought as the price for improved social status; a fabric of work and daily living routinized and increasingly based on money; in short, increasing fragmentation, less freethinking, and a loss of community.

When appointed head of the Small City Survey project from which *Middletown* grew, Robert Lynd had no special training in anthropology or social research. Born in New Albany, Indiana, he grew up across the Ohio River in Louisville, Kentucky, the son of an affluent banker and reliably Calvinist Presbyterian. Lynd graduated from Princeton in 1914 and worked for the next six years in journalism and publishing, joining the staff of *Publisher's Weekly* and managing trade books for Scribner's in New York City. He met

Helen in 1919 while hiking on a Mount Washington trail (he was attracted when she dropped a reference to Thorstein Veblen), and they married in 1921. She had an undergraduate degree from Wellesley College and a master's degree in philosophy from Columbia University. Robert served in the Army for five months in 1918, during part of which he was hospitalized with an illness. Lying in bed, he determined to reorient his life toward serving others. He began studying at Union Theological Seminary in fall 1920 and joined the liberal Unitarian congregation of John Haynes Holmes. During this period, he took a course in philosophy from John Dewey, which deeply impressed him.[50]

On a summer mission in 1921, Lynd gained employment as a pick-and-shovel man in the oil fields of Elk Basin, Wyoming, immersing himself as a participant observer in the rough-hewn community of these workers. He reveled in the camaraderie and at the same time successfully organized a small congregation around a liberal religious message of practical problem solving. He published an account of his experience in *Harper's*; it revealed his pleasure at the face-to-face interaction he encountered and his own success in creating a viable community. At the same time he wrote an exposé of the conditions in Elk Basin in *Survey* in 1922, emphasizing the lack of community, exhaustion, and fragmentation among the workers and drawing attention to (and a rebuttal from) the Rockefeller interests that employed the workers. Lynd had queried John D. Rockefeller Jr. about conditions at Elk Basin, but resisted his efforts to suppress the article, which drew much notice. A year later, remarkably, John D. Rockefeller Jr. approved hiring Lynd, now a freshly graduated seminarian, to take over the Small City Survey, which was funded by a Rockefeller philanthropy, the Institute of Social and Religious Research.[51]

Lynd's religious and social beliefs evolved during his years at the seminary, as he gradually abandoned his belief in the church and the capacity of religious preaching to promote social change. Instead, influenced by secular social scientists such as Dewey, Thorstein Veblen, and Wesley Mitchell, he now put his faith in the accumulation and dissemination of knowledge and facts. The bringing of facts into people's view would be the catalyst for social reconstruction. Over time, this put Lynd at odds with some members of the Institute. The aim of the study was to gain knowledge that would inform Protestant ministers and strengthen their churches. Lynd produced a study wholly different in orientation, and mollifying his supervisors at the Institute required adept political maneuvering. As it was, upon receiving the finished manuscript in 1927, the Institute deemed it unpublishable, although it eventually released it to Lynd.[52]

The Lynds, supplemented by a statistician, stenographer, and interviewer, began work in their "typical city," Muncie, in January 1924. The study was originally slated as a study of South Bend, Indiana, but Lynd, wanting a more homogenous city so as to focus on native-born Protestant Americans, shifted the site to Muncie, population approximately 35,000, which actually had an atypically large percentage of that group. Lynd plunged into the study with alacrity, cutting an odd figure for the locals due to his preference for bicycling around town, but attending church, singing in the choir, befriending one of the three local socialists, holding a weekly dinner with a doctor, banker, and real-estate agent, and, with his wife and colleagues, pursuing his research, which included lengthy interviews with 164 families. Many local people acted as advisors to the project. The Lynds relished their time in Muncie, making many friends and enjoying the community.[53]

The Lynds organized the book around inquiries into six basic aspects of social activity in a small city: getting a living, making a home, training the young, leisure, religion, and community activities (including government). They framed the study, however, with a comparison of contemporary Muncie with the city thirty years before, using interviews and historical research to recreate the life of the small town as it had been after the discovery of important natural gas reserves in the late nineteenth century—a circumstance that would launch the town on a process of industrial growth. This analytical choice emphasized the fact of change and the question of adjustment. "Middletown's life exhibits at almost every point either some change or some stress arising from failure to change," they observed. Often writing in engrossing prose, the authors effectively evoked the relatively recent nature of this change and the nostalgia many would feel for it in detailing the memories of a local physician who had lived in the town since the 1840s:

> Within the lifetime of this one man local transportation has changed from virtually the "hoof and sail" methods in use in the time of Homer; grain has ceased to be cut in the state by thrusting a sickle into the ripened grain as in the days of Ruth and threshing done by trampling out by horses on the threshing-floor or by flail; getting a living and making a home have ceased to be conducted under one roof by the majority of the American people; education has ceased to be a luxury accessible only to the few; in his own field of medicine the X-ray, anaesthetics, asepsis, and other developments have tended to make the healing art a science; electricity, the telephone, telegraph, and radio have appeared; and the theory of evolution has shaken the theological cosmogony that had reigned for centuries.[54]

Throughout the study, they referenced what had characterized Middletown of old but was now absent or replaced: gone was home-baked bread and canning; now commercially prepared foods were more common. Unions had declined, and there was more debt and less neighborliness. There were fewer stem-winding speeches, religious talks, or lectures. Men's discussion societies, including a freethinking Ethical Society, had faded, as had lodges, replaced by a variety of clubs the Lynds found less than impressive.[55]

The primary change was in how men and women got a living: machines had replaced craft labor. Now people purchased food and clothing rather than being self-sufficient, and Middletown was divided into two classes, the working class and the business class. One's class status was the "most significant single factor" influencing "what one does all day long throughout one's life; whom one marries; when one gets up in the morning; whether one belongs to the Holy Roller or Presbyterian church; or drives a Ford or a Buick; whether or not one's daughter makes the desirable high school Violet Club; or one's wife meets with the Sew We Do Club or with the Art Students' League; whether one belongs to the Odd Fellows or to the Masonic Shrine; whether one sits about evenings with one's necktie off; and so on indefinitely throughout the daily comings and goings of a Middletown man, woman, or child." Much work was now routinized, as emphasized in the comments of one personnel executive on the work of a machine tender: "There's a man who's ground diameters on gears here for fifteen years and done nothing else. It's a fairly highly skilled job and takes more than six months to learn. But it's so endlessly monotonous! That man is dead, just dead! And there's a lot of others like him, and I don't know what to do for them."[56]

The ramifications of industrial change were evident: specialty stores replacing general stores on Main Street, the pressure national chain stores were bringing to bear on local stores, the new reliance on credit for purchases, a uniformity in business class politics (Republican Party) and leisure (golf), ubiquitous advertising, the large percentage (85 percent) of workers who now worked for others and were closely supervised, the role of education as essential for success ("a faith, a religion, to Middletown"), above all the signal importance of money in measuring social status. One informant explained the habit by which locals placed people by their neighborhood, lifestyle, car, and possessions; it was "perfectly natural"—"You see, they know money, and they don't know you." Money became all-important, as "more and more of the activities of living are coming to be strained through the bars of the dollar sign."[57]

Although the Lynds professed that the book would have no thesis, and although their tone was relentlessly evenhanded and generally nonjudgmental, the message of the book was overpowering. Time and again, they emphasized the ways in which national, large-scale trends were making experience more uniform, how local forces pushed conformity to these trends, and how an unthinking booster attitude toward city and state characterized civic life. Movies and magazines, the Lynds pointed out, were diffusing new attitudes; fashionableness dictated higher standards of dress (the business world was seeing a "decrease in individualism and increase in type-consciousness"); the schools were becoming regimented; high school questionnaires revealed a high degree of chauvinism and uniformity of opinion among the students; and leisure was increasingly standardized ("being 'different' is rare even among the young"). Americans were now consumers but unprepared for this social role:

> As more and more of the things utilized as food, clothing, and shelter are be-ing shifted from home production to purchase for a price and as standards of living shift and varieties multiply, the housewife must distinguish among vari-ous grades of milk, bread, vacuum cleaners, and fireless cookers, must decide against rugs made of grass for another type or vice versa, and so on through hundreds of items. At a time when growing industrial units in Middletown are more and more entrusting their purchasing to specialized skill, the home is, as in 1890, an essentially isolated, small-unit purchaser served by an untrained, amateur purchasing agent exposed to competing, highly organized channels of diffusion.

Consumers were suffering from a type of "social illiteracy," bred both by high-pressure advertising aimed at emotions and the "stifling of self-appraisal and self-criticism" entailed in the urge to "local solidarity" and "city-boosting" and fostered in the schools. "Civic loyalty and patriotism are but two of the pressures tending to mold Middletown into common habits of thought and action," the Lynds argued. "Every aspect of Middletown's life has felt some-thing of this same tendency: standardized processes in industry; nationally advertised products used, eaten, worn in Middletown homes; standardized curriculum, text-books, teachers in the schools; the very play-time of the people running into certain molds, with nation-wide films, nationally edited magazines, and standardized music contests."[58]

They city was not just bifurcated between the "two worlds" of the working class and the business class, but, in fact, the city had fragmented, resulting in a "multitude" of worlds. "Small worlds of all sorts are forever forming, shifting, and dissolving," the Lynds observed, defined by the factory one worked at, or the department within the factory, or class in high school, or neighborhood, or union, or chamber of commerce, and so forth. The result was a more isolated population—less calling and visiting, a decline in the neighborhood as a source of friends, a significant minority of the population without friends, and higher "social isolation."[59]

The growth in size and scope of American life and the eclipse of local community that fostered an undercurrent of nostalgia in many Americans prompted anxiety about narrow-mindedness and conformity among intellectuals. In the opportunities of urban culture, the loosening of sexual mores, and new and assertive roles for women, liberal-minded intellectuals saw Americans embracing a new way of living, one that they believed was freer, more open, and more fulfilling. They were impatient with those who failed to see that the restrictive imperatives of gentility were outmoded, but they found themselves even more troubled that those who did shuck off the old morality seemed vulnerable to new and unanticipated forms of conformity. *Middletown* was a great success—it sold well, many colleges and universities adopted it as a textbook, market researchers pored over it for insights, and generations of social scientists read it avidly. It also reflected the ambivalence of the emerging generation of modernist cultural critics, desiring freedom and openness but unsettled at the choices Americans made and the institutions they discarded. The Lynds' heartfelt "secular jeremiad" reflected an emerging consensus among a large segment of public intellectuals that the commercialized entertainment and advertising industries were producing a standardized and materialistic culture that bred conformity in the behavior and thinking of Americans.[60]

CHAPTER TWO

~

Navigating Mass Society

The journalist Bruce Bliven developed a casual, even breezy style that he used for miniature freelance sociological analyses of middle-class manners and mores published in the *New Republic*, a magazine for which he went to work in 1923. In his reports, Bliven commented on movies, radio, night-clubs, flappers, and jazz music, adopting an attitude both of genial delight in their charms and middlebrow annoyance at their crudity. His perspective on middle America was respectful but sometimes condescending, marked by a distinct anxiety at the standardization and materialism of America's business-oriented culture. When visiting New Orleans, he fretted at the eroding of its cultural distinctiveness. The jangling, vertiginous commercial pleasures of Coney Island—where souls battered by "our industrial civilization" slath-ered hot dogs with mustard in a "rite" that was "symbolic of the place"—left him cold. "A palate dulled with condiments must be over-stimulated before it can taste it all," he declared. "A mind buffeted by the whirlwind of life in New York, assaulted by the roar of machinery, dizzied by the pace at which we spin along, learns to regard a shout as the normal tone, and cannot hear with comfort anything less strident."[1]

Bliven grew up in a small town in Iowa, the son of a hardworking but not especially successful farmer. He seems to have adopted the tough agrarian radicalism of the populist West, even though he had two uncles who were successful bankers and he would remember fondly the "orderly, disciplined, and authoritarian world" of his youth.[2] He graduated from Stanford University in 1911, married, and spent the following six years in San Francisco and Los Angeles. Exhibiting a Franklinesque talent for self-promotion, he cultivated acquaintances: the veteran progressive crusader Fremont Older (his editor while working at the *San Francisco Bulletin* in college), Van Wyck Brooks (a visiting faculty member at Stanford for one year), the veteran socialist intellectual W. J. Ghent (who inspired a lifelong taste for informal suppertime discussion clubs), and Charlie Chaplin (whom Bliven chanced to see in his last vaudeville performances while living in Los Angeles and later met through a mutual friend). After only one year of graduate work at Stanford and various odd writing, teaching, and advertising jobs, Bliven talked officials at the University of Southern California into establishing a department of journalism, which he headed for two years. He eventually made his way to New York City.[3]

Although a successful metropolitan journalist, Bliven cultivated his identity as a midwesterner, observing the tourist appeal of Greenwich Village in the early 1920s as if he and his wife were themselves ones. "Not only out-of-towners but middle-class couples from other parts of the city journeyed there to dine in dimly lit cellars and speculate whether the oddly dressed man at the corner table might not be Floyd Dell or Max Eastman (he was probably a Wall Street clerk from Brooklyn)," he wrote in his memoir. "We went there often, though like the other trippers we were never more than onlookers at the real Bohemian life of the place." His account of a trip to The Roof, a New York nightclub, evokes an overcrowded dancing floor, "hideous" jazz music from a black orchestra, uninspired dancing, and a less-than-first-rate floor show that began at 11:30 p.m. "[W]e want noise—any quantity of noise—noise which shall beat in upon our ear-drum and drown out for a space the ceaseless uproar which has been put there by this tumultuous iron-bound civilization of ours," he declared, speaking for the middle-class Rotarians who comprised the audience.[4]

Bliven appreciated the decency of Americans and delighted in the demotic pleasures of American mass amusements, yet he questioned the moral premises of the consumption ethic and brought an ironist's eye to bear on modern culture. Assessing the "uniform" of a young friend he called "Flapper Jane," Bliven mused on the progress of fashion—the heavy makeup, the bobbed hair, and the insubstantial outfit—"one dress, one step-in" (a slip), "two stockings, two shoes" (the year's fashions, Bliven noted, "have gone quite a long step toward genuine nudity"). Costume is "A Moral," Bliven observed, warning against mistaking fashion for reality. Because merely fashionable, Jane's flapper behavior actually was a sign of reassuring conventionality, not an alarming change in mores. At the same time, the real Jane's sarcasm, frank and carefree manner (her commitment to just being "honest"), and sexual independence were welcome repudiations of social gamesmanship.[5]

Writing up his experiences as a participant observer in American culture, Bliven reflected the biases of the intellectuals of his time. The mass amusements and consumer culture of America fascinated and repelled him at the same time. Bliven wrote of middle-class America with empathy yet skewered their shortsighted materialism. His embrace of modern America was decidedly ambivalent. What intellectuals confronted at every turn was the force of change, or, as they saw clearly at times, the aggressive engine of capitalist growth. The arts, culture, and leisure presented entrepreneurs new fields of commercial endeavor. As an amateur cultural anthropologist, Bliven saw a people moving rapidly and aggressively into a complex, fragmented, and yet oddly uniform industrial society. The American people were eager to navigate the flow of mass culture, often consuming it in a far less passive and inert way than Bliven imagined. All the same, he and those like him had good reason to fret. Americans were in thrall to "growth, growth for its own sake, growth of any kind," whether in Iowa or Los Angeles (inhabited as it was by midwestern migrants). Bliven remained skeptical of the "easy optimism" and "lax prosperity" that dominated the lives of his erstwhile fellow citizens in Los Angeles: "Those who live in this intoxication of success, of course, cherish two delusions: first, that they are personally responsible for it; and, second, that it will last forever."[6]

In the thirty years preceding the 1920s, Americans had created a startlingly new culture—one in which many of the goods of life, whether material, artistic, or spiritual, were mediated by commercial interests; in which social success was increasingly defined by wealth and social authority measured in dollars; and in which both pleasure and power, indeed ever more wondrous and astounding pleasures and powers, were available for purchase, with no barriers to acquisition other than the ability to pay. The cities became lands of desire—sprawling, bustling meccas of advertisement, garish display, dazzling lights and color, and ornate, even palatial, department stores, movie houses, and hotels, which beckoned all comers into public, respectable spaces, men, women, and children alike, to experience the unprecedented splendors of modern life, the fruits of mankind's technical ingenuity. Pleasures were to be had—good things, enjoyable diversions, mechanical conveniences that could be purchased (even on credit) and taken home—that would enliven and ease one's life. Entrepreneurs ensured that public entertainments like nightclubs, cabarets, and carnival-like amusements, even sporting events and prizefights, previously associated with the working class or otherwise considered disreputable and decadent, increasingly gained acceptance by the middle classes. As did Bruce Bliven and his wife, one could stroll the boardwalk or dance in a trendy nightspot, comfortably anonymous among strangers, attaining privacy in public while at the same time establishing membership in an elective community, whether it be the lovers of jazz, the fans of the Red Sox, or the patrons of Marshall Field's department store. With the coming of movies and sound recordings and, in the 1920s, broadcasting technology, the ability to surround oneself with mechanically reproduced images and sound furthered still more the individual's ability as a consumer to privatize one's pleasures while at the same time sharing them on a democratic basis with an even greater number of citizens.[7]

Americans approached the liberating potential of consumer society and mass amusements with curiosity, independence, and increasing avidity. As cultural authority slipped through their fingers, the guardians of Victorian values complained, and new critics attacked the hypercommercialized confusion of modern America—one in which citizens so casually threw off the restraints of tradition and standards of cultivation in the greedy pursuit of more pleasure and freedom. From the inception of these new mass amusements, consumer pleasures, and mass arts, the businessman's desire for profit conflicted with the artist's ambitions. The application of rationalizing forms of industrial production to culture was often at odds with artistic quality and the vision of the individual author. All the same, the new forms of commercialized culture, products of a society that defined happiness and success in terms of acquiring goods and gaining wealth, provided new ways for individuals to pursue dreams of upward mobility. As the historian Steven J. Ross pointed out, movies, which were first popular among workers and immigrants in storefront nickelodeons in the first decade of the century, had gained a solid middle-class following by the late 1910s and, in the 1920s, became "cross-class fantasies of luxury, comfort and consumption."[8]

Americans embraced leisure pursuits in the 1920s. Expenditures on recreation increased 300 percent over the course of the decade. Movie theater owners sold forty million tickets every week in 1922 (a year in which movie attendance dropped) and one hundred million per week in 1930, after Hollywood had turned to "talkies" to increase film's popularity.[9] While products of a consumer culture, movies, as much as the other popular new mass media artifacts of the era, such as hillbilly, blues, or jazz music, reflected the varied sensibilities of the American people. They were complex, even skeptical, containers of mass marketing messages. In silent comedies, such as the anarchic Keystone comedies of Mack Sennett, messages about modernity were decidedly ambiguous. Snub Pollard parodied the mechanical conveniences of the home in the Hal Roach comedy short *It's a Gift* (1923). The audience sees his character, upon waking, begin his day with minimal physical effort, relying on a series of handmade, rope-operated mechanical devices by which he can have, for example, a hen lay an egg and deposit it in boiling water, or his breakfast delivered to him in bed, or himself dressed mechanically without rising.

Likewise, in Buster Keaton's *The Navigator* (1924), two scions of wealthy families, a man and the woman who has rejected his proposal of marriage, are stranded and adrift on a vast ship named the *Navigator*. Having never been required to cook for themselves, they are at first incompetent in the ship's galley, but, over time, as in the Snub Pollard comedy, they, too, automate the routines of food preparation with homemade efficiency devices, eventually operating them in a somewhat mechanical fashion themselves, approximating automatons as they move through the routines of their unorthodox domesticity, the actors affecting deadpan expressions, bored and casual in demeanor, as if in fact the long-married couple that they are not yet. Cast off from civilization (the climax of the film entails Keaton fighting off dark-skinned, head-hunting primitives, a typically racist film image of the era), the two plucky moderns at sea contrive their own improvised contraptions to navigate the modern age, replicating industrialism's achievement of replacing human skills with machines. The movie echoes a theme previously pursued by Keaton: in a short entitled *The Electric House* (1922), Keaton's character installs a variety of electric gimmicks in a home only to have them all malfunction to comic effect. In *One Week* (1921), Keaton and his wife, newlyweds, construct a new home from a premanufactured kit, unaware that one of Keaton's rivals has spitefully renumbered the pieces. The product of their ingenuity is an absurdly misshapen house with doors, windows, and angles all wrong, but which they, nevertheless, continue to navigate, no matter how nonfunctional and inconvenient. In a climactic storm, the wind spins the house on its base like a merry-go-round, the do-it-yourself creation buffeted helplessly by the elements, an emblem of the chaotic natural and social forces constantly sweeping up the helpless individual, a theme to which the silent comics were highly attuned.

Consumer goods can be liberating—or not. It all depends on what they are and how they are used. A general message of silent comedy, particularly slapstick, was to beware the calamitous potential of prosaic objects—and fellow citizens. The slapstick comedy of physical violence—pratfalls, slaps, punches, thrown pies, and the rest—so characteristic of silent film derived from vaudeville, from which came the paddle-like devices used by clowns to hit each other and make a loud crack that gave the genre its name. (Two comics outlined the gags guaranteed to get the loudest laughs in 1913: "(a) when a man sticks one finger into another man's eyes; (b) when a man sticks two fingers into another man's eyes; (c) when a man chokes another man and shakes his head from side to side; (d) when a man kicks another man; (e) when a man bumps up suddenly against another man and knocks him off his feet; (f) when a man steps on another man's foot.")[10] In slapstick, humans are confounded by everyday objects: things do not work right, they escape one's grasp, they spill liquid or powder or they combust, they simply do not cooperate, which is exasperating. The film clown, the everyman hero, persists in attempting to work with the recalcitrant object all the same.[11]

Slapstick connoted the recalcitrance of the everyday world as well as an underlying anarchy in the social order and a latent challenge to authority. In slapstick films, cops looked silly, acted absurdly, often fell or slipped, and were generally ineffectual. Mack Sennett defined the art. A protégé of the pioneering film director D. W. Griffith at Biograph, Sennett founded his own studio, Keystone, in 1912, and produced comedies under that name through 1917 and as Sennett comedies into the 1920s. Notorious for the crudeness of his humor and the lowbrow character of his work, which also involved the heavy deployment of bathing beauties, Sennett conceived himself to be challenging the pomposity of those with authority. "The round, fat girls in nothing much doing their bumps and grinds, the German-dialect comedians, and especially the cops and tramps with their bed slats and bladders appealed to me as being funny people," he recalled in an autobiography he coauthored in the 1950s. "Their approach to life was earthy and understandable. They whaled the daylights out of pretension. They made fun of themselves and the human race. They reduced convention, dogma, stuffed shirts, and Authority to nonsense, and then blossomed into Pandemonium."[12]

The four masters of silent comedy in the 1920s were Charlie Chaplin, Buster Keaton, Harold Lloyd, and Harry Langdon.[13] Chaplin's body of work in the 1920s was small, as he focused on feature-length films, which he meticulously produced. He had slowly discovered his film alter ego, the Tramp, in the previous decade; originally aggressive and more prone to typical slapstick violence, the timid and often-frustrated Tramp was a marker of modern anonymity, everyone and no one at the same time, whom Chaplin invested with more sentimentality and serious emotions over time. Lloyd's defining character was the bespectacled, young man, a social climber (and physical climber, as Lloyd was first and foremost a stunt comedian) who displayed aggression but not for bad motives and typically as an act of desperation.

Spunky and full of grit, Lloyd was cocky but vulnerable. Of the group, Lloyd made the most films and had the greatest audience in the 1920s. Keaton was a formalist, eschewing camera tricks and performing his own, often dangerous, stunts. He was obsessed with the nature of the form: his comedy was one of geometry (the wall falls on Keaton, who is saved only by virtue of a precisely placed window); space (Keaton is on a curve, which inevitably brings him to where he began, or returns him to what he intended to escape, as when in *The General* (1926), after lighting the fuse on a nineteenth-century mortar during a train chase, the mortar becomes detached; the barrel, jarred loose, lowers its aim; and the curve of the track puts his own engine in its sights); and physical objects (they become functional when Keaton grasps them, even if in absurd ways). Keaton's character unflappably confronts the unpredictable effects of forces he knows he cannot control. The least remembered figure, Harry Langdon, established a man-child persona. His character was obviously an adult man, yet he acted as a child—appetitive but shy, alternately blithe and carefree or bored and peevish, often fretful and timid. Langdon drastically slowed the action of film comedy, his comedy bits comprised of long sequences in which his character builds up to some act of decisive action, his physical gestures tentative and provisional. Langdon briefly attained great popularity and, with his sweet-natured and somewhat tramp-like character, seemed poised as an heir to Chaplin before taking over the production of his own films, with disastrous results for his art and his career.

Film comedy itself, so built on physical humor and gags and guided by no purpose other than getting a laugh, reflected the "new humor" of the twentieth century—the nondidactic and aggressive joking derived from working-class life. Vaudeville had decisively shaped American tastes in light theatrical entertainment and survived into the 1920s. Over 1500 theaters across the nation featured vaudeville shows, with programs repeated throughout the afternoon and evening. Vaudeville provided a variety of acts in a safe and respectable venue, only gently testing the limits of vulgarity with ethnic humor or salacious material. To attract the broadest audience of men and women, no act lasted longer than twenty minutes. The producer assembled a program of performers who were essentially freelancers, with complete authority over their acts and responsibility for acquiring sets, props, and costumes. There was no logic or broader theme imposed on the material, and the booking agent often stocked shows with celebrities, whether figures from sports (boxers and swimmers were popular) or notorious figures, such as Evelyn Nesbit, whose husband had murdered her ex-lover, architect Stanford White. Vaudeville absorbed fading theatrical forms, taking acts from minstrel shows, burlesque, and showboats, and incorporated circus acts, magicians, freak show performers, blackface sketch artists, and medicine show acts as well as classical musicians, opera performers, and actors from legitimate theater who performed dramatic scenes, musical numbers, and comedy acts. Many times silent films were incorporated into the bill. Because the show itself was under constant revision, with acts constantly shuffling in or out, and given their limited performance time, vaudeville performers learned to play to types, often using ethnic stereotypes or developing a favorite stock character, which they exploited time and again in various skits. Vaudevillians frequently went on to legitimate theater, movies, and radio, having learned broad styles of performance and the necessity of charisma, force, and sharply defined character to connect with a theater crowd.[14]

To a remarkable degree, products of the mass arts depicted individual vulnerability, even as that image was often paired with dogged strength and the ability to survive. The bustling crowd became the emblem of the city, with the hero or heroine momentarily an insignificant figure in an onrushing, indifferent, and potentially hazardous mass. Silent comedians like Keaton or Lloyd often used this trope to good effect, with Keaton's late film *The Cameraman* (1928) opening and closing with his character overwhelmed and physically manhandled by a sudden surging crowd developing as suddenly as a cloudburst, resulting from a ticker tape parade to mark some unknown official happening or celebrity. Throughout the film, Keaton feels the physical pressing of humanity—riding on the side of a streetcar having failed to find a seat, sharing a very small dressing room with a very large man, seeing people tumble out of a taxi upon the door opening. In *Safety Last!* (1923), Harold Lloyd, desperate to avoid being late at work, like Keaton cannot ride the crowded trolley as he is physically unable to gain a toehold. As an emasculated clerk at the fabric counter of an urban department store, he faces a frenzied mob of women shoppers clutching, shouting, and demanding his attention. Having taken off his jacket and with his clothing askew, Lloyd's character is chastised by his manager for a lack of refinement that would shock the women shoppers—who, however, have been anything but refined in their mad scramble for a bargain.

In King Vidor's *The Crowd* (1928), a late classic of the silent era, the ever-present and indifferent crowds that haunt the hero, Jimmy, in his failed pursuit for success (defined in the film as standing out from the crowd) become the very emblem of a mass society, which looms in the film almost as an independent force of human nature. The epiphany for the feckless hero—an ambitious everyman dreamer lacking the talent and focus to raise his status—occurs when he hits bottom, unemployed and unable to find a job, recognizing himself as a failure. "We do not know how big the crowd is, and what opposition it is. . . . until we get out of step with it," a title card announces.

Literary humorists, comic strip artists, and film comedians worked the "little man" vein of comedy, developing weak, insecure, anxiety-ridden men who are dominated by the various forces in their life, whether the boss, his wife, the kids, or simply gadgets. The New York wit Robert Benchley adopted just such a mask, repeatedly humiliated and defeated in the contests of daily life by 1929. The *New Yorker* writers E. B. White and James Thurber also excelled in the form; comic strip writers exploited it, with characters such as Caspar Milquetoast, Andy Gump, and Barney Google.[15] Film comics like Keaton, Lloyd, Langdon, and even Chaplin played the part, although with more complexity, as they often depicted elements of insouciance, aggression, and cockiness as well. Lloyd's young, ambitious striver, whether in a rural or urban setting, was determined to get ahead. Lloyd was neat and unassuming, and although often depicted as naive, fearful, or insecure, in fact he was often also spunky, even cocky, quick-witted, assertive, and sometimes a con man. In *Safety Last!*, Lloyd plays a young man determined to make enough money in the city to marry his small-town sweetheart, but he also perpetrates an elaborate con, writing her that he manages a large department store when he actually is a low-ranking clerk. When she arrives in person, Lloyd decides to maintain the false front, which requires elaborate acts of deceit and dissimulation. On a certain level, Lloyd's character simply did not make sense: a put-upon, sometimes shy individual who was also daring and tremendously self-confident, a vulnerable little man who was quite competent when circumstances demanded.

Vulnerability was an important theme of the blues as well, an African American musical tradition fundamentally concerned with hardship. The popularity of blues and jazz in the 1920s reflects the possibilities for a plebeian and arguably oppositional sensibility even within what was by that time a highly professionalized music industry. Blues and jazz evolved across the South. They were hybridized and impure folk music forms that incorporated black and white cultural elements, including African survivals, as well as various aspects of commercial music. (Indeed, African American blues and jazz and the poor, working-class southern white "old-time" or hillbilly music evolved together in the late nineteenth-century South, utterly hybridized and intermixed.) Central to their development were the rural areas stretching from the Delta region in Mississippi through Louisiana and into east Texas, the core region of the blues. Jazz developed in the city, at first New Orleans but after 1917 primarily in northern cities—Chicago being the most fertile center of jazz innovation through the mid-1920s and New York there-after. The music originated in the plantation country—often among amateur bands, sometimes family bands and at times others comprised exclusively of kids. Musicians sometimes fashioned homemade instruments. Many jazz pioneers did unskilled labor during the day (Louis Armstrong hauled coal) and pursued music part-time or as amateurs.[16]

Jazz and blues were both new types of music, developing as distinct genres only in the 1890s and the first decade of the twentieth century. Some black bands used the label "jazz" in the 1910s in their names but not to identify a new form of music; the term was rare in New Orleans before 1920. After 1917, with the first recordings and touring of the white Dixieland-style jazz group the Original Dixieland Jazz Band, it was primarily whites who used the term, and it gained general usage first in the North. It remained rare among white and black musicians through the 1930s.[17] Jazz was a style of performance as much as a genre before the 1920s, an instrumental music marked by a syncopated, or irregularly accented, beat that began to "swing," a quality difficult to explain in words but which was the fruit of jazz musicians' obsession with how to accent the beat in a rhythm, combining the African impulse to polyrhythms with European traditions of a single, ground beat. When music swung, as it started to do regularly in Chicago, one simply knew it. Remembered the pianist Art Hodes, "We lived with a beat. . . . I'd wake up with 'Muskrat Rumble' on the vic, and immediately I was back in time, walking to the music, dressing to it, and being walked out of the house."[18] Jazz music was based on improvisation around the rhythm and melody, which required great skill, practice, and creativity and was one of the elements separating "hot jazz" from the popular syncopated dance music, or "sweet jazz," which was the music that white observers labeled jazz in the 1920s. (Mainstream dance music syncopated but rarely used blues, stressed improvisation, or swung.) Finally, hot jazz incorporated elements of the peculiar blues timbre derived from African tonal systems, which in the European diatonic scale entailed the bending or flattening of certain notes (what became known as "blue" notes). Moreover, jazz musicians freely adapted to their instruments the characteristic weirding vocal effects of rural bluesmen, who moaned and howled and used guttural tones, slurs, melisma, or falsetto to give a distinctive and sometimes otherworldly quality to their singing.[19]

Blues was a vocal music, and although featuring cross-rhythms, blues harmonics, and an often strange and effective performance style, it was also defined by lyrics, most typically written in a twelve-bar, AAB pattern (the first lyric repeated twice followed by a second phrase) that was, however, subject to constant variation. The blues derived from black rural penury and were built around compressed metaphors or images. The lyrics were indelibly associated with the rural life of African Americans and conveyed themes of longing, loss, regret, desire for escape, embittered love, and violent passion (although there was also much humor, self-parody, double entendre, erotic fantasy, hedonism, rowdiness, and talk of rambling as well). Hardship and vulnerability were constant themes, exemplified in many of the floating lyrics that rural folks blues singers used repetitively, borrowing and adopting as they pleased (e.g., "I'm worried now but I won't be worried long," "Out in dis wide worl' alone," "I got de blues an' can't be satisfied," "I'm laughing to keep from cryin'," "I been down so long, it seems like up to me").[20] The Delta blues, exemplified by blues musicians like the flamboyant and often-married Charley Patton and the alcohol-addicted Tommy Johnson (who would drink the denatured alcohol in shoe polish or Sterno, if need be, inspiring the "Canned Heat Blues"), featured many local references, folk sayings, and vignettes of Delta life. The bluesmen learned their craft in informal networks, akin to schools. Patton learned the blues on the plantation of Will Dockery, where Willie Brown, Tommy Johnson, and Son House also studied the music. (Tommy Johnson promulgated the African-derived legend, as another Delta bluesman Robert Johnson later did, that he gained his talent by selling his soul to the devil at a midnight crossroads meeting. Fiddle players had a similar legend.)[21]

Interpreting the precise import of the blues, as African American musicians sang of poverty, sexual frustration, emotional crisis, and desperation, is difficult. Though conveying messages of vulnerability, both to the vagaries of sexual partners and a social order hostile to their ambitions, blues protagonists were not "little men" (nor "little women," as the most commercially popular blues of the 1920s were sung by blues divas, immensely popular female singers such as Bessie Smith, Ma Rainey, Ida Cox, Alberta Hunter, Lucille Bogan, Ethel Waters, and Clara Smith). Though vulnerable ("Everyday seems like murder here," Patton sang in "Down the Dirt Road Blues"), they were not incapable. Indeed, much of the blues entailed a lusty appetite for life. Moreover, blues musicians often expressed anger and defiance, sometimes fantasies of extreme violence ("Want to set this world on fire," Julia Moody sang in "Mad Mama's Blues," and "Now if I could see blood running through the streets/Could see everybody lying dead at my feet"), with many men declaring their determination to escape by running away.[22] Moreover, as a communal performative art, marked by improvisation, the blues were a verbalization of deeds not enacted, in which the mere statement of an unconsummated act by the performer and the audience's response became cathartic. Saying you will wreck the city, or abandon a lover, or hop on the train, is not the same as doing so, which is the point.

Indeed, with references to the voodoo charms, animal totems, and demonic influences characteristic of African American folk tradition as well as the occasional imputing of independent power to the blues, the music could take on a theological dimension, the expression of an Old Testament fatalism, in which the feeble human is subject to the arbitrary wrath of an angry God. "Jazz originated with the American Negro. It was his way of expressing his religious emotions," the black songwriters Eubie Blake and Noble Sissle declared in the *Baltimore Afro-American* in 1924. In her study of "mongrelized" white and black Manhattan in the 1920s, Ann Douglas compared the blues to Proverbs and Ecclesiastes, arguing that they had "a purchase on what feels like universal and absolute truth"; they expressed the radical incomprehensibility of the universe. "If religion means the direct apprehension of the precise workings of things," Douglas argued, "of their reality-power, their ability to arouse terror and desire, an apprehension taken at a level so deep, though not necessarily so serious, that some term not altogether limited by historical circumstance is mandated to describe it," then the blues were religious. At times, blues singers presented the blues as a malign force in life, a living, embodied presence. In "Mama, 'Tain't Long fo' Day," the Georgia bluesman Blind Willie McTell (who evidently went blind slowly in his teens), recounted an evening of night terrors:

> Wake up, mama, don't you sleep so hard,
> Wake up, mama, don't you sleep so hard,
> For it's these old blues walkin' all on your yard.
> . . .
> Blues grabbed me at midnight and didn't turn me loose 'til day,
> Blues grabbed me at midnight, didn't turn me loose 'til day,
> I didn't have no mama to drive these blues away.

Or, as Ida Cox sang in "Rambling Blues":

> Early this morning the blues came walkin' in my room,
> Early this morning the blues came walkin' in my room,
> I said, "Blues, please tell me what you are doing here so soon."
>
> They looked at me and smiled but yet they refused to say,
> They looked at me and smiled but yet they refused to say,
> I came again and they turned and walked away.[23]

Although many male blues singers recorded their songs in the 1920s, blues sung by women were greater sellers. The vaudeville singer Mamie Smith's 1920 recording of "Crazy Blues," which was a version of a blues composed by the vaudeville performer Perry Bradford originally to have been recorded by the popular white singer Sophie Tucker, sparked the craze, selling 75,000 records in the first month and one million by the end of one year. "The people at that time were blues crazy," Alberta Hunter remembered of her experience singing in blues clubs in Chicago in the 1920s. A Los Angeles storeowner claimed his stock of a new blues recording (anywhere from fifty to one hundred copies) would sell out within an hour; if it was a Bessie Smith record, a half-block-long line would form two or three hours early. "Colored people would form a line twice around the block when the latest record of Bessie or Ma or Clara or Mamie came in," remembered pianist Clarence Williams. "Sometimes these records they was bootlegged, sold in the alley for four or five dollars apiece."[24]

Although professional songwriters, most often men, composed most of their songs, and the women performed a variety of types of songs, sometimes including original compositions, traditional blues, commercial vaudeville/blues hybrids, and Tin Pan Alley sentimental tunes, the female blues singers of the decade left audiences with little doubt about their power and authority and often defiance of conventions. They developed a reputation for their regal bearing, pointedly taking the stage in the rich and expensive accoutrements of ladyhood, in defiance of the reputation of the blues as a lower art form and the demeaning attitudes toward African Americans in white society. The minstrel show and vaudeville veteran Ma Rainey wore floor-length gowns, a diamond tiara and, at times, a necklace and earrings made of gold-eagle dollars, and used an ostrich fan. Bessie Smith performed in flamboyant attire as well, sometimes wearing headdresses that could weigh up to fifty pounds; on tour, she traveled in a private, bright-yellow, two-story railroad car, opulently appointed and with hot and cold running water.[25]

Raised in poverty in Tennessee, the daughter of a Baptist minister, Bessie Smith began performing at age eighteen in 1912, touring in minstrel troupes, where she befriended Ma Rainey. Eventually becoming the most renowned of the women blues singers of the era, the "Empress" of the blues, well-known in the South by 1918, the bisexual Smith became known too for her voracious appetites, for food as well as sex, which she indulged openly, and her volatile, even violent, temperament. She once shot at her husband and reportedly attacked her fellow blues singer Clara Smith. Invited to perform at the Fifty-Fifth Street apartment of Carl Van Vechten, the white impresario of the Harlem Renaissance, known for his expertise on Harlem nightlife and a penchant for primitivizing African Americans in print, a drunken Smith rebuffed his wife, Fania Marinoff, when she offered a polite embrace, knocking her down and exclaiming, "Get the fuck away from me! I never heard of such shit!" Obnoxious as her behavior was in this instance, her Harlem audience interpreted it as satisfying defiance. Indeed, the women blues artists exuded a proud independence of character. When blueswomen sang of leaving an abusive relationship, it was an act of autonomy, a theme exemplified in many of their lyrics. "Ya hear me talkin' to ya, I don't bite my tongue./Ya want to be my man, ya got to fetch it with ya when ya come," Ma Rainey declared in pride, defiance, and anger. Likewise, Bessie Smith affirmed her freedom in "Young Woman's Blues":

> I ain't no high yellow, I'm deep yellow brown,
> I ain't gonna marry, ain't gonna settle down,
> I'm gonna drink good moonshine and run these browns around.
> See that long lonesome road, don't you know it's gotta end,
> And I'm a good woman and I can get plenty of men.

Ida Cox's "Wild Women Don't Get the Blues" was an explicit repudiation of respectable sexual morality in the name of personal autonomy:

> I've got a different system and a way of my own,
> When my man starts kicking, I let him find another home,
> I get full of good liquor and walk the streets all night,
> Go home and put my man out if he don't treat me right,
> Wild women don't worry, wild women don't have the blues.
>
> You never get nothing by being an angel child,
> You better change your ways and get real wild,
> I want to tell you something and I wouldn't tell you no lie,
> Wild women are the only kind that really get by,
> 'Cause wild women don't worry, wild women don't have the blues.

For most women, in fact, this type of sexual autonomy was more easily asserted than enacted, a fact conveyed by Clara Smith in "Freight Train Blues," in which she points out the options available to men that were unavailable for women: "When a woman gets the blues, she goes to her room and hides,/When a man gets the blues, he catches a freight train and rides."[26]

The blues sung by both men and women in the 1920s often featured ribald lyrics. Producers eager to appeal to the prurience of potential record buyers encouraged the songwriters' penchant for vulgar sexual metaphors. Developing metaphors for sexual intercourse or male or female genitalia inspired the ingenuity of blues composers, who deployed lyrics about automobiles, weapons, trains, animals, cigarettes, and especially food in creative double entendre. Men sang of wanting women's jelly roll, angel food cake, and shortening bread; Bessie Smith announced her desire for a hot dog in her bun. "Don't forget, mama, please save my sweet jelly roll," Blind Blake sang as a steelworker on the job in "Steel Mill Blues"; "I wear my skirt up to my knees,/And whip that jelly with who I please," Clara Smith replied in "Whip It to a Jelly." The daughter of a Louisville attorney who made her first recording in 1923 at the age of fourteen, Helen Humes remembers puzzling over the lyrics of songs like "Papa Has Outside Lovin' and Mama Has Outside Lovin'" and "Do What You Did Last Night" but deciding to "pay no mind" to them. Despite opposition from elements of the black community, even the most accomplished women blues singers sang and recorded these raunchy songs, which were lascivious but also sometimes parodic. The great Texas bluesman Blind Lemon Jefferson sang, "Ummm better find my mama soon, better find my mama soon,/I woke up this morning, black snake was making such a ruckus in my room," while Lil Johnson, in "Hottest Gal in Town," explained her expectations for her kind of man at length:

> He's got to wake me every morning 'bout half past three,
> Kick up my furnace and turn on my heat,
> Churn up my milk, cream my wheat,
> Brown my biscuits, and chop my meat,
> He's long and tall, and that ain't all,
> He's got to be just like a cannonball,
> That's why I want him around,
> 'Cause I'm the hottest gal in town.

True to the tradition of female blues empowerment, Ida Cox in "One Hour Mama" made clear her expectations of male stamina:

> I want a slow and easy man,
> He needn't ever take the lead,
> 'Cause I work on that long time plan
> And I ain't a looking for no speed.
>
> I'm a one hour mama, so no one minute papa
> Ain't the kind of man for me.
> Set your alarm clock papa, one hour that's proper
> Then love me like I like to be.[27]

Though blues and jazz were considered disreputable by genteel critics, their popularity proves their mass appeal, and their sexual assertiveness put them in the vanguard of the decisive shift in sexual mores in the 1920s, led by the increasing sexual frankness (or, as Flapper Jane said, "honesty") of women. Among the female blues divas, several were lesbian or bisexual, sometimes rather openly, including Rainey, Bessie Smith, Ethel Waters, Alberta Hunter, and Gladys Bentley, the last of whom performed in tuxedo and top hat and openly married her lesbian lover.[28]

～

The leisure culture that white middle-class Americans had created by the 1920s was a peculiar blend of openness and repression. It bridged social and cultural barriers while simultaneously reinforcing them, provided new forms of mixed-sex and intimate leisure activities in public spaces but with increased expectations of privacy and social distance, and encouraged improvisation and anarchic fun within a system built on formulas and stereotypes. As with vaudeville, which remained popular throughout the period, Americans embraced variety but in predictable forms and uniform servings. By the 1920s, nightclubs and cabarets, like The Roof, which Bliven and his wife visited, emerged as popular and sophisticated urban venues for drinking, casual socializing, dancing, and the enjoyment of musical entertainment (often featuring pretty chorus girls). The clubs were intimate, with the performing space abutting the dance floor, which was surrounded by tables. Performers mingled easily with the crowd, which occasionally featured celebrities or fellow performers (sometimes planted) who were, in turn, invited to perform for the crowd. Cabaret performers like Sophie Tucker, a large and brassy singer of sentimental ballads and lightly risqué tunes (she was dubbed the Last of the Red Hot Mamas) of Russian Jewish heritage, learned how to win over a crowd with a friendly demeanor and attractive personality. Likewise, club owners such as Texas Guinan became famous for the colorful personalities they displayed as hosts and masters of ceremonies for their trendy nightspots. Some clubs trafficked in fantastic, stereotyped decor, sometimes egregiously racist, as in the Plantation Club, made up as a southern plantation with log cabins (one of which contained Aunt Jemima herself flipping pancakes), black mammies, a picket fence encircling the dance floor, and a summer sky above. Don Dickerman's Pirate's Den in the Village trafficked in a more elaborate if less offensive kitsch; patrons entered through a bolted iron door and ventured to the club through lantern-lit twisting passageways, ship's balconies, and tunnel-like passages, strewn with cutlasses, pistols, ropes and tackle, irons, cannon, parrots, and monkeys and attended by pirate-costumed employees.[29]

These clubs offered safe opportunities for adult fantasy play, whether as pirates, southern aristocrats, or urban sophisticates—venues for the much-sought-after commingling of different audiences. Gender and class boundaries were relaxed, and sometimes those of race were relaxed as well (in black-and-tan clubs in Chicago and Harlem). The clubs allowed informality and relaxed sociability as well as a sense of intimacy between performers and audience (chorus girls would sometimes engage in sexual teasing with the audience, and aggressive comic acts, such as that featuring the comic Jimmy Durante, would also pull in audience members, testing whether they were good sports).[30] Boundaries were observed: the clubs were special places of relaxation; normal rules applied outside their precincts.

One of the most popular forms of theatrical entertainment in New York was the revue, an elaborate stage show exemplified by the Follies staged by Florenz Ziegfeld between 1909 and 1931, featuring song and dance, comedy, and displays of feminine beauty. Unlike vaudeville shows, the revues reflected the energy and vision of the producer, who shaped the revue around a central theme, sometimes commissioning sketches and tunes from star performers. Between 1920 and 1930, producers such as Ziegfeld, Earl Carroll, Earl White, and the songwriter Irving Berlin produced 154 revues on Broadway. Nudity or the illusion of nudity was essential, as Ziegfeld and his peers basically presented lavish and high-toned versions of burlesque shows. In the 1920s, the revue producers appeased the local censors and abided by the rule that allowed topless showgirls so long as they did not move. (Carroll impishly mounted one of his showgirls on a swing in his 1924 *Vanities*, in technical compliance with the rule; in 1926, he featured an onstage champagne bath for one of his chorus girls before a selected audience, only to end up jailed for violating Prohibition.) Social norms were expanded, but boundaries maintained.[31]

The producers of mass entertainment gravitated to typecasting and formulas, as was seen in the evolution of vaudeville: the performer perfected a schtick and stuck to it, satisfying audience's expectations, guaranteeing his or her success in the allotted twenty-minute performance, and allowing the booking agent to make reliable predictions of ticket sales. Crowd-pleasing was the essence of "the show business," as it was known in the late nineteenth and early twentieth century. In the 1910s, producers began to identify film actors by name, thus adopting the "star system" already prevalent in theater. Actors such as Mary Pickford became enormously popular, playing more or less the same role film after film, to the audience's delight. They literally became bankable. Because popular stars like Pickford, Chaplin, Fairbanks, and Valentino ensured a larger audience and reliable profit, banks accepted their contracts as collateral for loans to movie companies. The public made silent film stars "semimythological" figures, according to the critic Walter Kerr, and by 1920 one journalist was moved to analyze Hollywood as a new kingdom, with the youthful and beautiful stars its royalty, trailed by entourages and sacrificing privacy for wealth and lavish excess.[32]

Whatever the emotional costs for this pioneering generation of celebrities, for whom screen image and public ardor bled into private life and eliminated their privacy, the artistic results were formulaic films, whether the top-of-the-bill features or the "program" films used to fill out the evening's movie show. The critic and future documentary filmmaker Pare Lorentz complained in 1928 that the businessmen who ran Hollywood had made films technically accomplished but uniform in content. As the power of financiers and businessmen grew, producers increased in importance and assembly line–style films began to appear. When looking for film extras, as one assistant director confided to a reporter, "We're not looking for raving beauties—we're looking for types. . . . It's the distinctive type of person that we're looking for." He displayed an information card on which an aspiring actress had written "society girl" next to "suitable role"; the assistant director had penciled in "French maid."[33] Joseph von Sternberg's ambitious *The Last Command* (1928), about an exiled former Russian general who ends up seeking work as an extra in Hollywood, parodies this process, as a pushy and aggressive mob of extras move through a sort of assembly line to pick up their costumes and props from ostentatiously bored studio workers. (The exiled grand duke corrects an ungrateful and officious assistant on the details of the Russian uniform.)

The recording industry, which was challenging the entrenched power of the Tin Pan Alley song publishing industry in the music business in the 1920s, pursued a similar strategy as performers became the subjects of public adulation and record labels created new genres to identify and meet public tastes. The creation of country music illustrates the process. Ralph Peer worked for the General Phonograph Corporation, which issued records under the Okeh label. In the early 1920s, he helped pioneer the marketing of African American blues music as "race records" for Okeh. Eventually leaving Okeh, Peer essentially worked as a talent scout and independent producer (although he contracted to record artists for Victor for a nominal salary). He developed a lucrative business model based on negotiating copyrights to the songs his artists wrote (either new songs or reworked old songs not yet copyrighted). Performers received a share in the royalties (and Peer would advance royalties on future profits, thus ensuring his musicians would continue to produce new music). Peer pioneered field recording in the 1920s, traveling to various cities with recording engineers, working to arrange publicity through local papers and contacts, and turning up blues and country music artists. Peer traveled to large cities like St. Louis, Dallas, and Atlanta but also to smaller towns and cities, such as Asheville, North Carolina, and Bristol and Johnson City, Tennessee. The head of the phonograph department in an Atlanta furniture store and the Okeh regional distributor, named Polk Brockman, helped instigate the recording of southern white rural music in 1923, when he persuaded Peer, who was in Atlanta searching for black artists, to record a famous local musician named Fiddlin' John Carson. A skeptical Peer released the recording unadvertised and unlabeled in Atlanta, and it proved an immediate hit. Peer and others went on to record many other folk, amateur, and small-time vaudeville fiddlers, singers, and string bands from the South, inventing country music, or what at the time was most often labeled hillbilly music, in the process.[34]

One of Peer's most fruitful field sessions took place in Bristol on the Tennessee-Virginia border. There in July and August 1927, the Carter Family— A. P., his wife Sara, and his sister-in-law Maybelle Addington Carter—made their first recordings. The Carter Family unearthed and recorded nostalgic songs about small-town and rural life, death, sorrow, and loss, which became country music staples. A. P. worked as a blacksmith, carpenter, and traveling fruit salesman; even after beginning a recording career, the Carter family had to work other jobs to make a living (A. P. spent six months in Detroit looking for carpentry work in 1929), meeting for semiannual recording sessions. A. P. would travel the countryside in search of material, sometimes in the company of Leslie Riddles, a black guitarist and singer who could learn a melody on first hearing and who taught Maybelle a guitar technique for playing melody and picking the rhythm at the same time, for which she became well known. He would then copyright his arrangements, as required by Peer.[35]

Peer also recorded Jimmie Rodgers for the first time at the Bristol sessions. The ambitious Rodgers eagerly pursued success in professional music, becoming the first major star in country music. Born in 1897 near Meridian, Mississippi, and raised primarily by his father, a railroadman required to make frequent moves, Rodgers determined to be an entertainer from his childhood, putting together a neighborhood carnival at the age of twelve and taking it on the road in a tent purchased on his father's credit, much to his consternation. He soon ran off with a traveling medicine show, then quit school at age thirteen and worked on the railroad. He had a brief early marriage and a later elopement with a minister's daughter but primarily lived as an itinerant worker, sometimes on railroads, sometimes as a musician (playing fairs, picnics, and political rallies, as a blackface entertainer, and at one point in a Hawaiian carnival). Influenced by vaudeville, Tin Pan Alley, and the black men with whom he worked on the railroad, Rodgers's musical style was the result of an amalgam of musical influences, including the blues. Audiences found his bent melody and broken-meter style of singing expressive, and he became known for melding the blues aesthetic with country yodeling and, during his brief career after 1927 (he died of tuberculosis in 1933), he performed on radio, in vaudeville, and in tent shows singing nostalgic songs of home, the hobo life, and unrequited love and recording blues, lullabies, and popular standards. Many of Rodgers's most popular songs were blues numbers, and some were jazz; in mixing blues, jazz, and traditional country music, Rodgers prefigured early rock and roll. Like the Hollywood stars, Rodgers became famous for his high style of living, which included lavish expenditures on his home, clothing, guitars, and automobiles.[36]

From its origin, hillbilly music was a commercial phenomenon, created by recording companies marketing sentimental songs and ballads popular among poor, rural white southerners to middle-class farmers and eventually southern migrants transplanted in northern cities. Comprised of a mix of folk and commercial influences from the beginning, hillbilly brought together a dizzying variety of musical sources, from English ballads to southern black blues and jazz to religious hymns, Tin Pan Alley standards, vaudeville, and Hawaiian music (which was in vogue after the Great War, resulting in the presence of ukuleles in many households and steel guitars in country music). Country fiddlers were given to improvisation, as were jazz players and silent comics, and were particularly influenced by recordings of the Hot Club of France, which featured Stéphane Grappelli and Django Reinhardt. The Texas-born Vernon Dalhart, a conservatory-trained singer who performed in light opera in New York City and recorded popular songs under a variety of names in the late 1910s and early 1920s, salvaged his career by recording "The Wreck of the Southern Old 97" and "The Prisoner's Song" in 1923, immense hits which established him as one of the most commercially successful hillbilly artists of the late 1920s. The hard-living and hard-drinking hillbilly singer Charlie Poole, who led a group called the North Carolina Ramblers, performed vaudeville and ragtime songs as well as rural music and idolized the Broadway star Al Jolson.[37]

Businessmen packaged country musicians as hillbilly performers and were careful to segregate white recordings from "race" records intended for black audiences. The term *hillbilly*, probably rooted in the late nineteenth-century southern vernacular, became a popular image of white southerners from Appalachia and the Ozarks in books, movies, and comics after 1900; connoting both positive (natural, strong, pure, stalwart) and negative (ignorant, lazy, violent, primitive) traits, record promoters found it a convenient way to provide a visual and linguistic analogue for the quality essential to the old-time music they were marketing—authenticity. Urbanites and music industry executives had little feeling for country music, nor respect for hillbillies. (A writer in *Variety* described the hillbilly as a "mountaineer type of illiterate white whose creed and allegiance are to the Bible, the Chautauqua, and the phonograph"; they were "illiterate and ignorant, with the intelligence of morons.") Yet the performers exuded no such disdain, and the audience valued those musicians who showed respect for the tradition and a credible knowledge of it yet were original, not merely imitating what had become popular. Authenticity was not a statement about the folk origins of these musicians (many were not "folk") nor about the music, which was highly complex and commercial, but about an attitude toward southern rural culture. Recording executives seemed to have understood this to some degree: the musicians were wont to perform in suit and tie—their Sunday-best, going-to-town outfits (although many early country performers were not poor and lived in cities); it was executives who concocted names such as the Hill Billies, Fruit Jar Drinkers, Gully Jumpers, and Dr. Bate's Possum Hunters for the country string bands and required the musicians to dress in countrified gear.[38]

The formulaic, typing, and genre-defining imperatives of commercialized mass art oftentimes disguised the profound cultural and racial hybridity of the raw material.[39] Folkish purity is hard to identify in the music of the 1920s, even as romantic folk enthusiasts would later make a fetish of it. Blackface performance—the nineteenth-century tradition of white people wearing black paint to perform comedic skits and African American music as egregiously stereotyped African Americans—remained popular in film, radio, and live performance in the 1920s and well beyond, serving to belittle black contributions to the popular arts. Stereotyped characters were common in mainstream Hollywood films (the small segment of black-produced films providing a complex exception to the dominant trend), oftentimes played by white actors wearing black makeup.

Many white musicians emulated black jazz, including Jack Teagarden in north central Texas, Hoagy Carmichael in Indiana, and the Austin High Gang, a group of high school students from a middle-class neighborhood on the west side of Chicago who spent hours listening to and discussing jazz records, including those of the New Orleans Rhythm Kings, a white group that tried to play in the black style. The Austin High Gang included the saxophonist Bud Freeman, trumpeter Jimmy McPartland, clarinetist Frank Teschemacher, and drummer Dave Tough. Other white players who eventually gravitated to the Chicago scene included saxophonist Mezz Mezzrow (originally Milton Mesirow), pianist Art Hodes, legendary clarinetist Benny Goodman, guitarist Eddie Condon, and cornetist Bix Beiderbecke. They comprised a hyperarticulate, intellectual, and artsy set: Beiderbecke was an avid reader, especially fond of Marcel Proust; Tough and Freeman frequented the Chicago Art Institute; Tough attended concerts of avant-garde compos- ers such as Igor Stravinsky and championed the work of his fellow native of the Chicago suburb Oak Park, Ernest Hemingway. Many were interested in Eastern philosophy; the iconoclastic *American Mercury* was the Austin High Gang's bible.[40]

All the same, jazz performance remained generally segregated. Although white Chicago jazzmen traveled to Chicago's South Side to see jazz played by black musicians and there were some rare interracial jazz sessions, out- side of Chicago, many whites remained ignorant of the black foundations of jazz. (Iowa-born and Denver-raised band leader Glenn Miller thought Benny Goodman the first jazz clarinetist.) Tentative efforts at integrating jazz performance picked up only in the 1930s, and many white jazz players (often ethnics eagerly leaving their roots and assimilating into mainstream America) were indifferent to the black foundations of jazz and happy to exploit their white skin privilege for commercial success. Players of popular "sweet jazz" dance music almost never mentioned its black roots; most no- toriously, Paul Whiteman, the hugely popular bandleader and impresario of lightly syncopated jazz dance music who claimed to be the King of Jazz, did not mention blacks or their music in his 1926 book, *Jazz*. Nick LaRocca, who led the white Original Dixieland Jazz Band, insisted that blacks played no role in the creation of jazz. Another Dixieland player, Tom Brown, claimed "niggers ain't no good on clarinet. Them thick, blubbery lips can't make a decent tone. . . . They aren't smart enough to tell where the harmony is, neither. After all, they niggers." The claims seemed to be rooted in a belief that Dixieland music, a syncopated style of traditional two-step music similar to early black jazz, was the only jazz music, despite the dominant legacy of black performers in New Orleans, including Louis Armstrong. Armstrong was perhaps the most influential jazz musician of the 1920s; one instructor required his trumpet students to play a horn dangling in the air by a string so that they might learn the posture, embouchure, and breathing necessary for Armstrong's warm, open sound. The white cornetist Bill Davison remem- bered a Sunset Café competition, or "cutting contest," between Armstrong and his mentor Joe "King" Oliver in Chicago: "they played about 125 cho- ruses of 'Tiger Rag'—exchanging choruses. . . . People went insane—they threw their clothes on the floor. . . . it was the most exciting thing I ever heard in my life."[41]

Rather, ethnic and Jewish white performers embraced popular white jazz, "the show business," and blackface routines as paths to an assimilated Ameri- can identity. Such a journey comprised the theme of *The Jazz Singer* (1927), starring the hugely popular singer Al Jolson, noteworthy as the first picture featuring recorded sound to become a major hit. (The movie was actually mostly silent, with sound provided only for Jolson's musical numbers.) In the film, Jolson plays Jakie Rabinowitz, the son of a cantor raised to follow in his father's profession. Defying his father's wishes, Jakie pursued an individualistic path to success by becoming Jack Robin and working his way up as a singer, in the process falling for a blonde shiksa. The film's climax occurs when Jack must decide, after failed attempts to reconcile with his dying father, whether to perform on opening night in a show that will vault him to fame or sing in the synagogue in his father's place, as his father wishes. Although melodramatic, the film effectively dramatized the tension between the authority of communal tradition and the personal autonomy promised by mainstream American society. Jack identifies his father as of the old world: "—tradition is all right, but this is another day! I'll live my life as I see fit!" His father regards such talk as "sacrilege." "You taught me that music is the voice of God!" Jack insists. "It is as honorable to sing in the theatre as in the synagogue!" Over the course of the argument, Jolson's character identifies his choice of a career in popular music not as a pursuit of wealth and success or a rite of independence but as a vocation. "My song means as much to *my* audience as yours to *your* congregation!" he insists, before being banished from the house by his father. He later explains to a friend of his father: "We in the show business have our religion, too—on every day—the *show must go on!*" Both his girlfriend and mother understand his sense of mission. Jack is "not *my* boy anymore—he belongs to the whole world now," his mother observes. As it happens, Jack is able to reconcile with his father, performing as a cantor before his death and singing the hit song "Mammy" in the big show, the opening night of which was fortuitously delayed.

Many popular and elite critics reacted with hostility to the quality of silent movies and jazz music and fretted at their moral effects. Jazz did, in fact, originate in vice districts, and many clubs where jazz musicians played were associated with organized crime. As a result, it gained a bad reputation within the bourgeois segments of the black community, at least initially. Whites wrote about jazz extensively, with many warning about the deleterious effects it would have on its auditors. It was often compared to a virus and a dangerous intoxicant; in both cases, it had the capacity to morally debilitate its listeners, encouraging promiscuity and race mixing, and degrade their tastes. Dr. E. Elliott Rawlings described the intoxication caused by jazz as "a continuous whirl of impressionable stimulations to the brain, producing thought and imaginations which overpower the will. Reason and reflection are lost and the actions of the persons are directed by the stronger animal passions." The General Federation of Women's Clubs pledged to "annihilate" jazz, feeling it an intoxicant as worthy of prohibition as alcohol. Over fifty cities, including Detroit, Cleveland, Kansas City, Omaha, and Philadelphia, banned jazz in public dance halls, and in New York, the city commissioner of licenses gained the authority to regulate jazz and dancing. In 1931, the National Association of Teachers of Speech listed *jazz* as one of the ten most offensive words in the English language.[42]

This perception was dramatized in Percy Marks's melodramatic tale of corrupted college youth, *The Plastic Age* (1924). The "terrible tom-tom" beat of a jazz band arouses the instinctual passions of young Hugh Carver and his date Cynthia Day, both inebriated at a dance. "Always the drums beating their terrible tom-tom, their primitive, blood-maddening tom-tom . . . Boom, boom, boom, boom," wrote Marks. The "weirdly sensuous" music, "rhythmic wailing of the fiddles," and "syncopated passion screaming with lust" combined with the "boom, boom, boom, booming" of the tom-toms to ill effect: "Blues, sobbing, despairing blues. . . . Orgiastic music—beautiful, hideous!" It is no wonder that Hugh's genteel (and somewhat prissy) roommate, an aspiring poet given to apostrophizing the beauty of love, found Hugh's behavior dispiriting. "I don't want beauty debased. I want to fight when orchestras jazz famous arias. Well, petting is jazzing love; and I hate it," he declared, to Hugh's mortification.[43]

Movies also aroused concern. The Reverend William L. Stidger, in praising the value of books in moral instruction, lamented the phenomenon of "Motion Picture Mind." Norman E. Richardson worried that "Our children are rapidly becoming what they see in the movies." The critic Burton Rascoe lambasted the quality of motion pictures in 1921, accusing movie producers of catering to the low intelligence of the average man. "The movie industry in America is a commercial and speculative enterprise and nothing more," he declared. Movies were mass-marketed merchandise, no more or less than canned beans, "dental creams," or the "depilator." If they were eliminated, the nation's intelligence would improve, Rascoe averred. The diversion they provide "was and is the mirror of the aspirations of a peculiarly unimaginative, repressed, and mentally starved people, a people who have in the overwhelming main been taught to value only a devitalizing and despiritualizing material success, arrived at by a curious duality of ethical teaching and practice." In 1929, responding to assorted critics who were now lamenting the fading art of the silent film as sound technology became the norm, the playwright Robert Sherwood sounded a note of optimism, predicting an artistic rebirth because a new crop of more competent corporate executives from the world of radio (General Electric, Western Electric, AT&T, and RCA) would bring a superior form of industrialization to the crop of low-quality producers, directors, and stars controlling Hollywood at the time.[44]

The writer and critic Gilbert Seldes became a significant defender of the "lively arts" in the 1920s. Born in 1893 to secularized Russian Jewish parents, Gilbert and his brother George (who had a long and noteworthy career as a radical journalist) grew up in an utopian farm colony shaped by both philosophical anarchism and the cooperativist beliefs of Edward Bellamy and Henry George in Alliance, New Jersey. His father was one of the colony's leaders, pushing his sons to read broadly and bringing them into contact with a wide variety of famous radicals. The sons became freethinkers; unattracted to socialism, Gilbert instead became a devoted Emersonian, given to pronouncements of his own divine nature. After high school in Philadelphia, Seldes graduated from Harvard in 1914, having befriended the poet E. E. Cummings, critic Harold Stearns, and novelist John Dos Passos. He worked as a journalist, stationed in London for part of the war; he and his brother were strong supporters of the Allied cause, and Gilbert joined the United States Army, serving stateside. Determined on a career as a writer, Seldes worked as an editor of the influential arts journal the *Dial* from 1919 to 1924, writing slashing critical essays there and elsewhere and earning the enmity of Ernest Hemingway, who mistakenly believed Seldes rejected one of his stories. In 1923, Seldes went to Paris to write a book on mass amusements drawing on appreciative critical essays he had been publishing in *Vanity Fair*, the *Dial*, and the *Freeman*. The following year his most famous work, *The Seven Lively Arts*, appeared.[45]

Seldes began the book by declaring his love of slapstick films, which he praised for their vulgarity and lack of pretense. In the book, Seldes established himself as a critic of the genteel tradition. The lively arts—movies, comic strips, musical comedy, vaudeville, radio, popular music, and dance—were lower forms, but they had what the fine arts of his time lacked: life, vitality, intensity, and (in a favorite phrase that Hemingway cruelly mocked in *The Sun Also Rises*) "irony and pity." "What makes Chaplin great," Seldes declared, "is that he has irony and pity, he knows that you must not have one without the other; he has both piety and wit." Seldes detested pretense and the "poison of culture." The Keystone comedies were "one of the few places where the genteel tradition does not operate, where fantasy is liberated, where imagination is still riotous and healthy." Irony, in his view, counteracted sentiment. Throughout the book, Seldes lavished praise on forms of popular art, treating them as works of genius and condemning out of hand "bogus" and "counterfeit" examples of high art. He praised George Her-riman's comic strip *Krazy Kat*, which he (and E. E. Cummings) considered brilliant; he credited jazz, which he equated with ragtime, with the "gaiety and liveliness" of the times; he admired Broadway comedians Eddie Cantor and Fanny Brice for their daemonic "intensity of action"; he liked the news-paper "colyumist" FPA (Franklin P. Adams) because he "recognizes fake." His admiration for Al Jolson was unabashed: "To have heard Al Jolson sing this song ["Swanee"] is to have had one of the few great experiences which the minor arts are capable of giving; to have heard it without feeling some-thing obscure and powerful and rich with a separate life of its own coming into being, is—I should say it is not to be alive."[46]

At times Seldes betrayed the limit of his taste and knowledge, as when, for example, he made the typical white critic's equation of jazz with synco-pated dance music, declaring Paul Whiteman's orchestra to be the best jazz orchestra. While crediting "negro music" for its role in the development of jazz ("our whole present music is derived from the negro," he observed), he also clearly distinguished "the negro and the intellectual" (the two strands of jazz, he believed), and "we" Americans from him, the negro. "In words and music the negro side expresses something which underlies a great deal of America—our independence, our carelessness, our frankness, and gaiety," Seldes wrote. "In each of these the negro is more intense than we are, and we surpass him when we combine a more varied and more intelligent life with his instinctive qualities." Despite his admiration for blacks' instinctive offer-ings and "desirable indifference to our set of conventions about emotional decency," Seldes commented, "I am on the side of civilization."[47]

While at times Seldes seemed to be indulging a deep passion for American kitsch, he was in fact taking the modernist critique of the ersatz and fabricated qualities of American industrialized culture and turning it against the middle-brow. He distinguished the artists working in popular media whom he deemed worthy. His enemies were members of the middle-class audience, he declared, who "blow neither hot nor cold" and who quail before the robust life of the lower arts merely because of their vulgarity. He attacked lifeless vocal concerts, classical dances, intellectual dramas, civic masques, grand operas, and high-toned films that were "counterfeit" currency, "the apparently good, essentially bad, which is the enemy of the good." Great works of art, he argued, produce the rare moments of "halcyon perfection" we all desire in life, like the aroma of a good wine. In daily life, with no leisure, we crave the intensity that comes at a tragic moment or experience of beauty, yet tend to guard against it for fear of being overwhelmed. For this reason, Seldes attributed a valuable function to the moments of authentic emotion in the lively arts:

The minor arts are, to an extent, an opiate—or rather they trick our hunger for a moment and we are able to sleep. They do not wholly satisfy, but they do not corrupt. And they, too, have their moments of intensity. Our experience of perfection is so limited that even when it occurs in a secondary field we hail its coming.

He also discerned a purity in specific examples of mass art, which provided a secondary rationale for his reappraisal of their value (one, ironically, echoed by Hemingway in his admiration for the technique of the bullfighter in *The Sun Also Rises*). "The part that is pure, I am convinced, is rarely matched on our other stages," he observed of vaudeville. "Certainly not in the legitimate, nor in the serious artistic playhouse where knowing one's job perfectly and doing it simply and unpretentiously are the rarest things in the world."[48]

In sallying forth so strongly in defense of the lowbrow and, further, implying that highbrow arts might actually pale in creativity and intelligence, Seldes touched one of the liveliest currents of debate among cultural critics of the 1920s. Moreover, he was honing in on topics and themes—popular artistic creation, the basis for ranking certain modes of artistic endeavor above others, authenticity versus pretense—central to the emerging critical discourse about industrial civilization developing among cultural critics in the world of letters and more academically inclined social scientists.

There were many explorations of such assumptions in the 1920s and beyond, but many of the early critics of mass culture missed a crucial dynamic. The emergence of radio provides an example. Confined to hobbyists in the early 1920s, radio listening at first focused on "DXing," testing one's equipment by tracking the most distant broadcast signal one could receive. The first broadcast station—KDKA in Pittsburgh, which began in 1920—grew out of the discovery by Westinghouse officials that an amateur broadcaster was gaining a popular audience by playing records for two hours on Wednesday and Saturday nights. Although there was an explosion of radio stations in 1922 (more than five hundred received licenses) and the diffusion of radio equipment was relatively rapid (by 1929, 40 percent of American families had receivers), there was much debate among intellectuals, policymakers, and corporations vying to profit from radio (AT&T, which led a "telephone group" that controlled transmitting technology and the phone lines necessary for national network broadcasting, fought with a "radio group" led by General Electric, RCA, and Westinghouse, which controlled patents for radio receivers) about who should control access to the airwaves, whether broadcasting should be commercial or publicly financed, and what the content should be.[49]

The debates were complex, with much opposition to advertising on the airwaves and resistance to commercialization, even from advertisers. Moreover, genteel technological enthusiasts believed radio would be an unprecedented bearer of high culture, as in the vision of one commentator who foresaw in 1924 a "super radio university educating the world," a "super orchestra bringing out the beauty of Beethoven's Ninth Symphony to millions," a "super newspaper reaching whole continents not by printed word but by the living voice." "We think not, thanks," Bruce Bliven had written two years earlier, after receiving an early demonstration of radio. He feared the homogenization such a vision entailed as well as the invasiveness of mass media (in a commentary more prescient if applied to the twenty-first century of social media), shuddering at "the civilization of 1930, when there will be only one orchestra left on earth, giving nightly world-wide concerts; when all the universities will be combined into one super-institution conducting courses by radio for students in Zanzibar, Kamchatka and Oskaloosa; when instead of newspapers, trained orators will dictate the news of the world day and night, and the bed-time story will be told every evening from Paris to the sleepy children of a weary world; when every person will be instantly accessible day or night to all the bores he knows, and will know them all; when the last vestiges of privacy, solitude and contemplation will have vanished into limbo."[50]

In fact, neither vision was fulfilled. Commercial broadcasting financed by paid advertisements came, not because imposed by larger corporations or major advertising agencies, but because small, independent broadcasters started using it, and the public accepted it, even liked it, eagerly tuning in stations run by department stores, newspapers, schools and universities, schools of chiropractic, and a variety of businesses (a stockyard, a marble company, a laundry, a steel foundry). Advertising, wrote one South Dakota listener to *Radio Digest*, "is interesting and helps lower the prices of what we need. . . . Why not let the farmers have a few stations that will give the programs of old-time singing and talks about things we need." Listeners had a taste for eccentric broadcasters such as John Rumulus Brinkley, who ran KFKB in Kansas and pedaled his own brand of medical flimflam, claiming that transplanted testicular tissue from live goats would increase sexual potency, or William K. "Doggone" Henderson, a profane disk jockey in Shreveport who specialized in "rustic insult comedy" and ranted against the government.[51]

Mass media need not be homogenizing nor were listeners' cultural identities easily changed. Movie fans actively sought to influence and control the films they loved. Movie studios invested large sums in administering fan-mail departments, which received millions of letters. Studio executives were attentive to the letters (and box-office receipts) when crafting the public personae of their stars. Working-class ethnics in Chicago listened to ethnic stations, sometimes listening together, actively and as a group. Italian immigrants in Chicago used Victrolas to play recordings of Italian opera and folk songs. Mass media actually reinforced ethnic identities, or fashioned regional ones, as when stations in Fort Worth, Chicago, and Nashville discovered that "barn dance" programs featuring rural and hillbilly music along with comic sketches and vaudeville-style entertainment drew large audiences of displaced rural southern whites. Such realities notwithstanding, the proliferating and unpredictable explosion of commercialized mass entertainment, and the fascination and alarm it stirred in intellectuals over what now increasingly seemed a tenuous and compromised American "culture," presaged future debates. Mass culture provoked the anxieties of modernist intellectuals, who tended to see conformity and uniformity everywhere. It also highlighted their ambivalence: Attuned to the immense power of culture, eager to repudiate the role of moral guardians, and avid proponents of personal freedom, they were profoundly distressed when the choices audiences made failed to reflect their own values or advance their aspirations for America.[52]

CHAPTER THREE

~

The Bridge

In the prewar years, Randolph Bourne was central to the circle of Young Intellectuals led by Van Wyck Brooks who were dedicated to creating a culture that would close, or at least bridge, the gap between a public caught up in the "catchpenny realities" of daily life and the genteel elite in their replica colonial mansions, that would unite Americans and foster community rather than reinforcing the distance between the refined and the masses. The "founder of the modern tradition of the New York literary intellectual," Bourne embraced the vibrancy of city life and evidenced an especially strong devotion to the ideal of "personality," the notion of self as fulfilled in social contact. Physically deformed from birth, Bourne was uniquely attuned to the emotional costs of outsiderhood and the imperative of friendship for personal fulfillment. The artistic "little renaissance" of bohemian Greenwich Village in the early 1910s succored Bourne, and he came alive in the free-flowing café talk that defined that place and period. Remaking America into a nourishing community, capable of sustaining "the good life of personality lived in the environment of the Beloved Community," was his foremost ideal. His lonely opposition to the Great War and premature death in the 1918 flu epidemic made him an icon of courageous dissent to subsequent generations of intellectuals.[1]

That the gap was not bridged in the 1920s and that the bifurcation between the new class of intellectuals and the broader public only widened and became characteristic of American public life perhaps should not be blamed on the literary intellectuals, for they surely expended much energy imagining how to accomplish the task. Indeed, American artists and writers became somewhat bifurcated themselves, with two distinct positions evolving over the course of the decade. The "Young American" critics (most notably Bourne, Van Wyck Brooks, Waldo Frank, Paul Rosenfeld, and Lewis Mumford) and the artistic coterie assembled by the photographer and art impresario Alfred Stieglitz, two groups sharing some common members and a loose intellectual affinity, vociferously and repeatedly declared their intention to turn from the alienating features of industrial and urban life to truer and more authentic representations of American ideals as inspiration for their work. Their rivals, most notably youthful proponents of the Dadaist provocations of the early 1920s, declared in equally passionate terms their intention to find a new, modern folklore inchoate in urban culture—the advertisements, the popular music, even the machines and buildings so often found distasteful by elite critics.

What both sides shared was an impulse to formulate a cultural politics defined ultimately by powerful images, symbols, and myths. Randolph Bourne likely would not have bridged this artistic and intellectual divide (between cultural nationalist and avant-garde modernist, between the artist eager to represent the nation in an epic work and the indifferent public, between the intellectual and the masses), but he would have enjoyed the extended conversation, undertaken by Americans and Europeans in cafés, salons, and lecture halls on both sides of the Atlantic.

In the 1920s, literary intellectuals were oftentimes alienated from America, and the measure of their alienation was the degree of their obsession with American culture. Alienation became the "essential" condition for literary Americans; American modernism, according to the critic Alfred Kazin in *On Native Grounds* (1942), grew out of literature's "surprise before the forces making a new world" and drew on the writers' "absorption in every last detail of their American world together with their deep and subtle alienation from it."[2] Alienation and engagement were opposing sides of the same coin.

The novelist Sinclair Lewis, enormously popular in the 1920s, exemplifies the often caustic disdain intellectuals displayed for middle America (and the wide public appetite for it). The heroine of *Main Street* (1920), Carol Kennicott, scathingly denounced her husband's small hometown, Gopher Prairie, as intellectually and culturally dead, its denizens a "savorless people, gulping tasteless food, and sitting afterward, coatless and thoughtless, in rocking-chairs prickly with inane decorations, listening to mechanical music, saying mechanical things about the excellence of Ford automobiles, and viewing themselves as the greatest race in the world." Lewis Mumford identified mass consumption as the engine of cultural homogenization, which to him was a disaster. Every town had its "Promenade," a commercial strip inspired ultimately by Broadway: "Up and down these second-hand Broadways, from one in the afternoon until past ten at night, drifts a more or less aimless mass of human beings, bent upon extracting such joy as is possible from the sights in the windows, the contacts with other human beings, the occasional or systematic flirtations, and the risks and adventures of purchase." Mumford's jaundiced view of American popular culture—the roller coasters and shoot-the-chutes of Coney Island that merely communicated the mechanical pressures of the workplace into the leisure realm—was characteristic of many critics. The movies, "White Ways," and Coney Islands in their various provincial iterations were merely "means of giving jaded and throttled people the sensations of living without the direct experience of life—a sort of spiritual masturbation."[3]

Mumford's commentary on American consumerism appeared in *Civilization in the United States*, a volume of critical essays edited by Harold Stearns and published in 1922 that provided a collective portrait of a starved, depleted civilization, ruined by the money-grubbing commercial mentality. The universal thirst for monetary success bred conformity, not creativity. Ultimately, business trumped culture, with the result that a prosaic class of provincials now ran the country. Hope, such as it was in this pessimistic analysis, lay in American pluralism and the urge to give voice to the authentic America, to foster an "autochthonous" art. The possibilities of any immediate change, however, seemed dim to these naysaying intellectuals.

Mumford linked a critique of the relatively homogenized city, planned for commercial purposes only, with the aimlessness of consumer habits. "People who do not know how to spend their time must take what satisfaction they can in spending their money," he opined. He attributed the relative paucity of distinguished intellect, art, and architecture in many American towns to their pioneer heritage, suggesting that the founding New Englanders had exhausted their energies in settling the Ohio River Valley. The legendary Johnny Appleseed, he averred, had "planted dry apple seeds, instead of slips from the living tree, and hedged the roads he travelled with wild apples, harsh and puny and inedible."[4] Pioneering allowed for no leisure, hence no critical self-reflection, and the rigors of frontier life precluded questions about the meaning and ends of life. An exclusive concern for business and practicality, absent culture, resulted in the physical blight and "desolateness" of the "common American industrial town," with its heaps of "rubbish and rusty metal" and "general disorder and vileness." As Mumford observed:

These qualities are indicative of the fact that we have centred attention not upon the process but upon the return; not upon the task but the emoluments; not upon what we can get out of our work but upon what we can achieve when we get away from our work. Our industrialism has been in the grip of business, and our industrial cities, and their institutions, have exhibited a major preoccupation with business. The coercive repression of an impersonal, mechanical technique was compensated by the pervasive will-to-power—or at least will-to-comfort—of commercialism.

Americans have "failed to react creatively upon their environment," Mumford believed. In the view of the young journalist Louis Raymond Read, echoing the complaint of *Main Street*, American cities were no different, spiritually, than American small towns, which set the tone of American civilization. He challenged those "few libertarians and cosmopolites" who saw dawning civilization in Eastern cities to deny his bleak scorn for the run of American popular culture:

They cannot watch the tremendous growth and power and influence of secret societies, of chambers of commerce, of boosters' clubs, of the Ford car, of moving pictures, of talking-machines, of evangelists, of nerve tonics, of the *Saturday Evening Post*, of Browning societies, of circuses, of church socials, of parades and pageants of every kind and description, of family reunions, of pioneer picnics, of county fairs, of firemen's conventions without secretly acknowledging it.[5]

Read listed the terms of daily American existence indiscriminately; they were for him self-evident signs of American cultural decline, self-enclosed synecdoches of American boobishness and philistinism (although one wonders, why be offended by a family reunion?). They reveal the particular colic that this type of criticism could sometimes foster. His reference to Model Ts and his assumption that one evangelist was much like the next betrayed a faith that American culture was standardized across the nation. Clarence Britten, an editor and professor, imagined a visiting explorer from Mars imparting his impressions of the United States: "in nothing are you so alike as in your universal desire to be alike—to be inconspicuous, to put on straw hats on the same day, to change your clothes in Texas in accordance with the seasons in New York, to read the books everybody else is reading, to adopt the opinions a weekly digests for you from the almost uniform opinions of the whole of the daily press, in war and peace to be incontestably and entirely American."[6]

In general, Stearns's symposium reflected a simplification of critical terms. Recycling George Santayana somewhat crudely, Stearns derided a feminized culture. The American pioneers had handed responsibility for art, music, religion, literature, and intellectual life to women, with baleful effects. "The spinster school-marm has settled in the impressionable, adolescent minds of boys the conviction that the cultural interests are largely an affair of the other sex; the intellectual life can have no connection with native gaiety, with sexual curiosity, with play, with creative dreaming, or with adventure." Students from the west at Harvard, he recalled, felt only "sissies" took courses in poetry. Would-be young intellectuals, he averred, are crippled by Santayana's "genteel tradition," squeamish before the body and palsied by an "essentially American (and essentially feminine) timorousness before life itself"—a prim, fussy, sour, fearful, and humorless culture.[7]

Lewis's heavy-handed satire *Babbit* (1922) tracked the viewpoint of *Civilization in the United States* closely, including the antifeminism of its critique. The novel narrates the fortunes of George F. Babbitt, social climber, conformist, indifferent father, moderately corrupt real estate agent, and modern consumer extraordinaire, in his brief rebellion against the limits of his existence. A midlife crisis drives Babbitt to temporarily fling caution aside and dabble in bohemianism and liberal thinking. One form of freedom is escape from a feminized domesticity: Babbitt's youthful friend and surrogate kid brother, Paul Riesling, was trapped in an unfortunate marriage. Paul's nagging wife precipitates Babbitt's own crisis, for was not Babbitt himself also trapped in a seemingly loveless marriage, having married more from pity than passion? Driving his car to work becomes Babbitt's pale surrogate for manly adventure; the preferred mode of escape in his life is to don "he-togs" and head to the "he-world" of outdoor adventure for a homosocial bonding with Paul and their guide Joe Paradise at a camp in the Maine woods. (Babbitt's fantasy escape from domesticity involves rugged hiking and hunting with Paradise, whom he assimilates in his mind to a trapper seen in a movie, only to discover the older Paradise cranky at the long hiking and dreaming of opening a shoe store.)

Throughout the novel, Lewis savagely caricatures the hypocritical Babbitt and his philistine companions. Conformity, standardization of living, and the absence of wit and verve define their lives. The showpiece of the book is Babbitt's address to the Zenith Real Estate Board boosting the appeal of Zenith and highlighting the virtues of the average citizen, whom Babbitt variously labels the "plain Solid American Citizen," "Our Ideal Citizen," "Sane Citizen," "Regular Guy," and, finally, the "Standardized Citizen." In Zenith, Lewis provided a detailed and vivid version of the undistinguished midwestern town already created by Mumford, with its "jaded and throttled people" and "spiritual masturbation." Babbitt hails the "new type of civilization" in Zenith and her "sister-cities": "There are many resemblances between Zenith and these other burgs, and I'm darn glad of it! The extraordinary, growing, and sane standardization of stores, offices, streets, hotels, clothes, and newspapers throughout the United States shows how strong and enduring a type is ours." The Standardized Citizens of America were culturally impoverished in Lewis's telling, although their condition seems more foolish than pathetic. Confronted by his son Ted with a preference for "home study" courses from the Shortcut Educational Publishing Co. of Sandpit, Iowa, the ever-equivocating Babbitt, whose own reading interests do not extend beyond the comics page, initially defends Shakespeare as a prerequisite to college entrance but eventually relents, commenting sympathetically to Ted on the time lost at universities "studying poetry and French and such subjects that never brought in anybody a cent. I don't know but what maybe these correspondence-courses might prove to be one of the most important American inventions."[8]

While Stearns expatriated himself to Paris, there to earn the scorn of Ernest Hemingway for being a lazy alcoholic, the caustic and debunking criticism of *Civilization in the United States* and Lewis's novels gained a broad audience and left an indelible image of 1920s criticism for later generations. However, the one person who most embodied this attitude at the time, for good and ill, was H. L. Mencken.

Mencken exemplified the new authority claimed by critics—and he represented the breed well. His prose was sparkling and witty, he was serious and wide-ranging, and he could hold forth on political, literary, social, and cultural matters with conviction and authority. He became famous, and he made criticism more salient in American culture.[9] Mencken was born in Baltimore, Maryland, in 1880, to an upper-middle-class German American family. His father, August Mencken, coowned a successful cigar factory with his brother and loomed as a powerful patriarch in the Mencken household. A fiercely antiunion, high-tariff, conservative Republican who also was an agnostic and opposed to conventional religion, August Mencken figured in his son's life as both a barrier to his ambitions and the model for many of his own conservative habits and beliefs. Mencken's father and paternal grandfather also communicated family prejudices to Henry: his grandfather was careful to stay separate from most of Baltimore's German population (the city was about one-fourth German at the time of Mencken's birth), and H. L. Mencken later snobbishly disdained most German Americans. His father took pains to emphasize that his family was not Jewish, often signaling this clearly by writing "We are not *Jews*" in business letters.[10]

His father also was a sporting man, however, and part owner of the Washington baseball club. As a youth, Henry Mencken would sometimes accompany

H. L. Mencken, 1928.
Courtesy Enoch Pratt Free Library, Maryland's State Library
Resource Center, Baltimore, Maryland.

him on his frequent trips to Washington. August introduced him to the life of relaxation and pleasure described by the German term *Gemutlichkeit*, however he opposed his son's vocational ambitions, which were to be a journalist and writer, enrolling him instead in a local polytechnic high school anathema to Henry. In three years spent working for the family business, Mencken occasionally approached despair. He was only released from paternal authority by chance, with the sudden and premature death of August Mencken from kidney disease in 1899, an event that, even at the time, young Henry Mencken understood as a fortunate tragedy that freed him to pursue his life's ambition. Almost immediately, he entered journalism, starting as city reporter for the *Baltimore Herald*, soon writing stories and poetry on the side, and eventually becoming the paper's city editor. By the mid-1910s, Mencken was an established newspaperman and columnist and had already developed a distinctive literary style.

Mencken lived his entire life, aside for a few married years, in his family's Baltimore row house. Even when dividing his time between his Baltimore newspaper work and editorial responsibilities with the *Smart Set* and later *American Mercury* in New York City, Mencken remained essentially a homebody, scrupulously caring for his mother and two unmarried siblings and often working late in his upstairs bedroom. He was a creature of habit, inured to his Baltimore routine, which included a weekly musical group that he attended faithfully. He enjoyed the pleasures of numerous female companions yet possessed a peerless ability to bifurcate his personal life between a libertine existence drinking on the town with fellow writers and dating young women (sometimes Broadway women, often while carrying on other relationships, even though outwardly the gentleman in his demeanor) and maintaining a genteel home in which he followed an arduous work routine. From the time he began reviewing for the *Smart Set* in 1908, Mencken reviewed two thousand books over fifteen years and wrote 182 essays and, on average, 1500 letters a year—a marvel of productivity.

Mencken was profoundly, if idiosyncratically, conservative. The hallmarks of his thinking were a commitment to reasoned inquiry and science as he understood it: thus, he was convinced on theory and from his own observation that blacks were inferior, in part due to what he took to be scientific proof of smaller brain sizes. He remained a lifelong social Darwinist, yet, all the same, before the Great War he supported many progressive reforms, such as industrial safety, workers' compensation, antitrust, an expanded electorate, opposition to capital punishment, and, in particular, public health reforms. (Mencken himself was something of a hypochondriac, minutely sensitized to the many physical complaints he meticulously recorded in letters and diary entries.)

At the same time, Mencken was dyspeptic and a man given to strong prejudices. Combined with his deep commitment to honesty, frankness, and free speech (late in life, he styled himself a libertarian), this dyspepsia, amounting almost to misanthropy, resulted in the Mencken of public caricature, dispensing caustic judgments in prose touched with hyperbole. In the fourth of his six volumes of *Prejudices*, which were published between 1919 and 1927, Mencken skewered political pandering to agrarian constituents. His point was unsurprising, given his complete devotion to city life, but his attack demonstrates well the comic excess of his vituperative iconoclasm, as he inverted traditional images of the virtuous husbandmen. He excoriated American veneration of the farmer, whom he accused of laying siege to the public treasury: "No more grasping, selfish and dishonest animal, indeed, is known to the students of the Anthropoidea," Mencken proclaimed. "When the going is good for him he robs the rest of us up to the extreme limit of our endurance; when the going is bad he comes bawling for help out of the public till." Mencken denounced the populist tradition of the Greenback Party and late nineteenth-century silver campaigns, all the "complex fiscal imbecilities of the cow State John Baptists," declaring, "There has never been a time, in good seasons, or bad, when his hands were not itching for more; there has never been a time when he was not ready to support any charlatan, however grotesque, who promised to get it for him." Far from being a model of civic virtue, the farmer, in Mencken's description, was uniquely avaricious as well as a "prehensile moron," condemned to live with "unclean and ill-natured wives."[11] (Mencken's animus was motivated in part, it should be noted, by Prohibition, which he credited to rural America. Mencken detested Prohibition, and opposing it was a personal crusade; he maintained a healthy stock of alcohol in his home and became an avid home brewer.)

Mencken was an elitist—convinced that the great mass of Americans were timid and fearful sheep, desperately seeking security and comfort by conforming to the going fashion. He reveled in sweeping judgments of ethnic groups (Mencken decried others' prejudices but treasured his own). His private papers, which were opened to the public beginning in 1971, revealed his severe prejudices; he was a private, and occasionally public, bigot—racist, anti-Semitic, intolerant, and cranky. Yet, he was also a racial paternalist, publishing and championing black authors, calling for black civil rights and the humane treatment of African Americans, and pushing the *Sun* newspapers to hire a black reporter and cover black topics. He accepted the racial theories of his time and considered blacks inferior, as late as 1926 suggesting that blacks were one or two inches from "gorillas" and, in dealing with matters regarding his house, capable, as he recorded, of getting a "Jew lawyer to induce the neighboring owners to sign an anti-coon agreement." Moreover, he reserved as much scorn for Anglo-Saxons as for blacks. Commenting on anti-German prejudice during the Great War and after, Mencken parsed the bloodlines of Anglo-Saxons in detail, attributing certain characteristics, such as religious fanaticism (leading to Methodist revivalism) and Prohibitionism, to their Scotch blood and generally passing a negative judgment on them. "The Anglo-Saxon of the great herd is, in many important respects, the least civilized of men and the least capable of true civilization," he declared. He found him shallow in political ideals, lacking aesthetic feeling, and prone to alarm about the world. "His blood, I believe, is running thin; perhaps it was not much to boast of at the start; in order that he may exercise any functions above those of a trader, a pedagogue or a mob orator, it needs the stimulus of other and less exhausted strains."[12]

In his famous essay attacking the South, "The Sahara of the Bozart," not only did Mencken denigrate southern cultural aspirations ("In all that gargantuan paradise of the fourth-rate there is not a single picture gallery worth going into, or a single orchestra capable of playing the nine symphonies of Beethoven, or a single opera-house, or single theater devoted to decent plays") but also speculated that the long-term effects of the Civil War were to enhance the power of "white trash" by depleting the "best blood" and argued that the upper-class white predilection for black mistresses had created a class of superior mulattoes.[13] For Mencken, class divisions reflected congenital traits identifiable by race, not just differences of wealth. In his hierarchical worldview, such class distinctions reflected a justly ordered society.

Offensive as Mencken is to modern sensibilities, he was enormously popular in his day—a particular favorite of college students. "You have no idea the enormous vogue Mencken has among students," a correspondent wrote to the president of the University of Virginia in 1925. In 1926, when Mencken's cultural authority and popularity peaked—indeed, when Mencken was a new and unprecedented cultural celebrity—his American Mercury ranked first among magazines sold in the college bookstores of Harvard, Columbia, and other universities across the country. As Philip M. Wagner, an editor at the Baltimore Evening Sun, reminisced, "It is hard to describe the way we felt, I mean our generation on the campuses about Mencken. For one thing, he gave us an attitude. . . . He shook the dust from early literature. He persuaded us that good writing didn't have to follow old models, although it might take the best of them. He knocked down a whole shooting gallery of sacred literary sheep and cows."[14]

Mencken intended American Mercury for the "civilized minority" and returned time and again to his belief that the masses were inferior and that only an aristocratic elite were capable of culture. "No sound art, in fact, could possibly be democratic. . . . The only art that is capable of reaching the Homo Boobus is art that is already debased and polluted—band music, official sculpture, Pears' Soap painting, the popular novel," Mencken wrote in his first volume of Prejudices. He lashed Americans for their conformity, assessing the struggle to attain membership in America's reigning "bugaboo" aristocracy as an exercise in servility and obedience to prescribed opinion. America lacked what Europe possessed by virtue of its history: an aristocracy. Only an elite secure in status and self-confident can preserve civilization in the face of popular philistinism. The "lower orders" quail before challenging ideas and fall prey to superstition. Mencken envisioned literary and artistic revolt as a revolt of the elites against the masses. (The American people, he observed, "taking one with another, constitute the most timorous, sniveling, poltroonish, ignominious mob of serfs and goose-steppers ever gathered under one flag in Christendom since the end of the Middle Ages," and, he believed, "they grow more timorous, more sniveling, more poltroonish, more ignominious every day.")[15] Mencken scorned a literature responsive to the dictates of the masses. A true elite did not shrink before the gross physical realities of life and did not embrace the treacly satisfactions of conventional church services and religion. Moreover, an enlightened elite embraced the world's pleasures and would superintend an open-ended, raucous culture, secure in their own status.

Mencken's hyperbolic prose style, so over-the-top and sometimes offensive to readers today, should not obscure his temerity, at a time when cultural repression was high—an age of nativism, Klan organizing, Red hunts, and dominant conservatism—in challenging popular prejudices. After 1920, at the peak of American reaction, Mencken railed against censorship, Prohibition, and the denial of civil liberties; he defended immigrant anarchists, including the eventually deported Emma Goldman (to whom he sent a check), Nicola Sacco and Bartolomeo Vanzetti, and Carlo Tresca.

Ultimately, Mencken's critical reach was limited: he did not analyze thinkers or works as a whole, but nibbled at the edges, picking out weak formulations or ripe rhetoric on which to base his critique, which often took the form of a sweeping judgment. He covered ideas as fashions only. In his relentless deflation of ideas—the debunking spirit which he exemplified—he also deflated the intellectual world. The greatest denouncer of American puritanism, he was something of a puritan in private, as one of his biographers, Fred Hobson, observed—living an austere, quiet life when at home, tending his garden, and working assiduously in his upstairs room. Scorning the genteel tradition publicly, in private he embraced what he considered the more civilized customs and manners of the upper class. He published the *Smart Set*, and helped launch silly and salacious magazines on the side to help support it, and yet ultimately he disdained the social and sexual habits of bohemians, valued hard work, and judged the poor lazy. While his libidinous side came out in trips to New York City, in Baltimore, his mother, an exemplar of Victorian gentility, superintended his home until her death in 1926. He grew steadily more conservative over time, yet he always remained tolerant and an advocate of private freedom and a freer, more open culture. All was reduced to his Nietzschean individualism and nonconformity; he treasured being his own man, toiling in his upper-floor room, casting a jaundiced eye at a foolish world. His views were leavened by a basic sense of decency and fair play, qualities which, along with his steadfast commitment to literary realism and naturalism and his stalwart defense of freedom in writing and the arts, more often than not aligned him with the literary avant-garde and liberalism. It did not hurt that, as an editor, Mencken published and promoted writers he deemed interesting and of high quality, not those who matched an ideological test. As such, his basic intellectual stance was rather simple, even if maddeningly complex as he worked it out in regular contributions to public debate.

⌒

Brooks's *America's Coming-of-Age* had been a distinctly more hopeful manifesto. Brooks felt the nation needed a centralized intellectual life to achieve organic community, a "race-life," a *"focal centre,"* a "middle ground" now absent, which could mediate between the institutions of culture and commerce. In the pioneering stage, the nation may have lacked the time and resources for civilization, but as a people, Americans have acquired a "competence," the physical necessities required for maintaining body and mind. Now the American can cultivate the personality, and this can only come with an end to pioneering and an establishment of roots. In an essay entitled "On Creating a Usable Past," published in the *Dial* in 1918, Brooks outlined the program to find this middle ground: reconstruct the "racial past" and create a "usable past" for the budding artist.[16] Although sharing in the general antipathy to America's commercial culture, the Young American group felt cultural revitalization to be possible, even imminent, for the resources lay at hand in America's own literary and artistic traditions. In *Our America* (1919), an essay in cultural self-analysis in response to the queries of two French friends, Waldo Frank imagined the task of modern American artists as cultural creation more than reconstruction. Beneath "the steel towers and the shrill accents of New York," the imposing but essentially false surface of modern, prosperous America, lay a hidden America, and in contemplating the task of explaining this nation to his friends, Frank realized that "America was a conception to be created."[17]

The goal of Frank, Brooks, and their circle was to restore the kind of organic community in American life that could foster art and develop a whole "personality," a term which had great meaning in their cultural criticism. The term *personality* was a late nineteenth-century and early twentieth-century way to speak of character. (In a more broadly popular sense, "personality" evoked the charisma and personal magnetism increasingly important to a metropolitan society and corporate economy.) It suggested the development of an individual's capacity to live a fulfilled and efficacious life—potency, the ability to lead others, and individualism—which could only be achieved in society, through democratically linking oneself to the broader community.[18]

In Frank's hopeful vision, his peers were to be a new generation of *spiritual* pioneers fighting through the cultural deprivations enforced by earlier generations of *physical* pioneers to reconstruct American culture. Religious moralism, the single-minded greed for national expansion, and the increased production of goods were oppressive. "The pioneer must do violence upon himself," Waldo Frank declared in *Our America* (1919). "Whole departments of his psychic life must be repressed. Categories of desire must be inhibited. Reaches of consciousness must be lopped off. Old, half-forgotten intuitions must be called out from the buried depths of his mind, and made governors of his life." The pioneer became, in Frank's telling, an emotionally locked up individual with no time allotted for the pursuit of harmony with nature or aesthetic fulfillment. The Young Intellectuals linked their dour and repressed stereotype of the American pioneer to the Puritan: the astringent asceticism of the Puritan became a complement to the spiritually bereft pioneer. Puritan and pioneer were temperamentally one, Frank declared. Puritanism became the religious rationale for continental expansion and imperial exploitation. "The Puritan movement was simply a chapter in the long history of religious decadence. . . . It was essentially an irreligious force: it was in practice a component of pioneering." "American Industrialism is the new Puritanism, the true Puritanism of our day," Frank declared.[19]

As Frederick J. Hoffman observed in his survey of writing from the decade, the double image of the "Puritan-pioneer" became the essential American problematic: "This conviction all but dominated American criticism throughout the 1920s. The American was an industrial giant, an emotional dwarf; having repressed his love of life (that is, his emotional predisposition to things, animals, fellow creatures), he came through with ingenious inventions, processes, methods; he built bigger, better, and faster locomotives, and was experimenting with automobiles and playing with airplanes; but the nearer India seemed, the more difficult the passage to it became." Or, in James Truslow Adams's pungent 1929 observation, "When one is busy killing Indians, clearing the forest, and trekking farther westward every decade, a strong arm, an axe, and a rifle are worth more than all the culture of all the ages. Not only has the frontiersman no leisure or opportunity to acquire manners and culture but, because of their apparent uselessness, and in true class spirit, he comes to despise them." Adams felt America to be a *"business man's civilization"* at its root, and linked the superficiality of American culture to a general lack of ideas, relatively weak religious and university establishments, and the failure of the political, military, and civil service elite to provide a counterweight to American business. As a result, the United States had developed an "economic" as opposed to a "humanistic" civilization.[20]

The most complete expression of the Young American ambition to mine American cultural history in the hopes of creating an organic, "humanistic" culture that would bridge rather than exacerbate the gap between the elite and the broader public occurred in the work of Lewis Mumford. After the death of Bourne, the extended illness of Brooks resulting from a breakdown, and the increasingly mystical flights of Frank as the decade progressed, Mumford remained to carry on the Young Intellectuals' cultural criticism. His *The Golden Day* (1926) marked a culmination of the cultural criticism of the Young Americans and presented Mumford's mature theories on cultural change in the form of a sweeping account of American cultural development.

Much of Mumford's education as a youth was the result of his self-directed explorations of prewar, bourgeois New York, which still bore physical signs of the rural hinterlands that supported it. He took various college courses in New York City during the 1910s before enrolling in the navy during the war, after which he returned home to make his living as a writer, editor, and critic. He drew on the ideas of Brooks, Bourne, and Frank and had connections with the Stieglitz circle, but was also influenced by the biologically and ecologically minded theories of the Scottish regional planner and theorist Patrick Geddes. Mumford became an advocate for regional planning, helping to found the Regional Planning Association of America and envisioning decentralized, small-scale communities organically connecting urban and rural living. In a special issue of *Survey Graphic* in May 1925, Mumford, the conservationist Benton MacKaye, and their compatriots urged a shift away from the soaring, modern megalopolis to carefully developed regional communities. Mumford wanted to ruralize cities and encouraged a return migration from the cities into the surrounding region. He published two books embodying his organic visions for the American landscape: *The Story of Utopias* (1922), in which the ideal city organically connected to the region, and *Sticks and Stones: A Study of American Architecture and Civilization* (1924), which lionized the New England town. *The Golden Day* carried on this criticism, identifying the New England renaissance stretching from Emerson to Melville as an embodiment of regional achievement. The "Golden Day" was both a moment in time and a specific place of cultural equipoise between an old order and a new, an "organic break" in which American intellectuals drew from their regional soil elements that could be preserved and reused and, at the same time, created anew, achieving—for a "day"—a renewed, vital, and balanced culture.[21]

In part, Mumford's book was also a critique of pragmatists such as John Dewey. He articulated a by then timeworn attack on the pragmatic acquiescence to modern industrialism and the pragmatists' transformation into utilitarian technocrats. They were concerned only for material abundance and devoid of vision and ideals, in this line of attack. More than this, the book was a call for the adoption of symbolic forms that might again civilize America. Mumford unfolded an interpretation of American civilization based on the image of pioneering, which became an emblem for hyperindividualism and excessive acquisitiveness. It was a critique grounded in the Young Intellectuals' dictum that personality must be achieved through a democratic engagement in community life. Mumford traced Western disintegration to the thirteenth century, a process driven by the ostensibly liberating forces of science, Protestantism, and the "new financial order." Instead of liberation, these transformative forces vouchsafed a new culture that was "thin, partial, abstract, and deliberately indifferent to man's proper interests"—an anemic and threadbare culture most fully realized in America. For Mumford, symbols and forms impelled social action. Historically, European Romanticism's symbol of the pioneer created the myth of pioneering and the actual pioneer who settled America. As pioneers, Europeans turned into savages and individualists: "with the drift to the West, America became . . . a place where the European could be swiftly transformed into something different: where the civil man could become a hardy savage, where the social man could become an 'individual,' where the settled man could become a nomad, and the family man could forget his old connections."[22]

In short, Mumford told a tale of westerners who stripped themselves of culture in a colonial outpost and put nothing in its place—the original self-created exiles, for whom Mumford had nothing but pity and regret. Civilization represents the culmination of humans' historical ability to cultivate the earth; in wild, uncivilized America, absent careful cultivations, the fruits were puny and insipid. "Cultivation is man's natural and proper condition; for life in the raw is empty," Mumford declared. He articulated the Young Americans' conception of culture: "The mission of creative thought is to gather into it all the living sources of its day, all that is vital in the practical life, all that is intelligible in science, all that is relevant in the social heritage and, recasting these things into new forms and symbols, to react upon the blind drift of convention and habit and routine." Human culture, he argued, is a "continuous process of choosing, selecting, nurturing, a process also of cutting down and exterminating those merely hardy and fecund weeds which have no value except their own rank life." The pioneer refused culture: singing of home, but moving away from it to the west; hymning the tree, but cutting the forest; romanticizing the Indians only to kill them. The pioneers' legacy was "deserted villages, bleak cities, depleted soils, and sick and exhausted souls."[23]

Mumford called for cultural renewal, hearkening to the Golden Day of Emerson, Thoreau, Whitman, and Melville, the moment of equipoise between two worlds, the disintegrating European culture and emerging American one, which allowed for a renaissance in which writers could develop symbols to underwrite a "modern basis of culture." In Mumford's view, contemporary Americans lived on only the fragments of older cultures, lacking the symbols that would foster useful and productive social action and artistic creation. "Men are sustained, in faith and work, not by what they find in the universe, but by what man has built there," Mumford argued, in a crucial passage, invoking Melville, the rediscovered American great author of the 1920s. "Man gave the word: he gave the symbol: he gave the form: he believed in his ejaculations and created language; he believed in his form and wrought cities; he believed in his symbols, and created myth, poetry, science, philosophy. Deny this initial act of faith, tear aside the veil man has thrown between his own experience and the blank reality of the universe and everything else becomes meaningless: depend upon one's private self alone and though the renunciation be heroic, the result is inevitable: the White Whale will swallow at one gulp."[24] It was a piquant call to the modern writer not to depict the "blank reality" of the universe but to create the veils that sustain humans in their faith and work; to undertake the task of building culture, not to recreate exile; to halt the pioneering and instead cultivate, recover, and retrieve past forms; and to create the symbols that would endow a new age of personality.

The Young American project aimed to tap into American cultural roots— a project echoed by African American writers such as Jean Toomer and Langston Hughes in the 1920s and various regionalist artists in the 1920s and 1930s. Despite the temporary migration of many writers to Paris in the 1920s (seeking artistic inspiration and a congenial and affordable setting), many European modernists courted American artists and floated claims of American artistic leadership during and after the Great War. They initiated an "intercontinental dance" with American artists, cultivating a transatlantic *américanisme* driven by fascination with American technology and mass culture. Many avant-garde artists embraced "machine-age idealism" and saw in technology and mass production the distinctive forms their generation was fated to engage. Skyscrapers, billboards, brand-name products, factories, plumbing fixtures, comic books, jazz, the Charleston, Coney Island, rush-hour crowds, store window displays, the Great White Way of Broadway, film, and ragtime—all became elements of an alternative symbology of modernity, the new, awakened America born into the machine age, trailing no past. Matthew Josephson, launching his career as a writer and critic, lived in Paris from 1921 to 1923. He recalled, "I was observing a young France that, to my surprise, was passionately concerned with the civilization of the U.S.A., and stood in a fair way to being *Americanized!*" As art historian Wanda Corn noted, "[W]here outposts of cultural *américanisme* began to crop up after the war around avant-garde activity, the young idolized American women, skyscrapers, jazz, and pop culture. . . . Their reading of American comic books and their fascination with Whitman, Henry Ford, Thomas Edison, and Charlie Chaplin would not be lost on the American expatriates in Paris, who found themselves in the curious position of having gone abroad to study great European literature and art only to discover that the French were engaged in a serious romance with America."[25]

The impulse to an expressive Americanness originated in the 1910s and merged with Euro-American machine-age idealism. The New York art dealer Robert J. Coady briefly published a little magazine called *The Soil* in 1916 and 1917, in which he complained of the sterile work produced by contemporary American artists who slavishly imitated European avant-garde fashions. "Our 'new men' are the 'ismists' who are more interested in theories than art," declared Coady. "None of this is American; none of it has come from the soil." Seemingly any cultural form that was the pure expression of a people's impulses or needs, whether high art or popular entertainment, was automatically superior to that derived from a school or movement. Because too beholden to European models, America lacked genuine art, which must be spontaneous and expressive. Not well known during his foreshortened lifetime (he died at age thirty-nine in January 1921), Coady rose from obscurity at the hand of Robert Alden Sanborn, who wrote about him for the Dadaist periodical *Broom*. He loved the popular amusements of New York City and proclaimed them the true basis of a new folk culture. Sanborn wrote of Coady sampling the low-rent amusements of the city, frequenting "smelly little East Side movie theatres" and delighting in burlesque houses, baseball games, and prizefights. Coady bitterly lamented the closing of an old Chinese theater on Doyer Street and seriously admired African American children's songs, cartoons, slapstick comedy, and the sports pages.[26]

An article in the December 1916 issue of *The Soil* contained Coady's views of American art; much of it was an indiscriminant listing of all that he judged to be art. Among the items: "The Panama Canal, the Sky-scraper and Colonial Architecture. The East River, the Battery and the 'Fish Theatre.' The Tug Boat and the Steam-shovel. The Steam Lighter. The Steel Plants, the Washing Plants and the Electrical Shops. The Bridges . . . the '3000.' Gary. The Polarine and the Portland Cement Works. Wright's and Curtiss' Aeroplanes and the Aeronauts. . . . Jack Johnson, Charlie Chaplin, and 'Spike' in 'The Girl in the Game.' . . . Bert Williams, Rag-time, the Buck and Wing and the Clog. . . . The Window Dressers." Before he died, Coady touted plans for an American Tradition League and hoped to publish a monthly magazine on the development of American culture. The poet William Carlos Williams and expatriate writer Robert McAlmon published *Contact* for five issues from 1920 to 1923, a journal which shared the spirit of Coady's project and heralded an indigenous art that would be in "contact" with the American people, even in the face of their indifference. The editors believed that, as art historian Dickran Tashjian observed, "a live art requires contact with the local environment in terms of particular experience." Williams's concept of "Contact" was, the young critic Kenneth Burke wrote in 1922, "man without the syllogism . . . man with nothing but the thing and the feeling of that thing."[27]

The group of artists and writers around Alfred Stieglitz shared the impulse to create the "Great American Thing," in Georgia O'Keeffe's words. The members of the circle included O'Keeffe (who became Stieglitz's wife), Arthur Dove, Marsden Hartley, John Marin, Paul Strand, and often Charles Demuth. "American," as Wanda Corn observed, became almost a "brand" for this circle, as they relentlessly used the term in their public showings and as part of their own elaborate critical vocabulary in essays (they published a short-lived journal, MSS, in 1922–1923) and private letters.[28] Stieglitz and his associates shared a vitalist rhetoric of "spirit" and "soil" and infused their work with spiritual and religious pretensions, positioning the older and accomplished Stieglitz as a prophet and seer, a heroic visionary of a new art rooted in the loam of the American countryside.

Stieglitz collected writers such as the midwestern novelist Sherwood Anderson; the art and music critic Paul Rosenfeld, who effusively promoted the circle and its "Americanist" cause in *Port of New York* (1923); and Waldo Frank, who was given to a mystical program of cultural renewal and who adopted Stieglitz as an important mentor. Other writers, such as Williams, the poet Hart Crane, and Lewis Mumford, maintained more peripheral connections to the group. The Stieglitz circle shared the embrace of new aesthetic practices, such as abstraction, as well as the impulse to sink roots in native soil with their Dadaist contemporaries, yet they rejected Dadaism and the stark aesthetic of mechanical objects favored by the Precisionist school. (Stieglitz and several artists associated with him, notably Charles Sheeler before he fell out of favor in 1923, were linked to Precisionism, which featured the smooth-surfaced and hard-edged reproduction of objects, often industrial objects and machines, in a manner that made structure the subject of the work. Precisionist art appeared alongside examples of modern architecture, engineering, and the industrial arts at the Machine Age Exposition organized by Jane Heap in New York in 1927, another attempt to bridge the divide between modern artists and the public.)[29]

There was no embrace of the rush-hour crowd, billboards, Coney Island, or the popular culture of jazz and blues music in the Stieglitz group. Rosenfeld disdained mass culture in especially strong terms. Stieglitz so disdained modernity that he only belatedly learned to drive, insisting, "Every time I see a Ford car something in me revolts. I hate the sight of one because of its absolute lack of any kind of quality feeling. . . . They are just *ugly* things in line & texture—in every sense of sensibility in spite of the virtue of so called usefulness." (O'Keeffe embraced the automobile earlier, some indication of her desire to be free of her husband's charismatic power.) Strand, Dove, Marin, and O'Keeffe—even eventually Stieglitz—used images of machines, the bridge, and skyscrapers in their work, appreciating their aesthetic power, but they did not embrace the spirit or the culture that grew around them. Stieglitz photographed the rising, angular shafts of skyscrapers in harsh daylight, while all the humanity at their bases were obscured in black shadow. Lights, towers, and bridges appeared in colorful and striking form but not as indicative of a vibrant culture. They disdained the machine-age idealism of various modern artists even as, like Frank, they embedded their art in a serious and consistently maintained program of organic cultural renewal, one that took account of industrial realities but insisted on finding the spiritual America in other sources.[30]

Leftist critics insisted that the path to a better society ran first and foremost through revolutionary politics, and that artists should submit their talents to its imperatives. Ideology would bridge the gap between artist and public. Prior to the Great War, the cultural left was loose and undogmatic, best represented by their revered literary organ, the *Masses*, a journal intended to meld the gay insouciance of the prewar "Rebellion" with radical politics. Writers and artists who gravitated to radical politics prior to the war tended to be undogmatic and eclectic in their critical and aesthetic principles. Social and cultural revolution would proceed together. Even those most committed to radical political change, such as Max Eastman, a young philosopher and writer trained at Columbia University who served as editor of the *Masses* from 1913 to 1918, could respect artistic freedom and feel at ease in bohemia. Yet, Eastman declared his skepticism toward any revolutionary project essentially cultural in nature, citing the idiosyncratic radical economist Thorstein Veblen, who mocked culture as the wasteful and meaningless accoutrement of wealth, and declaring that his generation suspected culture of the "taint of pecuniary elegance." The phrase echoed Veblen's scornful analysis of elite excesses and petty competition for social attention in *The Theory of the Leisure Class* (1899). This analysis, Eastman argued, "taught us how to see through 'culture.' We know something about knowledge. We have been 'put wise' to sophistication."[31]

In the early 1920s, the Soviet Union seemed the potential realization of revolutionary aims. The *Masses* was defunct, another victim of the war, and Eastman now coedited the *Liberator* with his sister Crystal. Aggressive young leftists like Mike Gold (born Irwin Granich in New York's east side slums), subordinated art to politics. Having quit school at age twelve, Gold cultivated an image of urban ghetto authenticity and toughness. He hung around the Village and other bohemian centers (including Cape Cod, where he dabbled in theater with the Provincetown Players), and adopted a bohemian-anarchist stance before the war and through 1921. To avoid the draft, he went to Mexico (as did Sacco and Vanzetti, among other anarchists) and worked in the oil fields, flaunting rough corduroy trousers, heavy shoes, and unkempt hair when he returned to Manhattan. He also began a long career as the most ardent spokesman for proletarian literature and an art submitted to revolutionary necessity, dismissing the assumption of coordinated social and cultural revolution characteristic of the prewar "lyrical left." His particular commitments came to characterize the *New Masses*, the radical successor to the *Masses* and *Liberator* that began publication in 1926. Art should serve the revolution. "Life" is realized more profoundly in recording its details. Gold advocated the creation of a proletarian culture—one by and about the working classes. "When there is singing and music rising in every American street, when in every American factory there is a drama-group of workers, when mechanics paint in their leisure, and farmers write sonnets, the greater art will grow and only then," he predicted. The revolutionary left opposed the cultural critics who would reconceptualize culture under their own aegis. No program of cultural change should be disengaged from the larger project of political and social revolution. Even as Eastman expressed the desire that artists retain "creative autonomy," he rejected efforts by artists to proclaim their intellectual independence, insisting that they ought to submit to the guidance of the revolutionary party: if radicals "wish to achieve liberty and democracy for the world we must place ourselves and all our powers unreservedly upon the side of the working class in its conflict with the owners of capital," he declared in the *Liberator* in December 1919.[32]

More influential were a group of American proponents of the European antiart movement, Dada, who challenged the prevalent disdain for American commercial culture not as an act of revolutionary praxis but as an expression of contempt for the established arbiters of artistic taste. Rather than bridge the divide between art and public life through the creation of a new, organic culture rooted in American traditions, advocates of Dada sought to explode the distinction between art and life itself, to make various forms of action—histrionic gestures, demonstrations, ideological pronouncements—take the place of art. American "Dada," principally the product of visiting French artists Francis Picabia, who arrived in 1913, and Marcel Duchamp, who arrived in 1915, predated the European movement of that name by a few months. Emerging in Zurich, Switzerland, in 1916, Dada was a calculated affront to the art world's critical establishment, a joyful and irreverent exercise in absurdity, and, in Europe, an anguished, nihilistic commentary on what the Dadaists perceived to be Europe's bankrupt civilization at the moment it was destroying itself. A typical and classic Dada expression was Duchamp's entry of a urinal upon which he had written "R. Mutt" and entitled *Fountain* in the exhibition of the Society of Independent Artists in New York in spring 1917. The entry provoked an uproar for its violation of good taste. Duchamp called such works "ready-mades"; the artistry lay in the creativity of shifting the object between contexts, which raised fundamental questions about the nature of art. Dada was antiart. The word *dada* was "yes-yes" in Romanian, the native tongue of Tristan Tzara, one of the founders and chief apologists of the movement, and meant a rocking horse in French. Tzara declared, "DADA MEANS NOTHING." It offered itself as an alternative culture to that which bred catastrophic war in Europe: it also extended modern experimentalism in art—in addition to the ready-made, adopting automatic writing, chance poetry, collage, photomontage, Rayographs (the American artist Man Ray's practice of placing objects directly on unexposed photograph paper and exposing them to light), assemblage, and events (sometimes violent—in a pale reflection of anarchists' "propaganda of the deed," Dadaists hailed an extreme act against decorum, even an assault, as a significant gesture, a work of art) as well as film, photography, painting, and poetry. Dada elicited responses ranging from disgust to delight and, inevitably, ridicule. A mischievous sketch in the June 1925 *Vanity Fair* described an imaginary "great dada composition by the fictional Oswald Brockle: ' . . . 14" x 7 ¾,' Beaver Board, painted pink, to which is appliquéd 3 sprays of pussy willow, a razor blade, a snapshot of Gilda Gray taken in 1918, page 3 of the *Congressional Record*, and a teaspoonful of Worcestershire sauce."[33]

Picabia and Duchamp irritated and impressed many in the art world in the 1910s: a small circle emanating from the salon of poet and art collector Walter Arensberg and including such figures as John Covert, Morton Schamburg, Charles Demuth, Man Ray, Joseph Stella, and Charles Sheeler showed interest; a few publications—the *Blind Man*, *Rongwrong*, and *New York Dada*—briefly appeared. There was some resonance between the antiart aesthetic of Dada and ideas circulated in *Camera Work*, Stieglitz's photography and art journal. Dada fed impulses to experimentalism in individuals like poet E. E. Cummings, who had arrived at his own love of elements of popular culture (most notably the cartoon character Krazy Kat) and antiart attitudes independently, or Sheeler's impulse to the precise visual rendering of an object (by the late 1920s, Sheeler was pursuing, in his own words, a "precision of statement set down directly with the least possible amount of painting"). William Carlos Williams, a full-time physician who wrote at night, found encouragement for his own experiments in automatic writing, what he called "Improvisations," and his own brand of Precisionism, paring down his poetry of ordinary objects to a minimum of direct and simple description as if, as suggested by the literary historian Frederick J. Hoffman, the verbal equivalent of a still life. Williams declaimed in *Kora in Hell* (1920): "There is nothing sacred about literature, it is damned from one end to the other. There is nothing in literature but change and change is mockery. I'll write whatever I damn please, whenever I damn please and as I damn please and it'll be good if the authentic spirit of change is on it."[34]

Matthew Josephson became the primary American exponent of Dada, primarily through his involvement with *Broom*, an avant-garde magazine founded by Harold Loeb, a young Princeton graduate who financed it with his inheritance and published it as an expatriate from Rome and Berlin, and dedicated to advancing "militant modernism" after Josephson became assistant editor in 1922. *Broom* was to be subversive—the obscure title came from an incident in Herman Melville's *Moby Dick* in which Ishmael both obeys and subverts a command to sweep—and was to showcase experimental prose. Initially opposed to Dada and open to Waldo Frank's declamations on the spiritual poverty of industrial America, the journal switched positions in its short career due to the particular influence of the charming, outspoken, and combative young critic Josephson. Born into a prosperous, middle-class Jewish family in Brooklyn (his father was a successful banker and local political eminence), Josephson attended Columbia University, where he helped establish a circle of rebellious literary outsiders who claimed to speak for the younger generation in the 1920s, beginning with a classmate, Kenneth Burke. Originally from Pittsburgh, Burke attended Columbia briefly before establishing himself in Greenwich Village and embarking on a career as a poet, critic, and editor. He and Josephson rubbed shoulders with some of the leading lights of the prewar Village bohemian scene, including the figures behind the Provincetown Players, George Cram Cook, Susan Glaspell, and Eugene O'Neill. Two of Burke's high school classmates from Pittsburgh, Malcolm Cowley, who became a poet and literary journalist, and James Light, who became a theater director, gravitated to the Village. Josephson worked in a shipyard during the Great War (he was drafted but saw no service) and enjoyed the life of bohemian New York at its apex (not especially promiscuous but gossipy—"love affairs were conducted in a fish bowl"). Having married Hannah Geffen, a former reporter, and working at a variety of jobs, including as a journalist, Josephson and his wife moved to Paris to inaugurate a more serious literary career.[35]

In Europe, Josephson collaborated with Gorham Munson, a private school teacher who had moved to Greenwich Village after the war and befriended the fledgling poet Hart Crane at Joseph Kling's Pagan bookshop. Munson considered Josephson intellectually shallow and manipulative and claimed to have introduced him to Dadaism through the person of Tristan Tzara at the Café de la Rotonde in Paris. Initially disdainful, Munson recalled, within weeks Josephson "reversed his stand and swallowed Dada, calipash and calipee." For his part, Josephson thought Munson brittle, pompous, self-aggrandizing, lacking in literary taste, and hapless—"a priceless comic figure of the literary scene of that period." He felt Munson constantly in need of guidance from an intellectual guru, the latter charge having some merit, as Munson seemed ever in search of an intellectual mentor to lead him and the nation to spiritual enlightenment. Initially under the spell of Waldo Frank, Munson later fell in with the Greek Armenian mystic George Ivanovitch Gurdjieff and his popularizer, the Englishman A. R. Orage, before shifting to the conservative new humanist critics Irving Babbitt and Paul Elmer More at the end of the decade. By June 1922, Josephson had helped pull Loeb and *Broom* into forthright defense of literary experimentation and Dadaism and a repudiation of Frank's cultural program of spiritual pioneering and cultural nationalism. Writing in *Broom* in November 1922, Josephson welcomed an America "where the Billposters enunciate their wisdom, the Cinema transports us, the newspapers intone their gaudy jargon; where athletes play upon the frenetic passions of baseball crowds, and skyscrapers rise lyrically to the exotic rhythms of jazz bands which upon waking up we find to be nothing but the drilling of pneumatic hammers on steel girders."[36]

Taking advantage of the cheap production costs of Europe, Munson established his own journal, *Secession*, in 1922, as an organ for a group of younger writers that he ambitiously hoped to mold into a school, what he considered the "youngest generation of American writers." *Secession* was successful as a little magazine, gaining attention and interest that belied its small circulation. Munson published serious, experimental prose and verse and promised an outlet for those interested in literary innovation. "*Secession* exists for those writers who are preoccupied with researches for new forms," he wrote in the first issue. Josephson, Munson, Cowley, Waldo Frank, William Carlos

Williams, Slater Brown, E. E. Cummings, Dadaists Louis Aragon and Tzara, Wallace Stevens, and Hart Crane, among others, appeared in its pages. The purpose of the magazine, Munson declared in another little magazine, *S4N*, in November 1922, was to secede from the flabby criticism, aesthetic sterility, and negativism toward life of America.[37]

Josephson arrived in Paris after Dadaism had already attracted much notice in New York and was reaching its peak in Paris. Finding little interaction between the American expatriates and the French, Josephson self-consciously cultivated relations with the Dadaist provocateurs gathered around André Breton, their autocratic leader. To Josephson, Dada was the recognition that art in the West was dead after the Great War. Breton's circle intended to "wage war upon society," not make art or literature. They were to be "terrorists of art and culture" through the creation of scandals and sensations. Josephson witnessed Dada festivals, events that featured a variety of provocations. The performance might begin with a lecture but then proceed to shouted interventions from the audience, plays comprised of disconnected passages from newspapers, and the reading of manifestoes and conclude with the audience exiting in outrage or expressing their displeasure with volleys of rotten vegetables, eggs, and meat. Breton forbid anyone from making a living from writing. Dadaists would travel to various French quarters and disrupt gatherings with vulgar behavior, perhaps reading a menu aloud or hurling insults at the guests, or they would engage in random stunts on the streets of Paris. One time, the group, including some wives, spontaneously visited a brothel, inviting the working women to perform their "tricks," a somewhat distasteful display of power that quickly disgusted Breton. The spirit of subversion with mockery and ridicule, even if harsh, eventually degenerated into nihilism in Josephson's view, entailing a fascination with suicide and debates as to whether the petty theft of a waiter's cash counted as a "revolt against common morality" or an act of cowardice.[38]

To Josephson, Dada breathed the rebellious spirit into an otherwise listless and staid avant-garde. (Bohemianism meant sophisticated chatter; the café culture of hard-up American expatriates was "a substitute for life, a wishful fantasy, a mirage.") The French writer Louis Aragon introduced Josephson to a literary tradition of which he was previously ignorant: "It was as if he had opened a door for me, leading to a whole new zone of art and all its rebellious works." Dadaist antics seemed a solution to genteel irrelevance. "At least we writers would leave our sedentary lives in our studies, cafés, or the parlors where we used to read our poems to old ladies, and go forth into the streets to confront the public and strike great blows at its stupid face," Josephson recalled. He drew inspiration from the French author Guillaume

Apollinaire, who had died in 1918. "The poet is to stop at nothing in his quest for novelty of form and material; he is to take advantage of all the infinite new combinations afforded by the mechanism of every-day life," Apollinaire declared. "What he creates out of these new instruments, or the repercussions which these elements will have upon our lives, will form the material, the folklore, out of which the myths and fables of the future will be created. . . . The recent conquests of man over nature have in many cases surpassed the fables of ancient times. It is for the modern poet to create the fairy tales which are to be harvested in ages to come." Writing about Apollinaire to friends in America, Josephson declared his new faith: "We must write for *our age* . . . the poets should be no less daring or inventive than the mechanical engineers of wartime; our literature should reflect the influences of the cinema . . . the saxophone."[39]

Dada offered Josephson a visceral and immediate response to the intellectual's desire for contact with society, for a middle ground that would ensure relevance, as it did for others in his circle, who could express a profound disdain for the pretensions of bohemia and the avant-garde. Burke, Cowley, and Josephson, as well as others in their literary circle, including William Slater Brown and his wife Susan, the young southern poet Allen Tate (who arrived in 1924), and even the peripatetic Hart Crane, tended to live outside New York City, in rural New York or New Jersey (although their lives outside the city were interspersed with regular dinners at Squarcialupi's Italian restaurant and drinks at speakeasies such as the Sullivan Street tavern or the Poncino Palace in the Village). Their stays abroad were relatively brief. Rather, they displayed great affection for the American countryside: Cowley remembered rural Pennsylvania fondly, and Tate eventually moved back to Tennessee. After a failed effort to publish *Broom* in the United States, Josephson eschewed bohemia and went to work as a stockbroker on Wall Street and later worked in publishing. Although embracing modernist experimentation in the arts, this group's patience for actual artists, let alone bohemian fellow travelers, was thin.

After attending Harvard and service in a French ambulance corps, Cowley attempted to earn his living as a poet and writer. He moved to Montpellier, France, to study French literature on an American Field Service fellowship in 1921 and 1922. He relished life in the French provinces and was disdainful of life in the American artists' colony in Paris, disapproving of the sexual license and laziness of the artists and writers there. Although dabbling in Dada when in Paris (at one point Cowley obtained local notoriety after punching the proprietor of the Rotonde in a Dadaist "significant gesture"), Cowley used his fellowship time to delve into classic French literature. He evinced hostility to avant-garde aesthetics in a letter to Kenneth Burke, whom he had known from high school: "I wish to hold the ideas of others and ourselves up to a mild ridicule; for example the fashion in which Art is taking the place of Religion—the desire that the artist should be poor and chaste. The fear of Being Understood, which I wish to tie up with Rosicrucianism. The Search for Originality, and all these other ridiculous ambitions of our times." Dada made great sense to Cowley. In a letter to Burke in 1923, he proclaimed, "I am now officially a Dada," defined as the "negation of all motives for writing, such as the Desire for Expression, the Will to Create, the Wish to Aid. A Dada has only one legitimate excuse for writing: because he wants to, because it amuses him." Burke's own views, it should be noted, were more measured. He agreed with Cowley, who had written that America was a "land of promise, something barbaric, and rich," but this was not, Burke noted, the "dignified richness" that "makes for peasants, household gods, traditions." "We *will* build a literature out of advertising, we *will* build a literature out of economy, directness, psychological salesmanship, and the like," Burke affirmed, but the "refined artist" does not simply exploit this material; it is "so subtilized, so deepened" as to be unrecognizable. "That is the thing you do not take into account. And to me it is the only important thing."[40]

In his memoir of the 1920s, *Exile's Return: A Literary Odyssey of the 1920s* (1934), Malcolm Cowley used his own life to analyze the imperatives of his literary generation and establish convergences between those who sought to root themselves in American traditions and those who embraced popular culture. He was trained, he claimed, to a false cosmopolitanism, which tended toward the destruction of "whatever roots we had in the soil." While attending Harvard, he wandered the old sections of Beacon Hill and the North End of Boston, admiring the closed doors but ignorant of the Armenians and Jews now living behind them. He failed even to learn of the literary inheritance of New England, to explore Longfellow's house or Brook Farm. Cowley condemned the elitism of the "salesrooms and fitting rooms of culture" from which he benefited, ones in which culture was a consumer good that garnered distinction but which was closed to the "life of the street."[41]

Thus, Cowley's generation were exiles well before the war and their postwar expatriate adventures. Of the period from fall 1923 and early 1924 when, just returned from France, Cowley and Josephson attempted to revitalize *Broom*, Cowley wrote of his cohort's unsuccessful attempt "to substitute moral for mechanical values, to create a background that would render their own lives more exciting and rewarding." That is, they had ignored the material conditions of cultural production. Only after being "stripped of their ambitions" did the exiles surrender to the city and make the necessary accommodation to a subterranean life that was the only avenue for spiritual exiles from modern American society, a life that provided pleasures enough in lunchtime meetings, coffeehouse talk, and "modest plans for the future."[42]

Writing late in the decade, Cowley figured his 1920s life as a rejection of bohemia and acceptance of the vocation of the professional writer, not the visionary cultural seer. As early as July 1922, while working from France, Cowley recounted the history of bohemia, discounting its most recent incarnation, the "new Bohemia," as a faddish and essentially commercial pose, an "end and not a means," a romantic fashion enjoyed for its own rewards. "Bohemia is a vast enterprise which could be capitalized at several millions," he observed. "Starting as a revolt against the bourgeoisie, it has become as much the property of the bourgeoisie as any other business-venture." He repeated the criticism in *Exile's Return*, suggesting that 1920s Village bohemianism was a bourgeois affectation, one that supported a "*consumption* ethic," which replaced a "*production* ethic":

> Thus, *self-expression* and *paganism* encouraged a demand for all sorts of products— modern furniture, beach pajamas, cosmetics, colored bathrooms with toilet paper to match. *Living for the moment* meant buying an automobile, radio or house, using it now and paying for it tomorrow. *Female equality* was capable of doubling the consumption of products—cigarettes, for example—that had formerly been used by men alone. Even *changing place* would help to stimulate business in the country from which the artist was being expatriated. The exiles of art were also trade missionaries: involuntarily they increased the foreign demand for fountain pens, silk stockings, grapefruit and portable typewriters. They drew after them an invading army of tourists, thus swelling the profits of steamship lines and travel agencies.

Cowley evinced no taste for the grand cultural projects of the prewar cultural rebellion.[43]

Writing for the *Toronto Star Weekly* in March 1922, the young newspaperman and aspiring novelist Ernest Hemingway made points resonant with Cowley, savagely denigrating many of his fellow American expatriates in Paris, declaring they turned his stomach. "The scum of Greenwich Village, New York, has been skimmed off and deposited in large ladleful on that section of Paris adjacent to the Cafe Rotonde," Hemingway reported. They strove "so hard for a careless individuality of clothing that they have achieved a sort of uniformity of eccentricity." The real artists of Paris "resent and loathe" the Rotonde crowd, he averred. "They are nearly all loafers expending the energy that an artist puts into his creative work in talking about what they are going to do and condemning the work of all artists who have gained any degree of recognition," he wrote, expressing disdain for the art of lively conversation so central to prewar bohemianism. "By talking about art they obtain the same satisfaction that the real artist does in his work."[44]

Although Hemingway had little affection for Cowley, both men came to a similarly jaundiced view of bohemianism, choosing to cultivate an alternative identity as literary craftsmen, hardworking and unillusioned men of letters, writing on the margins of, or even against, the avant-garde cultural establishment. In *Exile's Return*, Cowley explicitly contrasted his literary generation of New York writers with the previous one: "They" had been rebels, "full of proud illusions"; "we" were not. "We had lost our ideals at a very early age, and painlessly," declared Cowley, summoning the image of the Great War, which had for many registered the savage collapse of nineteenth-century civilization. "The truth is that 'we,' the newcomers to the Village, were not bohemians," Cowley flatly declared. His generation saw little use crusading against "puritanism," for it was no longer able to interfere with their personal lives. He and his ilk were "men on the make, the humble citizens not of bohemia but of Grub Street."[45]

As it happened, Josephson's and Cowley's attempt to publish *Broom* as an avant-garde magazine of the arts in New York, after Loeb could no longer underwrite its publication, was short-lived. Gorham Munson had left the production of *Secession* in the hands of Josephson in Europe, hoping to maintain editorial control of it from afar with the aid of Burke, who joined as an editor. The arrangement proved a disaster: Josephson and Munson were attuned neither personally nor critically—Josephson a stalwart spokesman for a waning Dadaism, Munson increasingly interested in Waldo Frank, about whom he published his first book-length critical work in 1923. (Josephson rejected Munson's work on Frank for publication in *Broom* and instead satirized Frank in a review of his latest book.) Josephson and Cowley saw *Broom* as the serious journal and Munson's *Secession* as a venue for Dadaist stunts and polemics and jointly hijacked (in Munson's later embittered characterization) the magazine in 1923, most notoriously editing a poem accepted for publication by Munson and Burke to its final two lines, an affront to the poet and other editors that they presented as a good-natured caprice (as evidently did the poet).[46]

Judging *Broom* intellectually tapped out, Cowley engineered a dinner meeting of its supporters and those of the rival *Secession* on October 19, 1923, to clear the air and consider options for the future. The result was a dispiriting fiasco, as the assembled broke into angry disputes, prompted in part by a letter from the absent Munson denouncing Josephson as an intellectual fraud and opportunist, which Cowley presented in open mockery. Partisans on both sides reacted angrily, including Crane, who out of loyalty to Munson shouted insults at Cowley and fought with Josephson; in true Dadaist fashion, ten days later, an angry (but physically slight) Josephson demanded satisfaction from (somewhat heavier) Munson. They grappled on the ground, both later acknowledging with embarrassment the absurdity of the encounter, but both also claiming to have had the better of the fight. In December, Mencken published "Aesthete: Model 1924," a sharp satire of the younger intellectuals by the journalist Ernest Boyd, in the *American Mercury*. In Menckenian fashion, Boyd treated the literary conflicts of that year superficially, focusing on style more than anything, and Cowley and his friends published a satirical rejoinder, *Aesthete 1925*, the next year, skewering, among other targets, Mencken as a smirking, middlebrow conservative. Boyd's article stung, however, particularly for Cowley, who felt he was personally caricatured and subsequently harangued Boyd on the phone. Cowley, Burke, and Crane responded to Boyd in the same spirit of hostility as Josephson did to Munson: they phoned Boyd with threats, abused him, threw stinking garbage into his home, and otherwise harassed him for three days, according to the (quite possibly exaggerated) account of newspaper columnist Burton Rascoe. As it was, the January 1924 issue of *Broom* was withheld from the mails by the post office on the charge that a story by Kenneth Burke contained obscenity, leading to the collapse of the magazine.[47]

The incidents signaled a frustrating end to one attempt to bridge the gap between high and low in American culture. In April 1924, the young critic Edmund Wilson published an evenhanded treatment of the larger literary issue, imagining a conversation between Paul Rosenfeld and Matthew Josephson representing opposite sides of the debate (and ably mimicking the distinctive styles of each). He quoted from Matthew Josephson's review of the poet Elinor Wylie, which had appeared in *Broom*: "The large imaginative, daring, formidable people in America are mostly to be found on the vaudeville stage, in the movies, the advertising business, prize-fighting, railroads, Wall Street. . . . Art is purveyed for small persecuted colonies, dispersed throughout this continent, and hidden away among its stone walls and steel foundations." In Wilson's telling, the Dadaists insisted that one had to either embrace the crudely demotic or consign oneself to being out of touch and irrelevant. He had Rosenfeld accuse Josephson of discrediting art that is fine in order to hail what is vulgar. Rosenfeld appeals to timeless principles and the "language of the heart," at which Josephson scoffs, remarking that the subway and modern shower are "more magnificent poems than anything by Schubert or Goethe." Culture as an enterprise leavening modern industrial society with moral values retreats before the Dadaist embrace of "mechanical life" and "hawking taxis, the screaming sirens." "And what is painting? What is sculpture?" Wilson's Josephson asks:

> A bad monument to celebrate a battle, a landscape not much larger than a playing-card in a gallery like a mausoleum, which only a handful of people in New York will ever come in to see and which the millions in the rest of the country will not even hear about! How can you set up these trivialities as rivals to the electric sign, which thousands of people see every day—a triumph of ingenuity, of color, of imagination!—which slings its great gold-green-red symbol across the face of the heavens themselves and tells the world that it has made a new Chewing Gum or a Pickle or a Cigarette that will give you a new sensation! I tell you that culture as you understand it is no longer of any value; the human race no longer believes in it.

In the end, Wilson's Rosenfeld warns Josephson that, as a poet and critic, he is a partisan of art and will be a victim if it is defeated. "You can never march with that procession; they have no place for critics or poets."[48]

Two writers provide a concluding perspective on the critical debates of the 1920s, one evincing an utterly personal and individualistic code, the other struggling to achieve in art the dreams of cultural union advanced by so many critics of the period. Eschewing college for a job as a reporter on the *Kansas City Star* in 1917, Ernest Hemingway got into the Great War not through enlistment in the United States Army but by volunteering to serve in the American Red Cross ambulance service and was eventually stationed in Italy, where he was seriously wounded in his legs by shrapnel from an artillery shell, thus bringing his short experience of war to a conclusion. Far from being embittered by his wound and the subsequent hospital love affair made famous in *A Farewell to Arms* (1929), Hemingway returned home a proud conquering hero, telling exaggerated tales of his exploits and displaying only "rapturous nostalgia" for the war, in the judgment of biographer Kenneth Lynn.[49]

Attractive, charismatic, bold, and a superb storyteller, Hemingway married and moved to Paris, armed with contacts from Sherwood Anderson, whom he met in Chicago and who became something of a mentor to him. (Typical of Hemingway, who often turned viciously on his friends, especially those to whom he was most indebted, he later broke with Anderson, savagely satirizing his writing style.) Due to chronic inflation, France was extraordinarily cheap to American writers, and its economic stagnation ensured them immersion into a world redolent of the recently bygone past, as many apartments lacked electricity and horse-drawn carriages remained common into the mid-1930s. In Spain, particularly in Pamplona, at the fest Fermin, Hemingway could absorb nineteenth-century peasant folk culture pure along with the atavistic and manly combat of the bullring, which he did much to make famous through his first novel, *The Sun Also Rises* (1926), and in his stories. Hemingway was a reporter and demonstrated an immensely detailed understanding of the rituals of bullfighting and the intricacies, in both geography and manners, of European cities and towns in which he lived. His stories and novels derived from his own experiences; *The Sun Also Rises* was rooted in thinly disguised friends and associates and events from the Paris expatriate scene, obvious to those in his circle and offensive to many of them. His spare and economic writing style, long on plain description and flat, sometimes oblique dialogue but little given to overt philosophizing or interior characterization of his protagonists, may have been influenced by Gertrude Stein, the longtime American expatriate who for a while enfolded Hemingway in her formidable intellectual embrace, but was as strongly indebted to his early lessons as a newswriter in Kansas City.[50]

In *The Sun Also Rises*, a meandering tale of reckless and hedonistic pleasure seeking among American and British expatriates living in Paris, Hemingway repudiated the moral choices of most of these dissolute characters. Hemingway's own worldview was decidedly naturalistic and his work is replete with the manly posturing of an avid (if perhaps insecure) sportsman and adventurer: life was conflict, meaning is derived from how one plays the game, and value is derived from bearing oneself with honor, whether this means, as in *The Sun Also Rises*, paying one's debts or, slightly more elevated, pursuing ritualized combat with absolute purity of motive. In the world-weary philosophy of life maintained by Hemingway's maimed hero, Jake Barnes, we must somehow pay for all we take from life. "You paid some way for everything that was any good," he observes. "Enjoying living was learning to get your money's worth and knowing when you had it."[51] The more powerful moralizing in the book, however, involves the purity of motive of the talented young bullfighter, Pedro Romero. Romero's purity, in Hemingway's rendition, comes from an inward, nonsocial fidelity; that is, he is faithful to his own understanding of the aesthetic of bullfighting, never faking, never cheaply playing to the ignorant audience's desire for thrills. Romero's expertise can only be understood and fully appreciated by an *aficion*, someone highly knowledgeable and passionate about the sport, as Barnes has become:

> Romero never made any contortions, always it was straight and pure and natural in line. The others twisted themselves like cork-screws, their elbows raised, and leaned against the flanks of the bull after his horns had passed, to give a faked look of danger. Afterward, all that was fake turned bad and gave an

unpleasant feeling. Romero's bull-fighting gave real emotion, because he kept the absolute purity of line in his movements and always quietly and calmly let the horns pass him close each time.[52]

Hemingway presents moral value in intensely individualistic terms, not only in the relativistic sense that value is derived from loyalty to any particular code chosen by an individual, the rules of any suitably dignified and challenging game, but also because Hemingway assumes a world in which culture, generally, has collapsed. Moral value and meaning are only gotten on the periphery of a thoroughly corrupted and aimless world, one characterized by fakery, cheating, and dishonesty, even with oneself. Such are the dominant traits of the particular individuals in Jake Barnes's crowd. Ironically but perhaps not unexpectedly, the great success of Hemingway's novel was among a cognoscenti of youth and would-be expatriates who found in him a new kind of style (not bohemian but rather that of the cool and precise connoisseur of life's pleasures), the life of gaiety, and, in literal terms, a guide to travel in Europe, where to take drink and dine and how to find one's way around the streets of Paris and Pamplona.

Hemingway himself began to emerge as a celebrity, at first as something of a sporting hero, as early as 1924; by 1928, everything in his life was judged newsworthy. The ambitious Hemingway embraced this life even as, by his own chosen code of professional writing discipline, such celebrity was potentially destructive.

He scorned bohemians and their expatriate equivalents. Jake Barnes's particular moral failure in the novel is to bring his corrupting friends and by extension, their corrupted moral universe—the shabby worldview of pleasures measured in cash payments and grounded in painful disillusionment—to the natural beauty of Pamplona, inhabited by peasants whose pleasures are both pure and robust, uncontaminated by the immoral hedonism of the urban denizens. Jake's friends lack his commitment to paying his own bills and his *aficion*, or passion, for the professionalism and craftsmanship of the dedicated bullfighter. The moral meaning of *The Sun Also Rises* lies in its indictment of the fashionable cultural milieu of expatriate Paris, the very title alluding to the book's epigraph from Ecclesiastes ("One generation passeth away, and another generation cometh; but the earth abideth forever"), which highlights the perdurable values of land and sea amidst natural cycles of change—values evident in peasant Spain but absent in the fashionable and gay flux of Paris in the 1920s. Although informed by a moral credo, Hemingway's book represented a stark repudiation of culture itself, a willingness to repudiate nineteenth-century didacticism and uplift much closer to the spirit of European Dada than that of more earnest American critics. The fact that the best-selling *The Sun Also Rises* could be read against his own moral meaning reveals its intentional limitations as a source of civilizing and a work of cultural criticism: Hemingway's parents disapproved of it on moral grounds; its surface pleasures, even the overlay of associations with the Great War—not only Barnes's outrageous wound from the war, which provides the nexus of much action, but also Gertrude Stein's epigraph citing the "lost generation" of young, male war veterans—led the reader away from Hemingway's particular moral criticism. It is a work upholding stoicism designed for an audience interested in leisured pleasure, gay life, and an essay on modern sexual politics.

The decade's dominant literary currents—the search for symbols from the American past with which to fashion an organic American culture and the elevation of modern technology and commercial enterprise to the level of a new folklore—converged in the person of Hart Crane, who maintained contacts with the Stieglitz circle as well as Josephson and Cowley's crowd of young writers. In his epic poem, *The Bridge* (1930), Crane attempted to reconcile the competing critical perspectives, utilizing the Brooklyn Bridge as an emblem for artistic possibility and a symbol for the interior journey to which Americans were now called.

He was not the first to try it. The Italian immigrant artist Joseph Stella's large five-panel work, *The Voice of the City of New York Interpreted*, completed between 1920 and 1922 and measuring nearly twenty-two feet long and almost eight and a half feet high at its highest point, depicts a journey through nighttime New York, beginning (starting at the leftmost panel) at the port of New York and Battery Park, continuing with views of the Great White Way and skyscrapers, and finishing with a panel depicting the Brooklyn Bridge. Influenced by Italian futurism as well as transatlantic *américanisme*, Stella's canvas also reflected the artistic ambition to capture New York City—and modernity—in one work. Like many Precisionist canvases, Stella's work depicts the material reality of industrialized, garish New York (depicting buildings; the residents are excised) in a stylized and abstract way. The dominant color in the overall work was black; individual panels were dominated by a palette either of blue, purple, and black or (Stella's vivid renderings of Broadway) orange, red, yellow, and white. The painting is like an Italian Renaissance altarpiece, with the modern city of New York artfully linked to Roman Catholic Church and liturgical motifs—cathedral-like arches in the Brooklyn Bridge, the brilliant colors of the White Way panels evoking stained glass, splashes of light and beacons evoking halos and crowns, and the use of many vertical lines (skyscrapers, the suspension cables of the Brooklyn Bridge) suggesting the faithful's upward appeal to heaven. Stella's spiritualized vision of the city was evident in his comments on the Brooklyn Bridge, which he described as a "weird metallic Apparition under a metallic sky" when seen for the first time, "out of proportion with the winged lightness of its arch, traced for the conjunction of WORLDS, supported by the massive dark towers dominating the surrounding tumult of the surging sky-scrapers with their gothic majesty." The bridge's cables, he imagined, were "like divine messages from above." The bridge "impressed me as the shrine containing all the efforts of the new civilization of AMERICA."[53]

Crane wanted to use Stella's Brooklyn Bridge panel as a frontispiece to *The Bridge* and wrote Stella of the "remarkable coincidence" that he shared similar sentiments regarding the Brooklyn Bridge, "which inspired the main theme and pattern of my poem." Crane's epic consisted of seven poems and a prologue, which chronicled the poet's journey throughout the day, starting and ending at the Brooklyn Bridge, which was contrasted with evocations of Columbus's voyage home after the discovery of the New World, the American pioneer's journey across the continent seeking opportunity, and the nation's history from the colonial period forward. Crane worked on the poem for a large part of the 1920s and was deeply indebted to Waldo Frank among others. In the poem, he was groping for new American mythology capable of enabling Americans to achieve the sort of spiritual transcendence about which Frank preached. Crane's focus on the travails of the pioneer reflected his primary goal, which was, as he indicated in letter to his patron, Otto Kahn, to treat the "Myth of America."[54]

Crane intermingled references to American history (Columbus's voyage, the Virginia colony, the westward migration) with apparent references to his own remembered personal traumas (a whipping, a cold and demand-ing mother). The pioneer's journey intercuts with his own daily routine, although his day's circuitous path from Brooklyn to Manhattan and back again (the bridge is at the beginning and end of his story) becomes a more complex and profound exploration of his consciousness. In the "Cape Hat-teras" section, he imagines Walt Whitman as the good and faithful guide for this spiritual (and poetic) inner journey. Whitman is an explicit precursor for Crane, whom the poet directly addresses:

> Our Meistersinger, thou set breath in steel;
> And it was thou who on the boldest heel
> Stood up and flung the span on even wing
> Of that great Bridge, our Myth, whereof I sing![55]

He imagines Whitman entered upon a cosmic journey: "To course that span of consciousness thou'st named/The Open Road—thy vision is reclaimed!/ What heritage thou's signaled to our hands!" (60).

"We are in the childhood of a new age, we are, by the chronological ac- cident of our birth, chosen to create the simple forms, the folk-tales and folk-music, the preliminary art that our descendants may utilize in the vast struggle to put positive and glowing spiritual content into Machinery," Mun- son had written in a study of Waldo Frank. Such was Crane's aim, and he was steeped in the critical vocabulary of "puritan-pioneer-industrial America" of Frank's circle. He intended *The Bridge*, he wrote Kahn, as "a new cultural synthesis of values in terms of our America." The importance of the pioneer lay in the journey taken. The pioneers' world has disappeared. Even as the pioneers traversed the continent, telegraph wires followed in their wake, advancing modernity. The wires "span the mountain stream."

> Keen instruments, strung to a vast precision
> Bind town to town and dream to ticking dream. (41–42)

Despite the jarring contrast between the poet's round of daily pleasures (in- cluding a visit to a burlesque house) and the rigors of pioneering—the poet's prosaic life seems a world removed from the heroic exploits of American history—Crane suggests that the past lies available for exploitation. He pres- ents a Native American "Medicine-man" as another spiritual guide. "Dance, Maquokeeta," the poet addresses the figure. He calls on him to "relent" and "restore," to "Lie to us," and in dispensing a cultural myth to "dance us back to the tribal morn!" (47). The pioneer functions for modern man as a symbol for his *spiritual* journey of self-discovery.[56]

The poet's daily round takes him underground on the subway, which be- comes an image for his own journey to the subconscious, skirting madness and self-destruction. He imagines the face of Edgar Allan Poe looming among the otherwise anonymous and blank faces of his fellow passengers. (After returning from two years in Paris, the New York subway shocked Matthew Josephson: "at the end of the day the people all looked stupefied and never glanced at anybody as if he were a human being, but stared at the floor of the car or de- voured their newspapers. Later, when I myself began to move at the American tempo, I never gave a thought to the faceless people in the subway.") "Whose head is swinging from the swollen strap?" the poet thinks, as he confronts the "interborough fissures of the mind" (69). Redemption occurs upon rising to the surface and seeing an Italian washerwoman, an image of earthy but healthy maternity. Ultimately, it is the wondrous man-made construction of the

Brooklyn Bridge that becomes a symbol for the transcendent aspirations of the modern spiritual pioneer. In the final "Atlantis" section of the poem, having recovered the necessary knowledge from the hidden world of his subconscious, the poet is drawn forward and upward by the majestic arches and ascending cables of the Brooklyn Bridge and the monitory and benevolent "steeled Cognizance" it represents, his inner trip successfully completed (73).[57]

In contrast to Hemingway, who with F. Scott Fitzgerald became an acclaimed and dominant literary success, both of them writing frankly of new morals and disillusioned heroes living in an age devoid of faith, Crane struggled even to gain time for his craft (for a period, he was forced to work in advertising) and faced a mixed critical reaction, with, dishearteningly, damaging reviews coming from his friends, many of whom felt that his ambition overreached his materials and that his sanctifying mythology was stillborn. His own life in disarray and in the throes of severe alcoholism, Crane committed suicide two years after the publication of his epic, one of the markers for the end of the 1920s in Cowley's *Exile's Return*. The cultural middle ground that would bridge the gap between intellectuals and the public remained out of reach.

CHAPTER FOUR

Mulatto America

In 1925, Anzia Yezierska published *Bread Givers*, a fictional treatment of the world that Jewish immigrants from Russian Poland made on the Lower East Side in New York City. Yezierska emigrated with her family in 1893 when she was a girl and she had, in a somewhat wrenching process, broken with the constricting traditionalism of her culture and become a successful writer. In the first half of *Bread Givers*, Yezierska provides a searing account of the emotional and spiritual costs of patriarchal tyranny. The father of the Smolinsky clan, a Jewish scholar and teacher, imperiously rules the lives of his four daughters, arbitrarily dashing their youthful and romantic dreams through insensitive and stubborn treatment of their suitors and selfish demands for support. In Jewish culture, a learned man—one who is to spread the "light of the Torah"—is not to work but rather be supported in his studies. Reb Smolinsky demanded that his daughters earn wages or otherwise make provision for him through prosperous marriages. Ultimately, he ruins their lives by making poor and foolish marriage choices for each, which they have little power to resist. "[E]ach time he killed the heart from one of his children, he grew louder with his preaching on us all," the narrator, his rebellious youngest daughter Sara, reports.[1]

Sara becomes the exception, defiantly repudiating her heritage ("I'm not from the old country," she rages at her father, "I'm American!") and escaping the home to lead the life of an independent woman. It is a punishing solo immersion in American life, marked by poverty, isolation, and insecurity. Her obsessive desire for education and autonomy, free of the obligations to a husband, clashes with the superficial ambitions of her college peers and the crass materialism of other assimilating Jews. Initially, she finds freedom in the bare single room she rents; the door, shut tight to the outside world, was "life. . . . [t]he bottom starting-point of becoming a person." However, separation does not eliminate the deep yearning for "light," for something more than bread, which animated her immigrant family and her father as well. The maddening figure of her father—hypocritical, cruel, improvident, unseeing, and naive, a failure in America, holding stubbornly to beliefs unsuited to the new society—dominates her consciousness. Like her, like them all, Reb Smolinsky lived for light and not bread, even as he hurt his children out of vanity and desperation. At the end of the novel, she develops a romantic bond with Hugo Seelig, a man of her own background; they spoke "one language" and sprang from "one soil." "You and I, we are of one blood," Hugo tells her. Ultimately, she forgives her now pathetic father, seeing him as a vulnerable child: "How could I have hated him and tried to blot him out of my life? Can I hate my arm, my hand that is part of me? Can a tree hate the roots from which it sprang? . . . If I grow, if I rise, if I ever amount to something, is it not his spirit burning in me?"[2]

Yezierska's tale—and the struggles of her heroine, Sara Smolinsky—were not unlike the actual struggles of intellectuals in this era. After all, both Yezierska and her fictional alter ego struggled to get a college education, and in becoming educated they became estranged from their ethnic community and tradition. Assimilation provided an exemplum of the peculiar dissociation that intellectuals took to be an essential problem of modernity—perhaps more accurately, the essential problem of the intelligentsia: with cultural transformation comes estrangement from the group. In her novels and stories, Yezierska pursued reconciliation with her heritage and tradition, albeit on her own terms. African American writers, too, sought such a reconciliation, even as culture also became the immediately available means for African Americans to pursue equality in America.

Ethnicity and race became vital and essential elements of the cultural crisis of the era. America had changed: European immigrants in the East and Midwest, Mexicans in the Southwest and West, and Asians in the West were transforming the nation's cities and rural areas, provoking an anti-immigrant backlash. As nativism waxed, immigrants created broad, new ethnic identities and ethnic institutions in self-defense. Group by group, those who stayed in the United States established ethnic identities—Polish American, Slovak American, Mexican American—that asserted a claim on America but also articulated an ethic of loyalty, solidarity, and reciprocity within the group. Roman Catholic and Jewish leaders urged assimilation and Americanization even as they cultivated traditional culture and practices. The problem of assimilation defined immigrant lives: To what extent does one adopt the culture and values of American culture (itself in flux), and to what extent does one maintain the old?

African Americans moving north consolidated a cultural identity as well, even as they faced a more vicious and intransigent form of discrimination. For the first time, blacks in large numbers moved outside the South. The freedom they found (hemmed in, as it was, by discrimination) fed hopes of racial progress. These were hopes often dashed: as African Americans found a foothold in the heterogeneous settings of northern cities, Americans and immigrants of European descent consolidated a new Caucasian identity in opposition to their own; the 1920 United States Census eliminated the category of "mulatto," an official refusal to recognize the hybrid character of many Americans. As the stark polarity of black/white emerged, African Americans faced an even more unforgiving color line. Americans' intense racial consciousness and concern for thwarting racial intermixture were everywhere on display in the 1920s—the "Negro Renaissance" based in Harlem; the keen appeal of Marcus Garvey's black nationalism; the success of the revived Ku Klux Klan; the sensational coverage of such minor cases as the 1925 trial of an annulment suit brought by Leonard Kip Rhinelander, the rather feckless scion of a wealthy New York family, against his lower-class, mixed-race bride, Alice, whom he had rather recklessly married; the passage of immigration restriction legislation; the cultural authority of theorists of "Nordic" racial superiority, such as the lawyer and conservationist Madison Grant and his protégé Lothrop Stoddard; and the success of eugenics (the science of racial breeding)—thirty-one states eventually passed laws allowing the involuntary sterilization of supposed social defectives in prisons, hospitals, and mental institutions.[3]

To American social scientists, attuned to the dynamics of group association in modern life, immigrants reflected the contest between conformity and personal autonomy that formed one of the chief features of modern life. Assimilation dramatized the individual's potential alienation from the group (in this case, the group of one's heritage) and the fraught nature of selfhood in the United States. Immigrants had to choose between traditional structures of authority (family and church) and the individualism of modern America. In focusing so much on the conflicted relation of group to individual, sociologists missed much—including an emerging hybridized identity, both immigrant and American, white and black. All the same, they created a language and articulated a set of problems relating to race and ethnicity that crystallized the disconcerting effects of change and gave form to the profound encounter between Americans who shared an identity but felt immeasurably distant from one another.[4]

⌒

The life of the emergent cities and the interaction of social groups comprised the chosen subject matter of the sociologists gathered at the University of Chicago—scholars who played a crucial role in replacing academic sociology's early ethos of Christian reform and social uplift with scientific, disinterested intellectual inquiry. Albion Small founded the department in 1892, but William I. Thomas and Robert Park defined the agenda that established its reputation: urban sociology and ecological succession (the study of the ways in which population groups and social activities develop, interact, and displace or succeed one another). A Tennessean Methodist by birth, Thomas initially studied literature in Germany before enrolling at Chicago in 1893 to earn a doctorate in sociology. He adumbrated many of the crucial theoretical notions for the Chicago school. In the landmark *The Polish Peasant in Europe and America* (five volumes, 1918–1920), Thomas and his coauthor, Florian Znaniecki, a younger Polish scholar of emigrants in Warsaw who came to Chicago to work as Thomas's translator, established theories and methodologies that defined the Chicago school for generations. They made social movement, contact, and change the focus of sociological inquiry. Moreover, the immigrant became the center of their analysis as they used qualitative sources such as letters, autobiographies, and life histories to develop a theoretical framework for understanding the effects of modern, industrial, and urban life on traditional and family-centered communities. They emphasized the immigrants' own predilection for creative adaptation.[5]

The university fired Thomas and even stopped publication of *The Polish Peasant* after an illicit sexual affair in 1918. (Although Thomas did most of the research and writing of a study of immigration on the Lower East Side, *Old World Traits Examined*, which appeared in 1921, the book appeared under the names of Robert Park and Herbert Miller due to the scandal.) An iconoclastic thinker with a variegated intellectual background, Robert Park emerged as the leader and public face of the department. With Ernest W. Burgess, he published *Introduction to the Science of Sociology*, which first appeared in 1921, an anthology of current writings that became a seminal textbook in the field, the "green bible" to subsequent generations of students.[6]

Born in Pennsylvania in 1864, Park grew up in Minnesota and attended the University of Minnesota and the University of Michigan. At Michigan, he studied under John Dewey and gravitated to German philosophy and literature, eventually opting for postgraduate training at German universities. Like many of the younger literary rebels of the 1910s and 1920s, Park developed a special devotion to Walt Whitman. Park's personality was a mix of restless intellectualism and careerism (instilled by his commerce-oriented family). Reform-minded yet scornful of reformers and intellectuals, Park struggled to find a vocation, eventually matriculating at Harvard and then traveling to Berlin and Heidelberg, where he studied with the sociologist Georg Simmel, among others. A "phenomenologist of everyday life," Simmel eschewed the organicism of much German sociology and focused instead on the social interactions of modern individuals, how they lived free lives as they mediated between their particular interests and the social forms in which they lived.[7]

After earning a doctorate in Germany, Park worked as a publicist for the Congo Reform Association and, later, as publicity director for Booker T. Washington at the Tuskegee Institute. Park shared Washington's conservative racial philosophy and worked with him until Washington died, continuing the connection even after accepting a position at the University of Chicago in 1914. "I feel and shall always feel that I belong, in a sort of way, to the Negro race and shall continue to share, through good and evil, all its joys and sorrows," he wrote Washington in 1912. At the same time, Park and Burgess's *Introduction to the Science of Sociology* characterized blacks as having a "genial, sunny, and social disposition" and being concerned with external and physical things rather than introspective. "He is primarily an artist, loving life for its own sake," the authors observed, providing an odd racial echo to the contemporary dig at the "genteel tradition." "His *métier* is expression rather than action. He is, so to speak, the lady among the races." At Chicago, Park inspired a generation of American sociologists. A relentless theorizer, Park's own work took the form of suggestive essays, often densely packed with social observation and somewhat loosely developed theoretical insights. The sociologist Edward Shils remembered him as hunched over and growling, like a bear. Heavily built with brown hair and ruddy skin, he often was untidy in appearance and intense, often blunt in interactions, sometimes taking students sternly to task for some deficiency in performance. He prowled the streets, striking up conversations avidly; he once rented a room in a Chicago slum to gain firsthand knowledge of the urban jungle.[8]

Using prevalent notions of race at the time, in the early decades of the twentieth century Americans equated nationality with race or otherwise affixed quite imprecise racial definitions based mainly on current prejudices. Popular race theorists, for example, divided Europeans into Teutonic (or Nordic), Alpine, and Mediterranean racial stocks based on locality and physical appearance. At the same time, scientists in universities were beginning to dispense with theories of human behavior based on biological or genetic factors and were increasingly turning to culture or environmental factors as explanations, a shift in part driven by the work of African American and ethnic scholars. Franz Boas and his students relentlessly attacked anthropological theories that attributed differences in mental and social capacities of particular groups to race. Boas expended a great amount of energy measuring and analyzing the head shapes of immigrants in America. Racial scientists had presumed that head shapes were a stable measure of race. Boas's measurements suggested that, in fact, head shapes of different ethnic (at the time, "racial") groups changed significantly after only ten years in the differing social environment of the United States. Given this discovery, racial differences, Boas contended, can be explained by the distinct physical and historical factors affecting particular groups. In other words "social factors," or culture, explain much of what people characterized as race. By the 1910s, it was becoming common for anthropologists and other social scientists to speak of "cultures" where previously they had spoken of "races."[9]

Boas's student Alfred L. Kroeber, an anthropologist at the University of California, played a crucial role in the triumph of cultural over biological explanations of behavior. In the nineteenth century Jean-Baptiste Lamarck had promulgated the "principle of acquired characters," the notion that parents transmitted behaviors they learned to their children. Modern genetics disposed of this theory. Between 1910 and 1917, Kroeber published a series of articles built on the collapse of Lamarckism. If achievements were not passed through inheritance, then biology could not explain the social and cultural achievements of advanced races. Only history—or, in essence, culture—did so. Kroeber posited cultural change as a form of nonorganic evolution, one which much more plausibly explained the differences between social groups than differences of race or biology. He was buttressed by another of Boas's students, Robert Lowie, who asserted in *Culture and Ethnology* that psychological research found no significant differences in mental capacities among races. The cultural diversity evident in peoples of the same race as well as their cultural variation over time defy racial or psychological explanation, Lowie insisted.[10]

The degree to which academics were questioning racial explanations of group differences emerged in the controversy over intelligence testing in the mid-1920s. During the Great War, the psychologists Robert Yerkes oversaw the development and administration of intelligence tests that were administered to almost two million draftees by the United States Army. The results were shocking, revealing that more than one-half of those tested registered below-normal levels of intelligence. Scholars compared the results by ethnic and racial group and concluded that northern European Nordics outperformed those of Alpine and Mediterranean stock and that whites outperformed blacks. "The most sinister development in the history of this continent," observed the Princeton psychologist Carl C. Brigham in *A Study of American Intelligence* (1923), was "the importation of the negro." Claims of racial disparities in intelligence generated controversy: critics argued that the tests measured learning more than intelligence. They challenged racial and ethnic interpretations of the data, pointing out that class standing explained differences in results better than race did. Boas and others challenged the assumption that blacks' intellects were inferior to whites', pointing out that northern blacks scored better than southern whites. By the end of the decade, Brigham repudiated his claims about the comparative intelligence of racial and ethnic groups based upon the tests.[11]

Likewise, the Chicago sociologists complicated the concept of race, making the term seem more subjective, more often attributing to culture what had previously been associated with biology and shifting the focus of analysis to more general group interactions and conflict. Neither Thomas nor Park was a crude racist; they both early rejected the impulse to attribute great differences in mental aptitude to race or biology. Thomas conceived racial prejudice to be an atavistic survival. The Chicago sociologists generally aligned with Boas.[12] Instead, influenced by German sociology and such American thinkers as Charles Horton Cooley, they gradually developed the concept of ethnicity as the group consciousness of urban minorities and embedded conflict between races and groups within a broader cycle of social relations leading to assimilation (a goal they deemed desirable). In fact, they conceived of this process "race neutrally," so to speak, describing problems of assimilation in modern city life as rooted in the adaptation of the peasant to urban life and not necessarily in racial competition per se.

In broader terms, the Chicago school adopted the German distinction, most notably articulated by Ferdinand Tönnies, between gemeinschaft and gesellschaft, or community and society. The community was organic and less dynamic; social bonds secure over time provided a person's identity in relation to unquestioned traditions. In *The Polish Peasant*, Thomas and Znaniecki argued that the individual immigrant still encountered modern society through the family even as current social conditions forced upon him or her more individualistic habits. What had been a very organized social system became, under the pressure of modern society, disorganized; individuals broke free of the values of the group, forming new attitudes to guide their behavior in society. Although this was a painful process, Thomas and Znaniecki argued that over time immigrants created their own solutions to social distress, established a new kind of ethnic community, and founded institutions such as mutual-benefit societies, churches, boardinghouses, schools, and cooperatives that enabled them to protect themselves. They adapted to the new world and internalized the values of an individualistic society. Thomas and Znaniecki endorsed the creation of ethnic institutions, finding them adjuncts, not barriers, to assimilation. Skeptical of well-intentioned efforts by reformers to change the immigrants' environment, their work endorsed an immigrant-led movement towards integration, even if inevitably marked by conflict and trauma.[13]

While focusing on immigration and assimilation, the Chicago sociologists created a broader template for understanding modern life as a natural and self-correcting process of adaptation to the disintegration of traditional forms of social authority. With change, social relations became objective, the economy money-based, and labor specialized and divided. In short, the peasant moved from gemeinschaft to city and to a social order based on rational design, not tradition. In doing so, the peasant became more independent and more autonomous. In Charles Horton Cooley's terms, this entailed moving from primary group relations (the face-to-face relations of family or community) to secondary institutions (in which many more contacts are made and many more individuals touched). As Charles S. Johnson, a student of Park's, observed: "Where once there were personal and intimate relations, in which individuals were in contact at practically all points of their lives, there are now group relations in which the whole structure is broken up and reassorted, casting them in contact at only one or two points of their lives."[14] In *Introduction to the Science of Sociology*, Park and Burgess outlined the interaction cycle—the race relations cycle when applied to racial groups, the assimilation or Americanization cycle when applied to immigrants. Groups in contact, Park believed, engaged first in competition, next conflict (resulting in boundary making and group definition), followed by accommodation (one group gaining dominance, or perhaps retreating to a ghetto), and finally acclimation, or assimilation. Recognizing that African Americans, Chinese, and Japanese experienced continued prejudice rather than acceptance, Park suggested a potential exceptional cycle ending in isolation rather than assimilation, although he did not consider racial prejudice different in kind from the broader hostility between insiders and outsiders in any social encounter. "In America . . . where economic and social opportunities were relatively abundant, individuals were emancipated from family conventions and had acquired a rational reflective morality," the historian Stow Persons observed of the Chicago school. "Here, among immigrant family groups the generations were divided, the children acquiring the new individualistic morality while the parents retained the older sense of family solidarity."[15]

Park and fellow Chicago sociologist Louis Wirth began to teach the first courses on racial and ethnic relations at the University of Chicago in the late 1920s. The Chicago school's theories and investigations moved discussions of racial and ethnic conflict away from debates about the purity of racial stock and a supposedly endangered American identity to a natural, predictable process of group conflict governed by the ethnic cycle of social relations. In the process of contact followed by adaptation, social relations and identities reveal themselves to be dynamic: immigrant groups of peasants created ethnicity as a transitional identity in adapting to America. The institutions of the ethnic enclave, which served to emphasize the national identity of immigrants, were not emblems of stubborn resistance to assimilation by a "new" immigrant population but rather invaluable tools in the long-term process of adaptation to American life. Eviscerating ethnic institutions and cultural networks would produce isolated and rootless immigrants.

A wave of racism, nativism, anti-Semitism, and anti-Catholicism crested during the Red Scare of 1919–1920 and the economic slowdown (1920–1922). Congress passed the Emergency Immigration Act in 1921, which for the first time limited immigration to the United States through the imposition of national quotas. Three years later, Congress passed the National Origins Act (or Johnson-Reed Act) of 1924, which permanently established national immigration quotas determined by the national origins of the current American population. The restrictive legislation of the 1920s eventually reduced immigration to the United States by approximately 85 percent.[16]

The Johnson-Reed Act, in particular, because of its reliance on a quota system based on nationality and the fact that persons legally recognized as ineligible for citizenship were excluded, advanced the creation of a bipolar racial system based on color. Between 1870 and 1923, congressional statutes and court decisions had declared immigrants from East and South Asia, including Chinese, Japanese, and Asian Indians, ineligible for citizenship. By barring these groups from the new quota system, the Johnson-Reed Act completed the process of excluding Asians from legal immigration to America that had begun with Chinese exclusion laws in the nineteenth century. Immigration from the Western Hemisphere (Canada, Mexico, and Central and South America) was exempted from the law's provisions. The law defined nationality as "country of birth," but specifically stated that for the purposes of the law, certain groups residing in the country were not counted as inhabitants of the United States, including immigrants from the Western Hemisphere and their descendants, aliens ineligible for citizenship (Asians) and their descendants, descendants of slave immigrants (African Americans), and descendants of "American aborigines." The government-appointed Quota Board simply discounted all blacks, mixed-race individuals, Chinese, Japanese, and South Asians from the population. As the historian Mae Ngai observed, the law "excised all nonwhite, non-European peoples" from American nationality.

Moreover, as Ngai observed, the ethnic and racial identities of European Americans were effectively "uncoupled" by immigration reform in the 1920s. Thus, a citizen born in the United States of European descent was simply classified as American (they now had a national identity distinct from their ethnicity), but other Americans were classified as members of "colored races"—identified not as Americans but as black, mulatto, Chinese, Japanese, and Indians in one 1924 table. Euro-Americans retained an ethnic identity but essentially gained a second racial identity as "white" (because being an American now meant not being "colored") and thus unquestionably capable of assimilation. Asian Americans (excluded from the system based on eligibility for citizenship) and Mexican Americans (exempted from the system, but soon caught up in the new visa and border-control policies created by the law and, in time, identified as a Mexican "racial problem") were not defined as part of the national identity. Their ethnicity and race remained "conjoined." Increasingly in the 1920s, race became a term denoting color divisions; whiteness, which had been fractured in the nineteenth century, was reconsolidated. A black-white binary system became conventional, with the scientific term Caucasian entering the vernacular as a new term (in contrast to Mongolian and Negroid) for whites.[17]

Many Americans continued to think of European ethnics as racially distinct and developed definitions of *American* that excluded them. Such was the case with the Ku Klux Klan, an organization taking its name and inspiration from the legendary southern paramilitary squad that attempted to enforce white supremacy in the years following the Civil War. A Methodist-Episcopal minister and war veteran named William J. Simmons established the second Klan in Georgia in 1915, hoping to create a nativist fraternal organization. In 1920, he employed the services of two experts in public relations, Edward Young Clarke and Mary Elizabeth Tyler of the Southern Publicity Association, who transformed the organization through the application of modern sales techniques, including the development of a system of sales representatives (known as Kleagles) who received four dollars of every ten-dollar initiation fee for every new member enrolled. The Klan promulgated a nativist, anti-Catholic, and racist message tailored to the heightened tensions of the early twenties and merchandised robes, masks, genuine Chattahoochee River water (to be used in initiations), and much else. The Klan varied by region: a reactionary civic group in many parts of the North, it was more violent and populist in the South. Klansmen revived cross burning and openly justified vigilantism, and the Klan prospered in a South still marked by racial lynchings and violent intimidation of blacks. The Klan used D. W. Griffith's *Birth of a Nation* (1915) in recruitment; the film's climactic sequence of heroic Klan retribution against a black male sexual predator aptly symbolized the spirit of the order for many. Klan members adopted time-honored techniques of violence and intimidation (most often used against white men and women) in their new role as self-appointed moral censors and social guardians. Negative publicity and congressional hearings in fall 1921 only improved recruitment. As the editors of the *New Republic* observed in 1921, Clarke outdid his sales and public-relations peers "in being able to sell religious bigotry and race hatred at the cost of $10 per bonehead."[18]

The Klan proved itself a tenacious and powerful presence in American life, with a membership potentially as high as five or six million (the organization's secrecy precludes accurate figures), the majority of which resided outside the South, and real political power, backing victorious gubernatorial candidates in states as diverse as Kansas and Georgia, Colorado and Indiana, Oregon and Oklahoma. The historian Leonard Moore estimates Indiana membership as perhaps as many as one-fourth to one-third of the state's native-born white men; many women affiliated with Klan auxiliary groups as well. Many Klan chapters drew membership broadly from the middle class, acted as decidedly mainstream civic reform organizations, and focused their energies on social and moral issues often tangential to the anti-Catholicism, bigotry, and nativism that comprised so much of the Klan's public message. Klan activists often targeted lax enforcement of the Prohibition laws, public vice and immorality, local political corruption, fading civic engagement, lower church attendance, and declining quality in the public schools. In one city, the Klan fought for higher taxes for road improvements, a new sewage system, and new school buildings; in Utah, the Klan challenged the power of the Mormon elite; in El Paso, Texas, the focus was on illegal alcohol and drug trafficking and violent crime. In Athens, Georgia, Klansmen were alarmed by alcohol consumption, gambling, and prostitution as well as dance halls, pool rooms, card games, jazz music, salacious books and movies, premarital sex, "parking," and petting parties.

Klan recruits were often a familiar type: dry activists who might also have joined the Anti-Saloon League; middle-aged Republicans, Methodists, or Masons; and critics of ball games and movies on Sundays. Strong in medium-sized cities, the Klan was a defensive reaction to the metropolitan and nationalizing forces transforming the nation at this time. Even its critics acknowledged the many average, well-meaning Americans who might reasonably find it attractive. At times, the organization seems a 1920s precursor to later "slow-growth" movements, urging its members to patronize local establishments affiliated with the Klan and turning its wrath on local elites who ignored bootlegging and corruption or sold out community interests to national corporations. As Stanley Coben observed, "Klansmen in the mid-1920s decidedly were not a fringe group of vigilantes; they were solid middle-class citizens and individuals of high Victorian character."[19]

Yet, the essential image of the Klan revolved around vigilantism, bigotry, and secrecy. The chauvinisms of the Klansmen (and Klanswomen) may have been broadly present in American society, as Leonard Moore observed, yet most Americans did not place them at the symbolic heart of their identity. Those who joined the Klan conceived themselves to be the subject of assault from those they opposed: "The order's basic message was that average white Protestants were under attack: their values and traditions were being undermined, their vision of America's national purpose and social order appeared to be threatened, and their ability to shape the course of public affairs seemed to have diminished." In the South, many members were drawn from the military and law enforcement. The flogging of men and sometimes women, often for bootlegging, adultery, prostitution, or (for men) the failure to support a family, were popular forms of vigilantism.[20]

In 1922, Hiram Wesley Evans, an ambitious Dallas dentist, seized control of the Klan from Simmons and his key aides, Clarke and Tyler (who had become embroiled in a morals scandal as their own faithlessness to the credo of family values with each other came to light). Believing a uniform and set national program would stifle organizational growth, Evans allowed local chapters to set their own agendas. However, he articulated a national ideology built around the Klan slogan of "Native, white, Protestant supremacy." The idea of equal rights was a theoretical notion only, he argued, contrary to facts and therefore invalid, "actually abhorrent in practice to the American mind." Racial equality, he argued, is practiced to no significant extent anywhere on earth. "Facts prove the idea unworkable. This beautiful philosophy, therefore, the Klan will not argue about. It merely rejects it, as almost all Americans do." In Evans's rhetoric, the descendants of the pioneers are the true Americans, those who have "the right of the children of the men who made America to own and control America." Immigrants must "become a part of us, adopt our ideas and ideals, and help in fulfilling our destiny along those lines."[21]

Evans provides an excellent case study of the orthodox mind. He explicitly opposed conviction to theory and hailed "racial instincts" and common sense as the basis of judgment, even labeling convictions, not science, the "fundamentals of our thought," backed by faith in the same way religious convictions are. Adhering to the logic of orthodoxy, Evans believed that strength came from suppressing contaminating ideas and persons. He noted distress among Nordic Americans: "confusion in thought and opinion," "futility in religion," the challenges posed by "strange ideas," and the "moral breakdown that has been going on for two decades." Yet, when turning from what he was against to what he supported, Evans could speak only platitudes: Americanism is, he declared in the *Forum*, "welded of convictions, independence, self-reliance, freedom, justice, achievement, courage, acceptance of responsibility, and the guidance of his own conscience by each man personally." Despite Evans's effort to formulate a national conservative ideology and American identity, he was unable to articulate any principles or substantive beliefs that would distinguish it from others. In the end, being American became essentially an ethnic claim, or a function of one's heritage and religion. Evans's efforts amounted to the chauvinistic assertion of the superiority of his race and the desire that white Americans' minds remain unchallenged. As a letter writer to the *Forum* noted, "Inside the mind of the Imperial Wizard I find passion instead of reason, assumptions instead of proofs."[22]

The most clearly articulated alternative to the nativism of the 1910s and 1920s was cultural pluralism, a term coined by the philosopher Horace Kallen in *Culture and Democracy in the United States*, which was published in 1924. The book consisted, in part, of previously published essays, the most important of which, "Democracy *versus* the Melting-Pot," originally appeared in the *Nation* in February 1915. Kallen immigrated to the United States at age five from Silesia in Germany. He grew up in Boston and attended Harvard, studying with literary historian Barrett Wendell, William James, and George Santayana. He eventually completed a doctorate in philosophy under James and lectured and taught at Harvard and the University of Wisconsin before helping to found the New School of Social Research in 1919, where he remained for over fifty years. Although his father was an Orthodox rabbi, Judaism became a secular if powerful commitment for Kallen.

In 1903, he became a Zionist, styling himself a "Hebraist." He remained an ardent nationalist at the same time.

Democracy was a prerequisite for culture, Kallen believed, and modernism in thought faced an onslaught from organizations such as the KKK panicked over perceived threats to native-born privilege, capitalists alarmed over liberalism in politics and economics, and orthodox religion stubbornly resistant to science and the Higher Criticism. The Klan represented the resistance of what is old against the things that are new. Kallen argued for a recognition and embrace of the autonomy and singularity of ethnicities, believing that the hope for democracy and a revived culture lay in the diversity of American communities. He envisioned an American culture "founded upon variation of racial groups and individual character; upon spontaneous differences of social heritage, institutional habit, mental attitude and emotional tone; upon the continuous, free and fruitful cross-fertilization of these by one another." The alternative was the "Kulture Klux Klan." Cultural pluralism took root only in a democratic culture, which fostered individuality, fellowship, and cooperation.[23]

To Kallen, no such thing as an American race existed. There was a superficial conformity in language and economic and political behavior, but the American republic actually enhanced group social consciousness rather than fostering a single race. The creative cultural response was not to compel unison in national affairs but to orchestrate a new harmony from the diverse constituents of American culture. The metaphor of the symphony replaced that of the melting pot. Kallen's version of cultural pluralism was more thoroughgoing than what went under this name after World War II, a call mainly for tolerance of a diversity of viewpoints and cultural backgrounds. To Kallen, national groups (such as the Irish, Poles, Scandinavians, or Jews) transmitted an essential "psycho-social inheritance," an intrinsic and unchanging personal quality. "Men may change their clothes, their politics, their wives, their religions; their philosophies, to a greater or lesser extent; they cannot change their grandfathers." Ethnic groups were permanent and ineradicable elements of the nation, and Kallen envisioned a "democracy of nationalities," a federal state built on the "cooperation of cultural diversities, as a federation or commonwealth of national cultures." Democracy, he believed, demanded not only that differences be tolerated but also that they be fostered and perfected. Hyphenation was not to be condemned, for it is a description of an inevitable feature of human society, pervading all of life. "A man is at once a son and a husband, a brother and a friend, a man of affairs and a student, a citizen of a state and a member of a church, one in an ethnic and social group and the citizen of a nation," Kallen observed. While it is true that one relationship of this kind may generate divided loyalties, it is also important to acknowledge "the truth that the hyphen unites very much more than it separates, and that in point of fact, the greater the hyphenation, the greater the unanimity."[24]

Although Kallen's book was not widely reviewed nor marked as influential at the time, Robert Park reported that the terms "racial and cultural pluralism" had attained some popularity by 1926. As John Higham observed, however, Kallen assumed that some kind of natural harmony existed beneath the various social conflicts of society. Were this assumption unwarranted, it was unclear how a nation of disparate ethnicities could achieve social peace, given the history of American social division and the ways in which pluralism promised to separate people and potentially increase inequality. Standing opposed to Kallen's pluralism, other intellectuals were beginning to develop the cosmopolitan stance more characteristic of later liberal modernists. The intellectual progenitor of cosmopolitanism was Randolph Bourne, but it was also articulated by critics such as Hutchins Hapgood, Floyd Dell, and Paul Rosenfeld. Cosmopolitans were suspicious of the ethnic particularisms that Kallen treasured, believing that while cultural differences should be preserved, Americans must avoid narrow parochialism. Instead of conceiving ethnic identity as a defining feature of the self, cosmopolitan intellectuals viewed subcultures "as repositories for insights and experiences that can be drawn upon in the interests of a more comprehensive outlook on the world," argued David Hollinger. Ethnic heritage remains valuable only insofar as it enhances individual experience.[25]

The African American philosopher and critic Alain Locke articulated a middle position between cultural pluralism and cosmopolitanism. Born in 1885 to Philadelphia schoolteachers, Locke attended Harvard from 1904 to 1907. He met Horace Kallen, who was a graduate assistant in one of Locke's courses, and they became friends. Kallen later traced the genesis of his notion of cultural pluralism to discussions he had with Locke at that time and the following year, when they both were Rhodes Scholars at Oxford. Intensely Anglophilic and more than a bit elitist, Locke must have been delighted to win the scholarship, becoming the first African American to do so; however, he faced some isolation at Oxford, where he failed to make the best colleges, was snubbed by some of the more color-conscious English, and was denied an invitation to the traditional Thanksgiving dinner at the American Club at the behest of his fellow scholars from the South. (Kallen refused to attend the dinner in protest; however, in correspondence surviving between Kallen and Barrett Wendell, one of his Harvard mentors and an acquaintance of Locke's as well, they both express distaste for blacks and repugnance at equal social relations.) Despite the persistence of racial prejudice beyond the nation's borders, Locke made the most of his time abroad, meeting young nationalist thinkers from India, Egypt, and South Africa, traveling to Eastern Europe, and studying social science at the University of Berlin. He returned to the United States in 1911. With the aid of Booker T. Washington, he gained a position in the Teachers College at Howard University in 1912, eventually completing a doctorate in philosophy at Harvard and joining Howard's philosophy department in 1917. He remained at Howard his entire career, although he briefly lost his position in the mid-1920s due to his open support for students seeking an end to compulsory chapel and Reserve Officers' Training Corps (ROTC) and his demands for a more equitable faculty pay scale.[26]

In a series of lectures in 1915 and 1916, Locke outlined his theories on race, arguing that races were the product of historical development and not biology. Neither race nor racism was a permanent feature of human affairs, in his view. Racial characteristics differed over time, and much variation existed even within racial groups. In a 1924 lecture, Locke distinguished between *race* used as a term for physical differences and *race* used in a social or ethnic sense. Most people's notions about race had to do with the types and accompanying traits that were the product of social development; indeed, Locke felt that what was meant when a social group was designated by "race types" was actually "culture-types," and that the term *culture-group* would better substitute for *race*. Like Boas and his students, to whom he was indebted, Locke repudiated the dominant pseudoscience of race, so influentially promulgated by popular race thinkers such as Madison Grant and Lothrop Stoddard. "Instead . . . of regarding culture as expressive of race, race by this interpretation is regarded as itself a cultural product," he explained. Race, he argued in his 1915–1916 lectures, was simply a metaphor to identify a social group that had been shaped by a common locale, history, and culture. What people associated with race had nothing to do with skin color; rather, Locke identified race-based domination of less powerful peoples as the essence of Western imperialism. In his analysis, racial prejudice came from economic competition and the ability of one group to dominate another.[27]

Even as he rejected the fundamental basis of racialist thinking, however, Locke, like Kallen, hailed racial consciousness as an effective tool of black cultural advance. He hoped African Americans could model themselves after European minorities such as the Irish, Czechs, or Poles, who were creating a national identity as a means of challenging repression. Race consciousness would give blacks self-respect; blacks could use the ethnic fiction of race every bit as effectively as immigrant groups. He urged race solidarity and loyalty. However, he also stressed the "highly composite" nature of culture.[28] Locke was a pluralist, but his pluralism always stressed interracial hybridity and cultural reciprocity.

In a 1930 lecture, he recognized the paradox of fostering racial conscious-ness while needing to fight racial prejudice and chauvinism. He analogized cultural interchange to free trade between nations, arguing that both races benefit in cultural development from mutual intercourse just as two nations benefit from reciprocity treaties in the form of reduced tariffs. Locke repudi-ated Kallen's ethnoracial essentialism, arguing that civilizations are always intermixtures. Race exists, he argued, but our attitudes toward it are wrong. When one group insists on a "vested ownership of culture goods," conflict and tragedy arise. "[D]o away with the idea of proprietorship and vested inter-est,—and face the natural fact of the limitless interchangeableness of culture goods, and the more significant historical facts of their more or less constant exchange, and we have, I think, a solution reconciling nationalism with internationalism, racialism with universalism," Locke declared. Culture is a folkish, organic growth, associated with a "particular people and place": "for all its subsequent universality, culture has root and grows in that social soil which, for want of a better term, we call 'race.'" In a 1927 *Forum* exchange with the racist Lothrop Stoddard (remarkably titled, "Should the Negro Be Encouraged to Cultural Equality?"), Locke argued that blacks deserved full "cultural recognition" for their contribution to American civilization, their "cultural gifts" to whites. Stoddard denied any such claim ("We know that *our* America is a *White* America," he declared, denying any black role in creating white institutions, ideals, and culture) and held that Locke wanted racial intermixtures, or hybrids, which were "disharmonic" and disruptive to the long-established and complex patterns of race. Were Locke's advice followed and blacks given social equality, the result would be a "mulatto America," he observed distastefully.[29]

Northern cities provided ambivalent promises of freedom to African Ameri-cans. When the tap dancer John Sublett (John W. Bubbles on stage) arrived in New York from the Midwest, he celebrated by roller-skating down Fifth Avenue, hanging onto the bumpers of cars. However, dangers lurked. In her novel of female African American self-discovery, *Quicksand* (1928), Nella Larsen provided a primer on the challenges of life in a big city for the newcomer: the dissatisfied heroine arrives on her own in Chicago, but, ab-sent friends willing to help and without an all-important letter of reference, she flails, quickly discovering the difficulties of making it alone in the city. The swarms of people on Chicago streets, "merging into little eddies and disengaging themselves to pursue their own individual ways," intrigue, even excite her, "as if she were tasting some agreeable, exotic food," but days with no work and encroaching hunger leave her lonely, shut off from life, "on the verge of weeping": "It made her feel small and insignificant that in all the climbing massed city no one cared one whit about her."[30]

In the 1920s, urban and rural African Americans vigorously pursued race consciousness as a strategy for reversing social and economic discrimination. The "Negro Renaissance" resulted, an efflorescence of black art, music, literature, and theater. The Renaissance received enormous stimulus from the rural migrant influx into the cities but also reflected black leaders' conviction that progress would come only if and when white leaders were convinced of the capability of their black peers. The leaders of the biracial National Association for the Advancement of Colored People (NAACP) and the National Urban League, both of which published important black journals, Crisis and Opportunity respectively, aimed to raise white consciousness of black achievements despite the challenges they faced. As middle-class leaders, they sought to resolve the vexing problems of African American self-consciousness (what W. E. B. Du Bois identified as a "double consciousness" of being both Negro and American, two separate souls struggling within one body) and intellectual insecurity. As it happened, the leading theme of the art and literature produced by Renaissance artists was precisely this legacy of African American self-division.

African American leaders appropriated the "New Negro" label that observers had begun to apply to the proud and defiant African American who refused to back down in the face of racial prejudice and discrimination. If hit, the New Negro hits back, Roland Lynde Hartt observed in the Independent. The bourgeois leaders of black America were also stealing a march on the black nationalist movement led by Jamaican-born Marcus Garvey, which gained a huge popular following among black rural tenant farmers and sharecroppers and the black working-class masses in the early 1920s. In 1925, Alain Locke published The New Negro (1925), an anthology assessing the state of black cultural production (Locke included poetry and fiction selections and illustrations and African-inspired design elements as well), analyzing the current state of the black community, highlighting black artistic achievements, suggesting areas of deficiency, and digging and sifting through the record of African American social and cultural life. "The American Negro must remake his past in order to make his future," declared the Puerto Rico–born collector Arthur Schomburg, betraying in his echoes of the language and sentiment of the Young American cultural nationalists a

An image of the New Negro by Aaron Douglas, featured on the cover of the American Negro issue of the *Annals of the American Academy of Political and Social Science*, edited by Donald Young (November 1928).
Collection of Richard and C. T. Woods-Powell.

shared conversation on American culture. "The New Negro has been a man without a history because he has been considered a man without a worthy culture." Locke pointed out that a "deep feeling of race" had become the "mainspring of Negro life," likening what he saw as a Negro Renaissance to insurgent global nationalisms.[31]

Although Locke lived in Washington, D.C., and drew inspiration from a small but vibrant intellectual community there, the center of black aspiration and cultural promotion lay in Harlem, an uptown section of Manhattan graced with solid brownstone homes that was experiencing racial turnover from white to black. Both southern rural blacks and a variety of Caribbean migrants flowed into the area, making visible every day the immense heterogeneity of black life in America. The distinguished black leader James Weldon Johnson claimed a "constant growth of group consciousness and community feeling" in Harlem. Locke decreed it to be the home of "the Negro's 'Zionism.'"[32]

Marcus Garvey made Harlem his home in America and the base of his brief but spectacular public career in black America. Unlike the bourgeois intellectuals collected around the NAACP and the Urban League, Garvey harbored a vision of the reorganization of black life international in scope. Born in Jamaica in 1887, Garvey traveled widely in Central America and Europe, doing some labor agitation and forming the Universal Negro Improvement Association (UNIA) in 1914. He was conversant with the strategies and philosophy of Booker T. Washington, with whom he corresponded and who invited him to Tuskegee. In 1916 Garvey arrived in the United States; in 1918, he reincorporated the UNIA in America.[33]

In less than ten years, Garvey created a political movement that unnerved the staid black leadership of America, alarmed not a few imperial capitals around the world (the UNIA established over one thousand divisions, or chapters, around the world, from the West Indies to Africa and even Europe), and evoked a repressive response from the federal government in the form of investigations by the relatively new General Intelligence Division of the Justice Department, headed by J. Edgar Hoover. Garvey's movement gained great support from the black public, particularly in 1921–1922. He built the UNIA in America to at least one hundred thousand dues-paying members and perhaps as many as two million (if rather vague estimates are to be believed). Close to 80 percent of the UNIA divisions were in the United States, with over four hundred in the South, where the UNIA was broadly popular among literate black tenant farmers and sharecroppers. The UNIA sponsored huge rallies and parades, promoting a message of Negro nationhood and the redemption of Africa, even advocating the return to Africa of all black peoples. Garvey insisted on fashioning the UNIA as an African government in waiting, replete with ministries (of labor, agriculture, and so on), orders of nobility (including Nile dukes and Ethiopian counts), paramilitary wings (a Black Star Navy and African Rifle Corps), and colors (red, black, and green). As president-general, Garvey often appeared decked out in elaborate military regalia. The UNIA published the *Negro World* and fostered an alternative church (the African Orthodox Church) and numerous business enterprises under the Negro Factories Corporation, including a grocery chain, laundry, restaurant, publishing house, and real estate firm, as well as the ill-fated Black Star Line, a shipping company so poorly run that it left Garvey open to the charges of mail fraud of which he was convicted in 1923.

Garvey reworked nationalist strands of nineteenth-century black thought, extolling a message of race consciousness and pride, African national identity, solidarity, economic independence, and self-help. Du Bois and other black leaders initially welcomed Garvey and maintained a wary respect for his achievements, but his ideology unsettled their core commitment to integration. Garvey called for the creation of a Negro nation in Africa, demanding that the continent be redeemed from the colonial powers. His economic projects were designed to build economic self-sufficiency and autonomy. Garvey provided a very direct and rude challenge to the middle-class leadership of the black community. Du Bois, James Weldon Johnson, and the socialist labor organizer A. Philip Randolph were not grassroots leaders. Booker T. Washington had organized a political machine; they viewed it as corrupt and stultifying. "They were not involved in the block and precinct work that might have given them the kind of political leverage that the American political system understood," observed Nathan Huggins. The result, he argued was that "Harlem intellectual leadership was epiphenomenal. It had no grass-roots attachments. Its success depended on its strategic placement, not its power."[34]

Initially welcomed by left-wing labor-oriented activists like Hubert Harrison and racial nationalists like Cyril Briggs (who had organized the African Blood Brotherhood, which mixed class-based and racial radicalism), Garvey's embrace of capitalism, opposition to unions, and support for lower wages, perhaps intended as strategic moves to build support among whites, alienated them. After 1921, Garvey emphasized racial purity and separatism, issues that opened the issue of skin-color prejudice within the black community and deeply distressed the established leadership, which was, in fact, generally light-skinned. The dark-skinned Garvey, though repudiating race prejudice and claims that any one race was superior to another, advocated race purity: "I believe in a pure black race, just as how all self-respecting whites believe in a pure white race, as far as that can be." He rejected interracial mixing. "I am conscious of the fact that slavery brought upon us the curse of many colors within the Negro race," he declared, "but there is no reason why we ourselves should perpetuate the evil."[35] Garvey's rivals, genuinely appalled at some of his ideas and aghast at the embarrassing financial disaster of the Black Star Line, cooperated in federal fraud investigations of Garvey, which led to his indictment in early 1922. Du Bois denounced him in print in April of that year. His fate was perhaps sealed in his miscalculated move to seek an alliance with white supremacists in America, meeting with Edward Y. Clarke, acting imperial wizard of the Ku Klux Klan in June 1922, perhaps to facilitate UNIA organizing in the South, and conferring with racist southern senators and the head of the Anglo-Saxon League. Garvey's actions alienated many rank-and-file blacks, who were the base of his support (although southern blacks remained loyal supporters). The black press turned against him in 1923, the year of his conviction on fraud charges. He was deported in 1927.

Nationalism remained a powerful force in American life. In 1925, the Communist Party organized the American Negro Labor Congress, which made an explicit cultural appeal to southern rural blacks and signaled a receptivity to black nationalism. The Congress only lasted five years, but it revealed the influence of Garvey's movement in black life, much to the frustration of some younger black radicals, such as Abram Harris Jr. and E. Franklin Frazier. Frazier grew up in working-class Baltimore; throughout the 1910s and 1920s, he attended college and pursued opportunities for graduate education as well as teaching and, occasionally, courting controversy. Frazier published an article on racial prejudice in Forum in 1927 that claimed, among other points, that white women's fantasies of attacks by black males reflected suppressed desires. The article's publication hastened his departure from Atlanta, where he had been teaching at Morehouse College and directing the Atlanta School of Social Work. Frazier eventually earned a doctorate in sociology under Robert Park at the University of Chicago. Both Harris and Frazier accepted teaching positions at Howard University and concluded that economic and class, as opposed to racial, analysis was the necessary basis of black social progress. In the 1920s, Frazier analyzed the class stratification of the black community, pointing to its lack of a unified racial viewpoint, and expressed skepticism of the New Negro movement.[36]

Harris was likewise skeptical of the New Negro, dismissing attempts to link American blacks to the African past. A Columbia-trained economist (he completed his doctorate in 1930) who had worked for the Urban League and the Messenger, a radical black journal published between 1917 and 1928, Harris believed that the American Negro cannot "be considered in any logical sense African." A student of black economic life and labor who prided himself on objective scientific analysis, Harris strongly opposed Garvey's racial nationalism, was critical of Du Bois's "racial subjectivism," and disliked the romanticism of The New Negro. Aware that his friend George Goetz (who wrote as V. F. Calverton) was agitating over Harris's exclusion from Locke's volume, Harris ordered him to desist, well aware of the disparity between his reputation and that of Du Bois, Locke, and the other contributors:

> Intellectually, I feel that with time and study, I could *clean* the whole bunch if we were simultaneously employed with a job that demands clear cut objective and philosophic thinking. They have me on these lyrical rhapsodies of racially inflected ebullience. Some time I wish I could sit on the Woolworth Building and say God-damn the Negro and his problems so loud that the pronunciation would ring to the ears of a universal audience.[37]

Garvey had presented a pointed challenge to black American leadership. "He had charisma, he was eloquent, he was black," recalled Benjamin E. Mays, the black educator and president of Morehouse College. "No other black leader, in my time, had attracted the masses as did Garvey." As David Levering Lewis noted, unlike much of the black elite in America, Garvey analyzed racism as a distinction in power, not color or religion or some other factor. Thus his program focused on economic and political mobilization, not cultural production. In Garvey's view, black American leaders were too committed to an unredeemable nation and system. As Lewis wrote, Garvey believed that "the error of leaders like Du Bois transcended skin color; they were rebels in American society only to the degree and duration of their exclusion from it."[38]

The "Negro Renaissance" grew from the ferment of ideas on race pride, the enormous influx of blacks into the northern industrial cities, and the calculations of middle-class black leaders casting about for any avenue of race progress. Black intellectuals knew and worked with white intellectuals, and the Renaissance paralleled their broader national project of cultural reconstruction. It was a joint white-black production. African American leaders leveraged the emerging autonomous institutions of Harlem and support from white and black donors into an appeal to talented blacks to come east. The intersection of 135th Street and Seventh Avenue, "The Campus," became a center of Harlem life. The 135th Street YMCA sponsored lectures by leading black and white intellectuals and mounted theatrical productions. Also important was the Harlem branch of the New York Public Library, which chief librarian Ernestine Rose transformed along progressive lines into a multiracial and multiethnic community cultural center for all Harlemites. Rose insisted on maintaining an interracial staff, resisting pressures from both black and white parties to make it all-black. The library sponsored poetry readings, book discussions, and a pioneering exhibition of Negro art in 1921.

Several black leaders assumed key roles in promoting black arts. Charles S. Johnson, national director of research and investigations for the National Urban League and editor of *Opportunity*, turned much of the magazine over to arts and letters. Trained as a sociologist under Robert Park at Chicago, Johnson believed that black literature could play a role in the objective social analysis of experience as well as foster interracial empathy, which would promote a national community. In 1924, *Opportunity* began sponsoring literary prizes, and the NAACP's *Crisis*, edited by Du Bois, soon followed suit. *Opportunity* also sponsored a gala dinner to honor Harlem writers at the Civic Club downtown on March 21, 1924—a key moment of introduction between the new black poets and novelists and white leaders in the publishing industry. At the dinner, Paul U. Kellogg, editor of the *Survey Graphic*, approached Charles Johnson about publishing a special issue on black culture, which appeared as "Harlem: Mecca of the New Negro" in March 1925. Alain Locke assembled the contents of the issue, which became the basis of *The New Negro*. Johnson worked to attract young talent to Harlem, enlisting the aid of his secretary, Ethel Ray Nance, a young woman from Minnesota whom he had also convinced to come east. She welcomed the recruited artists and provided food and sometimes a place to sleep in the flat she shared with two others at 580 St. Nicholas Avenue, an upscale apartment building in the affluent Sugar Hill neighborhood. Johnson cajoled Aaron Douglas, a young painter working as a high school teacher in Kansas City, to resign his position and migrate to Harlem. He stayed a week in Nance's flat while gaining his footing. The atmosphere encouraged experimentation and ambition; soon, white markets opened themselves to black work, and black authors were in demand.

The impulse to assert racial consciousness and race unity defined the New Negro, but what African American writers often returned to were the divisions within the black community and the ultimately illusory nature of race, the impossibility of defining a Negro consciousness neatly uniting a group of people within the American nation. Time and again, in personal lives and in literary politics, the Renaissance writers ran up against the hidden shoals of race identity and differentiation—the murky limits where black shaded into white, which permeated more of black life than most realized, or the cultural miscegenation between white and black (the "mulatto America" denounced by Stoddard) that may have seemed initially a rare offshoot of black cultural production but eventually loomed as something more like the root.

Jean Toomer provides a case in point: his largely absent father was the illegitimate mixed-race son of a North Carolina landowner; his mother died in 1909, leaving him to be raised in the home of his maternal grandfather, the distinguished P. B. S. Pinchback, former lieutenant governor of, and senator from, Louisiana who by the 1910s was a gambler and socialite in Washington, D.C. When at his grandfather's home, Toomer grew up in a wealthy white Washington neighborhood, not living amongst blacks until attending Dunbar High School, after Pinchback's declining economic fortunes necessitated a move. Toomer identified with neither white nor black but with the "colored," the well-off, mixed-race class of his Washington upbringing that sought to evade rigid racial classification. He fondly remembered the "unlabelled, unclassed, nonstratifiable, traditionless and yet cultured people" among whom he was raised. "Socially, though they were classified as colored, they had contacts in both groups, and were without any marked race-consciousness one way or another." Toomer bounced among various institutions of higher education in the country, studying agriculture briefly and later physical training, molding a fine physique through weight lifting in Chicago in 1916. After college, he meandered, taking odd jobs, hitchhiking, and doing some bodybuilding. By his late twenties, Toomer had no vocation and his jumble of cultural influences resulted only in alienation. He aspired to be a writer, inspired by Randolph Bourne, Waldo Frank, and the Young Intellectuals.[39]

A chance appointment to administer a small agricultural and industrial academy in rural Sparta, Georgia, in fall 1921 precipitated a decisive break in Toomer's hitherto aimless life. Here, the light-skinned young man who could pass for white and who spent much of his youth among whites discovered rural black folk culture, including African American spirituals and folk songs. "God, but they feel the thing," he wrote the next year. "Sometimes too violently for sensitive nerves; always sincerely, powerfully, deeply. And when they overflow in song, there is no singing that has so touched me." Toomer began writing and the next year publishing parts of what became *Cane* (1923), an experimental assemblage of poetry and prose written in an evocative, modernist style that received wide acclaim and established Toomer as a rising literary star. Writers befriended him; Waldo Frank became a particularly close friend, as they both shared a somewhat romantic and mystical sensibility. In Toomer's view, he had connected to his Negro identity: "My seed was planted in *myself* down there. Roots have grown and strengthened." *Cane* became an elegiac response from a formerly deracinated northern urbanite to what he interpreted as a fading cultural taproot; the book was sad, he wrote Frank, a "sadness derived from a sense of fading."

"Don't let us fool ourselves, brother: the Negro of the folk-song has all but passed away: the Negro of the emotional church is fading. A hundred years from now, these Negroes, if they exist at all will live in art."[40]

Much of the renewed racial consciousness in the Renaissance was similarly tied into a discovery of roots, whether a respectful attention to the southern black folk roots of Negro culture or the deeper African cultural tradition, which Locke, among others, pointed to proudly. Locke wrote respectfully of Negro spirituals and African art in *The New Negro*; an extensive thirty-two-page bibliography at the back of the book promoted further study of black culture and included extensive lists of sources on spirituals and "Negro Folk Lore." The clarion call was, as Schomburg had urged, for the American Negro to dig up his past. As the educator Montgomery Gregory urged about a projected National Negro Theater, "the only avenue of genuine achievement in American drama for the Negro lies in the development of rich veins of folk-tradition of the past and in the portrayal of the authentic life of the Negro masses to-day."[41]

Toomer himself soon strayed from the New Negro catechism, involving himself deeply in the mixed-race culture of Greenwich Village and in the spiritual-physical regimen of George Ivanovitch Gurdjieff, an Eastern European mystic who developed a strong following in the 1920s, especially among intellectuals. Under the influence of Gurdjieff's ideas, Toomer came to believe that finding the root of his Negro identity enabled him to be open to his white identity as well. "Prior to the present phase, because he was denied by others, the Negro denied them and necessarily denied himself," Toomer explained in an April 1925 lecture at the 135th Street library. "Forced to say nay to the white world, he was negative towards his own life." In turn, Toomer shucked off an identity as Negro and now felt himself multiracial, the spiritual pioneer of a new, American race. He was concerned to achieve a position above "the hypnotic division of Americans into black and white," he wrote Suzanne LaFollette in 1930.[42] He gradually drifted from the black literary scene and the Harlem Renaissance, never fulfilling the great promise once placed in him.

Another writer ensnared in the unexpected contradictions of black consciousness was Nella Larsen, author of two well-received novels.[43] Like Toomer, she was of mixed-race parentage and thrived in mixed-race social circles where racial consciousness in action could become a complex matter, worked out in the company of white, black, and multiracial pioneers. She and her husband, the physicist Richard Imes, were a noteworthy couple on the Harlem and Greenwich Village social scene, part of a group that embraced mixed-race sociability. Larsen's mother was white, an immigrant from

Denmark, and her father was an immigrant from the Danish West Indies and a person of color. He disappeared shortly after her birth in 1891. Her mother and a white stepfather raised Nella with a white stepsister in a poor section of Chicago, although she seems not to have gained full acceptance from all of the family. Her sister later disavowed their relationship.

Larsen's literary career blossomed in the hothouse atmosphere of the Harlem Renaissance. After serving as volunteer organizer of the 135th Street library Negro art show in 1921, she gravitated to the library field and, although a professional nurse, became the first black woman to earn a degree in it, working for Ernestine Rose in the children's section. In Larsen's two published novels, race drives the major characters to self-destructive and neurotic behaviors. Each concerned mixed-race women dissatisfied with the larger black community to which they are irresistibly drawn. ("They always come back," a character observes of light-skinned blacks who try to "pass" as white. "I've seen it happen time and time again.") Helga Crane, the part-Danish, mixed-race heroine of *Quicksand* (1928), shifts between a Tuskegee-like educational institution called Naxos, the cities of Chicago and Harlem, and Denmark, never to find satisfaction in a fulfilled, peaceful life. She finally makes the rash and unfortunate decision to marry a revival preacher, ending up unhappy, overburdened with children, and longing for escape in the small-town South—the very matrix of black culture. In *Passing* (1929) Irene Redfield and Clare Kendry are twinned light-skinned heroines, the former seemingly happily married and accepting of her black identity at the beginning of the novel, the second enjoying the financial security of passing for white but married to an egregious, black-hating racist. Although they had been childhood friends, when they are reacquainted as adults, Irene considers them "strangers" to each other: "Strangers in their desires and ambitions. Strangers even in their racial consciousness. Between them the barrier was just as high, just as broad, and just as firm as if in Clare did not run that strain of black blood."[44] Clare insists on reestablishing her connection to black culture despite the obvious danger of arousing the wrath of her racist husband. She cannot resist reconnecting to her roots, in the process seducing Irene's angry and unhappy husband Brian. In her desire for bourgeois comfort and respectability, Irene had thwarted Brian's plans to take the family to Argentina and escape the racial discrimination of America, which he loathed. His anger had not diminished over the years; the reader learns their sex life is less than fulfilling. By the end of the novel, the kinship between Irene and Clare is clear, as the reality of racial constructions in America destabilized both of their identities and compromised the security of both their homes.

The quantum of white or black blood in the veins does not effectively determine racial identity in either novel, as the principal characters in each are compelled to choose the race with which to identify. Whether or not one is a "stranger" to one race or the other has to do with consciousness and not blood. The decision to "come back" to the black race presupposes that color defines a home for everyone, which is not the case for the principal characters in Larsen's books and was not the case for Larsen herself. In *Quicksand*, Helga Crane scorns a certain type of black elite, which she finds secretly race-hating, yet she is unhappy herself when identifying as black and desirous of the freedoms of white life. Helga scorns the uptight educators at her Tuskegee-like Naxos. "These people yapped loudly of race, of race consciousness, of race pride, and yet suppressed its most delightful manifestations, love of color, joy of rhythmic motion, naïve, spontaneous laughter," she thinks. "Harmony, radiance, and simplicity, all the essentials of spiritual beauty in the race they had marked for destruction."[45] Her Harlem friend Anne is a race militant who hates white people but also scorns black culture (a model for the thwarted African American, according to Toomer's theory of racial consciousness).

In a book characterized by themes of suffocation, claustrophobia, and asphyxiation, Helga cannot abide Harlem when in Harlem but grows tired of being treated as an exotic primitive by the Danish. Aside from racial discrimination, black women authors faced the additional burden, placed on them by black men, to abide by a heightened code of bourgeois respectability in order to counter exaggerated stereotypes of black female sexuality. As a result, their writing often contained images of silence, entrapment, and paralysis, their characters marked by confinement and self-division as a consequence of a complex skein of race, gender, and class discriminations.[46] However, Helga also suffers from the same problem that Irene diagnoses in her son and her husband in *Passing*: always wanting what one cannot have. (The ambitious and restless home wrecker Clare, similarly, always had a "having way" about her.) In a society in which peoples are grouped by race, one will inevitably envy the other, Larsen seems to be saying. It was not a matter of race (the problem was more acute for the multiracial characters) but of the race line and cultural acceptance. Cultural pluralism would not have appealed to Larsen; she comments on the Danish idea of allowing each "his own mileu": "Enhance what was already in one's possession." Such a concept, Helga realizes, has no validity in the United States. "In America Negroes sometimes talked loudly of this, but in their hearts they repudiated it," she thinks. "In their lives too. They didn't want to be like themselves. What they wanted, asked for, begged for, was to be like their white overlords.

They were ashamed to be Negroes, but not ashamed to beg to be something else. Something inferior. Not quite genuine. Too bad!"[47]

The embrace of the rural black cultural root—the choice taken by Helga at the end of *Quicksand*—provides no adequate resolution, for it represents an extinction of identity, a choice for the "unknown world" and "nameless people" from which she initially recoiled and which ultimately brooks no satisfaction. Larsen evokes the impulse to transcend group identities based on race and therefore racial consciousness, denying the necessity of choosing one racial identity over another. She embraced social and cultural mongrelization.

Contributors to *The New Negro* asserted the unique spiritual or soulful gift that blacks gave the nation and the essentially American identity of American Negroes. Locke wrote of the "spiritual endowment" of the Negro as his "race-gift." The art collector Albert C. Barnes called him a "poet by birth." E. Franklin Frazier averred that blacks have an "artistic nature"; the white sociologist Melville Herskovits that blacks have an "emotional quality." Even Du Bois in *The Gift of Black Folk: The Negro in the Making of America* (1924) held blacks to be especially artistic, sensuous, joyful, spiritual, meek, and humble. Walter White disparaged segregation because it deprived both races of what the other could give. For whites, "there is the loss of that deep spirituality, that gift of song and art, that indefinable thing which perhaps can best be termed the over-soul of the Negro, which has given America the only genuinely artistic things which the world recognizes as distinctive American contributions to the arts." Other contributors to the volume similarly stressed this connection: Locke asserted that Negro spirituals were America's folk song. The journalist James A. Rogers declared jazz (in part "American" and in part "American Negro") as the "foremost exponent of modern Americanism." Or as the poet Langston Hughes wrote in "America": "I am America."[48]

After 1926, the Harlem Renaissance shifted somewhat in sensibility, as younger artists like Larsen challenged the middle-class leadership's liberal and integrationist race project. Evidence of self-division—within individual blacks and within the larger black community—multiplied. Larsen hearkened to a nonracialized, fluid, mulatto American culture, one already being realized in the immensely popular blues and jazz. Younger writers Langston Hughes, Zora Neale Hurston, Bruce Nugent, and Wallace Thurman valorized blues and jazz and hailed work that dealt frankly and openly with all aspects of black America, including Harlem's loose and erotic nightlife and its seamy underworld—subjects that reinforced white stereotypes of blacks as lusty and instinctual modern primitives.

A rooftop photo of young men of the Harlem Renaissance at a party thrown by Regina Andrews and Ethel Ray Nance to honor Langston Hughes, 580 St. Nicholas Avenue, Harlem, 1924. From left: Hughes, Charles S. Johnson, E. Franklin Frazier, Rudolph Fisher, and Hubert Delaney.
Courtesy Schomburg Center for Research in Black Culture, New York Public Library.

Carl Van Vechten's *Nigger Heaven* (1926) precipitated this debate, which also took place at a time in which whites were increasingly frequenting Harlem cabarets and clubs looking for "a tonic and a release" in hot jazz and sexualized entertainment. Harlem, Nathan Huggins observed, "was merely a taxi trip to the exotic for most white New Yorkers." In her analysis of "mongrel Manhattan" in the 1920s, Ann Douglas recounted the experience of George Tichenor, a white tourist to Harlem late in the heyday of black nightclubs. He felt he was taking off biases like layers of arctic overcoats, shouting and laughing "in the consciousness of an emotional holiday," only to button up again at the end of the evening and return to white respectability.[49] The immense Savoy Ballroom, capable of mounting shows for four thousand people at once, opened in March 1926, and commercialized black big-band jazz came to dominate popular tastes. An African American–inflected mass culture loomed as much more influential than the tender experiments in high culture launched by Harlem's black elite. Du Bois turned away from art and from the Renaissance, occupying his energies more in political topics and causes.

The center of gravity shifted from Sugar Hill to "267 House," the rent-free apartment of Wallace Thurman on 136th Street from which he, Hughes, Hurston, and other young artists launched a rebellion against the staid Victorian tastes of the dominant literary powers of Harlem. They produced a one-issue journal to espouse their views, calling it *Fire!!* and packing it with incendiary material. Thurman served as editor. Van Vechten's *Nigger Heaven* became notorious, a propagandistic novel of the color line but one which also frankly depicted a quite nonidealized and colorful Harlem underworld of criminality, sexual license, and vice. Thurman self-consciously embraced Van Vechten's novel, which in truth many Harlemites found distasteful, and generally endorsed the images of gyrating, sexualized, and instinctual blacks that trafficked in white tastes for primitivism. Behind *Fire!!* were at least two vital imperatives: The first was to present black cultural identity in terms of the values of everyday blacks, at work and at play, not elites. The second was to use an honest depiction of black life to emancipate the race from the false pretenses, condescending stereotypes (even when well-intentioned), and stultifying self-consciousness that thwarted black cultural achievement. Determined to stand up for "artistic and sexual freedom, a love of the black masses, a refusal to idealize black life, and a revolt against bourgeois hypocrisy," in Arnold Rampersad's words, a cadre of young Harlem writers were inspired to action by the abuse showered on Van Vechten, an impulse given voice by Langston Hughes in an essay entitled "The Negro Artist and the Racial Mountain," which appeared in the *Nation* in June 1926.[50]

Born in Joplin, Missouri, in 1902, Hughes grew up in the Midwest, spending his boyhood with his maternal grandparents in Lawrence, Kansas, and attending a mostly white high school in Cleveland, Ohio. Like so many Harlem Renaissance figures, he had both white and black ancestors. On his mother's side, he had a great-grandfather who was a white Virginia planter. His granduncle was John Mercer Langston, a distinguished African American congressman and diplomat who also served as the president of Howard University.

His maternal grandmother's first husband fought and died with John Brown at Harper's Ferry. (When former president Theodore Roosevelt delivered his "New Nationalism" speech at the dedication of the John Brown Memorial Battlefield in Osawatomie, Kansas, his grandmother and her grandson, Langston, were guests of honor on stage.)[51]

His parents' marriage had been brief: Hughes was united with his lively and vivacious mother only occasionally. His stern, ambitious father moved to Mexico, and Hughes paid some rather unsatisfactory visits to him as a teenager, in part to win his support to attend Columbia University upon graduation from high school. Early on Hughes determined to become a poet; he wrote "The Negro Speaks of Rivers" at age eighteen while traveling to see his father in the summer of 1920. Jessie Fauset, the literary editor of the *Crisis*, early spotted his talent, and he quickly gained influential friends in Harlem (he did briefly enroll at Columbia). Nevertheless, Hughes spent much of the decade working odd, often menial jobs to support himself. Only in 1926 did he return to college—this time to the prestigious if underfunded black college Lincoln University in rural Pennsylvania (where he became a classmate of the future NAACP lawyer and Supreme Court justice Thurgood Marshall). He graduated in 1929, already a noted and feted poet. Prior to this, Hughes worked as a steward on a rusty freighter at anchor up the Harlem River. In the summer of 1923, he shipped out on a merchant vessel bound for the coast of Africa (in his own account, dramatically throwing his accumulated books overboard—with the sole exception of his copy of Whitman). Unusual among Harlem intellectuals, Hughes had firsthand knowledge of Africa, initially feeling distant from Africans who seemed as exotic to him as they would to any white American but eventually becoming incensed at their exploitation. Africans did not accept Hughes as black, and perhaps the most important knowledge he gained was an awareness of the disjuncture between American blacks and Africans. On a later voyage, Hughes would travel to Europe, jump ship, and see Paris and London.

In the midst of final exams at Lincoln in early June 1926, the editor of the *Nation* forwarded Hughes proofs of an article by the iconoclastic black journalist George S. Schuyler entitled the "Negro-Art Hokum," asking for a reply. Within a week, Hughes forwarded his reply, "The Negro Artist and the Racial Mountain." Schuyler denied that there was such a thing as "Negro art" because he repudiated the idea of a black group identity based on race. There is no particular black soul or racial essence, he argued. The "Aframerican is merely a lampblacked Anglo-Saxon." What makes a person is environment, not race, and black artists reflect their nation, not their race. When the black man "responds to the same political, social, moral, and economic stimuli in precisely the same manner as his white neighbor, it is nonsense to talk about 'racial difference' as between the American black man and the American white man."[52]

Hughes's reply in some ways talked past Schuyler. Where Schuyler emphasized the error in assuming a unitary black consciousness and thus denied that something defined as *Negro* art can exist, Hughes attacked blacks who renounced the identity of Negro artist out of a covert shame at their race, which was not implicit in Schuyler's essay. While Hughes asserted a common folk consciousness for African Americans, he was more concerned to defend the autonomy of the artist and, even more, to repudiate black efforts to deny or disguise their true selves. He cited an unnamed young black poet (probably Countee Cullen) who declared, "I want to be a poet—not a Negro poet." This was, Hughes declared, a statement of the desire to be white, and this impulse to whiteness he decried as the "mountain standing in the way of any true Negro art in America."[53]

Unlike Larsen's impulse to transcend racial differences, Hughes simply repudiated an idolatry of whiteness, which he interpreted as the product of blacks' drive for material success, upward mobility, and standardization to the American type. Black artists should instead embrace the "low-down folks, the so-called common element" who comprise the majority of blacks and whom he characterized, romantically, as the "people who have their hip of gin on Saturday nights and are not too important to themselves or the community, or too well fed, or too learned to watch the lazy world go round." Hughes affirmed an essential folkish racial identity for blacks, linking it to the African American lower classes, and judged the success of the artist by his or her depiction of these folk. The great Negro artist will be the one courageous enough to depict blacks honestly, "the one who is not afraid to be himself."[54]

Hughes chided the black audience as well: blacks oppose their own, remaining indifferent to black art and betraying the same longing to mimic white tastes and to gain respectability in white eyes as the upwardly mobile, conformist black middle class. The black masses also opposed lower-class examples of black culture. Here, Hughes saw their defensiveness as symptomatic of an inferiority complex. Jazz culture was the great exception and an incipient modernist criticism: "jazz to me is one of the inherent expressions of Negro life in America: the eternal tom-tom beating in the Negro soul—the tom-tom of revolt against weariness in a white world, a world of subway trains, and work, work, work; the tom-tom of joy and laughter, and pain swallowed in a smile." In affirming the value of the plebeian culture of gin joints and jazz music, the black artist fostered racial pride. Hughes conflated whiteness with the soul-deadening work routines of American business. Blues culture represents spontaneity and life. He closed his essay with a ringing call for black cultural pride and integrity advanced by the autonomous and heroic artist-prophet:

> We younger Negro artists who create now intend to express our individual dark-skinned selves without fear or shame. If white people are pleased we are glad. If they are not, it doesn't matter. We know we are beautiful. And ugly too. The tom-tom cries and the tom-tom laughs. If colored people are pleased we are glad. If they are not, their displeasure doesn't matter either. We build our temples for tomorrow, strong as we know how, and we stand on top of the mountain, free within ourselves.[55]

Hughes urged an end to the time-honored black tradition of dissembling and trickery in the face of a more powerful white ruling class. Since slavery times, blacks had donned a mask in order to hide their true ambitions from the white master class. This was a "protective social mimicry forced upon him by the adverse circumstances of dependence," according to Locke. It was, arguably, as costly to blacks as it was helpful, confounding black identity and thwarting black self-understanding. Throwing off this mask, the expression of "our individual dark-skinned selves without fear or shame," represented a coming out, a final emancipatory act from the legacy of slavery. It was in this vein that Locke envisioned the New Negro consciousness working to heal the damaged race psychology of blacks. "The Negro to-day wishes to be known for what he is, even in his faults and shortcomings, and scorns a craven and precarious survival at the price of seeming to be what he is not."[56]

From his earliest poetry, Hughes adopted the Whitmanesque role of tribune of his people, writing in the first person in "The Negro Speaks of Rivers," his early assertion of a Negro soulfulness rooted in ancient racial knowledge. As the decade progressed, Hughes's interest in the blues tradition deepened as he attempted to incorporate the blues idiom into his own work as the redeeming heart of authentic black culture. When queried about jazz by Van Vechten, who was writing a piece for *Vanity Fair* designed to introduce jazz to a northern white audience, Hughes commented on the "animal sadness running through all Negro jazz," observing that the blues were especially sad "because their sadness is not softened with tears but hardened with laughter, the absurd, incongruous laughter of a sadness without even a god to appeal to." (When Hughes defended Van Vechten's *Nigger Heaven*, Van Vechten wrote him appreciatively, "You and I are the only coloured people who really love *niggers*.") In Hughes's depiction, the blues represented a sort of repository of racial experience for black Americans. "In the Gulf Coast Blues one can feel the cold northern snows, the memory of the melancholy mists of the Louisiana low-lands, the shack that is home, the worthless lovers with hands full of gimme, mouths full of much oblige, the eternal unsatisfied longings," he wrote Van Vechten.[57] Hughes evoked the culture-making role of folk stories in his early poem, "Aunt Sue's Stories," which depicts a child listening to an elder's stories gotten not from books but "Right out of her own life."[58]

Hughes reveled in the sensual depiction of low-down black characters, finding beauty in overt and blatant, even rough, sexuality. The dancing girl in "Jazzonia" has bold eyes and "Lifts high a dress of silken gold," yet her work in a Harlem cabaret does not disqualify comparison of her eyes to those of Eve or Cleopatra (34). Love, in "Beale Street Love," is accompanied by physical abuse, yet "Hit me again," declares the woman (80). Hughes consistently identifies with his race and relentlessly empathizes, internalizing the mind-set of the blues, which was both the subject of his work and eventually the form. Of Ruby Brown, a young and beautiful woman who chooses prostitution over domestic service, Hughes makes no judgment. He knows the questions she asked and for which the carnality and income of work as a prostitute provided the answer: What pleasures could be had on the wages of a black servant? "And ain't there any joy in this town?" (73).

On the one hand, he delineates the blues for the reader, often by mimicking them in verse. ("Midwinter Blues" and "Gypsy Man" are composed in AAB blues stanzaic form.) In the blues world, life is unpredictable and harsh, governed by fate (represented by images of fortune telling, luck, and gypsies by Hughes; in "Harlem Night Club," the speaker urges the band to play and the patrons to dance, "Tomorrow . . . who knows?" [90]); sex and pleasure provide short-term release and necessary joy in life (and the sexuality in the blues is no less beautiful or satisfying for its illicit or tawdry context); performing the blues becomes a shield against the outside world and provides healing, serving as a restorative (in "Hey!" the narrator feels the blues approaching as the sun sets; in the companion poem "Hey! Hey!," as the sun rises next morning, the narrator rejects the blues, for "I been blue all night long" [112]).

In "The Weary Blues," which incorporated a lyric fragment Hughes remembered hearing in Kansas City as a child, the narrator is an observer, listening to a bluesman sing the "Weary Blues." The bluesman remains cryptic, an object of fascination. While the blues he sings seemingly bares his soul, attesting to his spiritual desolation, he is self-evidently enjoying himself, even pleased at his music. The narrator notes that the bluesman goes home, sleeping like a "man that's dead," safe and secure (50). Here, the blues looms as a form of defense, a means by which one both performs his troubles but also fends off the world, thereby somehow gaining strength to persist and endure. The characters Hughes depicted move, but not in a trajectory steadily upward. Rather, like the "Elevator Boy," they move only up and down ("Guess I'll quit now" [85]). The rational choice in a world governed by fate and yielding little to even the ambitious African American becomes today's momentary dance of pleasure, to "fling my arms wide" as in "Dream Variations" (40). Or, as urged in "Song," "Open wide your arms to life" (45) and dance. Put in a blues argot, this meant relishing popular dances like the Charleston or the Eagle Rock.

All of this was too much for Du Bois.

Well into his late middle age in the 1920s, Du Bois had been a leader of his race since the late nineteenth century. Himself of mixed-race heritage, he had grown up poor but respectable in predominantly white Great Barrington, Massachusetts. As a student at Fisk University in Nashville, he established a connection with the rural mass of black America, particularly in summers teaching in the Tennessee countryside to earn money for his education. He went on to study at Harvard University and in Germany, establishing a brilliant record as a historian, political economist, and sociologist of black America, producing groundbreaking scholarship and establishing himself as a well-known intellectual among all African Americans with such works of analysis, criticism, and advocacy as *The Souls of Black Folk* (1903). From 1910, he edited the *Crisis* for the NAACP, an institution he helped found. Initially attracted to the self-help philosophy of Booker T. Washington, Du Bois had broken with Washington's accommodationism and asserted the need for racial agitation, gradually moving toward a socialist political economy. Du Bois had long thought in racial terms, feeling that blacks were a distinct race with particular gifts, but had insisted on maintaining a complex balance between Negro race pride and assimilation into Western culture. Blacks were legatees of both, and Du Bois wanted to preserve both souls. Even as he persistently fought for greater opportunities and an end to discrimination in America, he expended much energy in the 1920s on organizing international Pan-African conferences, which pushed for indigenous self-government in Africa, and reveled in his first visit to Africa—the conquering scholar-activist—in December 1923. At the same time, Du Bois remained elitist to the core, believing it necessary that the best of his race pave the way for mass success.[59]

He was appalled at Van Vechten's *Nigger Heaven* and the appearance of *Fire!!*, which could only be interpreted as backward steps in the long project of proving African American sophistication and equality with whites. Du Bois launched a symposium in *Crisis* on "The Negro in Art: How Shall He Be Portrayed" in 1926. He distributed a survey, the questions betraying his anxieties. One query: "What are Negroes to do when they are continually painted at their worst and judged by the public as they are painted?" Another: "Is not the continual portrayal of the sordid, foolish and criminal among Negroes convincing the world that this and this alone is really and essentially Negroid, preventing white artists from knowing any other types and preventing black artists from daring to paint them?" Many contributors hailed the role of the black artist in fostering the development of his race but also proclaimed the principles of artistic integrity and autonomy over and against race propaganda and asserted that good art will inevitably be recognized. "What's the use of saying anything—the true literary artist is going to write about what he chooses anyway regardless of outside opinions," Hughes coolly replied.[60]

Du Bois would have none of it. Black artists routinely face discrimination, he observed in "The Criteria of Art" in *Crisis* in October 1926, and had more difficulty receiving training and support. Moreover, white editors were not disinterested judges of aesthetic value. They purchased what sold, which was work about blacks that appealed to white prejudices. The purpose of art was not crudely propagandistic; Du Bois did not argue that art must inculcate morals or advance a social agenda, however, he did link the function of art to aesthetic value and identified its purpose as creating, preserving, and realizing beauty, enhancing "universal understanding" and "gaining sympathy and human interest." The artist's tools for accomplishing these aims are truth, which spurs imagination and builds understanding, and goodness, or justice, honor, and right, which build sympathy. The "apostle of beauty" is thus necessarily the "apostle of truth and right." "Thus all art is propaganda and ever must be, despite the wailing of the purists," Du Bois wrote. "I stand in utter shamelessness and say that whatever art I have for writing has been used always for propaganda for gaining the right of black folk to love and enjoy. I do not care a damn for any art that is not used for propaganda. But I do care when propaganda is confined to one side while the other is stripped and silent." All art shapes perceptions of a subject; it is efficacious, it has real effects. White editors refused to publish depictions of the white "underworld," he observed, but demanded distorted pictures of black life and refused to present alternative views.[61] The moral for him was obvious: a truthful picture of the black people demanded the recognition of upper-class social and cultural life.

~

For a long time, African American intellectuals and scholars were quite critical of the Harlem Renaissance: it failed to alter significantly the oppressive social conditions experienced by black Americans. Harlem did not thrive in the 1930s, but rather became an immiserated ghetto as the century progressed. In retrospect, the glamour of Harlem nightlife and jazz nightclubs faded in light of the ease with which white artists and producers coopted black music and culture. Too many blacks catered to white hedonist fantasies or fronted exploitative white club owners, who extracted profits from Harlem and gave nothing in return. Historians noted that famous attractions like the Cotton Club sometimes barred entry to blacks; the Plantation Club, with log-cabin decor, black mammies, and even an actress dressed as Aunt Jemima was comically racist; the ability of Josephine Baker to transfix Paris performing American numbers in nothing but a skirt adorned with bananas took stereotypes of black primitivism to absurd heights.

African Americans too often played into white stereotypes and appetites either for minstrel-style humor or jungle exoticism. The sad case of Bert Williams, one of the most sophisticated and refined comic sensibilities of his generation, consigned to performing Negro caricatures in blackface, became the paradigm. Even well-intentioned white patrons, such as the generous but controlling Charlotte Osgood Mason, who supported Zora Neale Hurston and Langston Hughes, compromised African American art by channeling it into representations of folk primitivism. "Whites have needed blacks as they have needed the blackface minstrel mask—a guise of alter ego," Nathan Huggins argued in *The Harlem Renaissance* (1971). "And blacks—sensing this psychic dependency—have been all too willing to join in the charade, hiding behind that minstrel mask, appearing to be what white men wanted them to be, and finding pleasure in the deception which often was a trick on themselves."[62] Instead of creating an art rooted in a complex development of the black folk cultural tradition, Renaissance artists too often ignored folk art in order to master Western forms, never moved beyond illustrating black problems to an ignorant white audience, or remained hidden behind the primitivist mask so comforting to white America.

Critics have reversed this assessment, incorporating the fertile and cre-ative black contributions to the popular arts into the Renaissance and find-ing subversion and satire where previous scholars have only seen minstrelsy. In his positive assessment of the Renaissance, Houston Baker declared Afri-can American modernism to be "first and foremost, the mastery of the min-strel mask by blacks."[63] Moreover, scholars have refused the project of black essentialism, much as did Harlem artists such as Nella Larsen. If blacks were masking, so were Jewish comics like Eddie Cantor and many others like him. Whites contaminated the black Renaissance no more than blacks infected white culture. America possessed a mongrelized culture built on hybrid cul-tural forms, Ann Douglas has argued, and the self-defined "Aframerican" art-ists and intellectuals realized this, declaring their postcolonial emancipation from white American domination through an assertion of their rightful place in the creation of American culture. Blacks and whites were contributing to each other's journals, engaging each other's ideas, and jointly formulating the cultural discourse on race in the 1920s. Surveying journalistic accounts of the New Negro, Rollin Lynde Hartt observed that "the Negro thinks as in identical circumstances a Caucasian would think" and would now act as Caucasians act. "For once—to that extent—black is white."[64]

White and black Americans eagerly crossed racial boundaries in pursuit of freedom, if only for an evening or in moments of imagination. Mixed-race individuals relished a new and distinctive racial identity that granted them autonomy and fulfillment, but all Americans could enjoy a racially mixed culture. Jazz artists, poets, and intellectuals as well as the street-level New Negroes pursued self-determination and pride regardless of group ascription, an impulse in line with the main thrust of American cultural development in the 1920s—the impulse to openness, tolerance, and autonomy—if at odds with cultural nationalists, spiritual excavators, and social theorists who feared fragmentation and dilution. To Robert Park, such conditions of cultural contact bred new civilizations and races; in studying Hawaii's cultural mélange, Park thought he glimpsed the disappearance of races and the origin of a new civilization. The migrant, he believed, was the type of the emancipated man—a cosmopolitan, an unsettled stranger able to look with enlightened detachment on the world in which he finds himself. Like the Jew in medieval Europe, he was a "cultural hybrid," living between the old and new, "a man on the margin of two cultures and two societies, which never completely interpenetrated and fused. . . . the marginal man, the first cosmopolite and citizen of the world."[65]

CHAPTER FIVE

~

The Eclipsed Public

At the peak of his popularity and influence, H. L. Mencken published *Notes on Democracy* (1926), a relentless and characteristically hyperbolic attack on the "theology" of democracy and an anathema on the majority of his fellow citizens for their weak will and instinctive conformity. In Mencken's view, prejudice, cowardice, resentment of his or her betters, and a predilection for emotional frenzies characterized the average American. Democratic government, "government by orgy, almost by orgasm," produced mediocrity, rule not by the talented and hardworking but by the losers, the incompetent and lazy masses who were unable to shimmy up the "greased poles" to claim the prized flag. The majority give up on the race after little struggle. "The effort is too much for them; it doesn't seem worth its agonies. Golf is easier; so is joining Rotary; so is Fundamentalism; so is osteopathy; so is Americanism." American politicians were cut from the same cloth and only provided what the voters wanted in any case. Though proclaiming civic-mindedness and unselfishness, the typical politician was, in fact, a "sturdy rogue," Mencken declared, "whose principal, and often sole aim in life is to butter his parsnips." Mencken ridiculed the servility of the American politician, whom he likened to a chorus girl sleeping with the producer to get a part, denouncing his boot-licking willingness "to embrace any issue, however idiotic, that will get him votes" and "sacrifice any principle, however sound, that will lose them for him."[1]

In Mencken's paradoxical analysis, Americans were both responsible for the state of American social and cultural life because they chose demagogic representatives and, at the same time, were manipulated by them. The masses reject liberty in favor of security, declared Mencken. The inferior man is a "natural slave," happy only when unfree, longing for the "warm, reassuring smell of the herd." The belief that men are capable of self-rule is an illusion, which no modern student of politics could fail to see absent a self-indulgent assertion of faith. The average American was lazy, jealous, and vindictive and had, by and large, the government he wanted and deserved. If American politics was corrupt and machine-ridden, it was so because Americans chose this type of government. In Mencken's shallow political theory, devoid of any analysis of power or interests, what the government did reflected exactly what Americans wanted; it presumably could be easily changed, if Americans were so inclined. Commenting on African American disfranchisement, Mencken callously observed that those unwilling to fight for the ballot do not deserve it: "If the blacks of the backwaters of the South keep away from the polls to-day it is only because they do not esteem the ballot highly enough to risk the dangers that go with trying to use it."[2]

Mencken's antidemocratic diatribe reflected a broader retreat not only from democracy but also from a Progressive Era belief in moral uplift as the basis of social reform, a corollary to intellectuals' general repudiation of the role of moral guardianship. The progressive reformers and intellectuals had never controlled an effective political party, despite the 1912 Bull Moose insurgent campaign. They had not constituted a social movement rightly considered, although many of the social policies they advocated had been implemented and the kind of professionalized, disinterested, expert advocacy they pioneered became a permanent feature of national life.

Moral disgust—at political corruption, irresponsible corporations, social degradation—had powered middle-class reform. Progressives imagined they spoke for a broad and inclusive "public." A favorite formulation was the "people's business," the work of balancing public against private good.[3] The progressives deprecated any narrow or specific loyalty that led to selfish or destructive public behavior and to the usurpation of public power, therefore condemning special interests that peddled influence invisibly, out of the public eye, as well as the corrupt mechanizations of shadowy bosses and machine politicians who thwarted good-government reforms. They had wanted to increase the power of the executive over and against corrupted legislatures, shift power to nonpartisan city managers or disinterested expert commissions, and bypass corrupted officeholders with direct democracy measures such as the initiative and referendum, all in the name of redeeming the public interest. Some of this passion lingered into the 1920s. The old progressive William Allen White identified "politics" as the "citizen's business" in 1924, this time training his criticism on what he saw as a new form of "invisible government," the new "extra-legal agencies," his term for lobbies, unions, trade groups, and advocacy organizations, which multiplied the votes of the few against the many. "The fiction of one vote for one person still is maintained politely in high-school classes in civil government; but men and women who touch practical politics, if only obliquely, know that men and women now may have as many votes in government as they have interests for which they are willing to sacrifice time and thought and money," White declared.[4]

At the heart of progressive activism lay a respect for the public and the good fortune that would result from mobilizing it. Direct democracy, Woodrow Wilson had declared in his 1912 presidential campaign, was the latch-key that would allow citizens to regain access to the house of government. Progressives put their faith in informing and enlightening the public, stirring their emotions, and convincing them to return to the house of government. They had assumed that a good faith, or sincerely benevolent social concern, rooted in a genuine empathy between the classes could animate a politics of reform and uplift. Such a fundamental commitment to bridging (although not erasing) divisions of social class and fostering public-spiritedness and a broader social loyalty (an ethic of association and reciprocity) comprised the activist moral core of the progressivism of figures such as Jane Addams and Walter Rauschenbusch.[5]

Yet, much of this faith in the public faded in the disillusioning decade that followed the Great War. What was left was a landscape dominated by the traditional political parties and the less established institutions of elite expertise: voluntary organizations, lobbying groups, government commissions, business and academic research institutes, and public-spirited philanthropies. In 1925 the veteran reformer Frederic C. Howe published an idealistic memoir, *The Confessions of a Reformer*, prompting a round of introspection about the fate of prewar radicalism, including a *Survey* magazine symposium featuring many veteran progressive reformers reflecting on the past and present state of reform politics. "Liberalism is a state of mind and not a creed," declared former Secretary of War Newton Baker. "A liberal uses his fellow men for their benefit and not for his own. He judges political purposes by their effect on the common good and he has in his mind's eye, as the ultimate object of his concern, 'the forgotten man,' remote, obscure and inaudible in high places." "The progressive movement, the liberal movement, the radical movement, all were largely moralistic," Howe somewhat wistfully observed. The righteousness and faith in converting others was, Howe now believed, childish. The tough-minded economist Stuart Chase was less charitable: the "Uplift Movement," as he described it, "as a dedication, as a religion, is comatose if not completely ossified—strangled both by the war and its own ineptitude. It was inept because its moral judgments took the place of sound analysis." Among other sins, it "deified a muzzy and mystical conception of democracy." "There is no 'Public'; the 'People' as a political party are unorganizable," declared Roger N. Baldwin of the American Civil Liberties Union. "Only economic classes can be organized. The only power that works is class power."[6] Cynicism coexisted with stubborn idealism in the years of postwar disillusionment.

Two important new strains of thinking related to the role of the intellectual in American thought blossomed in the 1920s. Social scientists consolidated their position of strength in universities and their access to funding from research institutes by basing their authority on scientific rigor, objectivity, and disinterestedness. Although hotly disputed, many propounded a more truly quantitative, antinormative science of society, becoming service intellectuals who gathered data, suggested ways to solve administrative problems, and predicted policy consequences but did not engage in uplift or advocate policy positions. William F. Ogburn had the following words chiseled on the side of the University of Chicago Social Science Research Building, dedicated in December 1929: "When you cannot measure . . . your knowledge is . . . meagre. . . and . . . unsatisfactory." This served as a credo for the objectivist service intellectual. It was a credo that drew plenty of opposition, not only from Boasian anthropologists, pragmatists working in the instrumentalist tradition of John Dewey, and those such as Robert Lynd who believed empirical scholarship must be infused with moral values, but also from economists, sociologists, and political scientists who saw theoretical and normative commitments as inevitable and legitimate elements in the acquisition of knowledge. Ogburn's more theoretically minded opponents were scornful of his motto, particularly his Chicago faculty colleagues in economics. "And if you cannot measure, measure it anyhow," scoffed Frank Knight. Added Jacob Viner: "And if you can measure . . . your knowledge will still be meager and unsatisfactory."[7]

A second strand of thought related to the role of group membership in society and was derived from the pragmatism of Dewey and William James as well as Charles Horton Cooley's theories of the social self. Speaking the language of social adjustment and group process, a variety of academics, educators, social welfare workers, and ministers imagined new forms of small-group, democratic decision making. Particularly strong at Columbia University Teachers College and Union Theological Seminary, the loose movement took inspiration from Deweyan instrumentalism but developed in the innumerable social clubs, recreation projects, community organizations, and discussion groups that settlement houses, women's organizations, schools, and religious denominations had sponsored for many years. An offshoot of the progressive drive for new forms of authority that could blend expertise with public engagement, the "process-based authority" of small groups where choices were circumscribed, participation mandated, and leaders appointed could take on the form, in historian William Graebner's phrase, of a kind of "democratic social engineering."[8]

Both social science objectivity and theories of group process dovetailed with the nascent field of management theory and broader trends to ever-larger, bureaucratized structures of authority in government and business. They presented liberal intellectuals with the prospect of social engineering, whether democratic or elite-driven. Postprogressive, reformist intellectuals spent the decade reimagining a liberal politics shaped now by a recognition of the bifurcation between reform-minded elites and an indifferent, enervated, or simply "eclipsed" public. The new liberalism preserved the crucial ideological recalibrations of the 1910s: an ideological repudiation of laissez-faire economics and a shift toward state interventionism, nationalism, and prolabor notions of "industrial democracy." Whether it could preserve a primary commitment to democracy, to bridging social divisions in the name of national unity, remained an open question.

While historians date the end of progressivism to the Great War, the older progressive faith in expert-driven and ameliorative reform remained strong in many precincts. On issues like poverty, workplace safety, industrial wages and hours, child labor, school reform, social insurance and unemployment, public housing, and slum clearance, the Progressive Era never ended. Reform intellectuals, social workers, and activists continued to advocate government regulation and social welfare programs at the state, municipal, and federal levels. Settlement houses, such as Jane Addams's Hull House and Lillian Wald's Henry Street in New York, remained engines for reform activism and ideas throughout the 1920s; *Survey* magazine provided a forum for debate. Longtime advocacy organizations, many led by women, such as the National Consumers' League and the Women's Trade Union League, remained active along with religiously sponsored organizations and social welfare groups.[9]

There was a significant interest in pluralist political theory, brought to the United States by the English political theorist Harold Laski, and varieties of syndicalist thought, such as the Englishman G. D. H. Cole's guild socialism. Pluralists wanted to organize politics by economic interests; the effective units of politics would not be parties or social classes but intermediate groups based on economic function or occupation. Proposed systems of occupational, as opposed to locality-based, representation were, as Robert D. Johnston observed in his study of Portland, Oregon, progressivism, "one of the burning issues in political theory in the immediate postwar period." In 1920, the People's Power League in Oregon proposed that state legislators be allocated by occupation (farmers, merchants, professionals, even housewives) rather than locality—a plan that would have given more than a third of the representation to housewives. In *American Labor and American Democracy* (1926), the veteran progressive publicist William English Walling provided a statement of principles for the American Federation of Labor (AFL). He embraced pluralist, interest-based politics, which he believed would shift congressional power to a labor-led bloc. To Walling, state ownership was unnecessary. Many intellectuals aligned with labor in the 1920s imagined corporations might become like public utilities, amenable to sharing control with organized interest groups representing labor, consumers, and the public and submitting to government regulation. Walling and the AFL anticipated much of the New Deal liberal synthesis, advocating countercyclical government spending, a shift to a consumption-based economy, and tying workers' wages to gains in productivity.[10]

The success of the new Labour Party in Britain spurred efforts to form an equivalent American labor party. The Socialist Party was not a viable alternative, having lost strength among native-born Americans in the Midwest and Southeast and splintered in the wake of the Bolshevik revolution. Disgruntled progressives (organizing as the Committee of Forty-Eight), upper midwestern agrarians and labor activists who tilted left, and some labor radicals (dissenting from the AFL's hostility to independent political action) worked vigorously to form such a party in the early 1920s and were on the cusp of success in spring 1924 when the obvious insurgent presidential candidate, the veteran Wisconsin progressive Robert La Follette, repudiated a new national progressive party and launched an independent progressive bid for the presidency instead. After 1924, hopes for a national progressive party faded.[11]

The representative thinker of this interregnum between the progressive movement and the New Deal was Walter Lippmann. By the time of his thirtieth birthday in 1919, Lippmann had already established himself as a major political journalist and thinker, acquired a wealth of experiences in radical politics and bohemian cultural circles, and become a noteworthy inside advisor to the Wilson administration during Great War; by his fortieth birthday, he had established himself as a political celebrity of sorts, editing the opinion page of one of the nation's leading papers and becoming a trusted political commentator to thousands of readers.

Born the only child of a well-to-do German Jewish couple in New York City in 1889, Lippmann enjoyed the splendid benefits of a cultured and cosmopolitan upbringing if not the solicitous devotion of his parents, who tended to cast their attentions elsewhere, marking the precocious and charismatic young Lippmann as insecure and emotionally reserved.[12] Although Lippmann faced anti-Semitic prejudice, most notably at Harvard, where it prevented him from making the *Crimson* and (along with his intellectualism) barred him from the most prestigious student clubs, he systematically submerged his Jewish identity. His family was assimilationist and attended

Walter Lippmann.
Courtesy Prints and Photographs Division, Library of Congress, LC-DIG-hec-21696.

the Reform Jewish Emanu-El temple (Lippmann did not have a bar mitzvah but rather a "confirmation") and as wealthy, second-generation immigrants displayed the haughty impulse to separate themselves from the newly arriving and much less assimilated Eastern European and Russian Jewish immigrants.[13]

Entering Harvard in 1906, Lippmann displayed a talent for cultivating the patronage of distinguished elders, impressing William James so much he was invited to weekly teas, becoming a dinner companion and assistant to George Santayana, and leaving the visiting Fabian socialist Graham Wallas enthralled. He dabbled in aestheticism and became a Fabian-type socialist himself—nonrevolutionary, elitist, and gradualist. He was also fiercely intelligent, an able debater, and a leader among his group of political and intellectual friends. After college he worked in reform journalism, became a habitué of the Greenwich Village bohemian scene, served as an assistant to the socialist mayor of Schenectady, New York, and published two much-admired political works: *Preface to Politics* (1913), a "hymn to Bull Moose progressivism," in the words of his biographer Ronald Steel; and *Drift and Mastery* (1914), a plea for science, planning, practicality, and discipline as the means of managing modern social change.[14] Herbert Croly convinced Lippmann to be a founding editor of the *New Republic*, which drew him into the circles of, first, Theodore Roosevelt, whom the magazine initially promoted, and later Woodrow Wilson. Lippmann became an advocate for American intervention in the Great War, eventually working for the administration and serving as an officer in military intelligence and a member of the postwar peace commission. Lippmann viewed the Treaty of Versailles as a betrayal of Wilson's announced democratic aspirations for the war and turned against it and the administration and worked to ensure its defeat.

After 1922, Lippmann edited the editorial page of the Pulitzer family's *New York World*, one of the most influential liberal papers of the day, for which he wrote 1200 editorials over the following nine years, solidifying his influence and importance as a public intellectual and shaper of opinion. It was from this vantage that he published his immensely influential studies of propaganda, public opinion, and democracy in the 1920s, most notably *Public Opinion* in 1922. Although these studies were often read as essential statements of progressive disillusionment with naive conceptions of democracy (which they were), Lippmann himself never wavered from an essential progressivism. He remained committed to democracy as rule by consent and was himself an inveterate and lifelong educator of public opinion.[15] Lippmann was intent, at least early in the 1920s, on reassessing the progressive legacy and renovating it. He outlined a path toward a refurbished, if elite-driven, politics based on the systematic application of intelligence to public problems.

In *Liberty and the News* (1920), a slim volume, much of which had appeared in the *Atlantic* magazine, he introduced the two problems of modern democracy that would draw his attention in these years: the peculiar nature of consent in a mass democracy and the problem of providing accurate knowledge to those responsible for decision making. His starting point, in the wake of his own propaganda work during the war and his experience as a journalist, was, as he wrote Ellery Sedgwick, editor of the *Atlantic*, in spring 1920, the "discovery that opinion can be manufactured." *Liberty and the News* was an example of early media criticism, expressing alarm at the power concentrated in what Lippmann considered a somewhat weak-willed press, too prone to subordinate the truth in the service of government propaganda. Men increasingly understand, he argued, that the complex questions of modern life are incomprehensible without a steady, quick, and reliable source of facts. "Increasingly they are baffled because the facts are not available; and they are wondering whether government by consent can survive in a time when the manufacture of consent is an unregulated private enterprise."[16]

To Lippmann, democracy, premised on the essential need for the consent of the public, simply was unworkable with a pliant press; for him, the preferred solution was to make information gathering and analysis somehow a public concern. In *Liberty and the News*, Lippmann evinced a faith, which he would shortly abandon, in the average citizen's ability to comprehend the complexities of the world if properly informed. All the same, he recognized that citizens lived in a "pseudoenvironment" of news reports, gossip, and secondhand chatter. Unless provided facts, men could not escape this pseudoenvironment and see through propaganda.[17]

In *Public Opinion* (1922), Lippmann provided a more vivid rendering of the individual citizen's reliance on images, or what he termed "stereotypes," to know the world and the role of censorship and propaganda in moving the public's attitudes. He seemed intent on shifting the way Americans thought about democracy as much as on prescribing progressive solutions to the challenges modern democracy posed. In *Liberty and the News*, Lippmann had stressed the newspaper, the "bible of democracy," as the source of the news: "The sights and sounds and meanings of nearly all that we deal with as 'politics' we learn, not by our own experience, but through the words of others," he observed. He evidently became an avid moviegoer, for in *Public Opinion* he dwelt on the power of pictures. We know the world only through pictures in our heads, he opined, and the visual dominated the modern imagination:

> Photographs have the kind of authority over imagination to-day which the printed word had yesterday, and the spoken world before that. They seem utterly real. They come, we imagine, directly to us without human meddling, and they are the most effortless food for the mind conceivable. Any description in words, or even any inert picture, requires an effort of memory before a picture exists in the mind. But on the screen the whole process of observing, describing, reporting, and then imagining, has been accomplished for you.

Lippmann drew on James and Dewey, among others, to explain how perception is necessarily shaped by preconceptions, or stereotypes. "For the most part we do not first see, and then define, we define first and then see," he wrote. "In the great blooming, buzzing confusion of the outer world we pick out what our culture has already defined for us, and we tend to perceive that which we have picked out in the form stereotyped for us by our culture." He explained the mind's creative role in creating the world by its choice of the stimuli to which it attends. ("A report is the joint product of the knower and known, in which the role of the observer is always selective and usually creative. The facts we see depend on where we are placed, and the habits of our eyes.")[18]

All the same, his conceptualization of stereotypes was remarkably loose, as he conflated a variety of different features of opinion formation—not only the notion of cognitive pathways that delimit our perception but also cultural attitudes, such as those associated with ethnic and national identity (for example, prejudices), as well as images from films, intellectual theories (such as the principles of classical economists), and broad intellectual constructs (the idea of progress or a moral code).[19] While Lippmann made it easy to see how the masses are susceptible to propaganda, in part as a function of cognitive limitations, it is clear as well that much of what Lippmann considered stereotyped cognition could be better thought of as acquired biases and ideological preconceptions or just plain ignorance, all of which could be dispelled with education, investigation, or simply healthy debate.

For the elites in his audience, Lippmann intended the book as a manual for modern citizenship and potential leadership. He believed the trained observer could use stereotypes in an educated and useful way, discarding them when counterproductive. He analyzed how to detect stereotypes, linking the varied potential viewpoints on an issue to the varying selves we bring to the table: how one viewed the issue of Japanese immigrants' rights in California depended on whether one interpreted their interests economically or socially (did they want to establish orchards or intermarry with the Anglo American population?). Lippmann posed as the Machiavelli to the modern prince, advising leaders on both the necessity of molding opinion and the means to do it. Leaders need to cultivate symbols to organize and build solidarity among their followers. Such symbol-making is essential to the ancient art of creating consent. Wise leaders, he instructed, seek consent by linking their policies to public emotions through symbols. This art, Lippmann argued, "has not died out. It has, in fact, improved enormously in technic, because it is now based on analysis rather than on rule of thumb. And so, as a result of psychological research, coupled with the modern means of communication, the practice of democracy has turned a corner. A revolution is taking place, infinitely more significant than any shifting of economic power."[20]

While Lippmann could adopt the pose of a tutor to the new leader, he also wanted to change how Americans thought about democracy. He decried the myth of the omnicompetent citizen—the notion that the typical citizen possessed the necessary knowledge and skills relating to the myriad issues that formed the national agenda to legislate and execute policy. The founding generation manipulated the "doctrine of sovereignty" to bolster their system. In fact, the constitutional system works against democratic self-government and popular rule, yet the illusions of rule by the people as a validating device only grew. Such illusions could no longer be afforded. "It is no longer possible, for example, to believe in the original dogma of democracy; that the knowledge needed for the management of human affairs comes up spontaneously from the human heart," Lippmann believed.[21]

Once they had abandoned this illusion, the public would be able to accept new institutions and forms of social organization to ensure effective governance and a new "machinery of knowledge." Lippmann proposed the creation of a new cadre of expert intelligence workers, many of whom were already working in research bureaus, legislative reference libraries, specialized lobbies funded by corporations and unions, advocacy groups, watchdog publications, and foundations. He proposed new intelligence divisions in each of the ten cabinet departments, guaranteed adequate funding, independence, and full access to relevant materials. The new intelligence worker was "there to represent the unseen," he declared. "He represents people who are not voters, functions of voters that are not evident, events that are out of sight, mute people, unborn people, relations between things and people. . . . By making the invisible visible, he confronts the people who exercise material force with a new environment, sets ideas and feelings at work in them, throws them out of position, and so, in the profoundest way, affects the decision."[22]

If his vision diminished the public's sense of popular sovereignty and limited their role to a kind of plebiscitary approval of their leaders' policies, Lippmann felt his new system democratic all the same. There is a give and take between leaders and the rank and file, measured by morale, a necessary limit on the leader's actions. The public-relations pioneer Edward L. Bernays provided an even more benign analysis of the new field of opinion management. Bernays was the son of Anna Freud, Sigmund's sister and fellow psychoanalyst. Although born in Vienna, he grew up in America from infancy, working as a journalist, as a publicist in the New York theater world, and for George Creel's Committee on Public Information during the war. To Bernays, advertising comprised a form of democratic debate. He became an astute student of public opinion and propaganda. "The advocacy of what we believe in is education," he wrote in *Crystallizing Public Opinion* (1923). "The advocacy of what we don't believe in is propaganda." However, Bernays believed the management of opinion to be fundamentally democratic because it was available now to anyone interested to learn its techniques. "Today the privilege of attempting to sway public opinion is everyone's," he declared. "It is one of the manifestations of democracy that anyone may try to convince others and to assume leadership on behalf of his own thesis." Acknowledging the danger of authoritarians' misuse of the power of propaganda, Bernays held education to be the antidote: "a public that learns more and more how to express itself will learn more and more how to overthrow tyranny of every sort."[23]

In *The Phantom Public* (1925), Lippmann embellished his analysis of the "mystical fallacy of democracy" with a more stark assertion of the essential absence of a reasoning and decisive public. It was, he declared, simply a "phantom." Much of the book iterated previous points, if more forcefully dismissing the "false ideal" of citizenship. "The individual man does not have opinions on all public affairs," Lippmann observed. "He does not know how to direct public affairs. He does not know what is happening, why it is happening, what ought to happen." "We must abandon the notion that the people govern," he stated flatly. He seemed to have given up the hope that intelligence workers would make the invisible government visible to the people, now simply reporting that public affairs was mostly invisible, which made a mockery of any notion of citizen "sovereignty." The citizen "lives in a world which he cannot see, does not understand, and is unable to direct." Lippmann analyzed elections as sublimated warfare, in which the public's role of voting yes or no becomes a decision to align either for or against a particular party, the "Ins" or the "Outs." Public opinion is a reserve force, and the role of the public becomes to "compose" a crisis by aligning for or against a political leader. There is no coherent public mind, Lippmann stressed, and imagining such organic, unified entities as society, the nation, or community is an error. The liberal's "appeal to this cosmopolitan, universal, disinterested intuition in everybody was equivalent to an appeal to nobody."[24]

Critics reviewed Lippmann's work favorably; his became a major voice among a wide variety of voices loudly and strongly questioning the validity of democracy. Low voter turnout in the 1920 and 1924 presidential elections inspired the delusional belief among middle-class civic organizations that working-class, black, ethnic, foreign-born, and female voters were becoming more likely to vote than middle-class white men, resulting in massive if ultimately ineffectual (because wrongly targeted) get-out-the-vote campaigns between 1923 and 1928. Academic political scientists became increasingly interested in psychology, using it to conclude that political behavior is nonrational and conditioned, as in the behaviorism propounded by John B. Watson. Charles Merriam, a political scientist based at the University of Chicago, became a leading proponent both of an objective, nonnormative science and the turn to psychology in the study of politics. One of his students, Harold Lasswell, pioneered the application of psychoanalytic theory to political behavior, concluding, for example, that antistatist radicalism resulted from displaced aggression against the father. A prodigy at the University of Chicago as an undergraduate before entering the graduate program in political science, Lasswell grew up in various towns in Illinois, following his ministerial father's peregrinations to various Presbyterian pulpits. Lasswell made an extensive study of propaganda, teaching a course on it with Merriam and publishing *Propaganda Technique in the World War* in 1927. He absorbed the Chicago school of sociology's emphasis on the origins of behavior in social relations from George Herbert Mead and Robert Park and studied Freudian psychoanalysis in Europe. Political movements, he argued in *Psychopathology and Politics* (1930), "derive their vitality from the displacement of private affects upon public objects, and political crises are complicated by the concurrent reactivation of specific primitive motives."[25]

The Australian émigré Elton Mayo became a pioneer in the field of industrial relations at the Harvard Business School in the 1920s and 1930s, establishing the human relations group, and exemplified these trends. Mayo had failed in medical school three separate times before receiving an appointment to teach philosophy at the University of Queensland in Brisbane, Australia. He lectured in psychology as well, becoming a self-taught psychotherapist, deeply influenced by the French psychologist Pierre Janet (who had theorized personality dissociation, or the existence of contradictory personalities in hysterical patients, which Mayo attributed to social deprivation). Traveling to the United States in 1922 to earn money lecturing, he ended up low on funds and desperately scrambling for positions in America, managed to win favor with Vernon Kellogg, secretary of the National Research Council, and secured a research appointment at the University of Pennsylvania's Wharton School. Something of an academic hustler, Mayo massaged his credentials, leaving the false impression with his employers that he had been a British colonial administrator, that his Queensland appointment was in psychology and physiology, and that he was, in fact, a physician.[26]

Prior to arriving in the United States, Mayo published *Democracy and Freedom* (1919), arguing that democracy actually promoted social disintegration. Parties polarized politics, and politicians trivialized the issues. Keenly interested in group harmony and social cohesion (the job of intellectuals, he believed, was to foster collaboration), Mayo was also skeptical of collective bargaining, which he felt reinforced class divisions. (In Australia, he diagnosed a labor radical's activism to neurosis resulting from an abusive father; once treated, the agitator became a happy clerk.) In Mayo's view, political disturbances and strikes were irrational and rooted ultimately in the unconscious; acceptance of authority indicated good mental health. "The plain fact is that class obsessions are continually cultivated in the name of democratic self-government," resulting in disorder, Mayo wrote in *Harper's* magazine in July 1925. At Merriam's behest, Lasswell worked with Mayo at Harvard in 1926 and 1927. Mayo influenced his psychological approach to politics. (He also psychoanalyzed the troubled Lasswell, who in turn tried his hand at analyzing some patients, a practice he kept up throughout his career.) Mayo's and Lasswell's skepticism of popular government was becoming more widespread among academics. The Smith College sociologist Harry Elmer Barnes concluded that empirical research proved popular government to be dangerously weak and that some men are born to rule over others. Mayo recommended rule by an "administrative elite." At the University of Texas, Benjamin F. Wright argued that the era of popular government, characteristic of only a relatively short historical period, was rightly passing. The advertising executive Earnest Elmo Calkins declared in *Business the Civilizer* (1928) that the "eternal job of administering the planet must be turned over to the business man. The work that religion and government have failed in must be done by business."[27]

The most remarkable example of America's antidemocrat
was the popularity of Italy's fascist dictator, Benito Mussoli
the decade. The charismatic authoritarian came to power in 1922 and be-
guiled American observers with his media-savvy antics—wrestling a bear
cub, stripping to the waist to harvest wheat, frolicking with his children.
The popular wave of "Mussolinism" was fed by friendly press coverage,
including notably profascist treatment in the *Saturday Evening Post*, which
serialized an autobiography of the dictator partially ghostwritten by the
American ambassador to Italy, Richard Washburn Child. Studebaker
named its Model EU Standard Six sedan the "Dictator"—a "brilliant
example of excess power." In a 1927 *Literary Digest* survey of newspapers
designed to answer the question "Is there a dearth of great men?" the figure
most often cited as evidence for a negative answer was Mussolini. Lincoln Steffens admired him, as did George Santayana; the banker Thomas
Lamont of J. P. Morgan helped arrange a loan of twenty-six million dollars
in 1926. Although many liberals and journals of opinion opposed him—
including Lippmann at the *World*—the *New Republic* counseled patience,
seeing potential in the fascist corporatist experiment. Horace Kallen
defended the regime in the *New Republic*, and historian Charles Beard
expressed interest, pointing out the American Founding Fathers' own hostility to democracy. Horace Kallen saw potential in Mussolini's economic,
educational, and administrative reforms. Others saw him as a bulwark of
the bourgeois values of order, duty, obedience, and loyalty in the face of
communism, or as an improvisatory and scientifically minded pragmatist
manipulating nationalism for the purpose of progressive reform, or as the
avatar of a more spiritual, antimaterialist form of politics. Mussolini's use
of violence and repression did not faze some of his admirers. The American
Legion commander, Alvin Owsley, publicly hailed his treatment of "de-
structionists" in the opposition. "The American Legion is fighting every
element that threatens our democratic government—soviets, anarchists,
I.W.W., revolutionary socialists and every other 'red.' . . . Do not forget
that the fascisti are to Italy what the American Legion is to the United
States."[28]

One of the most interesting and thoroughgoing critiques of Lippmann
came from Mary Parker Follett, a political and social theorist whose commitments and principles emerged from her career as a social worker in Progressive Era Boston. Follett straddled the divisions between academia and public
activism and between different disciplines; she attained much success in her
lifetime and has been lionized by managerial theorists more recently. Like
other liberal intellectuals from the period, Follett was both working within

Mary Parker Follett.
Courtesy Henley Business School.

the progressive tradition (in her case, on what she considered the creative capacity of the small group) and aggressively refashioning it to suit modern necessities.

Born in Quincy, Massachusetts, in 1868, Follett spent her career in and around Boston, although she lived in England for periods as well. She was close to her father, a craftsman and, later, a clerk, who had married into a wealthy business family; her father died when she was sixteen, leaving the family's finances and property in her capable hands. Follett attended college at the Harvard Annex, later Radcliffe College, over the span of ten years, with a year spent in study at Cambridge, where she had the chance to study with the philosopher Henry Sidgwick, and several years teaching at the progressive private school established by the reform-minded philanthropist Pauline Agassiz Shaw in Boston, the English headmistress of which, Isobel Briggs, became Follett's life partner. Influenced by Sidgwick and the Harvard historian Albert Bushnell Hart, she developed an interest in politics, publishing a well-regarded book on the speaker of the House of Representatives before her graduation in 1898. Beginning in 1900, Follett entered the world of social reform, becoming a settlement worker at Children's House (another institution established by Shaw) in Roxbury, an Irish neighborhood of Boston. Follett became a leader in social development and vocational education for boys and young men, establishing the Roxbury Industrial League, which provided social, civic, and vocational education for adolescent boys, and the Highland Union, a similar organization for young men. In part, her work was sponsored by the Boston Equal Suffrage Association for Good Government, and she became a leader in the community centers movement, in particular pushing the after-hours use of schools by neighborhood groups. She also led the effort to integrate vocational counseling and placement services into Boston schools and neighborhood centers.[29]

In 1918, Follett attracted positive attention, including from Lippmann, with *The New State* (1918), an idiosyncratic analysis of trends in political theory, including pluralism, and something of a landmark in the group-process movement. Like many progressive social thinkers who reconceptualized the individual as a social self, defined by varying persona and cultural attachments and not property or economic rationality, Follett treated the integrative group process as the basis of citizenship. She developed a battery of specialized terms, defining "interpenetration" as a type of integration of the individual with the group that enhanced individuality even while attaining something beyond it. "A man is ideally free only so far as he is interpermeated by every other human being; he gains his freedom through a perfect and complete relationship because thereby he achieves his whole nature," she observed. Interpenetration created personal freedom, and the neighborhood group, for Follett, should become the basis of a new state. "The group process contains the secret of collective life, it is the key to democracy, it is the master lesson for every individual to learn, it is our chief hope for the political, the social, the international life of the future."[30]

With the assistance of Herbert Croly, Follett received financial support from Dorothy Straight, his benefactor at the *New Republic*, for a collaborative study of social conflict conducted between 1922 and 1924 with the social theorist Eduard C. Lindeman. Her work informed *Creative Experience* (1924), as did two years of service on minimum wage boards in Massachusetts, which in tandem with the jurisprudence of certain progressive jurists seemed a model to her of conflict resolution based not on compromise or the victory of one side or the other but on careful social investigation and attention to the reciprocal relations of all parties.[31] Follett's brief for "creative experience," although couched in esoteric neologisms such as "plus-values," "plusvalents" as opposed to equivalents, "power-with" as opposed to "power-over," and "co-active," centered on her work as a community activist and advocate for community centers and her deep engagement with recent work in psychology. She believed the solution to social conflict lay in recognizing the dynamic process of group interaction. Opposed to the imposition of a solution from above, even if a fair-minded balancing of interests, she was convinced that dialogue, even on a starkly polarized issue, would generate creative solutions. Evading the complexities of mass politics treated by Lippmann, she focused on the small-scale confrontations that would occur in a community and workplace and extrapolated outward and upward, in the process placing a democratic faith in the citizens' willingness to "integrate" with one another and engage with experts. Her citizens, although no less abstract than in Lippmann's treatment, were assumed to be alive and eager for creative interaction.

Much of Follett's antagonism to contemporary assumptions in social and political theory represented a hopeful faith that conflicts may always be resolved to the advantage of both parties, that the complex "interweaving" taking place when one individual interacts with another—a type of interaction that was endlessly creative, as the two sides not only reacted to each other but to the new situation that was continuously unfolding, the "activity-between"—would inevitably create a new and unanticipated revelation that would make the existing conflict irrelevant. "The object of this book is to suggest that we seek a way by which desires may interweave," she wrote, "that we seek a method by which the full integrity of the individual shall be one with the social progress, that we try to make our daily experience yield for us larger and ever larger spiritual values." She did not want capitalism to "adjust" to labor organizing, she argued, but rather "we want something better than either of these. We want the plus values of the conflict. This is still adjustment, if you will, but with a more comprehensive meaning than of old." For this reason, Follett was given to paradoxical positions, such as opposing both compromise, because it "sacrifices the integrity of the individual," and balance of power, because it merely "rearranges what already exists." Compromise, she argued, does not foster change, promote interpenetration, or achieve integration. It represented suppression: "Suppression, the *bête noire* of modern psychology, is, in the form of compromise, the evil of our present constitution of society, politically, industrially and internationally."[32]

Follett opposed the language of social adjustment, as it implied one party submitting to another, suppressing his or her desires and interests. She even avoided using "social," preferring to talk of "interweaving *individual* activity" as she conceived of individuals as endlessly interwoven embodiments of an interaction between some subject and the surrounding elements in the environment. "Behavior is a function of the interweaving between activity of organism and activity of environment, that is, response is to a relating," she argued. In this "interlocking activity," the individual and situation are each "creating itself anew," thus "relating themselves anew," thus "giving us the evolving situation." In her view, integration always implied some gain, a plus value, never a loss, and always some creativity, a growth within the social interaction. The first step toward integration was actually disintegration, breaking down wholes. By this she meant the systematic deconstruction of accepted concepts. As an example, when dealing with conflict between labor and capital, one must first see that there is no labor or capital point of view. "These are imaginary wholes which must be broken up before capital and labor can cooperate," she argued. Likewise with a farmer or an artisan: they must be broken up: "Parts, aspects, factors, elements—all these words are too static; we must differentiate into *activities*."[33]

By seeing the parties to a conflict as made of parts and then analyzing the issue raised, for example, the worker's demand for an eight-hour day, in terms of what is really desired as well as as a symbol to be examined, creative solutions can be achieved:

> Is it an eight-hour day that the workman really wants? This is a whole which has to be split up to find what he really wants, and we have to split it not into ideas but into activities. In all wage controversies this is important. We can say, at the very least, that the workman does not "really want" wages above the point that will keep the factory open; that the employer does not "really want" wages low enough seriously to impair the productive power of the workman.

How this type of process does not result in compromise is a bit elusive, but Follett was convinced that such an approach, born of a social worker's commitment to dialogue, was transformative. Challenged by an audience member to resolve a conflict in which his mother insisted the dining-room table be in the middle of the room when he wanted it by the bay window, Follett thought to herself, "What is dining-table-in-middle-of-room a symbol of to you and what to your mother?" and "What did you and your mother *really* want?" Perhaps the mother wanted warmth from the radiator or proximity to the butler's pantry; the audience member may have wanted more light. If so, the answer might be taking down the curtains. Likewise, in the library, Follett wanted the window shut while another patron wanted it open. Opening the window in the next room integrated the situation, as the patron got fresh air and Follett was spared the north wind blowing directly on her. (In a somewhat dicier example, Follett pointed to Harvard's decision to admit the top seven graduates of approved schools without examination, an informal means of decreasing the number of Jewish students at the university. Both sides were happy, Follett concluded, as Jews faced no discrimination and "at the same time there will be fewer relatively if the expectation of largely increased numbers from west of the Mississippi is fulfilled." Follett's estimation of Jewish opinion was sadly lacking, and the policy was an "integration" in only a narrow and somewhat perverse sense.)[34]

For Follett, the movement to integration as opposed to compromise (let alone coercion, which she also deprecated) rested on the insights of modern psychology, including recognition of the reflex arc or circular response that depicted subject and object in dynamic and continuous interaction and Gestalt psychology, which suggested experience is the product of perceptions of wholes, of a complex field of relationships.

Circular response arrived at the "deepest truth of life," Follett declared. "We move always within a larger life than we are directly cognizant of. But many men have deliberately shut their eyes to that larger life because they felt that any view must be false which made the individual seem to 'transcend' what we know he can never transcend." The theory of creative experience disjoined creativity from the notion of transcendence. A man "expresses, brings into manifestation, powers which are the powers of the universe, and thereby those forces which he is himself helping to create, those which exist in and by and through him, are ever more ready to respond, and so Life expands and deepens; fulfils and at the same moment makes possible larger fulfillment."[35]

More powerfully, Follett likened her methods of conflict resolution, which entailed looking at the total picture and dynamic relationship, to the process of cultivation. Every human relation should entail a freeing, she argued.

> Last summer I noticed a strange plant in our pasture. I did not know what it was, I had no picture in my mind of what flower or fruit it would bear, but I freed it. That is, I dug around it and opened the soil that the rain might fall on its roots, I cleared out the thistles with which it was entangled so that it might have room to spread, I cut down the undergrowth of small maples near so that it could get the sun. In other words, I simply freed it. Every friendship which is not treated in this way will surely suffer; no human relation should serve an anticipatory purpose. Every relation should be a freeing relation with the "purpose" evolving.

Or, in a variation used later in the book, we "prune and graft and fertilize certain trees, and as our behavior becomes increasingly that of behavior towards apple-bearing trees, these become increasingly apple-bearing trees. The tree releases energy in me and I in it; it makes me think and plan and work, and I make it bear edible fruit. It is a process of freeing on both sides. And this is a creating process." It was analogous to the relationship between social worker and child and was premised on fundamental elements of the casework approach to social work advanced by social work pioneers such as Mary E. Richmond: respect for the dignity of the client, the cultivation of independence and self-reliance, and the creation of a positive social environment. The social worker's success depends upon "her ability to do her part in so freeing the life of the child that possibilities of child and possibilities of social environment may form a 'whole,' or working-unit, which shall make the child's life more happy and fruitful, and also make the social environment contain more possibilities for all young people." The breaking down of wholes, or the interactive dialogue regarding desires and needs, was, in Follett's ideas, both a process of freeing and integration. "As progress is through the release and integration of the action tendencies of each and every individual in society, way should be provided for such activity to take place normally," Follett observed. "This is perhaps the sentence in this book which I most want to emphasize."[36]

Follett's book was a democratic corrective to Lippmann, premised as it was on establishing group activity and the casework-style process of individual cultivation and interaction as the basis of social decision making. While she provided no explanation of how such processes could be applied to state-level decision making nor engagement with the arguments about propaganda and the manufacture of consent Lippmann advanced, she did vindicate an alternative progressive tradition—that of the social settlement and the promise of small-scale, cross-class social interaction and community-based deliberative democracy. "Democracy does not register various opinions; it is an attempt to create unity," she declared. She quibbled with Lippmann's emphasis on the "pictures" that constituted human perception, which she found static and untrue to the interactive nature of social reality. We do not "see with out minds," she declared, insisting on the connection of mind and body in the individual whole. "Life is not a movie for us; you can never watch life because you are always *in* life," she insisted.[37]

She rejected the expansive role Lippmann assigned to experts and the limited yes/no plebiscitary role assigned to the masses, just as she repudiated a leading role for "power-organizations" such as labor unions or employers' groups. Democracy means, she argued, that "the experience of all is necessary." She refused to romanticize the people, whom she did not hold to be instinctively good, but she held the experts themselves to be partial, biased, and prone to disagreement. What is more, information alone would not be sufficient to resolve all of the problems created by diverse interests. The workman's experience needed to be added to that of the expert. "The expert must find his place within the social process; he can never be made a substitute for it," she wrote. "Technical experience must be made a part of all the available experience. When we see expert and administrative official, legislator and judge, *and* the people, all integral parts of the social process, all learning how to make facts, how to view facts, how to develop criteria by which to judge facts, then only have we a vision of a genuine democracy."[38]

Thus, Follett disapproved of politics as a mode of public debate, persuasion, and interest-group contest. The "crowd-method" and "crowd-words" did not break up the debilitating social wholes—such as labor, management, or class identity—which, good progressive as she was, she believed deleterious to society. The form of government based on consent divided society between the experts and the people. One need not assume citizens to be omnicompetent nor desirous of self-government to recognize its necessity. She hailed community centers, cooperatives, and the workers' education movement as the "most democratic" in society, aiming to "train ourselves, to learn how to use the work of experts, to find our will, to educate our will, to integrate our wills." In Follett's conception, democracy was not so much a system of electoral representation or even direct democratic decision making as a form of community self-realization, not the ballot or factory suggestion box, but the "attempt to create unity." "Consent is not the technique of democracy. We want the information of expert or official, not to turn us into rubber stamps, but as the foundation for the social process. The 'consent of the governed' is intellectualistic doctrine; the will of the people is not to be found on this plane at all, but in the concrete activities of everyday life." Tightly connected to the Boston business elite and, after 1924, deeply engaged in management theory, Follett might have had this in mind when she observed that businessmen "are quietly . . . working out a system of organization which is not democratic in our old understanding of the word, but something better than that."[39]

Key aspects of progressivism informed Follett: social empathy, the centrality of primary group affiliation, the hope for deliberative democracy, and a social agenda based on eliminating conflict through manipulation of the environment. There was in Follett, too, a focus on group process that provided the basis of a theory of social engineering. The engineer (as well as the scientist) enjoyed great prestige in the early twentieth century, as did scientific management, and politicians and businessmen embraced attitudes implicit in the field. Alongside welfare-oriented social engineers who wanted to reshape the urban environment to counter social disintegration and impersonality and encourage self-reliance were technocratic advocates of a top-down and expert-driven vision of social progress, usually liberals but sometimes conservative progressives like Herbert Hoover, the Great Engineer.[40]

The conservative implications of this latter type of social engineering are most apparent in the emerging field of industrial psychology, led by Elton Mayo among others. By 1920 more than half of American psychologists engaged in some type of applied research. Trends toward rationalized corporate management and the development of personnel departments fed the development of this field. Psychological consulting firms blossomed, promising to aid employers in maintaining worker morale, and thus productivity, and developing optimal workplace conditions. The most significant advance in industrial psychology (as well as the fields of industrial sociology, social psychology, anthropology of work, and organizational and management theory) was a series of workplace experiments that took place at the Hawthorne Works of the Western Electric Company on Chicago's west side beginning in 1924 and lasting through the 1930s. Western Electric manufactured telephone parts for American Telephone and Telegraph; its managers made the factory complex a model of welfare capitalism. The Hawthorne Works featured lunch-hour concerts, company athletic fields with six baseball diamonds and thirteen tennis courts, and a gymnasium, as well as the Hawthorne Club, which organized social events, vacations, a beauty contest, a club store, and a savings and loan. Elections of Hawthorne Club officers were major annual events and featured lunchtime rallies and speeches relayed over the factory's public-address system.[41]

The experiments began in 1924 with a series of lighting tests, designed to examine the effects of variation in lighting on worker productivity. Inconclusive results whetted the researchers' appetite for more, and in 1927, a second set of experiments was begun designed around a special room where six young workers, all young women from Chicago's ethnic communities (four Poles, a Norwegian, and a Bohemian) were sequestered under controlled circumstances and close observation as they assembled electromagnetic relays, a highly repetitive task. In 1928, the company asked Mayo to advise their researchers, and he ultimately became the social scientist most identified with interpreting the results of the experiments.

What those results meant became a subject of much controversy and speculation. The lighting tests produced puzzling data, as the changes made—initially raising the lighting and then lowering the lighting to an extremely dim level in succeeding phases—all seemed to increase worker productivity. Likewise, the relay assembly room data seemed to indicate that every change in the work routine, whether positive, such as adding a rest break, or negative, such as taking it way, serially produced steadily rising productivity. The researchers were unable to isolate concrete environmental and social factors that could increase production. Those involved, including the workers, created competing interpretations of the results, and later researchers came to believe the true revelation was the effect the researchers unwittingly had on the workers being studied. The mere awareness of increased attention boosted output. As Richard Gillespie's exhaustive history of the experiments demonstrates, the managers were, in fact, well aware of the psychological effects of their presence and attempted to control for them as best they could. Mayo and his followers strongly emphasized the sociological factors involved in the relay assembly room tests, arguing that the fact of increasing small-group cohesion explained the increase in productivity. Mayo's interpretation affirmed the necessity of experts in personnel and industrial psychology who could understand worker attitudes and social organization, which he deemed features of the workplace as essential to worker satisfaction as pay rates and work conditions. (As Gillespie has also shown, Mayo's group understated the importance of intense supervision and increased pay rates on a small group of women, who were able to manipulate the experimental situation, both as individuals and a group, to their advantage. The evidence suggests that the increases in productivity documented by the researchers matched increases in pay, a result of little value to Western Electric, as it did not increase productivity in relation to cost.)[42]

After publishing *Creative Experience*, Follett turned her attention to management theory, preaching interactive concepts of leadership to progressive businessmen. It was "among business men (not all, but a few)," Follett declared, "that I find the greatest vitality of thinking to-day"; it was "in line with the deepest and best thinking we have ever had." In 1926–1927, she sponsored an interdisciplinary Harvard graduate seminar with Richard Cabot, her friend and chair of the Social Ethics Department, which drew distinguished speakers and included among its audience members Mayo and Harold Lasswell. Laswell later incorporated Follett's ideas into his own work on propaganda, arguing that the propagandist used cultural symbols to redefine social situations so as to produce integration, not victory or defeat for either party.[43]

A proponent of "self-government outside of government," Herbert Hoover, the energetic and immensely influential secretary of commerce for much of the 1920s, along with fellow Republican managerialists Charles Evan Hughes and Henry C. Wallace, advocated a new associationalism that would use the tools of the federal government to aid private development and corporate coordination through accurate economic data, expert commissions, government-sponsored conferences, and encouragement to

public-private collaboration.[44] Hoover placed great faith in quasiofficial public agreements within industries to reform work hours and safety standards,
codify trade practices, and standardize production and conserve resources
(over one hundred such agreements were approved by the federal government). The Federal Trade Commission eventually certified fifty fair-trade
practice codes, which remained essentially unenforceable.[45]

Corporate leaders wanted to solve endemic problems of overproduction
and destructive competition, which persisted into the 1920s. Industrial-
ists looked to welfare capitalism, trade associations, and even the embrace
of the business-style unionism of the American Federation of Labor, yet
no solution availed. While commercially oriented marketing cooperatives
flourished in agriculture (there were eleven thousand by 1927–1928), trade
associations generally failed to control competition or regulate prices. Top
producers tended to dominate the associations. Business remained opposed
to any federal economic regulation or planning, even as the federal structure
of American government, distributing power between federal authority and
the states, resulted in a fragmented and hypercompetitive political economy.
(Hoover complained that the nation consisted of 49 distinct regulatory
regimes, all conflicting with and weakening each other.) Most businessmen
opposed unions, even as the unions served to regulate a few relatively disorganized and labor-intensive industries; unionization declined precipitously in
the decade. Industrial leaders were opposed to centralized regulation, often
endorsing narrow solutions for their own problems but balking at similar
solutions for other industrial sectors.[46]

Hoover himself felt these stabs at state-sponsored associationalism ac-
corded with "American individualism," in his view a distinct political philosophy based on equality of opportunity and the absence of "frozen strata of
classes." Hoover eschewed laissez-faire liberalism, believing the government
had a role to play in facilitating business cooperation and self-regulation.
He acknowledged the imperfections of the American economy—economic
insecurity, long hours, employer domination of labor, unfair competition,
and deadening work routines—but saw them as diminishing and localized
problems. He even accepted some government responsibility to ensure social
justice and tax excessive wealth. Hoover welcomed the trend toward broader
stockholder ownership of large enterprises, seeing in it the emergence of a
"large capital" more beholden to small shareholders and more responsible
to the community, and saw no incompatibility between individual upward
mobility and greater economic, political, and social cooperation. Government fostered cooperation in business (Hoover endorsed cooperatives, trade
associations, unions, and chambers of commerce) only in order to encourage

individual initiative and counteract "overreckless competition in production and distribution." Hoover was untroubled by any possibility of conflict between the individual and the larger social institutions, seeing rising prosperity as an emollient for any potential social friction. "The only road to further advance in the standard of living is by greater invention, greater elimination of waste, greater production and better distribution of commodities and services," he advised, "for by increasing their ratio to our numbers and dividing them justly we each will have more of them."[47]

Hoover possessed a technocrat's social vision with the politics left out. Democracy had no value for him in and of itself, being merely one form of government. "Democracy is merely the mechanism which individualism invented as a device that would carry on the necessary political work of its social organization," Hoover believed. "Democracy arises out of individualism and prospers through it alone."[48] While in the progressive tradition, Hoover

John Dewey.
Courtesy Prints and Photographs Division, Library of Congress, LC-USZ62-51525.

had no commitment to collective democratic action, a commitment that, in one way or another, animated Lippmann and Follett. Nor did he seem troubled by the crisis in public action that interested Lippmann and John Dewey. Hoover's faith in economic opportunity, expert economic management, the tools of macroeconomic coordination, and economic growth found an audience with progressives, but his lack of imaginative identification with the democratic aspirations of the masses placed him outside their fold.

In his sixties as the 1920s opened and already vastly influential as the chief spokesman for pragmatism, or "instrumentalism" as he preferred, John Dewey devoted considerable effort to defining the conditions for effective popular social action. Shaken by the results of the Great War, which he had supported, to the consternation of young Deweyan leftists such as Randolph Bourne, and convinced by many of the particulars of Lippmann's diagnosis of public opinion and popular democracy, Dewey's response was to articulate a decentralist, left-leaning social democratic politics and, in *The Public and Its Problems* (1927), lay out a hopeful vision of democratic recovery.

Born in an industrializing Burlington, Vermont, in 1859, Dewey could see the signs of modernization while growing up. His father was a storekeeper, his mother a pious Congregationalist; New England social and religious traditions firmly enwrapped him. Educated at the University of Vermont and the new Johns Hopkins University, he moved through an early neo-Hegelianism to a scientifically oriented and experimental naturalism, shedding his earlier religious faith in the 1890s. After an initial teaching post at the University of Michigan, Dewey moved to the University of Chicago in 1894, establishing the Laboratory School, which embodied both his commitment to the application of science to society and his belief that education was the means by which to implement philosophical pragmatism and achieve genuine social change.[49]

Dewey left Chicago in 1904 in a dispute with the administration and moved to Columbia University in New York City, where he promulgated pragmatism, published prolifically, and established himself as a major public intellectual and liberal spokesman. In pragmatism Dewey and William James attacked inertia in American intellectual life and attempted to turn philosophy away from the kinds of problems and questions that were absorbing the energy of professional philosophers. They targeted encrusted assumptions about individualism and the rights of private property that had become dogma to so many Americans—beliefs so sanctified by supposedly natural laws and investigation as to defy any hopes of dislodging them. In the "matter of belief," James observed, "we are all extreme conservatives."[50] Pragmatism was premised on the belief that intellectual preconceptions were the foremost

barrier to human progress. The pragmatist would free the American mind, recasting timeworn philosophical debates in new ways, redefining ideas as tools
only, and asserting that truth need only be that which works, a provisional
hypothesis that will move us toward a satisfying result. James, Dewey pointed
out, saw the world as "still open, a world still in the making." The pragmatists
presented their ideas—which challenged belief in a single, real, unseen, and
unchanging world beyond our own that vouchsafed absolute truth—as the
means of intellectual and cultural regeneration. As such, pragmatism became
the philosophical armature of the more intellectual progressives and, by the
1920s, a de facto common sensibility, even a "faith," as Dewey observed in
1922. For pragmatists, Dewey argued, "consequences are the test and the to-
ken of responsibility in the operation of intelligence."[51]

In *Human Nature and Conduct* (1922), Dewey provided a pragmatic rationale for social scientific analysis, emphasizing the way in which human
action is governed by habits, the dispositions to action learned from the interaction of the person and the environment and which we call will. Much of
the book emphasizes the inclination to conformity. "The inert, stupid quality
of current customs perverts learning into a willingness to follow where others point the way, into conformity, constriction, surrender of scepticism and
experiment," Dewey complained. We resist change, Dewey charged, striving
"to retain action in ditches already dug" and regarding "novelties as dangerous." The "hankering for certainty," he believed, derived from a similar fear
of the new and thus an insistence on immutable moral law. While Dewey
recognized the necessity of habits, change is necessary, too, and social psychology promised a new discipline capable of analyzing and promoting helpful adjustments to new environments.[52]

Dewey put his hope on impulses or instincts, a feature of human conduct
secondary to habit but one that promised to push humans in a new direction
and break established habits. In Dewey's view, change and novelty comprised
the essence of life. As impulses interweave both with each other and the environment, new habits may arise. "In a definite sense, then, a human society
is always starting afresh," he wrote. "It is always in a process of renewing, and
it endures only because of renewal." The burden of Dewey's social psychology lay in defining the conditions that would most allow such needed inter-
weavings to occur, that would rekindle the experimental outlook we have as
children. "The first toddling is a romantic adventuring into the unknown;
and every gained power is a delightful discovery of one's own powers and
of the wonders of the world," Dewey wrote. "We may not be able to retain
in adult habits this zest of intelligence and this freshness of satisfaction in
newly discovered powers. But there is surely a middle term between a normal

exercise of power which includes some excursion into the unknown, and a mechanical activity hedged within a drab world."[53] If such could be found, it would be the condition of freedom.

To create such conditions is the aim of social action. In making this claim, Dewey was reaffirming the importance of shaping an environment that called forth effective personal action, a message aligned with that of Mary Parker Follett. Follett was herself critical of Dewey, whom she considered unoriginal. She saw her work as a corrective in its attention to the circular and dynamic nature of social interaction; the work of the Deweyans, she believed, had devolved into a stale empiricism, a focus on facts to the detriment of theory. Dewey's definition of social action also looked forward to the possibility of reshaping the conditions of public action, which was the theme of *The Public and Its Problems* (1927). Dewey provided a historical account both of the present democratic crisis and the development of nineteenth-century liberal individualism, which he long considered an impediment to progressive reform. Like Lippmann, Dewey considered the idea of the omni-competent citizen an "illusion," founded upon an equally mythological belief that men act independently of society and regularly base their actions on a rational calculus of self-interest.[54]

To Dewey, the nation's democratic institutions and its philosophy of individualism originated from specific and contingent historical circumstances. In the eighteenth and nineteenth centuries, the revolt against oppressive government and the constricting force of tradition took the form of theories of limited government and a reverence for inalienable rights. If only this revolt had taken the form of an assertion of group rights, Dewey felt; the result would have been equally legitimate. Moreover, the particular institutions of American electoral democracy, the general suffrage and frequent elections premised on the engaged citizen, were born of the social realities of a face-to-face community that no longer exists. "We have inherited, in short, local town-meeting practices and ideas," Dewey argued. "But we live and act and have our being in a continental national state." By definition, he asserted, a public is created when the product of social behavior creates broad, serious, ramifying, and indirect consequences that affect a large number of people. With the scale and scope of the modern "Great Society," the public has become "lost" or eclipsed. "The local face-to-face community has been invaded by forces so vast, so remote in initiation, so far-reaching in scope and so complexly indirect in operation, that they are, from the standpoint of the members of the local social units, unknown," Dewey believed.[55]

It was this leap forward in social interconnectedness and complexity that eclipsed the public. While technology integrated people into a single national community as never before, even imposing a unity despite social heterogeneity, the people's sense of themselves as a public, a cohesive, interacting group akin to a face-to-face community, had been lost. "It is not that there is no public, no large body of persons having a common interest in the consequences of social transactions," Dewey explained. "There is too much public, a public too diffused and scattered and too intricate in composition. And there are too many publics." Mobility has ensured that social bonds have atrophied. The result, in Dewey's view, was a "new era of human relationships," one "marked by mass production for remote markets, by cable and telephone, by cheap printing, by railway and steam navigation. Only geographically did Columbus discover a new world. The actual new world has been generated in the last hundred years."[56]

What is required, Dewey believed, is to convert our new Great Society into a "Great Community," a task to be done through communication of (unspecified) new signs and symbols that would convince people of their capacity for shared experience and action. The answer to the eclipse of the public was, pointedly, not an oligarchy of experts. The people must have a voice through the ballot: "The man who wears the shoe knows best that it pinches and where it pinches, even if the expert shoemaker is the best judge of how the trouble is to be remedied." All the same, Dewey saw "no sanctity in universal suffrage, frequent elections, majority rule, congressional and cabinet government."[57] Such may be the trappings of our historical political democracy, but political democracy represented only one form of a broader democratic ideal; moreover, suffrage and the rest were based on false assumptions of individualism. Moreover, Dewey shared the progressives' complaints against manipulative urban machine bosses who ignored the public good, political parties that were themselves undemocratic, and the rule of narrow self-interest.

Dewey provided no concrete alternatives to the established systems of representative democracy and general suffrage. He noted instead the need for greater communication within the nation, social research to create necessary knowledge, and improved methods and conditions of debate and discussion. In *Individualism, Old and New* (1930), he envisioned a new individualism that would reconstruct the self and create processes of socialization that would allow for an "integrated personality" suited to our current "era of integration." "Individuals who are not bound together in associations, whether domestic, economic, religious, political, artistic or educational, are monstrosities," Dewey declared. On a deeper level, however, he reached back to an older progressive yearning for a society governed by empathy and fellow feeling, declaring that democracy was, in fact, "the idea of community itself," the "clear consciousness of a communal life." More than a system of governance based on consent of the masses, as envisioned by Lippmann, democracy was the injunction to associated living that was necessary for self-sovereignty and social creativity, "a name for a life of free and enriching communion."[58]

The intensive rethinking of democracy reflected the political realities of the 1920s but also the yawning gap intellectuals and academic social scientists perceived between themselves and the general public. The public became an abstract thing, a topic of study as well as a subject of analysis. At the same time, it was indispensable to a liberal politics, and the progressive dream of community persisted in an age defined by social conflict and the massive new scale of social organization. Even such a cynic as Mencken could not avoid the rare admission of a desire for solidarity. The American people, he declared, are unhappy because they no longer trust one another. "The thing that makes life charming is not money, but the society of our fellow men," Mencken declared, "and the thing that draws us toward our fellow men is not admiration for their inner virtues, their hard striving to live according to the light that is in them, but admiration for their outer graces and decencies—in brief, confidence that they will always act generously and understandingly in their intercourse with us. We must trust men before we may enjoy them."[59] For all the scorn he heaped on the political system, Mencken seemed to possess a faint hope for civil society, if only American reformers would shake off the impulse to improve it.

~

CHAPTER SIX

The Inner Check

The greatest symbolic drama in American political culture in the 1920s concerned the case of Nicola Sacco and Bartolomeo Vanzetti, one a hardworking and successful family man originally from a prosperous peasant family in southern Italy, the other a gentle fish peddler originally from the Italian Piedmont who lived on the margins of American society. Both became dedicated anarchists in America, members of the Gruppo Autonomo anarchist cell in East Boston and followers of the anarchist-communist Luigi Galleani, a radical journalist and advocate of the use of revolutionary violence to overthrow capitalism, including the use of exemplary bombings and assassination, the propaganda of the deed, to publicize the anarchists' "beautiful Idea." They were undoubtedly involved in the 1919 spate of anarchist violence, although it is entirely likely that neither was involved in the bank robbery murders of which they were convicted in 1921. The two men languished in prison as their supporters waged an expert public-relations campaign protesting their innocence and revealing the biases of their trial judge and dubious prosecutorial conduct. They were eventually executed by electrocution in August 1927 to a worldwide outcry at the injustice of the proceedings.[1]

The execution became a revelatory moment for many younger radical writers, who found in the Sacco and Vanzetti case a symbol to differentiate themselves from the American majority. John Dos Passos portrayed Sacco and Vanzetti as philosophical anarchists, committed to the dream of a perfect city in a way analogous to the early Christians, victims of the popular prejudice against "garlic-smelling" foreigners.[2] In the stunning essay "Fear," poet

Edna St. Vincent Millay harnessed many of the tropes of 1920s alienation to a slashing attack on the complacent American majority. The public was ignorant, prejudiced, afraid, and morally bankrupt, willing to accept the conviction of anarchists for a capital crime simply on account of their political beliefs. There was no fellow feeling, no willingness to sacrifice. She identified the vindictive public who treated peaceful anarchists harshly with the older generation; the sympathizers, those with empathy and open minds living free of irrationality and fear, were the young.

Millay's mythologizing was of a piece of the larger modernist tale-telling of the 1920s, a knowing and powerful cultural politics which emerged fully developed as the culmination of the decade's cultural debates. A generation of liberal intellectuals came to identify with a new, critical, even adversarial mentality. The split emerged vividly in debates over religion, science, and intellectual life. In 1921, William Jennings Bryan, the Great Commoner, a fixture in politics and on the Chautauqua circuit, where he preached conservative Christian values as well as social reform, alerted Americans to a slackening of religious fervor among college students. He blamed the problem on secularism in education, for which he held college professors responsible.[3] Imagine a boy from a Christian family, he wrote, taught by his mother, as soon he was able, to "lisp the child's prayer: 'Now I lay me down to sleep; I pray the Lord my soul to keep; if I should die before I wake, I pray the Lord my soul to take.'" He attends Sunday school and begins a lifetime journey of faith, convinced he is precious in the sight of God. Off to college, he finds books with "no mention of religion, the only basis for morality; not a suggestion of a sense of responsibility to God—nothing but cold, clammy materialism." Rather, his instructor indoctrinates the boy in values that hollow out his simple Christian faith, setting him adrift, Bryan thundered, "WITH INFINITE CAPACITY FOR GOOD OR EVIL BUT WITH NO LIGHT TO GUIDE HIM, NO COMPASS TO DIRECT HIM AND NO CHART OF THE SEA OF LIFE!" Professors callously damaged their students, in Bryan's view, by leaving them bereft of the truth of religious revelation.[4]

Bryan soon launched a national effort to bar the teaching of the theory of evolution in schools, a project culminating in the Scopes trial in Dayton, Tennessee, in July 1925, which was designed to test the constitutionality of the state's antievolution law. A cocounsel for the prosecution, which was charged with finding John T. Scopes guilty of teaching evolution in violation of state law, Bryan confronted a team of liberal lawyers, including Dudley Field Malone, a twice-married Roman Catholic divorce lawyer who arrived in town with his current wife, the feminist writer Doris Stevens.[5] Early in the trial, Malone made the case for introducing expert testimony on the compat-

The intellectual and emotional (if legally irrelevant) climax of the Scopes trial, July 20, 1925: Clarence Darrow (standing, right) questions William Jennings Bryan (seated, left) on the scientific validity of the Bible.
Photo by Watson Davis. Courtesy Smithsonian Institution Archives, record unit 7091, box 405, image number SIA2007-0124.

ibility of evolution and religious faith—testimony essential to establishing that Scopes had not, in fact, endangered the faith of his students. Malone argued, in part, for openness and truth. "The truth always wins and we are not afraid of it," Malone declared.

> The truth is no coward. The truth does not need the law. The truth does not need the forces of government. The truth does not need Mr. Bryan. The truth is imperishable, eternal, and immortal and needs no human agency to support it. We are ready to tell the truth as we understand it and we do not fear all the truth that they can present as facts. We are ready. We are ready. We feel we stand with progress. We feel that we stand with science. We feel that we stand with intelligence. We feel that we stand with fundamental freedom in America. We are not afraid. Where is the fear? We met it. Where is the fear? We defy it.[6]

The courtroom audience broke into fervent applause, the most received by any attorney during the trial.[7]

The Scopes trial as well as the broader cultural divide over the theory of evolution, the authority of science in the schools, and the rise of fundamentalist evangelical Christianity accentuated the cultural divisions in America evident in the Sacco and Vanzetti case as well as in divisions over race, immigration, the labor movement, politics, music and art, women's roles, and sexual ethics. All were entangled with what liberal intellectuals deemed a popular fear of the new or different, of the truth. Fights on all of these issues revealed a deep divide among Americans. To Bryan, teachers and educators were cultural actors, charged with implanting and nurturing a religious faith too easily damaged by the currents of modern doubt, especially in the young. To Malone, American culture would be strongest when most open; no person ought to fear for his or her beliefs, for if they are true, they will survive and thrive in an open society. For the party of orthodoxy, culture serves as a spiritual discipline, a willed embrace of tradition, a closing off of distraction and temptation in recognition of human weakness and the tendency to confusion. For the modernists, culture embodied choices—choices of ideas and beliefs that were made in the past and the possibility of new choices in the future. They insisted that the individual remain open to new realities and the new perspectives revealed by science and experience. By 1930, the dividing line between a conservative and a modernist outlook was clear—and fell in part along the distinction drawn by Bryan and Malone: Shall we create a culture that nurtures and protects certain beliefs, that makes it hard for humans to doubt received tradition, or shall we cultivate a kind of critical inquiry that fosters skepticism, that makes it difficult to accept received tradition?

While the argument often took the form of debates on science and religion and the nature of free will, the key issues remained ones of culture and the role of intellectuals. When the dust had settled, a new framework for social debate was firmly established, as was a new and ascendant modernist liberalism, both of which would dominate American intellectual life for the next forty years. Out of the debates of the 1920s emerged a new class of cultural critics, intellectuals, and artists who renounced the authority to superintend public morals and to shape the character of youth but embraced the power of myth, symbol, and images—a language, modernists came to believe, in which cultural values are created and expressed.

By the 1920s, Protestant denominations were divided by factional splits between conservatives and liberals. The conflicts shattered the remaining cultural authority of liberal Protestantism. The American embrace of consumer pleasures, increased sexual freedom, and the frivolous, gay culture of adolescents and college students only emphasized the point. Women were emancipated, contraception and divorce were easier to obtain, and youth defied Victorian norms. "Old authorities crumble. The trusted landmarks drift. The God-man is merged in the crowd," a writer noted in *Methodist Review*. "To-day men possess knowledge and power. They do not wait for heaven." Ministers complained that church attendance, contributions, and missionaries had declined. Many were forced to cancel Sunday evening services. "There *is* no God," the captivating but unstable Eleanor declared to Amory Blaine in F. Scott Fitzgerald's seminal tale of unillusioned youth, *This Side of Paradise* (1920). Only a prig would not admit it.[8]

Originally dispatched to study religious institutions, Robert and Helen Lynd concluded that in Middletown, churches were becoming increasingly irrelevant; the confident boosterism of the civic speaker was supplanting the moral voice of the minister. (It is no wonder that the earnest advertising man Bruce Barton wrote a book depicting a "magnetic" and manly Jesus as the first businessman, an in-demand dinner guest, and an instinctive master of the sales pitch.) Meanwhile, the Lynds provided an accounting of declining orthodoxy in Middletown: the number of civil marriages and divorces was increasing, religious education declined in the home, church attendance was more irregular, Rotary excluded ministers (despite claiming to enlist all the city's leaders), and secular socializing increased (including leisure activities on Sunday). "In theory, religious beliefs dominate all other activities in Middletown; actually, large regions of Middletown's life appear uncontrolled by them."[9]

At the crux of liberal Protestantism lay a commitment to engaging the scientific and intellectual trends of the time. In adapting Christian teachings for a new historical moment, liberal ministers and theologians believed Protestants remained loyal to reason and relevant to modern life. In the nineteenth century, biblical scholars engaged in the Higher Criticism carefully assessed the Bible as a historical document, distinguishing between authors, tracing the likely provenance of its various books, and identifying contradictions. They historicized the Bible, linking it to the times in which it was composed. Anthropological, literary, and religious scholars identified commonalities between biblical religious beliefs and non-Judaic and non-Christian faiths and cults. Skeptics further armed with the empirical ethos of modern science denied claims of miracles, the virgin birth, or an afterlife. Finally, geologists and biologists, including Charles Darwin, presented accounts of the development of the earth and animal life that contradicted the Book of Genesis, including Darwin's theory that the origin of new species resulted from the long-term effects of inherited adaptations of particular animals to their environment. Religious liberals were inclined to accept the fruits of scientific and scholarly enterprise, identifying them with progress in general. To liberal Protestant theologians individual reason and experience must be the basis of all claims to truth; scriptural authority was not sufficient to make a truth claim. The Baptist scholar and theological modernist Shailer Mathews, dean of the University of Chicago Divinity School and a self-identified evangelical Christian (the last of the liberal theologians at Chicago to consider himself an evangelical, his subsequent work was naturalistic and empiricist), held in *The Faith of Modernism* (1924) that the genius of Christianity was not a set of beliefs about miracles or assumptions about creation but an essential set of convictions and a governing method.[10] "A religion is a way of living, and the modernist refuses to think of it as an accumulation of decrees," he wrote.[11]

To the modernists, Christianity could only survive if liberalized; otherwise, it lost its hold on the increasing number of educated people. Christians needed to recast Christianity to suit the times, recognizing that the terms of Christian revelation in each generation are shaped by particular historical conditions, even as the essential beliefs remain the same. The "social mind" of an age shapes its religious revelation. "The world needs new control of nature and society and is told that the Bible is verbally inerrant," Mathews declared in *The Faith of Modernism*. "It needs a means of composing class strife, and is told to believe in the substitutionary atonement. It needs a spirit of love and justice and is told that love without orthodoxy will not save from hell. . . . It needs faith in the divine presence in human affairs and is told it must accept the virgin birth of Jesus Christ."[12]

The problem lay in discriminating between the ephemeral and the timeless truth. Liberal Protestants asserted the need to interpret the Bible in light of modern biblical criticism, the theory of evolution, and the truths of other religious traditions in order to discern its essential meaning. The liberalism of the popular New York City preacher Harry Emerson Fosdick grew out of a crisis of faith experienced while at college. He preached a version of Christianity that dispensed with the virgin birth of Christ, which he found incredible, and the belief that Christ had to die to atone for human sinfulness. The resurrection of Christ, he argued, was purely spiritual.[13]

Ultimately, modernists like Mathews conceived of God as active in, if not the essential aspect of, secular progress. Cultural progress reveals the Kingdom of God. God is immanent in—revealed through—human cultural development. (Secularization came to be, in this view, a religious process.) While Mathews affirmed that Jesus is the revelation of a Savior God, that humans are in need of salvation from sin and death, and that life persists after death, he also affirmed that God is revealed in human experience. Indeed, the data of religious study is simply human experience, including the Bible, which, when interpreted historically, was a part of the "progressive revelation of God." "I believe in God, immanent in the forces and processes of nature, revealed in Jesus Christ and human history as love," declared Mathews in *The Faith of Modernism*. Modernism is the "evangelicalism of the scientific mind," a "phase of the scientific struggle for freedom in thought and belief."[14]

~

Theological conservatives strongly opposed Protestant liberalism and, in particular, the modernist variant represented by Mathews. Mathews's chief rival was J. Gresham Machen, a biblical scholar teaching at Princeton Theological Seminary. In Machen's view, modernist liberalism was no longer Christianity, and in his major defense of Christian orthodoxy, *Christianity and Liberalism* (1923), he beseeched liberals to choose between Christianity and liberalism. He would have the modernists leave the traditional Christian denominations, therefore relieving the churches of the constant pull to unorthodoxy. Machen's position was reflected in recurring battles within the major Protestant denominations, particularly in the North (and particularly among the Baptists and Presbyterians, although there was some conflict among Episcopalians and northern Methodists as well, and the Disciples of Christ split over baptism by immersion). For example, the Presbyterian General Assembly adopted a five-point declaration of "essential" doctrines in 1910— biblical inerrancy, the divinity of Christ, the virgin birth, Christ's substitutionary atonement for the sins of mankind, and the authenticity of miracle—in response to doubts raised about the orthodoxy of some graduates of Union Theological Seminary.[15]

Conservative evangelicals issued a series of Bible teachings between 1910 and 1915 called *The Fundamentals*. Funded by an oilman and written by leading conservative theologians, scholars, ministers, and lay leaders, the series eventually consisted of twelve inexpensive, paperback books of essays. Its backers distributed it free to pastors, missionaries, professors, students, and various other Protestant lay leaders and editors throughout the English-speaking world. *The Fundamentals* reflected conservative evangelical outreach; moderate in tone, the contributors exuded a confident and eager faith in their message, which was based above all on a proclamation of the literal and inerrant truth of the Bible. The revivalist Reuben A. Torrey presented Christ's promise of salvation as a balm for the discontented secularist, a "cure for loneliness." While the maintenance of the authority of scripture over that of science was the key issue, there were strong elements of moderation, particularly early in the series, even an acknowledgment of the possibility of theistic evolution. (The tone became more anti-intellectual and hostile to science and evolution as the series progressed.) One contributor proposed common ground between orthodox Christians and pragmatists, who, after all, aimed to "save men from pessimism."[16]

Fundamentalism emerged out of confrontations between liberals and conservatives during the Great War. In 1917, liberals at the University of Chicago Divinity School, led by Mathews, launched an intellectual assault on dispensational premillennialists, accusing them of being unpatriotic and dangerous to the nation. These attacks, somewhat bizarre in finding a remote connection between a supposed lack of civic responsibility and millennialist fatalism, derived in part from a crosstown rivalry with the conservative Moody Bible Institute and in part from the generally prowar zealotry embraced by the Chicago theologians. The war provoked a crisis for liberal Christians, as it did for liberals generally, dividing them on its wisdom (and provoking a similar postwar disillusionment among some). The liberal wartime attacks on dispensationalists bred an incipient fundamentalism, as premillennialists, in response to the liberal accusations, in turn attributed German militarism to the Higher Criticism, the critical scholarly study of the Bible pioneered by German scholars, which, they argued, undermined Christian faith and ethics.[17]

The fundamentalist movement, a "militantly antimodernist Protestant evangelicalism," in George M. Marsden's definition, was a decentralized, contentious, and often self-divided coalition of ministers, revivalist, writers, and evangelists that developed among moderately well-educated, middle-class evangelicals in the North (shifting to a base of support in the South later in the 1920s).[18] Several strands of conservative Protestantism shaped it, including the type of conservative orthodoxy espoused by Machen and his associates, which had long divided northern denominations. Also important were dispensational premillennialism and a revivalist impulse derived from a holiness movement that originated first among Methodists.

Premillenialists believed that human history was a struggle between the forces of Christ and Satan and that Christ would return to Earth to establish the millennium (his one-thousand-year reign of peace to be followed by the final judgment) after a cataclysmic confrontation between the forces of good and evil. The dispensationalist variant suggested that God had ordained seven "dispensations," or ages of man, that organized history; some believed that in the final years of tribulation before the Second Coming a "rapture" will occur, allowing the chosen few to escape the final evils of human history. Millennialism historically lent itself to a type of worldly engagement fed by the urgency of prophecy, the impulse to read into "signs of the times" prophetic claims that matched biblical suggestions. The holiness movement derived from beliefs about the spirit from John Wesley, founder of Method-ism. In Wesleyan doctrine the aim of Christian life was to obtain perfec-tion, or "perfect love." Such a doctrine accentuated human choice and free will and emphasized the power of the Holy Spirit, who Christians believed poured into the world at the first Pentecost shortly after Christ's resurrection and ascension to heaven. The Spirit is available in this world and can infuse and raise the individual just as air inflates a hot-air balloon, lifting it to the heavens. After 1901, Pentecostalism emerged as a self-conscious embodi-ment of this movement.[19]

Both dispensationalist premillennialism and holiness teachings figured prominently in evangelical teaching, as, for example, among some followers of the revivalist Dwight L. Moody. After the Great War, these trends—all focused on literal readings of the Bible and all opposed to the reigning Christian liberalism—formed the intellectual basis of the fundamentalist campaign to assert orthodoxy in Protestant denominations and reform a godless and hedonistic American culture. Guided by the Minneapolis Baptist minister William Bell Riley, conservative Christians established the World's Christian Fundamentals Association in May 1919. The Baptist editor Curtis Lee Laws coined the term *fundamentalists* to refer to those willing "to do battle royal for the Fundamentals" in 1920.[20]

While American Protestants faced crisis and division, Roman Catholics experienced renewal. Still facing deep anti-Catholic animosity, embodied to some extent in both Prohibition and immigration reform as well as the anti-Catholic Ku Klux Klan, Catholic leaders nevertheless began to assert Catholic doctrines in more public ways. Working within a hierarchical in-stitution governed from Rome, Catholic priests and lay leaders were neces-sarily cosmopolitan and traditionalist. At the same time, the Catholic laity, especially in England and France, sparked a Catholic intellectual "revival" in the postwar years. In 1922, Pope Pius XI, recognizing these trends, endorsed the "participation of the laity in the work of the apostolate," a powerful stimulus to what came to be known as "Catholic action." In the late nine-teenth century, the Vatican mandated that Scholasticism, which derived principally from the thirteenth-century Dominican Thomas Aquinas, was the fulcrum of Catholic intellectual life. Aquinas's adaptation of Aristotelian metaphysics to Christian revelation provided the basis for Neoscholasticism (or Neothomism). Catholic culture was deeply medievalist in the 1920s; a European "liturgical renaissance" spread in the United States, with the aim of breathing light into Catholic art, music, prayers, vesture, architecture, and ritual through creative borrowing from medieval examples, including plainsong and Gregorian chant. Thomism became a required part of the curriculum in American Catholic colleges, a "school philosophy," sometimes taught in a six-course mandated sequence. It blended theology and science, suggested rational proofs for God's existence, and posited an essential disjunction between the human mind and external reality. Thomists reconciled faith and reason through a careful reduction in the capacities of the intellect and a hedging in of faith. Humans must rely on intuition and experience as well as reason; we can know of God, but only by analogy, never directly. We find God in the natural world in the form of natural law, a construction of the rational mind that nevertheless reflected the order of the universe.[21]

Thomism enabled Catholic intellectuals to evade many of the tortuous conflicts between religion and science that split Protestant churches. They aligned with the top-down Catholic impulse to stand against modernity; there was no impulse to associate divinity with secular progress. (Pius X condemned modernism in 1907; priests were to take an "oath against modernism" after 1910.) Although Catholic medievalism and Neoscholasticism were self-marginalizing in some respects (Catholic Thomist philosophers were often relegated to the historical sections of the programs of professional conferences), the philosophical stances allowed reason to serve as a bulwark of faith and Catholics to identify with the American national project in important ways. In the 1920s, Neoscholastics briefly but energetically advocated the theory that American constitutionalism and democracy were rooted in medieval Scholasticism. While marginalized in academic philosophy and always differing from mainstream liberals on first principles (Catholic leaders were fundamentally critical of liberal individualism), Catholics found common ground with liberals on social welfare, most notably in the advocacy of Father John A. Ryan for a living wage for industrial workers. Ryan drafted the progressive Bishops' Program of Social Reconstruction in 1919, which advocated old-age insurance, a share for labor in the management of industry, municipal health clinics, and a minimum wage. At the same time, Catholic leaders, such as the Jesuit Daniel Lord, opposed the Equal Rights Amendment, birth control, and the reform of divorce law. Catholic prelates assumed leadership in censorship efforts; Lord drafted the movie production code in 1929.[22]

⁓

The crisis in Protestant liberalism reflected the more general crisis in cultural authority that dominated the decade. By the end of the decade, Walter Lippmann, in his impressive summation of religious, cultural, and intellectual trends, *A Preface to Morals* (1929), placed the loss of religious faith—what to him was a traumatic and perplexing emancipation—at the center of American moral debate and as the starting point for a new modernist humanism. The "acids of modernity," he declared, dissolved the old order, including the old religious faiths. Absent such faith, modern individuals no longer had a "sure" foundation for moral rules or values. The result, he believed, was a general discontent, unhappiness, and desperation. "For the modern man who has ceased to believe, without ceasing to be credulous, hangs, as it were, between heaven and earth, and is at rest nowhere," he claimed.[23]

J. Gresham Machen had insisted that the crisis in modern religious belief hinged on questions of science. Unlike many sympathetic liberals, Machen would not countenance the notion that religion and science were simply separate spheres of knowledge, each with valid but incommensurable claims to truth. Religion, he argued, is connected to convictions about the world, both scientific and historical, that are subject to scientific investigation. Empirical science represented a challenge Christians could not duck. If Jesus did not exist, there is no Christianity.[24]

Lippmann agreed, dismissing modernist Protestants and citing Machen respectfully; without belief in the factuality of Christian revelation and its historical narrative, the values of Christian faith are lost. Educated men may hold to an attenuated faith in a Christian spirit or an abstract, immanent God, but the masses needed authoritative belief and signs of the truth of their religion. As certainty dissolved, so did their faith and so did the basis of values. A Platonist might be satisfied with God as an immaterial spirituality or a religion of the spirit, Fosdick might discourse on God as if he were a hypothesis and reject any notion of immortality as the persistence of a person's physical form, but the "worldling" expects immortality to mean the persistence of this life into perpetuity.[25]

The critic Joseph Wood Krutch echoed the theme in *The Modern Temper* (1929), articulating the anxieties of an unhappy modernist who is consigned to live without the glories and comforts of religious myths that had historically imbued human life with dignity. As science reduced man to an unexceptional element of the natural world, he took up residence, involuntarily, in the "universe of nature," having fallen from the more amenable "universe of illusions." Nature is impersonal, indifferent to men's needs and even ruthlessly inimical to his desires; in a purely naturalistic worldview, in which humans are merely a species of mammal, there is no tragedy and no romance, both of which assume an exalted notion of man as a being in the image of God. The modernist intellect, insistent on God's nonexistence and man's cosmic demotion, is at odds with human emotions. "What man knows is everywhere at war with what he wants," Krutch observed.[26]

The Tennessee poet John Crowe Ransom likewise echoed these complaints. A professor of English at Vanderbilt University in Nashville, Ransom had been part of a group of poets, including the students Allen Tate and Robert Penn Warren as well as his faculty colleague Donald Davidson, who briefly published a magazine called the *Fugitive*. By 1930, part of the group had refashioned themselves as social critics and published a noteworthy anti-industrialist and antimodern symposium, *I'll Take My Stand: The South and the Agrarian Tradition*, under the collective name Twelve Southerners. In the same year, Ransom, the son and grandson of Methodist ministers, published *God without Thunder: An Unorthodox Defense of Orthodoxy*. It was a somewhat paradoxical defense of traditional faith, as Ransom himself believed neither in religious revelation, the idea of an afterlife, or the divinity of Christ. Nevertheless, Ransom expressed a devotion to the God of orthodox faith and, like Machen, dismissed the God promulgated by modernist Christians as the fruit of a new religion founded upon "scientific naturalism" and reflecting the values of efficiency and amelioration. The new God of science was soft and, reflecting men's liberal predilections, "amiable and understandable"; a true God is by definition "supernatural," Ransom argued. "We wanted a God who wouldn't hurt us; who would let us understand him; who would agree to scrap all the wicked thunderbolts in his armament," Ransom wrote dismissively, attributing the popularity of the new God to human frailty. "And this is just the God that has developed popularly out of the Christ of the New Testament: the embodiment mostly of the principle of social benevolence and of physical welfare." Ransom called modern man to resist the new dispensation: "Let him restore to God the thunder."[27]

Above all, Ransom was concerned to repudiate a progressive faith in a rational, benevolent world. He challenged the notion that science was sufficient to explain the universe in its totality, arguing that it, too, employed mythological, or "super-sensible," concepts, whether general principles of power, force, or cause or the modern theories of evolution, the ether, or electromagnetic energy. Following David Hume and Immanuel Kant, he interpreted these as artifacts of language, metaphysical assumptions that have unduly received unwarranted allegiance. Science cannot explain evil in the world but a good Calvinist could: the God of the Old Testament and of orthodox faiths authorized evil as well as good. Evil exists, Ransom held, and the universe itself is indifferent to human wishes, inhumane, irrational, and unrighteous. This was the lesson of Job. Material wealth does not guarantee well-being, prosperity is not necessarily the reward for virtue, the world is not committed to human morality or humane purposes, and God cannot be held accountable by humans for his acts. While Ransom would dispense with the notion of the divinity of Christ, he would keep the teachings on Adam's fall, predestination, and the essential evil present in the world.[28]

Ransom reflected theological shifts occurring within Protestant liberalism and the rise of what came to be called "neo-orthodoxy," which drew on German theological trends. Gustav Krüger introduced American theologians to the German "crisis theology" of Karl Barth, Emil Brunner, Friedrich Gogarten, Eduard Thurneyse, Rudolf Bultmann, and occasionally Paul Tillich, a more realistic, biblically based alternative to a failing liberalism, in a lecture at Union Theological Seminary. It was a bracing theology at once pietistic, modern, and scripturally based and also featured a God distant from man and disdainful of his values. Barth's theology of crisis, according to Walter Lowrie, was an act of protest to the reigning religious ideals of the time, a ringing corrective to liberal theology and the human-centered assumptions upon which it was based. For crisis theologians, faith could not be founded on human experience, man is not inherently good, scripture does not give men a role in creating the Kingdom of God, and the kingdom is not equivalent to social reform, progress, civilization, or culture. Barth taught that faith was based on paradox and, Lowrie declared, "made us perceive that in every article of our creed—in our exaltation of religion, of Christian experience, of mysticism, of the kingdom of God as a social Utopia, and of Jesus as the ideal of humanity—we were not thinking of God but of man." The war had already forced liberals to rethink their faith in progress and irenic commitments: Is not peace selfish if one is unwilling to make sacrifices for justice? Even Fosdick felt the war to be a lesson in the persistence of moral evil in the world. The individual may be unselfish, but the collective is not and promulgates illusions that disguise this self-interest. The dynamic, young Protestant theologian Reinhold Niebuhr, the pastor of Bethel Evangelical Church in Detroit from 1915 to 1928 and thereafter on the faculty of Union Seminary, enthralled his audiences, particularly youthful ones, with impassioned attacks on both social injustice and the corrupted optimism of theological liberalism. He decried a liberalism that replaced God with the worship of science, placed undue emphasis on reason in human affairs, mistook physical comfort for happiness, and missed the evil that existed even in the good. "Humanism as well as religion has been engulfed in the naturalism of our day," he wrote in 1926. "Our obsession with the physical sciences and with the physical world has enthroned the brute and blind forces of nature, and we follow the God of the earthquake and the fire rather than the God of the still small voice." Niebuhr's Christ was a paradoxical Christ of "irrational truths." Life is tragic, he declared: "You can't be happy in an easy way."

The world is not really Christian; to be happy, one must be afflicted. "The gospel of Jesus is not a gospel of obvious success, but of ultimate success through obvious failure," Niebuhr preached, dismissing the virile business-man Christ of Bruce Barton's imagination.[29]

～

The Scopes trial was a crucial moment in this crisis of Protestant liberalism. Amid the welter of discussion about science and religion, democracy, and the authority of scholarly expertise sparked by the case, there was also evidence of the overriding social and cultural division generated by the modernist commitment to an open-minded and critical intellectual temperament. Beginning in 1921, William Jennings Bryan made antievolution a public movement premised on the majority's right to determine the curriculum in public schools; from January 1922 he pushed state lawmakers to ban the teaching of evolution in schools. At the end of a long and principled career in public life, antievolution was Bryan's last reform crusade. Three times the Democratic Party's candidate for president and a former secretary of state, Bryan was supporting himself through public speaking and writing (supplemented by fortunate investments in Florida real estate). He was a tireless lecturer, averaging about two hundred speeches per year for many years, and an ardent proponent of reform, backing successful drives for the direct election of senators, Prohibition, a national income tax, and women's suffrage. In his view and those of the fundamentalists who embraced him as a leader, evolution and specifically Darwin's theory of natural selection undercut religious faith, public morals, and the integrity of marriage, family, and home life.[30]

Bryan and others conflated Darwin's teachings with "social Darwinism," the broader antireformist philosophy that posited social development as necessarily a competition between the weak and the strong. Any government efforts to ameliorate inequality or social misery violated the laws of nature and justice. (Bryan knew the difference but ignored it.) Bryan linked Darwinism to other social trends he loathed: laissez-faire capitalism, class conflict, imperialism, militarism, and eugenics. Darwinism substitutes the law of hate for the law of love, he declared, and promotes war. In his view, a local majority has the right to enact laws regarding education. "The hand that writes the pay check rules the school," he was fond of saying. Over the course of the decade, legislators in twenty-one states proposed forty-five antievolution bills, including the statute passed by the Tennessee legislature in 1925, first proposed by a Primitive Baptist (and thus nonfundamentalist) state senator named John W. Butler, which made it a misdemeanor subject to a maximum fine of five hundred dollars for a public school teacher "to teach any theory that denies the story of the Divine Creation of man as taught in the Bible, and to teach instead that man had descended from a lower order of animal."[31]

Prominent academics, scientists, and commentators such as H. L. Mencken (who kibitzed with the Scopes defense team and issued lacerating dispatches from Dayton, antagonizing the locals) interpreted the law as a threat to science and intellectual freedom if not rationality itself. The debate quickly took on broader cultural meaning, as city-based cosmopolitans trained their fire on supposedly rustic fundamentalists mobilized in an anti-intellectual populist crusade. Traditional Protestant revivalism, averred David Starr Jordan, the distinguished evolutionary biologist and president of Stanford University, was "simply a form of drunkenness no more worthy of respect than the drunkenness that lies in the gutter!" President Nicholas Murray Butler of Columbia University declared, "The notion that a majority must have its way, whether in matters of opinion or in matters of personal conduct, is as pestilent and antidemocratic a notion as can possibly be conceived."[32]

Roger Baldwin and other officers of the American Civil Liberties Union (ACLU), which had grown out of the National Civil Liberties Bureau founded in 1917 to protect conscientious objectors and antiwar protesters, saw the antievolution statute as an issue of civil liberties and determined to defend the academic freedom of public school teachers and their students. They advertised for a teacher in Tennessee who would violate the state law and thus become a litigant in a case testing the constitutionality of the statute. Local town boosters, including the chair of the county school board and school superintendent, eager to gain some recognition for Dayton, recruited the easygoing science teacher John Scopes, even though it was unclear whether he had actually taught evolution, having only led study sessions for exams as a substitute in the advanced biology course. (Scopes had to coach his students on the testimony they delivered against him at trial.)[33]

As it happened, the town received plenty of attention, perhaps more than desired. When the ACLU retained the famed criminal defense lawyer and notable agnostic Clarence Darrow for the defense and the prosecution added Bryan himself to their team of lawyers, public interest soared. Upwards of 150 journalists arrived in town in the sweltering midsummer weeks of July 1925. The townspeople eagerly accommodated them, assembling a movie platform in the courtroom for newsreel producers (an airstrip was made so that planes could fly out the footage) and installing a new switchboard capable of handling one hundred phone calls. The Chicago radio station WGN broadcast the proceedings live. The town eagerly courted publicity in the best tradition

of 1920s ballyhoo, staging a mock fistfight between an opponent and a supporter of the law and preparing for the masses: they built a barbecue pit behind the courthouse; vendors sold soft drinks, hot dogs, and ice cream; circus
performers, musicians, and itinerant preachers performed on the streets and
in tent shows; and local storeowners and advertisers decorated their stores
with images of apes and monkeys. Despite the press coverage, the city boosters who hoped the "monkey trial" would attract up to thirty thousand visitors
tallied the final total at around five hundred.[34]

The public displayed a great curiosity about evolution during the controversy; public debates on the issue were popular. In one sense, the antievolution controversy pitted the proponents of science against those of religion;
this certainly was an angle developed by the national press, which tended to
exaggerate positions on either extreme. However, evolutionary theory was
well established by 1900 and had been incorporated into the textbooks. Many
devout Christians (not just liberal Protestants but also Catholics) accepted
evolution as the means of God's action in the world and embraced allegorical
interpretations of scriptures. Fundamentalists denied any hostility to science.
Rather they argued speculative hypotheses were a distortion of true science,
which they defined, following Francis Bacon, the sixteenth-century founder
of deductive science, as careful observation and classification of facts. In this
sense, they saw themselves as the defenders of true science.[35]

The ACLU lawyers saw the issue as academic freedom and the constitutionality of the Tennessee statute, arguing that the law was unconstitutional
because it established a narrow religious viewpoint in the public schools.
Further, they argued that the law barred only instruction in evolution that
denied the biblical account, and so they planned to introduce expert testimony from scientists and religion scholars to prove that evolution could be
compatible with biblically based religious faith. It was Darrow and Bryan who
engaged in remarkably personal attacks on each other's beliefs and actions
and wanted to make the trial a showdown between faith and reason. (Indeed,
from the beginning the ACLU was wary of Darrow, who volunteered his
services for the case, and tried to ease him off the defense team for both the
initial trial and the appeal.) Prosecutors for the state endeavored to keep the
trial focused on the public's right to control public education; the meaning
of evolution or whether it conflicted with the Bible was irrelevant. The public had clearly stated in law that the theory of evolution ran counter to the
Bible and could not be taught, and the issue ended there.[36] They successfully
pushed to exclude expert testimony. When the judge excluded the experts,
the trial was essentially over; he ruled for the prosecution and fined Scopes.

The confrontation between Darrow as cross-examiner and Bryan as an expert Bible witness occurred after the judge had ruled to exclude expert testimony and so was largely irrelevant and later ruled inadmissible. Darrow tested Bryan with a series of questions drawing on the long village-atheist tradition of biblical skepticism: How could a whale swallow a man? Where did Cain find his wife? How could morning follow evening in the Genesis account prior to the creation of the sun? How could Joshua lengthen the day by making the sun stand still? Although the local audience sided with Bryan as he fended off the questions by professing either a lack of interest or ignorance (Bryan did acknowledge his belief in the "day-age" theory of creation, meaning that he interpreted the days of the Genesis account of creation to be symbolic of long periods of time, a view not uncommon among fundamentalists), Bryan was shaken and the larger public was faced with the spectacle of a lay religious leader who led the fight against evolution displaying shockingly little knowledge of the Bible and even less curiosity. Bryan could not even define agnosticism.[37]

The Tennessee Supreme Court upheld the antievolution law on appeal but overturned Scopes's conviction on a technicality, thus frustrating the ACLU's ambition to appeal the case to federal courts. Two more states, Mississippi and Arkansas, passed antievolution statutes in 1926 and 1928 respectively and by the end of the decade, in states and localities where fundamentalism was strong (mostly in the South and some areas of the West), laws, administrative rulings, or school board actions effectively restricted the teaching of evolution. (John Scopes's sister Lela lost her job teaching math in Paducah, Kentucky, when she refused to repudiate her brother's position on the teaching of evolution.) Optimistic and enthusiastic in the wake of the trial, Bryan died within a few days of a cerebral hemorrhage; he had long faced chronic health problems. Deprived of its leader, the antievolution movement petered out. Fundamentalists, divided as always, nevertheless thrived in the long term, establishing Bible colleges, seminaries, conferences, and radio and later television ministries even as they retreated from overt public controversy. It was Protestant liberals who continued to lose cultural authority. Church attendance and the number of missionaries declined, Protestant ministers felt their status declining, the centrality of Protestantism to American culture and its dominance in American religious life waned, and the "neo-orthodoxy" informed by German crisis theology gained wider appeal.[38]

In 1928, in a small volume entitled *American Inquisitors*, Lippmann considered the problem public teachers, loyal first of all to the truth, faced from both fundamentalists and superpatriots. Anticipating his arguments in *Preface to Morals* and still engaged in the debates about democracy that had preoccupied him earlier in the decade, Lippmann perceived the conflict as one between those loyal to a "modern spirit" and those adhering to an older mentality. Lippmann understood the complaints of the religiously orthodox (as well as the superpatriot "Americanists") even as he disagreed with their viewpoint, as evident in his belief that the prosecution of public teachers amounted to a new inquisition. People want security and the new modernist, scientific spirit inculcated doubt: "An easy and tolerant skepticism is not for them. They want ideas which they can count upon, sure cures, absolute promises, and no shilly-shallying with a lot of ifs and perhapses. The faith of the people is always hard, practical, and definite."[39]

The fundamentalists were correct to see the teaching of evolution as undercutting the authority of the Bible and weakening faith. Science does represent a new religion of the elite, and it was premised on teaching the "inquiring state of mind." Modernism was the "belief that human reason has the last word," and it was incompatible with fundamentalism, which held that religious faith cannot be subject to verification by reason and science. "Reason and free inquiry can be neutral and tolerant only of those opinions which submit to the test of reason and free inquiry." Lippmann's small volume represented a significant marker in liberal intellectuals' embrace of a modernist identity. Lippmann accepted the term as descriptive of a broader intellectual worldview based on open-mindedness, provisional truth, science, tolerance, free inquiry, and the critical spirit. In this mind-set, Lippmann argued, "The child is not taught to believe. He is taught to doubt and to inquire, to guess, to experiment, and to verify."[40]

The emergence of this new, modernist spirit lay at the root of the humanist controversy that flared between 1928 and 1930. Ostensibly a literary affair, pitting traditionalists against realists, naturalists, and modernists, the conflict sparked a large outpouring of commentary. It was a final rehearsal of the decade's many fraught contests over culture and the role of intellectuals, a secular analogue to the modernist-fundamentalist controversy, as it pitted partisans of two diametrically opposed outlooks, conservative and modernist, in a battle for what each side conceived of as the intellectual soul of the nation. Like the public fights over fundamentalism and evolution, it subsided with liberal modernists seemingly victorious; yet, as in the former controversy, the conservative principles articulated proved long lasting.

In Western thought, the term *humanism* refers to the Renaissance recovery of the secular learning of the pagan Greek philosophers, especially Plato. The scholarly adepts who pursued this kind of learning, founded on knowledge of ancient languages and close study of texts, were the humanists. They stood against the medieval Scholastics, bent on using Aristotelian philosophy to reconcile faith and reason. They hailed the powers of reason and aimed to instill a well-rounded character in their pupils, establishing a pedagogy based on the broad study of art, history, poetry, morals, the sciences, manners, and the classical texts. From the nineteenth century, "humanist" was the label attached to an education centered on classical literature and history.[41] In this literal sense, Irving Babbitt and Paul Elmer More were, professionally, humanists.

Born within a year of each other in the Midwest (Babbitt in Dayton, Ohio, in 1865; More in St. Louis in 1864), both men distinguished themselves in the study of ancient languages and culture but fit only uncomfortably in academia. Babbitt studied Greek and became an Orientalist at Harvard, enamored in particular of Buddhism. He completed only a master's degree but, after a few years teaching in Montana and then at Williams College, returned to Harvard to teach in 1894. He was a dynamic and successful teacher, having as students Van Wyck Brooks, Lippmann (who was critical of his stance even as an undergraduate), T. S. Eliot, Stuart Sherman, and Norman Foerster (the latter two of whom became prominent English professors allied with his "new humanist" cause). Babbitt developed his distinctive conservative cultural criticism in various volumes, most notably *Rousseau and Romanticism* (1919).

More earned a bachelor's and master's degree from Washington University in St. Louis and taught in a prep school before entering Harvard to study Sanskrit. He and Babbitt became friends, but More left academia in 1897 and spent the years between 1901 and 1914 as a literary editor at such journals as the *Nation* and *New York Evening Post*. He retired from this life in 1914, lecturing occasionally at Princeton University and splitting his time between Princeton and a cottage in Shelburne, New Hampshire. He collected his essays in a series of volumes that he entitled the Shelburne Essays between 1904 and 1921. He went on to publish a multivolume history of Greek thought and early Christian teaching.[42]

Babbitt and More differed in important ways from each other, as they did from followers, such as Sherman and Foerster. At the root of the new humanism they advocated was an assertion of discipline and tradition. The humanists attributed broad social and political change to particular ideas, even particular philosophers. Babbitt and More articulated the essentials of their program of cultural criticism, educational theory, and social and political philosophy before the 1920s, but the zeitgeist seized upon them in 1928 and a flurry of publicity followed. In 1930, dueling symposia appeared, *Humanism and America: Essays on the Outlook of Modern Civilisation*, edited by Foerster, and *The Critique of Humanism: A Symposium*, edited by C. Hartley Grattan.[43]

The humanists propounded the importance of self-discipline, self-control, and balance. "The characteristic evils of the present age arise from unrestraint and violation of the law of measure and not, as our modernists would have us believe, from the tyranny of taboos and traditional inhibitions," argued Babbitt. He promoted the "law of measure" by which men and women could obtain a harmonious development of all their faculties. "Nothing too much" was the dictum. Babbitt identified the balance between what is variable and what is permanent in human nature as "decorum." The more unusual premise of their work had to do with the faculty in humans that allowed such balance to be retained. The humanists returned repeatedly to the notion of an "inner check," in More's phrase, or "higher will" or *"frein vital"* (vital control or the will to refrain), in Babbitt's work. Despite the essentially secular grounding of humanism, they insisted that their distinctions between a higher and lower, or human and animal self, reflected a dualistic as opposed to monistic conception of reality. The inner check, or will to refrain, originated in some dimension of being beyond the physical, a nonmaterial level in which free will was possible, or from which it was endowed, that was not accessible to lower animals. Or, formulated alternately, one part of man was flux, the other—in which the higher will resided—was unchanging. The will to refrain, Babbitt argued, "is specifically human in man and ultimately divine."[44]

The humanists presented themselves as resisting the drift of the times, standing against a set of defective modern ideas—whether identified as "naturism" or "modernism" or "humanitarianism" or "rationalism"—that fed a soft-hearted, sentimental, and utilitarian individualism. Babbitt consistently traced the root of these ideas to the French philosopher Jean-Jacques Rousseau, to whom he attributed the self-indulgent characteristics of Romanticism and a flawed belief in the natural goodness of humankind. "Against those who reduce man to a chaos of sensations and instincts and desires checking and counter-checking one another in endlessly shifting patterns, the humanist points to a separate faculty of inhibition, the inner check or the *frein vital*, whereby these expansive impulses may be kept within bounds and ordered to a design not of their making," More declared. The humanists stand, too, he argued, against those who would exonerate human failings by declaring that the individual bears no responsibility for his character and is, rather, by nature morally good before being deformed by society.[45]

Although humanism was ostensibly a secular philosophy, the humanists opposed many of the same trends in modern intellectual life, such as the dominance of a scientific and naturalist point of view, that conservative

Christians and fundamentalists did. The debate over humanism was, in many ways, a secularist echo of the earlier fundamentalist-modernist debates, and the humanists could be decidedly ambiguous in the face of pointed complaints about their lack of religious faith. In 1928, T. S. Eliot challenged his former teacher Babbitt for the absence of religious doctrine in his philosophy. An expatriate in England, Eliot was a major figure in English letters, having published *The Waste Land* (1922), the supreme modernist treatment of modern spiritual desiccation, and established the *Criterion*, an influential literary magazine. In 1929, he would declare himself a "classicist in literature, royalist in politics, and anglo-catholic in religion." He took Babbitt to task for making humanism an alternative to religion. In Eliot's view, it was religion, not humanism, that held most promise for restoring a traditional society. "We must use our heredity, instead of denying it," he argued. "The religious habits of the race are still very strong, in all places, at all times, and for all people. There is no humanistic habit: humanism is, I think, merely the state of mind of a few persons in a few places at a few times." Humanism provides a needed critical perspective on religion, he allowed in his contribution to the humanist symposium, but humanism was futile without religion. Only dogmatic religion provided the "discipline" the humanists valued.[46]

The poet Allen Tate agreed, declaring that only religion could validate the values the humanists claimed to reverence. Norman Foerster explicitly denied that humanism was a religion, suggesting it was an appropriate alternative to religious belief, but Babbitt was considerably more flexible, arguing the compatibility and common cause of humanists and Christians, aligning the "religious-humanistic" against the "utilitarian-sentimental." If forced to choose between naturalism and supernaturalism, he declared his choice would be for the latter. More claimed that only religion could provide purpose and values; indeed, from 1917 onwards, he had been moving toward an explicit religious viewpoint. "In this world we have no abiding city; he who thinks to find peace in this mortal life is pursuing a phantom more elusive than the winds," More wrote. "It may be possible to achieve a kind of simulacrum of happiness by a dull or bovine acquiescence in things as they are, or by an indefatigable activity that leaves no time for reflection, or even by a cunningly managed pursuit of worldly pleasures; but such a state is precarious always, and at the best devoid of the 'high seriousness' . . . demanded by a genuine humanism."[47]

The revival of Babbitt and More's humanism at the end of the 1920s touched a nerve among a wide range of intellectuals, many of whom were aroused to sarcastic and scathing dismissals of their thought. Modernist liberals envisioned a final assault from the forces of Puritanism and Victorian conservatism. Alfred Kazin remembered them in *On Native Grounds* as a "violent counter-reformation against modern literature and thought." The editors of the *New Republic* depicted them, flippantly, as "clansmen" bringing the "flaming cross" to their academic outposts.[48]

Critics accused them, on the one hand, of simply upholding moderation and self-discipline, values with which few would disagree—"platitudes which my iceman, cigar dealer, grocer, butcher, bootlegger, garbage man and druggist already know: i.e., that it is best to keep temperate and thrifty, not to let your temper run away with you, not to make a nuisance of yourself, not to get up in the air over trifles, to see that your family gets properly fed and clothed, to pay your bills and not violate the laws," Burton Rascoe observed. "But what is new or Humanistic about that?" On the other hand, the humanists seemed simply to assert their own prejudices as true, unwilling to provide any further justification for their judgments (which were often sweepingly negative on modern literature) beyond their own authority. Katharine Fullerton Gerould felt little distinguished Babbitt and More from the callow young hedonist indulging a habit for nightclubs: they all "have decided what gives them most pleasure." More and Babbitt, "by accident of breeding, education, mental equipment," preferred reading Plato and "cursing Rousseau" to "drinking bootleg gin or clasping meretricious graces in their arms." However, "we must not be tricked into believing too wistfully," she concluded, that Babbitt and More "are wearing themselves out, like the great saints, in exercising that famous 'inner check.'"[49]

Edmund Wilson had no sympathy with the humanist project. In Wilson's view, the belief in God or any supernatural absolutes was no longer tenable for educated people. The humanism of Babbitt and More was unconvincing and even offensive. Wilson castigated Babbitt and More for the lack of passion and life in their work, marked as it was by incessant injunctions to self-discipline and the "will to refrain." "As if humanity were not, now as always, as much in need of being exhorted against coldness and indifference and routine as against irresponsible exuberance—especially Anglo-Saxon humanity," Wilson exclaimed. "As if it were not obvious that Boston and New York, Manchester and London, were not suffering rather from a lack of normal human fellowship and normal human hope and joy than from any demoralizing effects of unbridled 'humanitarian' sympathies, indiscriminate emotional 'expansiveness' or universal orgiastic dissipation—as if our clerks, our factory workers and our respectable professional and business classes were all in danger of falling victims to the rhapsodical enthusiasm and the lawless individualism of romanticism!"[50]

Henry Seidel Canby, a sympathetic but tough critic, found the humanist program overly negative: "It is a very porcupine hunched up against our familiar world." The humanists, many argued, were attempting to revive a way of thinking no longer suited for the world; they were men of the past, declaiming against modernity in safe and irrelevant academic outposts and self-consciously aligned with the existing order. Babbitt clearly articulated his skepticism about democracy, and More declared: "To the civilized man, *the rights of property are more important than the right to life.*" Lippmann expressed careful respect for More's achievements but dismissed Babbitt as a propagandist, recalling his days as one of his students at Harvard. "He is saying today what he was saying twenty years ago; he has multiplied his citations but he has not, so far as I can see, enlarged or deepened his insight." Linking the humanists to the Scopes trial, Lippmann accused them of being afraid to submit their values to scientific study despite the fact that science serves only truth. Their principles were untested by science and irrelevant to modern society. "I do not wish to lay too much stress on the analogy, but it is perhaps not unfair to say that the humanism of Aristotle is to the humanism which modern men will need, if they are to live by it, about what the atomism of Democritus is to the atomism of the modern physicist." According to Henry Hazlitt in the *Nation*: "They are trying to revive an outworn and discredited metaphysics." In his caustic address on American literature delivered upon accepting the Nobel Prize in Literature in 1930, Sinclair Lewis heaped special scorn upon the humanists, commenting sarcastically on their exclusive resort to ancient Greece for moral values and models of heroic action: "Oedipus is a tragic figure for the New Humanists; man, trying to maintain himself as the image of God under the pressure of dynamos, in a world of high pressure salesmanship, is not," he observed. To Lewis, the message amounted to the "not particularly novel doctrine that both art and life must be resigned and negative," a doctrine, he declared, "of the blackest reaction introduced into a stirringly revolutionary world."[51]

Lewis's characterization represents well the tempest the humanists stirred and the deep and angry reaction they sparked. The issue was not really modern art or literature, Canby observed: "It was the temper, the ethics, and the philosophy of living of the present age." Babbitt and More represented the party of order to younger critics, now self-consciously identifying themselves as modernists. They might as easily have been on the same side, were all parties to agree that it was the rationalizing of the "business civilization" that most threatened humane values in modern life. The new humanists derided rationalists, naturists, and humanitarians for self-indulgent individualism, but ignored the depredations of business.[52] Instead, the conservatives became "humanists"; their rivals, the "modernists." By 1930, all of the elements of the twentieth-century conservative movement were in place: a probusiness philosophy of minimal taxation and limited government, embodied in the administrations of presidents Coolidge and Harding and the policies of Treasury Secretary Andrew Mellon; a right-wing and middle-American populism, taking form in the Ku Klux Klan; fundamentalist evangelicalism; and, with the humanists, a traditionalist intellectual wing. Thus, while liberal and radical humanists inveighed against the American business civilization and the middlebrow culture of the Chautauqua, conservative humanists complained about sentimentalism, debased cultural standards, and hedonistic self-indulgence.

C. Hartley Grattan, editor of the antihumanist symposium, and Canby both affirmed their desire to find a "true humanism," and more than one critic accused the new humanists of stealing a term that maintained a broader allegiance. "A small clique of the self-anointed have arrogated to themselves a name that stood, in the fifteenth century, for a genuinely liberating attitude, and degraded it to a synonym for a hide-bound academicism," Hazlitt observed angrily. "The whole doctrine has become little more than a rationalization of neophobia and a piece of special pleading for the genteel tradition." Lewis Mumford declared new humanism to be "pseudo-Humanism." A true, organic humanism would provide "positive channels of effort, dignified tasks, fine and significant actions, and quiet states of beatitude, which by their very pursuit or enjoyment provide, incidentally, such checks and restrictions as may be necessary to their success." Mumford presented himself as a critic of both the new humanism and what he styled the "New Mechanism," the utilitarian and practical spirit that he associated with John Dewey and Charles Beard, which he believed subordinated human needs to material progress and endorsed the division of man from nature. He called for a "modern synthesis" or "modern ideology" to redress the flaws of the "two definite philosophies" (humanism and mechanism) he judged inadequate. John Dewey found the rationale for calling the movement "humanism" obscure and argued that a true humanism would embrace the natural sciences and the technologies humans have produced. "A humanism that flees from science as an enemy denies the means by which a liberal humanism might become a reality."[53]

"The burden of all sensible critiques of modern society must be against its economic structure," Grattan declared. Malcolm Cowley agreed, chiding the humanists for ignoring the social and economic realities of America, which continued to overproduce goods, foster inequality, standardize the work lives of industrial laborers, and consistently maintain high unemployment and misery. The humanists, he declared, had "produced the lamest utopia ever imagined." The "Chicago beer barons," he observed, "would continue to seek their fortunes and slaughter their rivals, revealing once more a deplorable ignorance of the Inner Check; the students in the new humanist university, after the two o'clock lecture on Plato, would spend an hour at the talkies with the It Girl—and meanwhile, because of a few thousand humanists, our society, our government, our arts, would be genuinely and ideally humanistic." Summarizing a decade of cultural criticism, Canby identified the sacrifice of quality to quantity and the ubiquity of "cheap comforts and cheap thinking" as the fruits of industrial progress. "Never have leisure, thought, the sense of beauty, and even pure physical enjoyment been so subordinated to the business of stimulating material wants and creating the goods to satisfy them." Nevertheless, the benefits of technology and "mechanism" cannot be denied. What is needed is a humanism that will tackle the realities of a machine civilization, one that will "ride" them rather than pretend they do not exist. What is needed is "humanism, not a cult, not a refusal of life as it is in favor of life as it is deduced from books."[54]

A similar criticism of humanism in this vein came from the circle of southern intellectuals, soon to be known as the southern agrarians, around John Crowe Ransom. *I'll Take My Stand*, steeped, unlike Canby's critique, in a rhetorical refusal of the machine age, was nevertheless the same in spirit. *I'll Take My Stand* was an extended defense of the values, customs, and way of life of small-town and rural life, posited as an alternative to, and indictment of, industrial society. There were elements of southern defensiveness and special pleading in the volume (Ransom declared that the southerner's goal was to be "reconstructed but unregenerate"), but the definition of their program in terms of the opposition of agrarian and industrial orders was very much an effort to recognize that preferred cultural values were grounded in a way of life dictated by economic decisions. The agrarians were both deeply conservative and, by contrast with the Humanists, quite radical. "It is strange, of course, that a majority of men anywhere could ever as with one mind become enamored of industrialism: a system that has so little regard for individual wants," they declared in their introductory "Statement of Principles." "If a community, or a section, or a race, or an age, is groaning under industrialism, and well aware that it is an evil dispensation, it must find the way to throw it off," they asserted. "To think that this cannot be done is pusillanimous."[55]

Modern society, focused on mass production and mass consumption, degraded the quality of labor and exhausted the laborers; individuals lost sight of the ends of social life as they rushed through a daily routine whose tempo continuously increased. Rehearsing the cultural criticism of the Young Intellectuals, Ransom argued that the American pioneering impulse worked against the settled, "establishment" culture of the South, which was otherwise rich in the "social arts" of dress, conversation, manners, the table, oratory. "The South took life easy, which is itself a tolerably comprehensive art," he wrote. In modern civilization, art was relegated to museums ("What is a picture for, if not to put on one's wall?" asked Davidson) and music commercialized ("Throw out the radio and take down the fiddle from the wall," urged Andrew Nelson Lytle).[56]

While preparing the volume, one of the organizers had been approached at a writers' retreat by Gorham Munson, who had become a convert to humanism and proposed that the southerners and the humanists join forces. The southerners spurned the offer, believing the humanist program inadequate, both in religious terms (Allen Tate was prominently associated with this argument) and material. In a favorite turn of phrase, the agrarians argued that cultural change cannot come from above, from indoctrination in the arts and humanities at college. "The trouble with the life-pattern is to be located at its economic base, and we cannot rebuild it by pouring in soft materials from the top." Social values, religion, and economic structure were inextricably linked, a belief captured in a phrase of Tate's: "The social structure depends on the economic structure, and economic conviction is the secular image of religion." Or as Davidson stated in a review of the humanist symposium, "A movement of reform must begin at the base of our life—that is, with its economic base. And the humanists have practically nothing to say on the subject of economics."[57]

The emerging modernist liberal intellectuals may have had some sympathy with the ambitions and complaints of the humanists, but they found their beliefs untenable if not unintelligible. The humanists confronted the profound force of modern change, what the critic Stark Young in *I'll Take My Stand* called the god of "Mutability," but could only preach to deracinated moderns the imperative of discipline and restraint, the need to check their desires in the name of values and ideals in which many modern Americans had lost faith. The "acids of modernity," in Lippmann's phrase, had burned away much of the old order, and new values, new institutions must be created. To Lippmann, the answer lay in the critical mind, free and open and honest inquiry into the realities of man and the universe. Herein lay the "modern spirit," and it rested on science and a repudiation of any notion that there exists "a supernatural kingdom from which ultimately all laws, all judgments, all rewards, all punishments, and all compensations are derived." Humans must turn toward a "humanism" that would define a system of morals—what is right and good, what conduces to happiness—grounded in human experience, rationally intelligible, and functioning by consent among humans, not the command of an otherworldly king. Lippmann believed that a cultivated disinterestedness, or stoic reserve, an acceptance of the world as it is and not as we would have it (his own version of the lesson of Job), will generate the values we need: courage, veracity, faithfulness, honor, love, magnanimity, justice, and temperance. Disinterested and realist experts—competent civil servants, jurists, statesmen, professional managers, and above all scientists— embodied the kind of character he admired. Humanism requires the ethic of the pure researcher; "pure science is high religion incarnate."[58]

Joseph Wood Krutch arrived at no such optimistic faith. Rather, *The Modern Temper* was a lamentation for the destructive effects of science and the loss of religious faith on the humanist project. Like the new humanists, Krutch held to the conviction that the essentially human was whatever within or about man separated him from animals (or the simply natural). Whereas Lippmann and John Dewey saw science as the heart of recon-structed liberal humanism, Krutch felt science reduced humans to the merely natural. Artifacts of the mind that defined humanism, such as intelligence, individualism, and sensibility, when conceived of as ends in themselves and not instrumentally, worked at cross purposes with nature. Nature had no use for art, love, romance; the higher one's mental organization, the more cultivated, the more vulnerable one is and the less suited for survival in a Darwinist universe. Human values and even the cultivation of sensibility itself are maladaptive, as a Darwinian would say: they make a person's situ-ation more precarious. To become human, in Krutch's way of thinking, was to court disaster.[59]

Krutch based his argument on another crucial premise of modernist liberalism, even as he remained pessimistic about the conditions of mod-ern society. The premise became clear in his discussion of love. In nature, sexual intercourse exists for the purpose of procreation and survival of the species. Animals handle it efficiently, and primitives treat it practically. But the cultivated human enshrouds the animal act of sex in layers of romance, making it about the high ideal of love, and thus ennobling it. Like chivalry, glory, or nobility, humans make the necessities of animal life meaningful, significant, even beautiful by shrouding them in illusion. In Krutch's conservative view, new ideas on "free love" destroyed love by emphasizing the physiological act and consequently downgrading it as an ideal. More generally, critical analysis destroyed illusions; the price of rationality, the lifting of the "veil of mystery," is the loss of illusions, but this entailed not emancipation in Krutch's view, but rather the loss of love, tragedy, and God in human life.[60]

Krutch's discussion of cultural values as "illusions" that humans create but do not apprehend in strictly rational ways reflected a modernist emphasis on symbols, images, and myths as the language of culture and value. Edmund Wilson rooted avant-garde literature in the work of the French symbolists and their particular unconventional use of symbols. Lewis Mumford based his critical theory on an analysis of the use and interaction of symbolic forms and language. "Man's ability to repeat and modify and pattern valuable experiences," he observed, "is achieved, chiefly, through the aid of symbols; and this is what releases him from the blind habit or even blinder chaos."[61]

This particular analysis of culture as myth and symbol became one way in which modernist liberals resolved the cultural crisis of the 1920s. They no longer conceptualized culture as a project to cultivate society's leaders but rather as a description of the accreted customs and habits of a people. Modernist intellectuals realized their inability to be pedagogues for the American masses, but they could be the analysts of symbols, myths, and images, and perhaps the creators of new ones. Such assumptions lay behind Ransom's analysis of the Old Testament God of thunder. Such a God was mythical, Ransom frankly admitted, but myths constituted religion. "Religion is the system of myths which gives a working definition of the relation of man to nature," he declared. Myths, ritual, and scripture constitute a religion, which determines a political economy, which, in turn, defines a community's sense of the relation of humans to the universe. The time is past, Ransom believed, when religious leaders can restore an appreciation of myth and the supernatural through preaching and claims of authority. Rather, the myth must be "defined for the modern unbeliever in terms of its psychic necessity—by a sort of natural history of supernaturalism."[62]

Malcolm Cowley thought in similar terms. "The world about us was alien in the beginning; vast portions of it are alien to us to-day. Before man can feel at ease in any milieu, whether that of forest, plain or city, he must transform the natural shapes about him by infusing them with myth," Cowley argued. He knew certain streets in New York City by a fragment of a ragtime song; a Charles Sheeler image of the telephone remained imprinted indelibly on his mind; he could not think of a New England village except through the lens provided by Hawthorne. "I might say that this creation of myth, by whatever name we call it, has continued since the earliest times; that it is, indeed, a necessity of the human mind. It is a sort of digestive process, one that transforms the inanimate world about us into food without which the imagination would starve."[63]

Cowley's generation became adept at creating and maintaining myths and images that held cultural power and represented to Americans their relation to the world. Chief among them was the carefully constructed image of the spiritual rebel, the voluntary exile from the meretricious mainstream, the intellectual forced to abandon philistine America for the freedom to create modernist literature. The expatriate legend became central to the cultural authority of this initial generation of American modernist writers. Ernest Hemingway's fictional world offered no possibility of a unifying Culture that could effectively instill an inner check. The overarching, civilizing force of culture was that which the men and women of Hemingway's generation had "lost," as is evident in the full statement of the Gertrude Stein epigraph that prefaced *The Sun Also Rises*. According to Stein, the phrase "lost generation" was a hotelkeeper's description of the war generation. "He said that every man becomes civilized between the ages of eighteen and twenty-five," she remembered. "If he does not go through a civilizing experience at that time in his life he will not be a civilized man. And the men who went to the war at eighteen missed the period of civilizing, and they could never be civilized. They were a lost generation. Naturally if they are at war they do not have the influences of women of parents and of preparation."[64]

It was in the 1920s that critics and intellectuals crafted a discourse relentlessly focused on individual autonomy and collective cultural self-rule, which resulted, in the succeeding decades, in the fear of conformity and totalitarianism becoming essential leitmotifs of American social thought.[65] The result was a characteristic mid-twentieth-century intellectual ambivalence—one defined by an uncomfortable realization of one's own marginality and yet a faith in the power of culture.

Culture marked the gap of knowledge and values—one that modernist liberals felt could be alleviated through training in making choices and the adoption of cultural myths and symbols that reinforced individual freedom and autonomy. To modernist liberals, the gap lay between those immured in orthodoxy and those willing to be critical-minded, to repudiate the "conspiracy of silence," to face the facts and not engage in genteel obfuscation, to be open-minded and not intolerant. It is in this way that a schism between highbrow and lowbrow, modernist and traditionalist, liberal elite and plain people emerged, only growing greater in the decades following the 1920s. The critical concerns of the 1920s—conformity, intolerance, materialism, mass culture, propaganda, cultural repression, censorship—and the liberal values proffered in response—sexual equality, free expression, personal fulfillment, pluralism, tolerance, critical inquiry, scientific rationality, and open-mindedness—came to define the next forty years of American intellectual life.

The 1920s intellectuals' intense focus on cultural criticism, often premised on an assumption of a shared "American" experience, spurred the creation of the academic field of American Studies, which developed in the 1930s. The first course, "American Thought and Civilization," was offered at Yale University in 1931. There was an American mind, early students of American studies presumed, and it could be approached through the close analysis of works of American cultural production—texts and images.[66] In social thought, these intellectuals instigated a body of work focused on culture and social organization, insistent on analyzing patterns of culture, the interaction of personality and culture, the deep ways in which civilization and psychosocial structures interrelate to produce conformity or rebellion. The outlook was distinctively postcapitalist in bent, rooted in the conviction that a "new age in social organization, for good or ill, had just dawned or was in the offing."[67]

Politically, modernist liberals were given to elitism and a penchant for centralization and planning. The result was a gaping vulnerability to populist resentment. By the 1950s, a conservative movement emerged that defended both a quasi-aristocratic notion of order and the authority of wealthy capitalists and at the same time presented itself as an anti-elitist attack on a technocratic elite. For the generation that had led the nation into the "American Century" of post–World War II power and influence, the decade of the 1920s was the time of their youth and the 1970s marked the end of their era: As the liberal consensus collapsed and the American economy faltered, the cultural authority of modernist liberals dissipated as well. The gap between the mid-century intellectual elite and the public now seemed generational as well as one of values, outlook, interests, and concerns. The public mind was fractured, with a diversity of radical and conservative positions articulated. A full panoply of dissident voices burst forth on the left, lacerating the older generation with the cruelest of blows—dismissal or simple indifference. By the 1970s, neoconservatives could lambaste liberalism as the preferred credo of a technocratic "new class" even as radicals dismissed liberals as corporate apologists. As the era of the liberal modernists drew to a close, the bifurcation of American society that so consumed them in the 1920s became a means to undercut their remaining authority.

~

Chronology

1919   Ratification of the Eighteenth Amendment, which prohibited the manufacture, sale, and transport of intoxicating liquors within the United States. Beginning of "Red Scare," an aggressive push by the Justice Department under Attorney General A. Mitchell Palmer to investigate and detain alleged radicals. More than four million workers participate in strikes, including national strikes in the coal and steel industry, a Boston Police strike, and a general strike in Seattle. A series of bombings occur targeting public officials, including Attorney General Palmer. Baptist minister William Bell Riley leads conservative Christians in establishing the World's Christian Fundamentals Association, May. Major outbreaks of racial violence, including a riot in Chicago, occur in late July and early August. President Woodrow Wilson suffers a severe stroke after campaigning for passage of the Treaty of Versailles, which he had helped negotiate at the Paris Peace Conference, October. Deportation of 249 suspected immigrant radicals, including Emma Goldman and Alexander Berkman, December.

1920   Under the direction of Attorney General A. Mitchell Palmer, the Justice Department, with assistance from deputized citizens and local police, detains more than three thousand suspected radicals in thirty cities (the "Palmer Raids"), January 2–3. The Senate fails to ratify the Treaty of Versailles. Establishment of first broadcast radio station in the United States (KDKA in Pittsburgh). Arrest of Nicola Sacco and Bartolomeo Vanzetti for the murder of two men in a payroll robbery in South Braintree, Massachusetts, May 3. Vaudeville singer Mamie Smith's recording of "Crazy Blues" sells 75,000 records in the first month and one million by the end of one year. The Baptist editor Curtis Lee Laws coins the term *fundamentalists* to refer to those willing "to do battle royal for the Fundamentals" in 1920. Ratification of the Nineteenth Amendment, which declared that the right of citizens to vote shall not be denied on account of sex. F. Scott Fitzgerald's *This Side of Paradise* and Sinclair Lewis's *Main Street* are published.

1921   Opening of *Shuffle Along* by Noble Sissle and Eubie Blake, the first Broadway musical acted, directed, and written by African Americans. Trial and conviction of Sacco and Vanzetti for the South Braintree crimes and beginning of their long series of appeals. Harold Loeb begins publishing *Broom* (1921–1924), an outlet for contemporary art and literature from the United States and Europe. Congress passes the Emergency Immigration Act of 1921, limiting immigration to the United States through the imposition of national quotas. Race riot in Tulsa, Oklahoma, leaving thirty-five African Americans dead. Charlie Chaplin releases *The Kid*.

1922   Harold Stearns edits the anthology *Civilization and the United States*, a caustic appraisal of America by younger intellectuals and a landmark in the emergence of a new cultural criticism; Gorham Munson begins publishing *Secession* (1922–1924) to promote younger writers. T. S. Eliot's "The Waste Land" appears in the *Dial*, November. Sinclair Lewis publishes *Babbitt*, the title of which becomes a byword for empty-headed American conformists.

1923   Jamaica-born black nationalist leader Marcus Garvey is convicted of charges of mail fraud, for which he was later deported from the United States. Equal Rights Amendment proposed in Congress for the first time. In Atlanta, Georgia, Ralph Peer records Fiddlin' John Carson, who became one of the first major country music star performers. Release of *The Covered Wagon*, directed by James Cruze, the first epic film western. Jean Toomer publishes *Cane*. James P. Johnson's "The Charleston" becomes a hit song and the music for a dance featuring the fast kicking of both feet, forward and backward, which becomes a craze. Another major hit: Frank Silver and Irving Cohn's "Yes! We Have No Bananas."

1924   H. L. Mencken and George Jean Nathan begin publishing the magazine *American Mercury*, which became an outlet for acerbic commentary and a favorite on campuses across the nation. Congress passes the National Origins Act (or Johnson-Reed Act) permanently establishing national immigration quotas determined by the national origins of the current American population. Mary Parker Follett publishes *Creative Experience*. Beginning of pioneering experiments in industrial psychology and workplace productivity at the Hawthorne Works of the Western Electric Company on Chicago's west side. Paul Whiteman mounts a concert featuring his white jazz orchestra, which played lightly syncopated jazz dance music, at Aeolian Hall in New York, in a bid for respectability and to celebrate the achievements of jazz musicians, capped with the premiere of George Gershwin's *Rhapsody in Blue*. Gilbert Seldes's appreciative assessment of popular culture, *The Seven Lively Arts*, appears.

1925 F. Scott Fitzgerald publishes *The Great Gatsby*, to modest success. Alain Locke publishes *The New Negro* (1925), an anthology on African American social and cultural life. The arrest of Indiana Grand Dragon D. C. Stephenson for kidnapping, rape, and second-degree murder, an event marking the declining influence of the Ku Klux Klan. Trial of John T. Scopes in Dayton, Tennessee, for violating state law prohibiting the teaching of evolution in Tennessee public schools, July 10–21. Charlie Chaplin releases *The Gold Rush*.

1926 Sophie Tucker's song "Some of These Days" becomes a popular record and her signature song. Appearance of the *New Masses* (1926–1948), a leftist journal of opinion. Wallace Thurman edits the sole issue to appear of the magazine *Fire!!*, an outlet for younger and more militant voices of the Harlem Renaissance. Ernest Hemingway publishes *The Sun Also Rises*, containing the following quotation from Gertrude Stein as an epigraph: "You are all a lost generation."

1927 Henry Ford closes his production line and stops production of the Model T to retool for a new model, the Model A, which was revealed later in the year. Charles A. Lindbergh completes the first solo, nonstop flight across the Atlantic Ocean in the *Spirit of St. Louis*, May 20–21. Report of the Lowell Committee, established to review the trial of Sacco and Vanzetti, concluding both men are guilty, July 27. Ralph Peer supervises the Bristol sessions, field recordings of unknown musicians in the small town of Bristol on the Tennessee-Virginia border, including the Carter Family and Jimmie Rodgers, July and August. Execution of Sacco and Vanzetti in the face of worldwide protests, August 23. Release of *The Jazz Singer* featuring Al Jolson, a mostly silent feature film that included some portions with sound. F. W. Murnau's expressionist film *Sunrise* released, an artistic peak for silent film, just as "talkies" were coming to be seen as the future of cinema.

1928   Election of Herbert Hoover, a devotee of planning and social science research, to the presidency, defeating Al Smith, the first Roman Catholic to be nominated for president on a major party ticket. Signing of the Kellogg-Briand Pact outlawing war as "instrument of national policy" by the United States. Awarding of the first Academy Awards by the Academy of Motion Picture Arts and Sciences, honoring films released in 1927 and 1928; a World War I war movie, *Wings*, released in 1927, won the first award for Best Picture. Release of King Vidor's film *The Crowd*.

1929   Point-blank murder of seven men, five associated with Bugs Moran's criminal gang, by men they believed to be police officers but who in fact were associates of Al Capone, an event that became known as the St. Valentine Day Massacre, February 14. William Faulkner's *The Sound and the Fury* and Thomas Wolfe's *Look Homeward, Angel* appear, landmarks in the renaissance of southern literature. Robert L. Ripley's *Believe It or Not*, based on a comic strip, becomes a best seller. Ernest Hemingway publishes *A Farewell to Arms*. Walter Lippmann's *A Preface to Morals* and Joseph Wood Krutch's *The Modern Temper* appear, both meditations on the contemporary crisis of values. Robert S. Lynd and Helen Merrell Lynd publish *Middletown*, a classic work of social criticism in the form of a study of an average, small American city—the nonaverage Muncie, Indiana. "Black Thursday," beginning of stock market collapse, October 24, 1929. "Black Tuesday," value of stocks plummeted $14 billion; at many points in the day, no buyers could be found for some stocks at any price, October 29.

1930   Hart Crane publishes his epic poem *The Bridge*. Appearance of dueling symposia, *Humanism and America: Essays on the Outlook of Modern Civilisation*, edited by Norman Foerster, and *The Critique of Humanism: A Symposium*, edited by C. Hartley Grattan, capping off an intense literary controversy over the new humanism. The Twelve Southerners publish *I'll Take My Stand: The South and the Agrarian Tradition*. Sinclair Lewis becomes the first American to win the Nobel Prize in Literature.

1931   Frederick Lewis Allen publishes *Only Yesterday: An Informal History of the 1920s*.

1932   Suicide of Hart Crane, April 27.

1933   Repeal of the Eighteenth Amendment, ending the nation's experiment with national prohibition.

Notes

Introduction:
The New Era

1. James Truslow Adams, *Our Business Civilization: Some Aspects of American Culture* (1929; reprint, New York, AMS Press, 1969), 292; Henry F. May, "Shifting Perspectives on the 1920s," *Mississippi Valley Historical Review*, 43, no. 4 (Dec. 1956), 406; Ellis W. Hawley, *The Great War and the Search for a Modern Order: A History of the American People and Their Institutions, 1917–1933* (New York: St. Martin's Press, 1979), v-vi, 8–9; Frederick Lewis Allen, *Only Yesterday: An Informal History of the 1920s* (1931; reprint, New York: Perennial Classics, 2000), 269.

2. William Fielding Ogburn, *Social Change: With Respect to Culture and Original Nature* (New York: Viking, 1927), 199; Booth Tarkington, *The Magnificent Ambersons* (1918; reprint, Bloomington: Indiana University Press, 1989), 498; John Dewey, *The Public and Its Problems* (1927; reprint, Athens, OH: Swallow Press, 1985), 140.

3. Hawley, *Great War*, 136; Lynn Dumenil, *The Modern Temper: American Culture and Society in the 1920s* (New York: Hill & Wang, 1995), 59; William Leuchtenburg, *The Perils of Prosperity, 1914–32* (Chicago: University of Chicago Press, 1958), 3; Willard B. Gatewood Jr., ed., *Controversy in the Twenties: Fundamentalism, Modernism, and Evolution* (Nashville, TN: Vanderbilt University Press, 1969), 81.

4. Sherwood Anderson, *Winesburg, Ohio* (New York: Dover), 34; Sinclair Lewis, *Main Street* (1920; reprint, New York: Bantam, 1996), 307–8.

5. On the impulse to consolidation, see Wilfred M. McClay, *The Masterless: Self and Society in Modern America* (Chapel Hill: University of North Carolina Press, 1994).

215

6. Wilfred M. McClay, "Do Ideas Matter in America?" *Wilson Quarterly*, 27, no. 3 (Summer 2003), 70; Douglas L. Wilson, ed., *The Genteel Tradition: Nine Essays by George Santayana* (Cambridge, MA: Harvard University Press, 1967), 39–40.

7. Van Wyck Brooks, *America's Coming of Age* (1915), in Claire Sprague, ed., *Van Wyck Brooks: The Early Years: A Selection of His Works, 1908–1925*, rev. ed. (Boston: Northeastern University Press, 1993), 79–158.

8. The following discussion is based on Daniel Joseph Singal, "Towards a Definition of American Modernism," *American Quarterly* 39, no. 1 (Spring 1987): 7–26; Malcolm Bradbury, "The Nonhomemade World: European and American Modernism," *American Quarterly* 39, no. 1 (Spring 1987):, 27–36; Malcolm Bradbury and James McFarlane, "The Name and Nature of Modernism," in *Modernism, 1890–1930*, ed. Malcolm Bradbury and James McFarlane (1976; reprint, London: Penguin, 1991), 20–50; McFarlane, "The Mind of Modernism," in *Modernism, 1890–1930*, 71–90; Michael Levenson, ed., *The Cambridge Companion to Modernism* (Cambridge: Cambridge University Press, 1999); T. J. Jackson Lears, *No Place of Grace: Antimodernism and the Transformation of American Culture, 1880–1920* (1981; reprint, Chicago: University of Chicago Press, 1994); Karl Frederick, *Modernity and Modernism: The Sovereignty of the Artist, 1885–1925* (New York: Atheneum, 1988); Andreas Huyssen, *After the Great Divide: Modernism, Mass Culture, and Postmodernism* (Bloomington: Indiana University Press, 1986); and Robert Genter, *Late Modernism: Art, Culture, and Politics in Cold War America* (Philadelphia: University of Pennsylvania Press, 2010).

9. The following discussion relies on Lewis Perry, *Intellectual Life in America: A History* (Chicago: University of Chicago Press, 1989), 263–81; Joan Shelley Rubin, *The Making of Middlebrow Culture* (Chapel Hill: University of North Carolina Press, 1992), 1–27; and Raymond Williams, *Culture and Society, 1780–1850* (New York: Columbia University Press, 1960), xvi-xviii, 38–39, 87–91.

10. See Daniel Walker Howe, *Making the American Self: Jonathan Edwards to Abraham Lincoln* (1997; reprint, New York: Oxford University Press, 2009).

11. Perry, *Intellectual Life in America*, 267; Rubin, *Making of Middlebrow Culture*, 2.

12. Edmund Wilson, *The Shores of Light: A Literary Chronicle of the Twenties and Thirties* (New York: Farrar, Straus and Young, 1952), 11, 22, 471–72; Lewis M. Dabney, *Edmund Wilson: A Life in Literature* (New York: Farrar, Straus and Giroux, 2005), 16, 38–40.

13. Casey Nelson Blake, "Overview: From the Great War through the Great Depression," in *Encyclopedia of Cultural & Intellectual History*, ed. Mary Kupiec Cayton and Peter W. Williams, 3 vols. (New York: Charles Scribner's Sons, 2001), I: 611. On intellectuals as a social class, see Christopher Lasch, *The New Radicalism in America, 1889–1963: The Intellectual as a Social Type* (New York: Norton, 1965); and Stanley Coben, *Revolt against Victorianism: The Impetus for Cultural Change in 1920s America* (New York: Oxford University Press, 1991), 36–47.

14. Dabney, *Wilson*, 56–57, 63–64, 106.

15. Harold E. Stearns, ed., *Civilization in the United States: An Inquiry by Thirty Americans* (1922; reprint, Westport: Greenwood Press, 6.

16. Wilson, *Shores of Light*, 54, 439, 450.

17. See Allen, *Only Yesterday*; Charles W. Eagles, "Urban-Rural Conflict in the 1920s: A Historiographical Assessment," *Historian* 49, no. 1 (Nov. 1986): 26–48; Burl Noggle, "The Twenties: A New Historiographical Frontier," *Journal of American History* 53, no. 2 (Sept. 1966): 299–314. For general studies of the 1920s that define the decade in terms of social, political, and culture conflict or the resistance to change, see Coben, *Rebellion against Victorianism*; Roderick Nash, *The Nervous Generation: American Thought, 1917–1930* (Chicago: Rand McNally, 1970); Lawrence Levine, "Progress and Nostalgia: The Self Image of the Nineteen Twenties," in *The Unpredictable Past: Explorations in American Cultural History* (New York: Oxford University Press, 1993), 189–205; Dumenil, *Modern Temper*; and David J. Goldberg, *Discontented America: The United States in the 1920s* (Baltimore, MD: Johns Hopkins Press, 1999). Studies that emphasize the replacement of local and small-town social and cultural authority with new, highly organized and increasingly bureaucratic elites (in business, government, lobbying groups, and social service agencies) include Leuchtenburg, *Perils of Prosperity*, which anticipated Hawley, *Great War*, and Dumenil, *Modern Temper*.

18. May, "Shifting Perspectives on the 1920s," 411, 407–8, 410–11, 425; Warren Susman, *Culture as History* (New York: Pantheon, 1985), 109, 111. In her study of "mongrel" Manhattan in the 1920s, Ann Douglas characterized the decade as the "first age of the media, of book clubs, best-sellers, and record charts, of radio and talking pictures." Ann Douglas, *Terrible Honesty: Mongrel Manhattan in the 1920s* (New York: Farrar, Straus, and Giroux, 1995), 20.

19. Susman, *Culture as History*, 107, 116. It is noteworthy that Henry May, writing in the 1950s, saw great continuity between postwar social thought and that of the 1920s, finding the sociologist David Riesman's "strikingly influential vision of the shift from inner-direction to other-direction" (his depiction of the "social self" that his contemporaries, such as May, took as a diagnosis of modern conformity) as indicative of the 1920s, a "description of the end of the genteel tradition and the birth of the New Era, the defeat of Wilsonian moralism and the victory of the Babbitts." Moreover, May found the rise of the "white-collar salariat," caustically analyzed by C. Wright Mills as "a regimented, rootless, and docile new middle class," to the "arbitral position in American society" as occurring "especially fast" in the 1920s. May, "Shifting Perspectives on the 1920s," 424–25. On David Riesman, see Genter, *Late Modernism*, 73–89.

20. Alfred Kazin, *On Native Grounds: An Interpretation of Modern American Prose Literature* (New York: Harcourt, Brace, and World, 1942), 265–66.

Chapter 1:
The Gay Table

1. Ernest Hemingway, *A Moveable Feast* (New York: Collier Books/Macmillan, 1964), 49; Richard Lingeman, *Sinclair Lewis: Rebel from Main Street* (New York: Random House, 2002), 89–90; Allen Tate, *Essays of Four Decades* (Chicago: Swallow Press, 1968), 545; Roderick Nash, *The Nervous Generation: American Thought, 1917–1930* (Chicago: Rand McNally, 1970), 75–76, 99, 160.

2. Nash, *Nervous Generation*, 127.

3. William Fielding Ogburn, *Social Change: With Respect to Culture and Original Nature* (New York: Viking, 1927), 200, 200–203, 278; Robert C. Bannister, *Sociology and Scientism: The American Quest for Objectivity, 1880–1940* (Chapel Hill: University of North Carolina Press, 1987), 170.

4. On the social tumult of the first half of the decade, see, in particular, David J. Goldberg, *Discontented America: The United States in the 1920s* (Baltimore, MD: Johns Hopkins University Press, 1999).

5. Clarke A. Chambers, *Seedtime of Reform: American Social Service and Social Action, 1918–1933* (Ann Arbor: University of Michigan Press, 1967), 10, 22; Nelson Lichtenstein and Howell John Harris, eds., *Industrial Democracy in America: The Ambiguous Promise* (Cambridge: Cambridge University Press, 1993), 3–4, 29–30, 41–42, 51; Charles Forcey, *The Crossroads of Liberalism: Croly, Weyl, Lippmann, and the Progressive Era, 1900–1925* (London: Oxford University Press, 1961), 34–36, 157–58, 164–65, 210–212, 221; Paul W. Glad, "Progressives and the Business Culture of the 1920s," *Journal of American History* 53, no. 1 (June 1966): 82, 84; Arthur S. Link, "What Happened to the Progressive Movement in the 1920's?" *American Historical Review* 64, no. 4 (July 1959): 839; Mark C. Smith, *Social Science in the Crucible: The American Debate over Objectivity and Purpose, 1918–1941* (Durham, NC: Duke University Press, 1994), 24.

6. John Dos Passos, *Novels, 1920–1925* (New York: Library of America, 2003), 106, 393; F. Scott Fitzgerald, *Novels and Stories, 1920–1922* (New York: Library of America, 2000), 247.

7. E. E. Cummings, *The Enormous Room*, ed. George James Firmage (1922; reprint, New York: Liveright, 1978), 83, 125.

8. For information on the American economy and data on wages, production levels, and growth, see Lynn Dumenil, *The Modern Temper: American Culture and Society in the 1920s* (New York: Hill & Wang, 1995), 58–59, 79–80; Frank Stricker, "Affluence for Whom?—Another Look at Prosperity and the Working Class in the 1920s," *Labor History* 24, no. 1 (Winter 1983): 5–33; William Leuchtenburg, *The Perils of Prosperity, 1914–1932* (Chicago: University of Chicago Press, 1958), 178–82, 186; James Livingston, *Pragmatism and the Political Economy of Cultural Revolution, 1850–1940* (Chapel Hill: University of North Carolina Press, 1997), 103, 107–108, 114–15; James Livingston, *The World Turned Inside Out: American Thought and Culture at the End of the Twentieth Century* (Lanham, MD: Rowman & Littlefield, 2010), 140–41; Ellis W. Hawley, *The Great War and the Search for a Modern Order: A*

History of the American People and Their Institutions, 1917–1933 (New York: St. Martin's Press, 1979), 81–90; and Nathan Miller, *New World Coming: The 1920s and the Making of Modern America* (Cambridge, MA: Da Capo Press, 2003), 149–50, 281–83.

9. Leuchtenburg, *Perils of Prosperity*, 225, 227.

10. Paul V. Murphy, *The Rebuke of History: The Southern Agrarians and American Conservative Thought* (Chapel Hill: University of North Carolina Press, 2001), 34.

11. F. Scott Fitzgerald, "Echoes of the Jazz Age," in *The Crack-Up*, ed. Edmund Wilson (1945; reprint, New York: New Directions, 1993), 18, 15.

12. John D'Emilio and Estelle B. Freedman, *Intimate Matters: A History of Sexuality in America* (New York: Harper & Row, 1988), 24, 240–42, 256–57; Beth Bailey, *From Front Porch to Back Seat: Courtship in Twentieth-Century America* (Baltimore: Johns Hopkins University Press, 1988), 13, 17–18; Paula Fass, *The Damned and the Beautiful: American Youth in the 1920s* (Oxford: Oxford University Press, 1977), 262–63, 265–66; Robert S. Lynd and Helen Merrell Lynd, *Middletown: A Study in American Culture* (1929; reprint, San Diego: Harcourt Brace Jovanovich, 1957), 137–39, 145. On the image of the flapper in film, see Patricia Erens, "The Flapper: Hollywood's First Liberated Woman," in *Dancing Fools and Weary Blues: The Great Escape of the Twenties*, ed. Lawrence R. Broer and John D. Walther (Bowling Green, KY: Bowling Green State University, 1990), 130–39.

13. Alan Nadel, "Film," in *Encyclopedia of American Cultural and Intellectual History*, vol. 3, ed. Mary Kupiec Cayton and Peter W. Williams (New York: Charles Scribner's Sons, 2001), 459; Mary P. Ryan, "The Projection of a New Womanhood: The Movie Moderns in the 1920s," in *Decades of Discontent: The Women's Movement, 1920–1940*, ed. Lois Scharf and Joan M. Jensen (Westport, CT: Greenwood, 1983), 116; Lynd and Lynd, *Middletown*, 266; Dumenil, *Modern Temper*, 133.

14. George Chauncey, *Gay New York: Gender, Urban Culture, and the Making of the Gay Male World, 1890–1940* (New York: Basic Books, 1994) , 2–3, 6–7, 13–15, 23, 155, 163, 227, 244–57, 276.

15. Chauncey, *Gay New York*, 227, 257–58, 291–99, 301.

16. Freda Kirchwey, ed., *Our Changing Morality: A Symposium* (1924; reprint, New York: Albert and Charles Boni, 1930), vi, 14–15, 100–1, 183–91.

17. Nathan G. Hale Jr., *The Rise and Crisis of Psychoanalysis in the United States: Freud and the Americans, 1917–1985* (New York: Oxford University Press, 1995), 66; Christina Simmons, *Making Marriage Modern: Women's Sexuality from the Progressive Era to World War II* (New York: Oxford University Press, 2009), 4, 7, 11, 58–60, 82–83, 102, 106–8, 121–27, 132–33, 143, 148–49; Rebecca L. Davis, "'Not Marriage at All, but Simple Harlotry': The Companionate Marriage Controversy," *Journal of American History* 94, no. 4 (March 2008): 1137–63.

18. Carl N. Degler, *In Search of Human Nature: Decline and Revival of Darwinism in American Social Thought* (New York: Oxford University Press, 1991), 155, 153–55; Hale, *Rise and Crisis of Psychoanalysis*, 5, 98; John Chynoweth Burnham, "The New Psychology: From Narcissism to Social Control," in *Change and Continuity in Twentieth-Century America: The 1920s*, ed. John Braeman, Robert H. Bremner, and David Brody (Columbus: Ohio State University Press, 1968), 353–57, 373–74, 387,

394. On the association of psychoanalysis with bohemian intellectuals and modern attitudes towards birth control and sex, in particular the release of sexual repression, see Hale, *Rise and Crisis of Psychoanalysis*, 5, 57–58, 62, 79–80.

19. Burnham, "The New Psychology," 367, 372, 374–75, 380; Hale, *Rise and Crisis of Psychoanalysis*, 24, 26–27, 32–33, 35, 57–58, 61–62, 64, 69–71, 74–76.

20. Hale, *Rise and Crisis of Psychoanalysis*, 5, 40–42, 49, 52–53, 75, 81, 96–97; Burnham, "The New Psychology," 370. Matthew Josephson, *Life among the Surrealists* (New York: Holt, Rinehart, and Winston, 1962), 214, mentions the practice of getting "psyched."

21. Paul Vanderham, *James Joyce and Censorship: The Trials of "Ulysses"* (New York: New York University Press, 1998), 8; Rochelle Gurstein, *The Repeal of Reticence: A History of America's Cultural and Legal Struggles over Free Speech, Obscenity, Sexual Liberation, and Modern Art* (New York: Hill & Wang, 1996), 28–29, 99–101, 129–35, 142–45, 182, 213; Marion Elizabeth Rodgers, *Mencken: The American Iconoclast* (New York: Oxford University Press, 2005), 302–5; William M. Halsey, *The Survival of American Innocence: Catholicism in an Era of Disillusionment, 1920–1940* (Notre Dame, IN: University of Notre Dame Press, 1980), 93.

22. Gurstein, *Repeal of Reticence*, 11–31, 104–15, 120, 138–39, 182, 179–212; Vanderham, *James Joyce and Censorship*, 8–12, 15.

23. Kirchwey, ed., *Our Changing Morality*, vi, viii, 236; Hale, *Rise and Crisis of Psychoanalysis*, 42; Paula Baker, "The Domestication of Politics: Women and American Political Society, 1780–1920," *American Historical Review* 89, no. 3 (June 1984): 620–67.

24. Nancy F. Cott, *The Grounding of Modern Feminism* (New Haven: Yale University Press, 1987), 233, 85, 264, 266–67; Jan Doolittle Wilson, *The Women's Joint Congressional Committee and the Politics of Maternalism, 1920–1930* (Urbana: University of Illinois Press, 2007), 1.

25. Cott, *Grounding of Modern Feminism*, 98–99; J. Stanley Lemons, *The Woman Citizen: Social Feminism in the 1920s* (Urbana: University of Illinois Press, 1973), 184; Doris Stevens, "Suffrage Does Not Give Equality," *Forum* 72, no. 2 (Aug. 1924): 147.

26. Lemons, *Woman Citizen*, 50–54, 90–91; Anne Martin, "Feminists and Future Political Action," *Nation*, Feb. 18, 1925, 185, 186.

27. Ann Butler, *Two Paths to Equality: Alice Paul and Ethel M. Smith in the ERA Debate, 1921–1929* (Albany: State University of New York Press, 2002), 68; Cott, *Grounding of Modern Feminism*, 13–15, 19–20, 49.

28. Cott, *Grounding of Modern Feminism*, 15, 36–37, 42–44, 49, 129, 157–58, 179, 181; Christine Lunardini, *From Equal Suffrage to Equal Rights: Alice Paul and the National Woman's Party, 1910–1928* (New York: New York University Press, 1986), 151–52, 154; Suzanne La Follette, *Concerning Women* (1926; reprint, New York: Arno Press, 1972), 16, 19–20, 68, 96, 109, 137.

29. Lunardini, *From Equal Suffrage to Equal Rights*, 166–67; Clarke A. Chambers, *Seedtime of Reform: American Social Service and Social Action, 1918–1933*, 78; Ethel

M. Smith, "What Is Sex Equality and What Are Feminists Trying to Accomplish," *Century Magazine*, May 1929, 100, 96–97. On the 1920s split in the women's movement generally, see Lunardini, *From Equal Suffrage to Equal Rights*, 150–68.

30. Cott, *Grounding of Modern Feminism*, 121, 124–25, 133–34, 139–40; Stevens, "Suffrage Does Not Give Equality," 146, 149; La Follette, *Concerning Women*, 170–71, 173; Butler, *Two Paths to Equality*, 56, 62–63.

31. Cott, *Grounding of Modern Feminism*, 72, 75–76.

32. Lunardini, *From Equal Suffrage to Equal Rights*, 156, 165.

33. On the spread of Franz Boaz's theory of culture, see Degler, *In Search of Human Nature*, vii–viii, 84, 102, 108.

34. The following paragraphs are based on George W. Stocking Jr., *Race, Culture, and Evolution: Essays in the History of Anthropology* (New York: Free Press, 1968), 195–233; George W. Stocking Jr., *The Ethnographer's Magic and Other Essays in the History of Anthropology* (Madison: University of Wisconsin Press, 1992), 114–77, 342–61; George W. Stocking Jr., *Delimiting Anthropology: Occasional Essays and Reflections* (Madison: University of Wisconsin Press, 2001), 24–48; Howard Brick, *Transcending Capitalism: Visions of a New Society in Modern American Thought* (Ithaca, NY: Cornell University Press, 2006), 86–92; Degler, *In Search of Human Nature*, 59–83; and Lois W. Banner, *Intertwined Lives: Margaret Mead, Ruth Benedict, and Their Circle* (New York: Knopf, 2003), 191–92.

35. Stocking, *Race, Culture, and Evolution*, 222.

36. Banner, *Intertwined Lives*, 191; Stocking, *Ethnographer's Magic*, 134, 159, 353.

37. Stocking, *Ethnographer's Magic*, 162, 152–53; 293–95; Susan Hegeman, *Patterns for America: Modernism and the Concept of Culture* (Princeton, NJ: Princeton University Press, 1999), 8–12; Richard Handler, *Critics against Culture: Anthropological Observers of Mass Society* (Madison: University of Wisconsin Press, 2005), 53, 76; Banner, *Intertwined Lives*, 17, 45, 47, 109, 124–25, 130–38, 143, 146, 152, 179–80.

38. Banner, *Intertwined Lives*, 18, 68–69, 70, 75, 101, 155–65, 173, 179–84, 192, 217–218, 219–220.

39. Banner, *Intertwined Lives*, 185, 199, 220, 225, 227, 230–31, 234, 245, 262, 268; Stocking, *Ethnographer's Magic*, 311.

40. Stocking, *Ethnographer's Magic*, 137, 214; Brick, *Transcending Capitalism*, 89–91; Handler, *Critics against Culture*, 49–50.

41. Edward Sapir, "Culture, Genuine and Spurious," *American Journal of Sociology* 29 (Jan. 1924): 403, 410, 421, 406, 409, 412–13.

42. Sapir, "Culture, Genuine and Spurious," 411–12; Handler, *Critics against Culture*, 77–81; Hegeman, *Patterns for America*, 67, 72–73.

43. Sapir, "Culture, Genuine and Spurious," 414–17, 428–29, 422; Hegeman, *Patterns for America*, 74, 78–79.

44. Nancy C. Lutkehaus, *Margaret Mead: The Making of an Icon* (Princeton, NJ: Princeton University Press, 2008), 45–46, 50–53, 84–89, 94; Stocking, *Ethnographer's Magic*, 318; Banner, *Intertwined Lives*, 239.

45. Stocking, *Ethnographer's Magic*, 311–12; Banner, *Intertwined Lives*, 234–40. For discussion of the challenges to Mead's research, driven by the accusations of the New Zealand anthropologist Derek Freeman, see Stocking, *Ethnographer's Magic*, 311–18, 325–40; Banner, *Intertwined Lives*, 235–45, 492n80; Lutkehaus, *Margaret Mead*, 242–52.

46. Margaret Mead, *Coming of Age in Samoa: A Psychological Study of Primitive Youth for Western Civilization* (1928; reprint, New York: Morrow Quill, 1961), 90–92, 108, 135–36, 148–49, 151, 195, 334–35, 201, 151.

47. Mead, *Coming of Age in Samoa*, 157, 198, 199.

48. Mead, *Coming of Age in Samoa*, 201–205, 207, 235, 244, 247, 242–44, 246.

49. The anthropologist Clark Wissler labeled the study a work in "social anthropology" in a foreword to the book. Lynd and Lynd, *Middletown*, vi. Sarah E. Igo, *The Averaged American: Surveys, Citizens, and the Making of a Mass Public* (Cambridge, MA: Harvard University Press, 2007), 37.

50. Richard Wightman Fox, "Epitaph for Middletown: Robert S. Lynd and the Analysis of Consumer Culture," in *The Culture of Consumption: Critical Essays in American History, 1880–1980*, ed. Richard Wightman Fox and T. J. Jackson Lears (New York: Pantheon, 1983), 106–108; Smith, *Social Science in the Crucible*. 134; Igo, *Averaged American*, 31–32.

51. Fox, "Epitaph for Middletown," 108–14; Smith, *Social Science in the Crucible*, 128–31.

52. Fox, "Epitaph for Middletown," 112, 114–22; Igo, *Averaged American*, 32–35.

53. Lynd and Lynd, *Middletown*, 3; Fox, "Epitaph for Middletown," 118–120, 124; Igo, *Averaged American*, 35, 42–44, 56–58.

54. Lynd and Lynd, *Middletown*, 498, 10.

55. Lynd and Lynd, *Middletown*, 61n18, 76–79, 155–56, 228–29, 285–301, 306.

56. Lynd and Lynd, *Middletown*, 24, 39–40, 75, 73–75.

57. Lynd and Lynd, *Middletown*, 45–47, 52, 80–81. On the role of education, see ibid., 60, 68, 80, 184, 219 (quotation), 220–21.

58. Lynd and Lynd, *Middletown*, 3,6, 139–40, 161, 176, 188, 197, 200–201, 222, 310, 490–91. On advertising, see ibid., 82n18.

59. Lynd and Lynd, *Middletown*, 478, 272, 275.

60. Igo, *Averaged American*, 68–69; Fox, "Epitaph for Middletown," 129.

Chapter 2:
Navigating Mass Society

1. Bruce Bliven, *Five Million Words Later: An Autobiography* (New York: John Day, 1970), 148. Biographical information is taken from this volume and from Bliven's profile in the *American National Biography*. Bruce Bliven, "New Orleans: The Nordic Goes Semi-Native," *New Republic*, Sept. 21, 1927, 119–21; Bruce Bliven, "Coney Island for Battered Souls," *New Republic*, Nov. 23, 1921, 372.

2. Bliven, *Five Million Words Later*, 23.

3. Bliven, *Five Million Words Later*, 50–59, 62, 72–73, 91–93.

4. Bliven, *Five Million Words Later*, 108–9; Bruce Bliven, "Slaves of the Roof," *New Republic*, March 22, 1922, 104, 106.

5. Bruce Bliven, "Flapper Jane," *New Republic*, Sept. 9, 1925, 65–66.

6. Bruce Bliven, "A Stroll on Main Street," *New Republic*, Dec. 12, 1923, 64; Bruce Bliven, "Los Angeles," *New Republic*, July 13, 1927, 197.

7. On the advent of a consumer culture, see William Leach, *Land of Desire: Merchants, Power, and the Rise of a New American Culture* (New York: Pantheon, 1993); Gary S. Cross, *An All-Consuming Century: Why Commercialism Won in Modern America* (New York: Columbia University Press, 2000); Roland Marchand, *Advertising the American Dream: Making Way for Modernity, 1920–1940* (Berkeley: University of California Press, 1985).

8. Steven J. Ross, *Working-Class Hollywood: Silent Film and the Shaping of Class in America* (Princeton, NJ: Princeton University Press, 1998), 175.

9. Lynn Dumenil, *The Modern Temper: American Culture and Society in the 1920s* (New York: Hill & Wang, 1995), 77; William Leuchtenburg, *The Perils of Prosperity, 1914–1932* (Chicago: University of Chicago Press, 1958), 196; Ellis W. Hawley, *The Great War and the Search for a Modern Order: A History of the American People and Their Institutions, 1917–1933* (New York: St. Martin's Press, 1979), 86; Robert Sklar, *Movie-Made America: A Cultural History of American Movies* (New York: Vintage, 1994), 82.

10. Henry Jenkins, *What Made Pistachio Nuts? Early Sound Comedy and the Vaudeville Aesthetic* (New York: Columbia University Press, 1992), 35.

11. Alan Dale, *Comedy Is a Man in Trouble: Slapstick in American Movies* (Minneapolis: University of Minnesota Press, 2000), 10–11.

12. Sklar, *Movie-Made America*, 106–7; Dale, *Comedy Is a Man in Trouble*, 16.

13. This paragraph is drawn from Walter Kerr, *The Silent Clowns* (New York: Knopf, 1975).

14. Jenkins, *What Made Pistachio Nuts?*, 27–28, 32–33, 37–38, 39, 61–64, 70–71, 85; Lawrence E. Mintz, "American Humor in the 1920s," in *Dancing Fools and Weary Blues: The Great Escape of the Twenties*, ed. Lawrence R. Broer and John D. Walther (Bowling Green, KY: Bowling Green State University Press, 1990), 165; David Nasaw, *Going Out: The Rise and Fall of Public Amusements* (Cambridge, MA: Harvard University Press, 1999), 21–28.

15. Mintz, "American Humor in the 1920s," 166–68; Walter Blair and Hamlin Hill, *America's Humor: From Poor Richard to Doonesbury* (New York: Oxford University Press, 1978), 421, 427–433, 438–47.

16. Burton W. Peretti, *The Creation of Jazz: Music, Race, and Culture in Urban America* (Urbana: University of Illinois Press, 1992), 7, 12, 16–21, 29, 46; William Barlow, *"Looking Up at Down": The Emergence of Blues Culture* (Philadelphia: Temple University Press, 1989), 3; Kathy J. Ogren, *The Jazz Revolution: Twenties America and the Meaning of Jazz* (New York: Oxford University Press, 1989), 40;

Robert M. Crunden, *Body and Soul: The Making of American Modernism* (New York: Basic Books, 2000), 148. On black secular song generally, see Lawrence W. Levine, *Black Culture and Black Consciousness: Afro-American Folk Thought from Slavery to Freedom* (Oxford: Oxford University Press, 1977), 190–297. On the broader southern context of blues and jazz as well as hillbilly and gospel music, see Richard A. Peterson, *Creating Country Music: Fabricating Authenticity* (Chicago: University of Chicago Press, 1997), 8, 236–37n10; Edward L. Ayers, *The Promise of the New South: Life after Reconstruction* (New York: Oxford University Press, 1992), 373–99.

17. Peretti, *Creation of Jazz*, 22, 71, 133; Crunden, *Body and Soul*, 165–66.

18. Peretti, *Creation of Jazz*, 21–22, 26, 108–9.

19. Peretti, *Creation of Jazz*, 16–17, 21–22, 94–95, 110; Barlow, "*Looking Up at Down*," 4, 140; Ogren, *Jazz Revolution*, 102, 108.

20. Barlow, "*Looking Up at Down*," 4, 6, 8–9, 27–28; Levine, *Black Culture and Black Consciousness*, 206–7; Daphne Duval Harrison, *Black Pearls: Blues Queens of the 1920s* (New Brunswick, NJ: Rutgers University Press, 1990), 68–74.

21. Barlow, "*Looking Up at Down*," 33–36, 40–41; Ogren, *Jazz Revolution*, 111–12.

22. Barlow, "*Looking Up at Down*," 37, 149.

23. Peretti, *Creation of Jazz*, 16, 53; Barlow, "*Looking Up at Down*," 6, 92–93; Ann Douglas, *Terrible Honesty: Mongrel Manhattan in the 1920s* (New York: Farrar, Straus, and Giroux, 1995), 400–1; Harrison, *Black Pearls*, 80.

24. Barlow, "*Looking Up at Down*," 127–28; Peretti, *Creation of Jazz*, 52. See also Barlow, "*Looking Up at Down*," 114–15; Ogren, *Jazz Revolution*, 92.

25. Harrison, *Black Pearls*, 67, 111, 37; Barlow, "*Looking Up at Down*," 125, 141, 157; Peretti, *Creation of Jazz*, 68; Douglas, *Terrible Honesty*, 411.

26. Barlow, "*Looking Up at Down*," 165–66, 168, 174, 176–77, 159–60, 175, 151–52; Harrison, *Black Pearls*, 53, 82, 87–90; Douglas, *Terrible Honesty*, 412–13. For an interpretation emphasizing the assertiveness of women blues singers, see Hazel V. Carby, "It Jus Be's Dat Way Sometime: The Sexual Politics of Women's Blues," in *The Jazz Cadence of American Culture*, ed. Robert G. O'Meally (New York: Columbia University Press, 1998), 471–82.

27. Barlow, "*Looking Up at Down*," 142, 88, 150, 69, 142; Levine, *Black Culture and Black Consciousness*, 242–44; Harrison, *Black Pearls*, 104–9; Peretti, *Creation of Jazz*, 68; Carby, "It Jus Be's Dat Way Sometimes," 481.

28. George Chauncey, *Gay New York: Gender, Urban Culture, and the Making of the Gay Male World, 1890–1940* (New York: Basic Books, 1994), 251.

29. Lewis A. Erenberg, *Steppin' Out: New York Nightlife and the Transformation of American Culture, 1890–1930* (Chicago: University of Chicago Press, 1984), 124–29, 177, 184, 187–88, 193–95, 254.

30. Erenberg, *Steppin' Out*, 216–19, 248–49.

31. Erenberg, *Steppin' Out*, 206, 213–14; Arnold Shaw, *The Jazz Age: Popular Music in the 1920's* (New York: Oxford University Press, 1987), 167, 231–32, 236–38, 242, 244; Jenkins, *What Made Pistachio Nuts?*, 87–89.

32. Nasaw, *Going Out*, 43, 197; Richard Schickel, *His Picture in the Papers: A Speculation on Celebrity in America Based on the Life of Douglas Fairbanks Sr.* (New York: Charterhouse, 1973), 8, 27; Kerr, *The Silent Clowns*, 31; Harrison Rhodes, "The High Kingdom of the Movies," *Harper's*, April 1920, 640, 646–47, 649.

33. Schickel, *His Picture in the Papers*, 6–8; Pare Lorentz, "The Stillborn Art," *Forum* 80, no. 3 (Sept. 1928): 364; "A Visit to Movieland: The Film Capital of the World—Los Angeles," *Forum* 63 (Jan. 1920): 20–21. On the effects of businessmen on Hollywood films, see David Robinson, *Hollywood in the Twenties* (London: A. Zwemmer, 1968), 30–31.

34. Peterson, *Creating Country Music*, 17–31, 33, 37–39, 46; Barlow, *"Looking Up at Down,"* 129; Bill C. Malone, *Country Music, USA*, rev. ed. (Austin: University of Texas Press, 1985), 36–39, 67, 80; Diane Pecknold, *The Selling Sound: The Rise of the Country Music Industry* (Durham, NC: Duke University Press, 2007), 26. Arnold Shaw highlights the centrality of the song in Tin Pan Alley. Shaw, *Jazz Age*, 115.

35. Malone, *Country Music*, 65–67; Peterson, *Creating Country Music*, 41–42.

36. Malone, *Country Music*, 77–91; Peterson, *Creating Country Music*, 42–51, 196, 247n34.

37. Pecknold, *Selling Sound*, 2, 14, 20, 22–23; Malone, *Country Music*, 4–6, 10–16, 23, 26, 61–64, 51–52; Peterson, *Creating Country Music*, 9.

38. Peterson, *Creating Country Music*, 4–5, 7–8, 66–71, 75–77, 80, 195–96, 209, 220; Anthony Harkins, *Hillbilly: A Cultural History of an American Icon* (New York: Oxford University Press, 2004), 3–7, 9, 48, 76–80.

39. Cultural hybridity is a major theme of Douglas, *Terrible Honesty*.

40. Peretti, *Creation of Jazz*, 82–83, 91–93.

41. Peretti, *Creation of Jazz*, 87, 89, 96, 178, 187–89, 198–99, 202, 79–80, 110, 52.

42. Peretti, *Creation of Jazz*, 26–28, 46–47, 146–47, 62–63, 69–71; Ogren, *Jazz Revolution*, 70–71, 112–113, 115, 140–41, 156–58; Macdonald Smith Moore, *Yankee Blues: Musical Culture and American Identity* (Bloomington: Indiana University Press, 1985), 66–68, 85–86, 88–89, 90, 86.

43. Percy Marks, *The Plastic Age* (New York: Century, 1924), 252–255, 271.

44. Joan Shelley Rubin, "Modernism in Practice: Public Readings of the New Poetry," in *A Modern Mosaic: Art and Modernism in the United States* (Chapel Hill: University of North Carolina Press, 2000), 145; Sklar, *Movie-Made America*, 125; Burton Rascoe, "The Motion Pictures: An Industry, Not an Art," *Bookman* 54, no. 3 (Nov. 1921): 194–98; R. E. Sherwood, "Renaissance in Hollywood," *American Mercury* 16 (April 1929): 431–33.

45. Michael Kammen, *The Lively Arts: Gilbert Seldes and the Transformation of Cultural Criticism in the United States* (New York: Oxford University Press, 1996), 17–23, 25–27, 31–33, 41–42, 56–57, 66, 70, 76–77, 106–7. For Hemingway's hostility, see ibid., 53–55, 416n27.

46. Gilbert Seldes, *The Seven Lively Arts* (1924; reprint, Mineola, NY: Dover, 2001), 3, 21, 15, 23–24, 60–61, 310, 231–45, 83, 85, 191, 281, 74.

47. Seldes, *Seven Lively Arts*, 99, 73, 93, 95, 98.

48. Seldes, *Seven Lively Arts*, 350, 310, 203–4, 255.

49. Michele Hilmes, *Radio Voices: American Broadcasting, 1922–1952* (Minneapolis: University of Minnesota Press, 1997), 43; Paul Starr, *The Creation of the Media: Political Origins of Modern Communications* (New York: Basic Books, 2004), 327–70; Susan Smulyan, *Selling Radio: The Commercialization of American Broadcasting, 1920–1934* (Washington, DC: Smithsonian Institution, 1994); Clifford J. Doerksen, *American Babel: Rogue Radio Broadcasters of the Jazz Age* (Philadelphia: University of Temple Press, 2005).

50. Doerksen, *American Babel*, 12; Bruce Bliven, "The Ether Will Now Oblige," *New Republic* Feb. 15, 1922, 330.

51. Doerksen, *American Babel*, viii–x, 11–17, 83–86, 92–97. See also Hilmes, *Radio Voices*, 17; Pecknold, *Selling Sound*, 18–19.

52. Samantha Barbas, *Movie Crazy: Fans, Stars, and the Cult of Celebrity* (New York: Palgrave Macmillan, 2001), 4, 6–7, 137–42; Lizabeth Cohen, *Making a New Deal: Industrial Workers in Chicago, 1919–1939* (Cambridge: Cambridge University Press, 1990), 105, 133–35, 138; Malone, *Country Music*, 33–34, 71–75; Pecknold, *Selling Sound*, 16.

Chapter 3:
The Bridge

1. Thomas Bender, *New York Intellect: A History of Intellectual Life in New York City, from 1750 to the Beginnings of Our Own Time* (Baltimore, MD: Johns Hopkins University Press, 1987), 232; Casey Nelson Blake, *Beloved Community: The Cultural Criticism of Randolph Bourne, Van Wyck Brooks, Waldo Frank, & Lewis Mumford* (Chapel Hill: University of North Carolina Press, 1990), 2.

2. Daniel H. Borus, ed., *These United States: Portraits of America from the 1920s* (Ithaca, NY: Cornell University Press, 1992), 9; Alfred Kazin, *On Native Grounds: An Interpretation of Modern American Prose Literature* (New York: Harcourt, Brace & World, 1942), ix.

3. Sinclair Lewis, *Main Street* (1920; reprint, New York: Bantam Books, 1996), 307–8; Harold E. Stearns, ed., *Civilization in the United States: An Inquiry by Thirty Americans* (1922; reprint, Westport: Greenwood Press, 1971), 8, 13.

4. Stearns, ed., *Civilization in the United States*, 9, 4.

5. Stearns, ed., *Civilization in the United States*, 12–13, 286.

6. Stearns, ed., *Civilization in the United States*, 109–10.

7. Stearns, ed., *Civilization in the United States*, 141–42, 147–48.

8. Sinclair Lewis, *Babbitt* (1922; reprint, New York: Bantam Classic, 1998), 188–90, 192, 80, 86.

9. My account of H. L. Mencken's life is drawn from Fred Hobson, *Mencken: A Life* (New York: Random House, 1994) and Marion Elizabeth Rodgers, *Mencken: The American Iconoclast* (New York: Oxford University Press, 2005).

10. Rodgers, *Mencken*, 17.

11. H. L. Mencken, *Prejudices: Fourth Series* (New York: Knopf, 1924), 46–4.

12. Hobson, *Mencken*, 248, 250; Mencken, *Prejudices: Fourth Series*, 40.

13. H. L. Mencken, *Prejudices: Third Series* (New York: Knopf, 1922), 145–50.

14. Rodgers, *Mencken*, 3, 308.

15. Hobson, *Mencken*, 243, 244; H. L. Mencken, *Prejudices: First Series* (New York: Knopf, 1919), 94; H. L. Mencken, *Prejudices: Second Series* (New York: Knopf, 1920), 68–69, 70; Mencken, *Prejudices: Third Series*, 10.

16. Claire Sprague, ed., *Van Wyck Brooks: The Early Years: A Selection from His Works, 1908–1925*, rev. ed. (Boston: Northeastern University Press, 1993), 83–86, 132, 221, 223–24.

17. Waldo Frank, *Our America* (New York: Boni & Liveright, 1919), 3–4.

18. Wilfred M. McClay, "Two Versions of the Genteel Tradition: Santayana and Brooks," *New England Quarterly* 55, no. 3 (Sept. 1983): 379; Claire Sprague, ed., *Van Wyck Brooks*, rev. ed., 95. On the contemporary concept of personality, see Casey Blake, "The Young Intellectuals and the Culture of Personality," *American Literary History* 1, no. 3 (Autumn 1989): 510–34; Richard Wightman Fox, "The Culture of Liberal Protestantism, 1875–1925," *Journal of Interdisciplinary History* 22, no. 3 (Winter 1993): 647–52. For an older meditation on the shift from "character" to "personality" that takes a somewhat different analytical direction, see Warren I. Susman, *Culture as History: The Transformation of American Society in the Twentieth Century* (New York: Pantheon, 1984), 271–85.

19. Waldo Frank, *Our America* (New York: Boni and Liveright, 1919), 18–19, 63, 66–67, 98.

20. Frederick J. Hoffman, *The Twenties: American Writing in the Postwar Decade*, rev. ed. (New York: Free Press, 1965), 29–30, 31; James Truslow Adams, *Our Business Civilization: Some Aspects of American Culture* (1929; reprint, New York: AMS Press, 1969), 240, 12–16, 25.

21. Blake, "Young Intellectuals and the Culture of Personality," 513, 524; Blake, *Beloved Community*, 220; Robert L. Dorman, *Revolt of the Provinces: The Regionalist Movement in America, 1920–1945* (Chapel Hill: University of North Carolina Press, 1993), 6–9, 52–53; John L. Thomas, "Lewis Mumford, Benton MacKaye, and the Regional Vision," in *Lewis Mumford: Public Intellectual*, ed. Thomas P. Hughes and Agatha C. Hughes (New York: Oxford University Press, 1990), 67, 75–83, 89–93. On the regionalist tradition, see Dorman, *Revolt of the Provinces* and Charles C. Alexander, *Here the Country Lies: Nationalism and the Arts in Twentieth-Century America* (Bloomington: Indiana University Press, 1980).

22. Lewis Mumford, *The Golden Day: A Study in American Literature and Culture* (1926; reprint, New York: Dover, 1953), 8–9, 11, 25–26. On Mumford's critique of pragmatism, see Robert Westbrook, "Lewis Mumford, John Dewey, and the 'Pragmatic Acquiescence,'" in *Lewis Mumford*, ed. Hughes and Hughes, 301–9.

23. Mumford, *Golden Day*, 90, 83, 89–90, 38.

24. Mumford, *Golden Day*, 44, 75, 5. On Mumford's interpretation of the "Golden Day," see John L. Thomas, "Theories of Catastrophism: Lewis Mumford, Vernon L. Parrington, Van Wyck Brooks, and the End of American Regionalism," *American Quarterly* 42, no. 2 (June 1990): 229–30, 241–42.

25. Wanda M. Corn, *The Great American Thing: Modern Art and National Identity, 1915–1935* (Berkeley: University of California Press, 1999), xviii, xv–xviii, 89, 43–89, 135; Matthew Josephson, *Life among the Surrealists* (New York: Holt, Rinehart, and Winston, 1962), 125.

26. Corn, *Great American Thing*, 85; Gorham Munson, *The Awakening Twenties: A Memoir-History of a Literary Period* (Baton Rouge: Louisiana State University Press, 1985), 40.

27. Dickran Tashjian, *Skyscraper Primitives: Dada and the American Avant-Garde, 1910–1925* (Middletown, CT: Wesleyan University Press, 1975), 73, 84; Jack Selzer, *Kenneth Burke in Greenwich Village: Conversing with the Moderns, 1915–1931* (Madison: University of Wisconsin Press, 1996), 211n33.

28. Corn, *Great American Thing*, 31.

29. On the Stieglitz group, see Corn, *Great American Thing*, xiii–xviii, 3–40. On the precisionists, see ibid., 295 and Charles J. Shindo, *1927 and the Rise of Modern America* (Lawrence: University Press of Kansas, 2010), 22–25.

30. Corn, *Great American Thing*, 23, 20–31.

31. Daniel Aaron, *Writers on the Left: Episodes in American Literary Communism* (New York: Columbia University Press, 1992), 34. My account of the 1920s literary left is based on Aaron's classic treatment. See also Richard H. Pells, *Radical Visions and American Dreams: Culture and Social Thought in the Depression Years* (Middletown, CT: Wesleyan University Press, 1973), 8–9, 22.

32. Aaron, *Writers on the Left*, 89, 50–51; Edward Abrahams, *The Lyrical Left: Randolph Bourne, Alfred Stieglitz, and the Origins of Cultural Radicalism in America* (Charlottesville: University Press of Virginia, 1986); Pells, *Radical Visions and American Dreams*, 14.

33. Tashjian, *Skyscraper Primitives*, 9; Selzer, *Kenneth Burke in Greenwich Village*, 9; Hoffman, *The Twenties*, 110.

34. Tahsjian, *Skyscraper Primitives*, 218. For additional information on the prewar avant-garde, see Arthur Frank Wertheim, *The New York Little Renaissance: Iconoclasm, Modernism, and Nationalism in American Culture, 1908–1917* (New York: New York University Press, 1976). Hoffman, *The Twenties*, 209; Tashjian, *Skyscraper Primitives*, 95.

35. Josephson, *Life among the Surrealists*, 17–39, 50, 188. See also Selzer, *Kenneth Burke in Greenwich Village*.

36. Munson, *Awakening Twenties*, 161; Tashjian, *Skyscraper Primitives*, 129–30; Josephson, *Life among the Surrealists*, 238, 100, 154–55, 158.

37. Munson, *Awakening Twenties*, 163–64.

38. Josephson, *Life among the Surrealists*, 114–15, 119, 128–29, 132, 134–37, 145.

39. Josephson, *Life among the Surrealists*, 87, 113, 116, 125.

40. James Kempf, "Encountering the Avant-Garde: Malcolm Cowley in France, 1921–1922," *Southern Review* 20, no. 1 (Jan. 1984): 18; Selzer, *Kenneth Burke in Greenwich Village*, 238n30, 131.

41. Malcolm Cowley, *Exile's Return: A Literary Odyssey of the 1920s*, rev. ed. (New York: Viking, 1951), 27, 29, 33.

42. Cowley, *Exile's Return*, 202, 204–5.

43. Malcolm Cowley, "A Brief History of Bohemia," *Freeman*, July 19, 1922, 439; Cowley, *Exile's Return*, 61–63.

44. Ernest Hemingway, "Artistic Poseurs," in *The Culture of the Twenties*, ed. Loren Baritz (Indianapolis: Bobbs-Merrill Educational Publishing, 1970), 297–99. On the role of conversation in early modernism, see Christine Stansell, *American Moderns: Bohemian New York and the Creation of a New Century* (New York: Owl Books/Holt, 2000), 73–119.

45. Cowley, *Exile's Return*, 72–73.

46. Josephson, *Life among the Surrealists*, 232, 234–37; Selzer, *Kenneth Burke in Greenwich Village*, 109–13.

47. Selzer, *Kenneth Burke in Greenwich Village*, 47–52, 109–14; Josephson, *Life among the Surrealists*, 262–67, 269–74.

48. Edmund Wilson, *The Shores of Light: A Literary Chronicle of the Twenties and Thirties* (New York: Farrar, Straus and Young, 1952), 126, 130, 132, 140.

49. Kenneth S. Lynn, *Hemingway* (New York: Simon & Schuster, 1987), 120. I have relied on Lynn for biographical details. On the modernist ethos of "terrible honesty," see Ann Douglas, *Terrible Honesty: Mongrel Manhattan in the 1920s* (New York: Farrar, Straus, and Giroux, 1995), 31–40.

50. On Ernest Hemingway's *The Sun Also Rises*, see Lynn, *Hemingway*; Michael S. Reynolds, *"The Sun Also Rises": A Novel of the Twenties* (New York: Twayne, 1995); and Earl Rovit, *Ernest Hemingway* (New York: Twayne, 1963).

51. Ernest Hemingway, *The Sun Also Rises* (1926; reprint, New York: Charles Scribner's Sons, 1954), 152.

52. Hemingway, *Sun Also Rises*, 171.

53. Corn, *Great American Thing*, 188, 135–53.

54. Corn, *Great American Thing*, 381n97; Sherman Paul, *Hart's Bridge* (Urbana: University of Illinois Press, 1972), 192.

55. Hart Crane, *Complete Poems and Selected Letters* (New York: Library of America, 2006), 59 (subsequent parenthetical citations from this text).

56. Tashjian, *Skyscraper Primitives*, ix; Paul, *Hart's Bridge*, 46, 166.

57. Josephson, *Life among the Surrealists*, 243; Paul, *Hart's Bridge*, 270–71.

Chapter 4:
Mulatto America

1. Anzia Yezierska, *Bread Givers: A Novel* (1925; reprint, New York: Persea Books, 2003), 24, 65. For biographical information on Anzia Yezierska, see Alice Kessler-Harris, "Introduction," in Yezierska, *Bread Givers*, xxi–xxxvi and Mary V. Dearborn,

Love in the Promised Land: The Story of Anzia Yezierska and John Dewey (New York: Free Press, 1988).

2. Yezierska, *Bread Givers*, 138, 159, 278, 286.

3. On the 1920 census, see Matthew Pratt Guterl, *The Color of Race in America, 1900–1940* (Cambridge, MA: Harvard University Press, 2001), 166. On Madison Grant, eugenics, and race theory, see Jonathan Peter Spiro, *Defending the Master Race: Conservation, Eugenics, and the Legacy of Madison Grant* (Burlington: University of Vermont Press, 2009) and Carl N. Degler, *In Search of Human Nature: Decline and Revival of Darwinism in American Social Thought* (New York: Oxford University Press, 1991), 41–49. On the consolidation of a new white, or "Caucasian," racial identity and the creation of a bipolar opposition between white and black, see two works in the field of whiteness studies most relevant for the 1920s: Matthew Frye Jacobson, *Whiteness of a Different Color: European Immigrants and the Alchemy of Race* (Cambridge, MA: Harvard University Press, 1998) and Guterl, *The Color of Race in America*. On the Rhinelander case, see Earl Lewis and Heidi Ardizzone, *Love on Trial: An American Scandal in Black and White* (New York: Norton, 2001).

4. For an articulation of ethnic biculturalism as an alternative to the bipolar model of cultural continuity or gradual acculturation, again particularly relevant to ethnic change in the 1920s, see George J. Sánchez, *Becoming Mexican American: Ethnicity, Culture, and Identity in Chicano Los Angeles, 1900–1945* (New York: Oxford University Press, 1993), 6–13. See also Kathleen Neils Conzen, "Thomas and Znaniecki and the Historiography of American Immigration," *Journal of American Ethnic Studies* 16, no. 1 (Fall 1996): 16–21.

5. Eli Zaretsky, "Editor's Introduction," in William I. Thomas and Florian Znaniecki, *The Polish Peasant in Europe and America*, ed. Eli Zaretsky (Urbana: University of Illinois Press, 1984), 1–4, 8–9; Henry Yu, *Thinking Orientals: Migration, Contact, and Exoticism in Modern America* (New York: Oxford University Press, 2001), 8; Conzen, "Thomas and Znaniecki," 16–18.

6. Yu, *Thinking Orientals*, 38–39, 224n14; Zaretsky, "Editor's Introduction," 23–24.

7. Fred H. Matthews, *Quest for an American Sociology: Robert E. Park and the Chicago School* (Montreal: McGill-Queen's University Press, 1977), 42, 48. For biographical information on Park in this and subsequent paragraphs, see Matthews, *Quest for an American Sociology*.

8. Yu, *Thinking Orientals*, 44; Jonathan Scott Holloway, *Confronting the Veil: Abram Harris, Jr., E. Franklin Frazier, and Ralph Bunche, 1919–1941* (Chapel Hill: University of North Carolina Press, 2002), 135–36; Edward Shils, "Some Academics, Mainly in Chicago," *American Scholar* 50, no. 2 (Spring 1981): 179, 188–89.

9. Degler, *In Search of Human Nature*, vii–viii, 61, 63–65, 67–71, 159–60, 196, 199–202.

10. Degler, *In Search of Human Nature*, 90–97, 100–101.

11. Degler, *In Search of Human Nature*, 48–51, 144, 168–79; John Chynoweth Burnham, "The New Psychology: From Narcissism to Social Control," in *Change and Continuity in Twentieth-Century America: The 1920s*, ed. John Braeman, Robert H. Bremner, and David Brody (Columbus: Ohio State University Press, 1968), 390.

12. The following account is based generally on Stow Persons, *Ethnic Studies at Chicago, 1905–1945* (Urbana: University of Illinois Press, 1987). On Park and the Chicago school's conception of race as a matter of group consciousness and culture, see Yu, *Thinking Orientals*, 8–11, 45.

13. Zaretsky, "Editor's Introduction," 2–5, 8, 14–18, 20, 24; Conzen, "Thomas and Znaniecki," 18.

14. Alain Locke, ed., *The New Negro* (1925; reprint, New York: Touchstone, 1999), 285.

15. Yu, *Thinking Orientals*, 40–42; Persons, *Ethnic Studies at Chicago*, 48.

16. On the National Origins Act, see David J. Goldberg, *Discontented America: The United States in the 1920s* (Baltimore: Johns Hopkins University Press, 1999), 151–66; John Higham, *Strangers in the Land: Patterns of American Nativism, 1860–1925*, 2nd ed. (New York: Atheneum, 1965), 153–65; and Gary Gerstle, *American Crucible: Race and Nation in the Twentieth Century* (Princeton, NJ: Princeton University Press, 2001), 94.

17. Mae M. Ngai, *Impossible Subjects: Illegal Aliens and the Making of Modern America* (Princeton, NJ: Princeton University Press, 2004), 7–8, 21–38; Guterl, *Color of Race in America*, 5–6; Jacobson, *Whiteness of a Different Color*, 8, 91–92.

18. "The KKK," *New Republic*, Sept. 21, 1921, 89. On the Klan generally, see Leonard J. Moore, *Citizen Klansmen: The Ku Klux Klan in Indiana, 1921–1928* (Chapel Hill: University of North Carolina Press, 1991); Nancy MacLean, *Behind the Mask of Chivalry: The Making of the Second Ku Klux Klan* (New York: Oxford University Press, 1994); Shaw Lay, ed., *The Invisible Empire of the West: Toward a New Historical Appraisal of the Ku Klux Klan of the 1920s* (Urbana: University of Illinois Press, 1992); Stanley Coben, *Rebellion against Victorianism: The Impetus for Cultural Change in 1920s America* (New York: Oxford University Press, 1991), 136–56; Goldberg, *Discontented America*, 117–39; Lynn Dumenil, *The Modern Temper: American Culture and Society in the 1920s* (New York: Hill & Wang, 1995), 235–49.

19. Coben, *Rebellion against Victorianism*, 142.

20. Moore, *Citizen Klansmen*, 23; MacLean, *Behind the Mask of Chivalry*, 21, 150, 152–53, 163–64.

21. Hiram Wesley Evans, "The Klan's Fight for Americanism," *North American Review*, March 1, 1926, 52, 50; Hiram Wesley Evans, "The Klan: Defender of Americanism," *Forum* 74, no. 6 (Dec. 1925): 803–4.

22. Evans, "Klan's Fight for Americanism," 52, 38; Evans, "The Klan," 805; letter to the editor, *Forum* 75 (Feb. 1926): 305.

23. Horace M. Kallen, *Culture and Democracy in the United States* (1924; reprint, New Brunswick, NJ: Transaction, 1998), 34–35.

24. Kallen, *Culture and Democracy*, 114, 116, 108, 54–55.

25. Robert Ezra Park, *Race and Culture* (Glencoe, IL: Free Press, 1950), 145; John Higham, *Send These to Me: Jews and Other Immigrants in Urban America* (New York: Atheneum, 1975), 200–1; David A. Hollinger, *In the American Province: Studies in the History and Historiography of Ideas* (Baltimore: Johns Hopkins University Press, 1985), 59.

26. Jeffrey C. Stewart, "Introduction," in Alain LeRoy Locke, *Race Contacts and Interracial Relations: Lectures on the Theory and Practice of Race*, ed. Jeffrey C. Stewart (Washington DC: Howard University Press, 1992), xxxv–xlii; Leonard Harris, "Rendering the Text," in *The Philosophy of Alain Locke: Harlem Renaissance and Beyond* (Philadelphia: Temple University Press, 1989), 3–6; Paul Allen Anderson, *Deep River: Music and Memory in Harlem Renaissance Thought* (Durham, NC: Duke University Press, 2001), 132–33.

27. Stewart, "Introduction," xx–xxviii; Alain Locke, "The Concept of Race as Applied to Self-Culture," in *Philosophy of Alain Locke*, ed. Leonard Harris, 193, 188–94.

28. Stewart, "Introduction," xxi, xxxi–xxxii; Locke, "Concept of Race," 195.

29. Anderson, *Deep River*, 119, 122, 134; Alain Locke, "The Contribution of Race to Culture," in *Philosophy of Alain Locke*, ed. Harris, 202–3, 206; Alain Locke, "The High Cost of Prejudice," *Forum* 78, no. 4 (Oct. 1927): 502–4; Lothrop Stoddard, "The Impasse at the Color-Line," *Forum* 78, no. 4 (Oct. 1927): 513–15.

30. Burton W. Peretti, *The Creation of Jazz: Music, Race, and Culture in Urban America* (Urbana: University of Illinois Press, 1992), 47; Charles R. Larson, ed., *The Complete Fiction of Nella Larsen* (New York: Anchor, 2001), 62, 66.

31. Rollin Lynde Hartt, "The New Negro," *Independent*, Jan. 15, 1921, 59; Locke, ed., *The New Negro*, 231, 237, 11.

32. Locke, ed., *The New Negro*, 309, 14. For the claim that Washington, D.C., was the center of African American intellectual life, see Holloway, *Confronting the Veil*, 35–50.

33. This discussion of Marcus Garvey and his movement is based on Alphonso Pinckney, *Red, Black, and Green: Black Nationalism in the United States* (Cambridge: Cambridge University Press, 1976); Judith Stein, *The World of Marcus Garvey: Race and Class in Modern Society* (Baton Rouge: Louisiana State University Press, 1986); Mary G. Rolinson, *Grassroots Garveyism: The Universal Negro Improvement Association in the Rural South, 1920–1927* (Chapel Hill: University of North Carolina Press, 2007); Nathan Irvin Huggins, *Harlem Renaissance* (London: Oxford University Press, 1971), 41–48; David Levering Lewis, *W. E. B. Du Bois: The Fight for Equality and the American Century, 1919–1963* (New York: Holt, 2000), 50–84; and David Levering Lewis, *When Harlem Was in Vogue* (New York: Penguin, 1997), 34–45.

34. Huggins, *Harlem Renaissance*, 48.

35. Pinckney, *Red, Black, and Green*, 48.

36. Holloway, *Confronting the Veil*, 3–4, 11, 84–88, 128–48.

37. Holloway, *Confronting the Veil*, 105, 109, 110–11, 114–16.

38. Rolinson, *Grassroots Garveyism*, 18; Lewis, *When Harlem Was in Vogue*, 42.

39. Guterl, *Color of Race in America*, 158. This interpretation of Jean Toomer is drawn from Lewis, *When Harlem Was in Vogue*, 59–75. See also Guterl, *Color of Race in America*, 154–83.

40. Lewis, *When Harlem Was in Vogue*, 64, 68; Guterl, *Color of Race in America*, 180.

41. Locke, ed., *The New Negro*, 159; Guterl, *Color of Race in America*, 176, 172, 155.

42. George Hutchinson, *In Search of Nella Larsen: A Biography of the Color Line* (Cambridge, MA: Harvard University Press, 2006), 183. Matthew Pratt Guterl, *The Color of Race in America, 1900–1940* (Cambridge, MA: Harvard University Press, 2001), 155.

43. For biographical information on Nella Larsen, see Hutchinson, *In Search of Nella Larsen* and Cheryl A. Wall, *Women of the Harlem Renaissance* (Bloomington: Indiana University Press, 1995).

44. Larson, ed., *Complete Fiction of Nella Larsen*, 215, 222–23.

45. Larson, ed., *Complete Fiction of Nella Larsen*, 51.

46. Wall, *Women of the Harlem Renaissance*.

47. Wall, *Women of the Harlem Renaissance*, 131; Larson, ed., *Complete Fiction of Nella Larsen*, 176, 182, 104.

48. Locke, ed., *The New Negro*, 47, 19, 339, 359, 364, 216; Arnold Rampersad, ed., *The Collected Poems of Langston Hughes* (New York: Knopf, 1995), 53.

49. Huggins, *Harlem Renaissance*, 89; Ann Douglas, *Terrible Honesty: Mongrel Manhattan in the 1920s* (New York: Farrar, Straus, and Giroux, 1995), 74.

50. Arnold Rampersad, *The Life of Langston Hughes*, vol. 1, *1902–1941, I, Too, Sing America* (New York: Oxford University Press, 1986), 135.

51. For biographical information on Langston Hughes, see Rampersad, *Life of Langston Hughes*, vol. 1.

52. David Levering Lewis, ed., *The Portable Harlem Renaissance Reader* (New York: Penguin, 1994), 97–98.

53. Lewis, ed., *Portable Harlem Renaissance Reader*, 91.

54. Lewis, ed., *Portable Harlem Renaissance Reader*, 92.

55. Lewis, ed., *Portable Harlem Renaissance Reader*, 94–95.

56. Locke, ed., *The New Negro*, 3, 11.

57. Arnold Rampersad, ed., *The Collected Poems of Langston Hughes* (New York: Knopf, 1994), 23–24; Anderson, *Deep River*, 177. All quotations in the text followed by pages in parentheses are from Rampersad, ed., *Collected Poems of Langston Hughes*.

58. Rampersad, *Life of Langston Hughes*, 111.

59. For biographical information on W. E. B. Du Bois, see David Levering Lewis, *W. E. B. Du Bois: Biography of a Race, 1868–1919* (New York: Holt, 1993) and Lewis, *W. E. B. Du Bois: The Fight for Equality*.

60. Henry Louis Gates Jr. and Gene Andrew Jarrett, eds., *The New Negro: Readings on Race, Representation, and African American Culture, 1892–1938* (Princeton, NJ: Princeton University Press, 2007), 190, 192.

61. Gates and Jarrett, eds., *New Negro*, 259.

62. Huggins, *Harlem Renaissance*, 84.

63. Houston A. Baker Jr., *Modernism and the Harlem Renaissance* (Chicago: University of Chicago Press, 1987), 17.

64. Rollin Lynde Hartt, "The New Negro," *Independent*, Jan. 15, 1921, 60.

65. Park, *Race and Culture*, 354; Yu, *Thinking Orientals*, 81.

Chapter 5:
The Eclipsed Public

1. H. L. Mencken, *Notes on Democracy* (New York: Knopf, 1926), 14, 16–19, 21–22, 24–25, 45, 16, 99, 104–5.

2. Mencken, *Notes on Democracy*, 44–45, 49, 51, 147, 87.

3. Arthur S. Link, "What Happened to the Progressive Movement in the 1920's?" *American Historical Review* 64, no. 4 (July 1959): 836, 839; Elisabeth S. Clemens, *The People's Lobby: Organizational Innovation and the Rise of Interest Group Politics in the United States, 1890–1925* (Chicago: University of Chicago Press, 1997); Otis L. Graham Jr., *An Encore for Reform: The Old Progressives and the New Deal* (New York: Oxford University Press, 1967). On the new lobbying of the 1920s, see Lynn Dumenil, *The Modern Temper: American Culture and Society in the 1920s* (New York: Hill & Wang, 1995), 40–51.

4. William Allen White, *Politics: The Citizens' Business* (New York: Macmillan, 1924), v–vi, 7, 14, 15.

5. Jane Addams, *Twenty Years at Hull-House* (New York: MacMillan, 1910). See Michael McGerr, *A Fierce Discontent: The Rise and Fall of the Progressive Movement, 1870–1920* (New York: Oxford University Press, 2003), 65–67.

6. "Where Are the Pre-War Radicals?" *Survey*, Feb. 1, 1926, 557, 563, 560; Frederick C. Howe, "Where Are the Pre-War Radicals? A Rejoinder," *Survey*, April 1, 1926, 33, 34.

7. Mark C. Smith, *Social Science in the Crucible: The American Debate over Objectivity and Purpose, 1918–1941* (Durham, NC: Duke University Press, 1994), 5–6, 8–10, 27–29, 38.

8. William Graebner, *The Engineering of Consent: Democracy and Authority in Twentieth-Century America* (Madison: University of Wisconsin Press, 1987), ix, 3–4, 9–11, 14–15, 18, 48–49. On the social self, see Daniel H. Borus, *Twentieth-Century Multiplicity: American Thought and Culture, 1900–1920* (Lanham, MD: Rowman & Littlefield, 2009), 130–44; Eugene McCarraher, "Me, Myself, Inc.: 'Social Selfhood,' Corporate Humanism, and Religious Longing in American Management Theory, 1908–1956," in *Figures in the Carpet: Finding the Human Person in the American Past*, ed. Wilfred McClay (Grand Rapids, MI: Eerdmans, 2007), 192–202; Jeffrey Sklansky, *The Soul's Economy: Market Society and Selfhood in American Thought, 1820–1920* (Chapel Hill: University of North Carolina Press, 2002); James Livingston, *Pragmatism and the Political Economy of Cultural Revolution, 1850–1940* (Chapel Hill: University of North Carolina Press, 1997); and Wilfred M. McClay, *The Masterless: Self and Society in Modern America* (Chapel Hill: University of North Carolina Press, 1994).

9. For a comprehensive account of social reform in the 1920s, see Clarke A. Chambers, *Seedtime of Reform: American Social Service and Social Action, 1918–1933* (Ann Arbor: University of Michigan Press, 1967).

10. Robert D. Johnston, *The Radical Middle Class: Populist Democracy and the Question of Capitalism in Progressive Era Portland, Oregon* (Princeton, NJ: Princeton University Press, 2003), 156, 152–56; Joan C. Tonn, *Mary P. Follett: Creating Democracy, Transforming Management* (New Haven, CT: Yale University Press, 2003), 293; Charles Forcey, *Crossroads of Liberalism: Croly, Weyl, Lippmann, and the Progressive Era, 1900–1925* (London: Oxford University Press, 1961), 198; Howard Brick, *Transcending Capitalism*, 59; Robert B. Westbrook, *John Dewey and American Democracy* (Ithaca, NY: Cornell University Press, 1991), 235, 301; Richard Schneirov, "The Odyssey of William English Walling: Revisionism, Social Democracy, and Evolutionary Pragmatism," *Journal of the Gilded Age and Progressive Era* 2, no. 4 (Oct. 2003): 405, 420–27.

11. James Weinstein, *The Decline of Socialism in America: 1912–1925* (1967; reprint, New Brunswick, NJ: Rutgers University Press, 1984); Schneirov, "Odyssey of William English Walling," 414.

12. Biographical details on Walter Lippmann are taken from Ronald Steel, *Walter Lippmann and the American Century* (New York: Vintage, 1980).

13. Steel, *Walter Lippmann*, 6–7, 9, 14, 28, 30, 193–95.

14. For Steel's comment on *Preface to Politics*, see Steel, *Walter Lippmann*, 49.

15. Steel, *Walter Lippmann*, 199, 40.

16. Steel, *Walter Lippmann*, 171; Walter Lippmann, *Liberty and the News* (New York: Harcourt, Brace and Howe, 1920), 4–5.

17. Lippmann, *Liberty and the News*, 55.

18. Lippmann, *Liberty and the News*, 47, 85; Walter Lippmann, *Public Opinion* (1922; reprint, New York: Free Press, 1965), 61, 54–55.

19. Lippmann, *Public Opinion*, 61, 69, 71, 77, 79, 81.

20. Lippmann, *Public Opinion*, 58, 60, 111–12, 156, 158.

21. Lippmann, *Public Opinion*, 162–84, 158.

22. Lippmann, *Public Opinion*, 230, 238, 243–44, 241. On the newspapers, see Lippmann, *Public Opinion*, 202–28.

23. Lippmann, *Public Opinion*, 153; Edward L. Bernays, "Manipulating Public Opinion: The Why and the How," *American Journal of Sociology* 33, no. 6 (May 1928): 959–60; Graebner, *Engineering of Consent*, 60, 65.

24. Walter Lippmann, *The Phantom Public* (New York: Harcourt, Brace and Company, 1925), 38, 77, 56–61, 14, 68–69, 126, 147, 156, 168–69.

25. Edward A. Purcell Jr., *The Crisis of Democratic Theory: Scientific Naturalism and the Problem of Value* (Lexington: University Press of Kentucky, 1973), 97–102, 103, 107; Liette Gidlow, *The Big Vote: Gender, Consumer Culture, and the Politics of Exclusion, 1890s–1920s* (Baltimore: Johns Hopkins University Press, 2004); Dorothy Ross, *The Origins of American Social Science* (Cambridge: Cambridge University Press, 1991), 395–96, 452, 455; Smith, *Social Science in the Crucible*, 215, 217–220,

222–23, 227–28. On the antidemocratic trend among intellectuals, see Purcell, *Crisis of Democratic Theory*, 95–114 and Merle Curti, *The Growth of American Thought*, 2nd ed. (New York: Harper & Row, 1951), 695–96.

26. James Hoopes, *False Prophets: The Gurus Who Created Modern Management and Why Their Ideas Are Bad for Business Today* (New York: Basic Books, 2003), 129–33, 137, 142–43.

27. Richard Gillespie, *Manufacturing Knowledge: A History of the Hawthorne Experiments* (Cambridge: Cambridge University Press, 1991), 97–99; Richard C. S. Trahair, "Elton Mayo and the Early Political Psychology of Harold D. Lasswell," *Political Psychology* 3 (Oct. 1, 1981): 170–73; Purcell, *Crisis of Democratic Government*, 100–102, 103, 109; McCarraher, "Me, Myself, and Inc.," 213; Smith, *Social Science in the Crucible*, 224–25.

28. John P. Diggins, *Mussolini and Fascism: The View from America* (Princeton, NJ: Princeton University Press, 1972), 20, 23–24, 27, 68, 72, 56, 58–60, 146–48, 209–11, 222–23, 226–28, 206; Benjamin L. Alpers, *Dictators, Democracy, and American Public Culture* (Chapel Hill: University of North Carolina Press, 2003), 15. On Lippmann's steadfast criticism of Mussolini, see Diggins, *Mussolini and Fascism*, 51–52; and Steel, *Walter Lippmann*, 252.

29. Biographical information is from Tonn, *Mary P. Follett*; Joan C. Tonn's entry on Mary Parker Follett in *American National Biography*; and Hoopes, *False Prophets*, 101–28. See also McCarraher, "Me, Myself, and Inc.," 219–23, for a critical perspective on Follett. Briggs predeceased Follett; the Englishwoman Katharine Furse became her partner of later years (Hoopes 126).

30. Tonn, *Mary P. Follett*, 304–10, 315, 301; Graebner, *Engineering of Consent*, 37, 71; Kevin Mattson, *Creating a Democratic Republic: The Struggle for Urban Participatory Democracy during the Progressive Era* (University Park: Pennsylvania State University Press, 1998), 95. On Follett's conceptions of citizenship, see Tonn, *Mary P. Follett*, 265–303 and Mattson, *Creating a Democratic Republic*, 87–104.

31. Tonn, *Mary P. Follett*, 332–33; Joan C. Tonn, "Follett, Mary Parker," *American National Biography*, ed. John A. Garraty and Mark C. Carnes (24 vols., New York: Oxford University Press, 1999), VIII, 176.

32. M. P. Follett, *Creative Experience* (1924; reprint, New York: Peter Smith, 1951), xiv, x, 160, 164.

33. Follett, *Creative Experience*, 48, 89, 45–46, 53, 156–57, 168.

34. Follett, *Creative Experience*, 169–70, 184, 161.

35. Follett, *Creative Experience*, 116.

36. Follett, *Creative Experience*, 82–83, 118–19, 97–98, 262–63, 106, 178, 224.

37. Follett, *Creative Experience*, 209, 148, 146–50, 134.

38. Follett, *Creative Experience*, 15, 19, 5–6, 20, 29.

39. Follett, *Creative Experience*, 22–23, 5, 209, 205–6; Graebner, *Engineering of Consent*, 72; Hoopes, *False Prophets*, 116–17; McCarraher, "Me, Myself, Inc.," 222.

40. Chambers, *Seedtime of Reform*, 115, 148–49, 181; John M. Jordan, *Machine-Age Ideology: Social Engineering and American Liberalism, 1911–1939* (Chapel Hill: University of North Carolina Press, 1994).

41. Loren Baritz, *The Servants of Power: A History of the Use of Social Science in American Industry* (1960; reprint, Westport, CT: Greenwood Press, 1974), 48–52, 62–74; Richard Gillespie, *Manufacturing Knowledge: A History of the Hawthorne Experiments* (Cambridge: Cambridge University Press, 1991), 1, 19–21.

42. For the Hawthorne experiments generally, see Gillespie, *Manufacturing Knowledge*, 37–95; for the interpretation of results, see, in particular, ibid., 2–3, 66–68, 89–95 and Hoopes, *False Prophets*, 146–53. For a brief, earlier account, betraying interpretations qualified by Gillespie, see Baritz, *Servants of Power*, 77–95.

43. Tonn, *Mary P. Follett*, 388, 428–37; Ross, *Origins of American Social Science*, 456.

44. Jordan, *Machine-Age Ideology*, 114; Ellis W. Hawley, *The Great War and the Search for a Modern Order: A History of the American People and Their Institutions, 1917–1933* (New York: St. Martin's Press, 1979), 59–62.

45. Daniel T. Rodgers, *Transatlantic Crossings: Social Politics in a Progressive Age* (Cambridge, MA: Harvard University Press, 1998), 341–42; Hawley, *Great War and Search for Modern Order*, 101–4; Colin Gordon, *New Deals: Business, Labor, and Politics in America, 1920–1935* (Cambridge: Cambridge University Press, 1994), 1, 15, 128–37.

46. Gordon, *New Deals*, 3, 5, 21–24, 86–87, 93, 96–97, 121.

47. Herbert Hoover, *American Individualism and The Challenge to Liberty* (West Branch, IA: Herbert Hoover Presidential Library Association, 1989), 34, 35, 56–57, 35, 47–50, 44–45.

48. Hoover, *American Individualism*, 51.

49. Alan Ryan, *John Dewey and the High Tide of American Liberalism* (New York: Norton, 1995), 156–57; Robert B. Westbrook, *John Dewey and American Democracy* (Ithaca, NY: Cornell University Press, 1991), 225–26. My account of John Dewey's life draws on Westbrook, *John Dewey and American Democracy*; Robert B. Westbrook, "Dewey, John," in *A Companion to American Thought*, ed. Richard Wightman Fox and James T. Kloppenberg (Oxford: Blackwell, 1995), 177–79; Ryan, *John Dewey*; and Bruce Kucklick, *A History of Philosophy in America, 1700–2000* (Oxford: Oxford University Press, 2001).

50. William James, *Writings, 1902–1910* (New York: Library of America, 1987), 513.

51. John Dewey, "Pragmatic America" (1922), in John Dewey, *The Middle Works, 1899–1924*, ed. Jo Ann Boydston, vol. 13, *1921–1922* (Carbondale: Southern Illinois University Press, 1983), 308–9.

52. John Dewey, *Human Nature and Conduct: An Introduction to Social Psychology*, in John Dewey, *The Middle Works, 1899–1924*, ed. Jo Ann Boydston, vol. 14, *1922* (Carbondale: Southern Illinois University Press, 1983), 15, 21, 33, 47, 159, 162–64, 54, 60.

53. Dewey, *Human Nature*, 65–69, 197, 212, 69, 72, 50–51.

54. Dewey, *Human Nature*, 203; Tonn, *Mary P. Follett*, 374–77; John Dewey, *The Public and Its Problems* (1927; reprint, Athens, OH: Swallow Press, 1985), 158–60.

55. Dewey, *Public and Its Problems*, 85–89, 113, 126, 116, 131.

56. Dewey, *Public and Its Problems*, 115–16, 137, 140, 141.

57. Dewey, *Public and Its Problems*, 142, 207, 144–45.

58. Dewey, *Public and Its Problems*, 166–68, 179, 180–81, 208, 148–49, 184; John Dewey, *Individualism, Old and New* (1930; reprint, New York: Capricorn, 1962), 32, 48–49, 66, 70–72, 81–82.

59. Mencken, *Notes on Democracy*, 174–75.

Chapter 6:
The Inner Check

1. See Paul Avrich, *Sacco and Vanzetti: The Anarchist Background* (Princeton, NJ: Princeton University Press, 1991) and Michael M. Topp, *The Sacco and Vanzetti Case: A Brief History with Documents* (New York: Bedford Books, 2005).

2. John Dos Passos, *Facing the Chair: Story of the Americanization of Two Foreign-born Workmen* (Boston: Sacco-Vanzetti Defense Committee, 1927), 56–57.

3. Michael Lienesch, *In the Beginning: Fundamentalism, the Scopes Trial, and the Making of the Antievolution Movement* (Chapel Hill: University of North Carolina Press, 2007), 59, 72, 112.

4. Lienesch, *In the Beginning*, 62, 64.

5. Edward J. Larson, *Summer for the Gods: The Scopes Trial and America's Continuing Debate over Science and Religion* (New York: Basic Books, 1997), 138; Lienesch, *In the Beginning*, 167.

6. Paul K. Conkin, *When All the Gods Trembled: Darwinism, Scopes, and American Intellectuals* (Lanham, MD: Rowman & Littlefield, 1998), 91–92.

7. Larson, *Summer for the Gods*, 179; Conkin, *When All the Gods Trembled*, 86.

8. Review of *The Quest of the Ages* by A. Eustace Haydon, in *Methodist Review* 46, no. 5 (Sept. 1930): 781; Lynn Dumenil, *The Modern Temper: American Culture and Society in the 1920s* (New York: Hill & Wang, 1995), 170; F. Scott Fitzgerald, *Novels and Stories, 1920–1922* (New York: Library of America, 2000), 208.

9. Bruce Barton, *The Man Nobody Knows: A Discovery of the Real Jesus* (1925; reprint, Chicago: Ivan R. Dee, 2000), 4–5, 23, 35–36, 52, 59–74; Robert S. and Helen Merrell Lynd, *Middletown: A Study in American Culture* (1929; San Diego: Harcourt Brace Jovanovich, 1957), 406.

10. William R. Hutchison, *The Modernist Impulse in American Protestantism* (Cambridge, MA: Harvard University Press, 1976), 275, 277–78; Gary Dorrien, *The Making of American Liberal Theology: Idealism, Realism, and Modernity, 1900–1950* (Louisville, KY: Westminster John Knox Press, 2003), 1, 3, 532.

11. Willard B. Gatewood Jr., ed., *Controversy in the Twenties: Fundamentalism, Modernism, and Evolution* (Nashville, TN: Vanderbilt University Press, 1969), 57.

12. Conkin, *When All the Gods Trembled*, 131–32; Hutchison, *Modernist Impulse in American Protestantism*, 275, 280–81.

13. Richard Wightman Fox, "The Culture of Liberal Protestantism, 1875–1925," *Journal of Interdisciplinary History* 25, no. 3 (Winter 1993): 645–46; Conkin, *When All the Gods Trembled*, 123–25.

14. George M. Marsden, *Fundamentalism and American Culture* (New York: Oxford University Press, 2006), 48, 177, 176; Hutchison, *Modernist Impulse in American Protestantism*, 2, 8, 277–78; Fox, " Culture of Liberal Protestantism," 645; Conkin, *When All the Gods Trembled*, 134, 137; Gatewood, ed., *Controversy in the Twenties*, 59, 60, 56.

15. Hutchison, *Modernist Impulse in American Protestantism*, 258, 262, 269; Conkin, *When All the Gods Trembled*, 119, 64–74; Marsden, *Fundamentalism and American Culture*, 117, 164–84.

16. Marsden, *Fundamentalism and American Culture*, 118–23; Lienesch, *In the Beginning*, 8, 13, 16–24, 28; Larson, *Summer for the Gods*, 20–21.

17. Marsden, *Fundamentalism and American Culture*, 141, 145–49; Hutchison, *Modernist Impulse in American Protestantism*, 226–28.

18. Marsden, *Fundamentalism and American Culture*, 4, 184–88; Lienesch, *In the Beginning*, 36, 38, 52, 57, 133.

19. Marsden, *Fundamentalism and American Culture*, 48–55, 72–80, 161; Conkin, *When All the Gods Trembled*, 60–61.

20. Marsden, *Fundamentalism and American Culture*, 72, 158–59; Lienesch, *In the Beginning*, 34, 40–41.

21. William M. Halsey, *The Survival of American Innocence: Catholicism in an Era of Disillusionment, 1920–1940* (Notre Dame, IN: University of Notre Dame Press, 1980), 1–2, 10, 20, 17–18; Philip Gleason, *Contending with Modernity: Catholic Higher Education in the Twentieth Century* (New York: Oxford University Press, 1995), 105, 112, 116–22; John T. McGreevy, *Catholicism and American Freedom: A History* (New York: Norton, 2003), 140; Eugene McCarraher, *Christian Critics: Religion and the Impasse in Modern American Social Thought* (Ithaca, NY: Cornell University Press, 2000), 36, 54. On the Catholic revival in general, see James Hitchcock, "Postmortem on a Rebirth: The Catholic Intellectual Renaissance," *American Scholar* 49 (Spring 1980): 211–25 and Peter A. Huff, *Allen Tate and the Catholic Revival* (New York: Paulist Press, 1996), 11–22.

22. Gleason, *Contending with Modernity*, 112, 125–27; McGreevy, *Catholicism and American Freedom*, 140–44, 153–63.

23. Walter Lippmann, *A Preface to Morals* (1929; reprint, New York: Macmillan, 1940), 3–4, 6, 8, 9.

24. Gatewood, ed., *Controversy in the Twenties*, 83.

25. Lippmann, *Preface to Morals*, 11–12, 14, 19, 21–28, 32–33, 41–44, 46–47, 119.

26. Joseph Wood Krutch, *The Modern Temper: A Study and a Confession* (1929; reprint, San Diego: Harcourt Brace, 1957), xviii, 6–9, 50, 10–11.

27. Paul V. Murphy, *The Rebuke of History: The Southern Agrarians and American Conservative Thought* (Chapel Hill: University of North Carolina Press, 2001), 54–55; John Crowe Ransom, *God without Thunder: An Unorthodox Defense of Orthodoxy* (New York: Harcourt, Brace, 1930), 4–5, 35, 48, 14, 25, 5, 328.

28. Ransom, *God without Thunder*, 76, 78, 82, 210–211, 248–50, 269, 39, 55, 47, 49, 53, 149–50, 305, 165.

29. Hutchison, *Modernist Impulse in American Protestantism*, 289–90, 233, 254–55; Gary Dorrien, *The Barthian Revolt in Modern Theology: Theology without Weapons* (Louisville, KY: Westminster John Knox Press, 2000), 2; Walter Lowrie, *Our Concern with the Theology of Crisis* (Boston: Meador Publishing Company, 1932), 37–38, 33–36, 43, 49; Gatewood, ed., *Controversy in the Twenties*, 97; Richard Wightman Fox, *Reinhold Niebuhr: A Biography* (San Francisco: Harper & Row, 1985), 84, 65–66, 89. For details on Niebuhr's career, see Fox, *Reinhold Niebuhr*.

30. Larson, *Summer for the Gods*, 37, 38–39, 41, 43, 46–47; Lienesch, *In the Beginning*, 62, 71, 88.

31. Lienesch, *In the Beginning*, 86–87, 115, 71, 87; Larson, *Summer for the Gods*, 27–29, 39–40, 115, 177, 44, 6, 104, 50; Conkin, *When All the Gods Trembled*, 80.

32. Larson, *Summer for the Gods*, 41, 56.

33. Larson, *Summer for the Gods*, 60–83, 88–89, 91, 108; Lienesch, *In the Beginning*, 139.

34. Larson, *Summer for the Gods*, 105, 140, 142, 145, 147, 152; Lienesch, *In the Beginning*, 143, 145–47.

35. Larson, *Summer for the Gods*, 21–22, 116, 119–22, 123, 126–27; Lienesch, *In the Beginning*, 83–84, 92–93, 95, 110, 278n90; Marsden, *Fundamentalism and American Culture*, 7, 121.

36. Larson, *Summer for the Gods*, 102, 128–29, 131, 133, 134, 136, 144, 163, 171, 174, 208, 220; Lienesch, *In the Beginning*, 144, 156–57, 158–59.

37. Larson, *Summer for the Gods*, 5, 187–90; Marsden, *Fundamentalism and American Culture*, 186–87; Conkin, *When All the Gods Trembled*, 96; Lienesch, *In the Beginning*, 162–63.

38. Larson, *Summer for the Gods*, 197, 199, 220, 230; Lienesch, *In the Beginning*, 167, 171, 178, 180; Conkin, *When All the Gods Trembled*, 96. On the decline of American Protestantism, see Robert T. Handy, "The American Religious Depression, 1925–1935," *Church History* 29, no. 1 (March 1960), 3–16.

39. Walter Lippmann, *American Inquisitors* (1928; reprint, New Brunswick, NJ: Transaction, 1993), 87, 45–46.

40. Lippmann, *American Inquisitors*, 51–55, 57, 40–41, 75, 85, 84.

41. On the medieval humanist tradition, see W. T. Jones, *A History of Western Philosophy*, vol. 3, *Hobbes to Hume*, 2nd ed. (San Diego, CA: Harcourt, Brace, Jovanovich, 1969), 33–43 and Richard H. Popkin, ed., *Columbia History of Western Philosophy*, 2nd ed. (New York: MJF Books, 1999), 292–303.

42. The best study of New Humanism is J. David Hoeveler Jr., *The New Humanism: A Critique of Modern America, 1900–1940* (Charlottesville: University Press of Virginia, 1977). For biographical details on Irving Babbitt, see ibid., 5, 8–9, and for details on Paul Elmer More, see ibid., 10–12; Daniel Aaron, ed., *Paul Elmer More's Shelburne Essays on American Literature* (New York: Harcourt, Brace, & World, 1963), 1; Byron C. Lambert, ed., *The Essential Paul Elmer More: A Selection of His Writings* (New Rochelle, NY: Arlington House, 1972), 15–16.

43. Norman Foerster, ed., *Humanism and America: Essays on the Outlook of Modern Civilisation* (New York: Farrar and Rinehart, 1930); C. Hartley Grattan, ed., *The Critique of Humanism: A Symposium* (1930; reprint, Freeport: Books for Libraries Press, 1968).

44. Irving Babbitt, "The Critic and American Life," *Forum* 79, no. 2 (Feb. 1928): 167; Irving Babbitt, "What I Believe: Rousseau and Religion," *Forum*, 38, no. 2 (Feb. 1930): 82, 83, 86; Irving Babbitt, *Democracy and Leadership* (1924; reprint, Indianapolis: Liberty Fund, 1979), 28; Foerster, ed., *Humanism and America*, 26, 40–44; Paul Elmer More, *The Demon of the Absolute* (Princeton, NJ: Princeton University Press, 1928), x, 23; Frederick J. Hoffman, *The Twenties: American Writing in the Postwar Decade* (New York: Free Press, 1962), 166; Hoeveler, *New Humanism*, 34.

45. Paul Elmer More, "A Revival of Humanism," *Bookman* 71, no. 1 (March 1930): 4. For a typical assault by Babbitt on Rousseau, see Babbitt, "What I Believe," 80–81. For the varying humanist terms of opposition, see Foerster, ed., *Humanism and America*, x, 31, 34, 268; Babbitt, *Democracy and Leadership*, 29; More, *Demon of the Absolute*, x, 1; More, "A Revival of Humanism," 2.

46. T. S. Eliot, *For Lancelot Andrewes: Essays on Style and Order* (Garden City, NY: Doubleday, Doran, 1929), vii; T. S. Eliot, "The Humanism of Irving Babbitt," *Forum* 80, no. 1 (July 1928): 39; Foerster, ed., *Humanism and America*, 105, 110.

47. Grattan, ed., *Critique of Humanism*, 160; Norman Foerster, "Humanism and Religion," *Forum* 82, no. 3 (Sept. 1929): 147; Babbitt, "What I Believe," 83; Foerster, ed., *Humanism and America*, 37, 39; More, "Revival of Humanism," 7–10; Hoeveler, *New Humanism*, 16–17, 152–53, 169–76.

48. Alfred Kazin, *On Native Grounds: An Interpretation of Modern American Prose Literature* (New York: Harcourt, Brace, & World, 1942), 291; "The Embattled Humanists," *New Republic*, Feb. 12, 1930, 315.

49. Grattan, ed., *Critique of Humanism*, 123; Katharine Fullerton Gerould, "Salvation by Invitation," *Yale Review* 20 (Dec. 1930): 264–65.

50. Edmund Wilson, *The Shores of Light: A Literary Chronicle of the Twenties and Thirties* (New York: Farrar, Straus and Young, 1952), 456–57.

51. Henry Seidel Canby, "The New Humanists," *Saturday Review of Literature*, Feb. 22, 1930, 750. See also Grattan, ed., *Critique of Humanism*, 113; Gerould, "Salvation by Invitation," 266. Babbitt, *Democracy and Leadership*, 38; Babbitt, "Critic and American Life," 163–64; Hoeveler, *New Humanism*, 132; Walter Lippmann, "Humanism as Dogma," *Saturday Review of Literature*, March 15, 1930, 817–18, 819; Henry Hazlitt, "The Pretensions of Humanism," *Nation*, March 5, 1930, 273. See also

Canby, "New Humanists," 750 and Henry Seidel Canby, "Post Mortem," *Saturday Review of Literature*, June 14, 1930, 1122–23. Sinclair Lewis, "The American Fear of Literature," in *The Rise of Sinclair Lewis, 1920–1930*, ed. James M. Hutchisson (University Park: Pennsylvania State University Press, 1996), 243.

52. Canby, "Post Mortem," 1121. For hints of a critique of the modern "one-sided cult of material efficiency" in Babbitt, see Babbitt, "Critic and American Life," 174–75. See also Babbitt, *Democracy and Leadership*, 25–26; and Foerster, ed., *Humanism and America*, 45. See also Gorham Munson in Foerster, ed., *Humanism and America*, 244.

53. Grattan, ed., *Critique of Humanism*, vii, 345, 350; Canby, "New Humanists," 751. See also Grattan, ed., *Critique of Humanism*, 63; and Lippmann, "Humanism as Dogma," 818. Henry Hazlitt, "All Too Humanism," *Nation*, Feb. 12, 1930, 182; Lewis Mumford, "A Modern Synthesis," *Saturday Review of Literature*, April 12, 1930, 920–21; John Dewey, *Individualism, Old and New* (1930; reprint, New York: Capricorn Books, 1962), 155–56.

54. Grattan, ed., *Critique of Humanism*, 9, 70–71; Canby, "New Humanists," 749, 751.

55. Twelve Southerners, *I'll Take My Stand: The South and the Agrarian Tradition* (1930; reprint, Baton Rouge: Louisiana State University Press, 1977), xxxvii, xlvi, xlviii, 1.

56. Twelve Southerners, *I'll Take My Stand*, 8–12, 39, 244. See, in general, Murphy, *Rebuke of History*, 11–30.

57. Murphy, *Rebuke of History*, 51–54, 56–57, 58–59; Twelve Southerners, *I'll Take My Stand*, xliii–xliv, 168.

58. Twelve Southerners, *I'll Take My Stand*, 359; Lippmann, *Preface to Morals*, 143, 137, 210, 214, 216, 221, 235–37, 239. See, generally, ibid., 256–58, 271–72, 282–83.

59. Krutch, *Modern Temper*, 19–38.

60. Krutch, *Modern Temper*, 60–61, 64, 67–70, 75.

61. Edmund Wilson, *Axel's Castle: A Study in the Imaginative Literature of 1870–1930* (New York: Charles Scribner's Sons, 1931); Grattan, ed., *Critique of Humanism*, 353. See Casey Nelson Blake, *Beloved Community: The Cultural Criticism of Randolph Bourne, Van Wyck Brooks, Waldo Frank, & Lewis Mumford* (Chapel Hill: University of North Carolina Press, 1990), 220–24.

62. Ransom, *God without Thunder*, x, 28, 116, 156, 81.

63. Grattan, ed., *Critique of Humanism*, 82–83.

64. Michael Soto, *The Modernist Nation: Generation, Renaissance, and Twentieth-Century American Literature* (Tuscaloosa: University of Alabama Press, 2004), 42.

65. For a recent study brightly illuminating this mindset, see Robert Genter, *Late Modernism: Art, Culture, and Politics in Cold War America* (Philadelphia: University of Pennsylvania Press, 2010).

66. Gene Wise, "'Paradigm Dramas' in American Studies: A Cultural and Intellectual History of the Movement," *American Quarterly* 31, no. 3 (1979): 305–6.

67. Howard Brick, *Transcending Capitalism: Visions of a New Society in Modern American Thought* (Ithaca, NY: Cornell University Press, 2006), 3–4.

~

Bibliographical Essay

There are many fine histories of the 1920s: Lynn Dumenil, *The Modern Temper: American Culture and Society in the 1920s* (New York: Hill & Wang, 1995); David J. Goldberg, *Discontented America: The United States in the 1920s* (Baltimore: Johns Hopkins University Press, 1999); Ellis W. Hawley, *The Great War and the Search for a Modern Order: A History of the American People and Their Institutions, 1917–1933* (New York: St. Martin's Press, 1979); and the older but still relevant William Leuchtenburg, *The Perils of Prosperity, 1914–1932* (Chicago: University of Chicago Press, 1958). For an especially stimulating treatment of American culture in the 1920s, see Ann Douglas, *Terrible Honesty: Mongrel Manhattan in the 1920s* (New York: Farrar, Straus, and Giroux, 1995) as well as Stanley Coben, *Rebellion against Victorianism: The Impetus for Cultural Change in 1920s America* (New York: Oxford University Press, 1991) and Robert M. Crunden, *Body and Soul: The Making of American Modernism* (New York: Basic Books, 2000). Two older but suggestive accounts of the cultural history of the decade include Roderick Nash, *The Nervous Generation: American Thought, 1917–1930* (Chicago: Rand McNally, 1970), the only book-length survey, and Lawrence Levine, "Progress and Nostalgia: The Self Image of the Nineteen Twenties," in *The Unpredictable Past: Explorations in American Cultural History* (New York: Oxford University Press, 1993), 189–205. Warren Susman's *Culture as History: The Transformation of American Society in the Twentieth Century* (New York: Pantheon, 1984) contains brilliant analytical essays relevant to any study of this period.

Frederick Lewis Allen's still rewarding popular history remains in print: *Only Yesterday: An Informal History of the 1920s* (1931; reprint, New York: Perennial Classics, 2000). For astute analyses of Allen's history, see David M. Kennedy, "Revisiting Frederick Lewis Allen's *Only Yesterday,*" *Reviews in American History* 14, no. 2 (June 1986): 309–18 and Kenneth S. Lynn, *The Air-Line to Seattle: Studies in Literary and Historical Writing about America* (Chicago: University of Chicago Press, 1983), 140–51. For an early scholarly history, see Preston William Slosson, *The Great Crusade and After, 1914–1928* (New York: Macmillan, 1930). An older but still interesting historiographical essay is Henry F. May, "Shifting Perspectives on the 1920s," *Mississippi Valley Historical Review* 43, no. 3 (Dec. 1956): 405–27. Still of interest as well are John Braeman, Robert H. Bremner, and David Brody, eds., *Change and Continuity in Twentieth-Century America: The 1920s* (Columbus: Ohio State University Press, 1968) and Paul A. Carter, *Another Part of the Twenties* (New York: Columbia, 1977). A recent popular history is Nathan Miller, *New World Coming: The 1920s and the Making of Modern America* (Cambridge, MA: Da Capo Press, 2003). See also the recent Charles Shindo, *1927 and the Rise of Modern America* (Lawrence: University Press of Kansas, 2010). Kathleen Drowne and Patrick Huber, *The 1920s* (Westport, CT: Greenwood, 2004) provides much descriptive information. See also Lawrence R. Broer and John D. Walther, eds., *Dancing Fools and Weary Blues: The Great Escape of the Twenties* (Bowling Green, KY: Bowling Green State University, 1990).

For the classic sociological study of Muncie, Indiana, see Robert S. Lynd and Helen Merrell Lynd, *Middletown: A Study in American Culture* (1929; reprint, San Diego: Harcourt Brace Jovanovich, 1957). On the Lynds and their work, see Richard Wightman Fox, "Epitaph for Middletown: Robert S. Lynd and the Analysis of Consumer Culture," in *The Culture of Consumption: Critical Essays in American History, 1880–1980*, ed. Richard Wightman Fox and T. J. Jackson Lears (New York: Pantheon, 1983), 103–41 and Sarah E. Igo, *The Averaged American: Surveys, Citizens, and the Making of a Mass Public* (Cambridge, MA: Harvard University Press, 2007). Two sets of state-by-state assessments of America from the period are Daniel H. Borus, ed., *These United States: Portraits of America from the 1920s* (Ithaca, NY: Cornell University Press, 1992) and Tom Lutz and Susanna Ashton, eds., *These "Colored" United States: African American Essays from the 1920s* (New Brunswick, NJ: Rutgers University Press, 1996).

For the 1910s cultural rebellion, which shaped the decade, see Henry F. May, *The End of American Innocence: A Study of the First Years of Our Time, 1912–1917* (New York: Knopf, 1959); Christine Stansell, *American Moderns: Bohemian New York and the Creation of a New Century* (New York: Owl Books/

Holt, 2000); Arthur Frank Wertheim, *The New York Little Renaissance: Icono-clasm, Modernism, and Nationalism in American Culture, 1908–1917* (New York: New York University Press, 1976); and Ross Wetzsteon, *Republic of Dreams: Greenwich Village; The American Bohemia, 1910–1960* (New York: Simon and Schuster, 2002). On the Young Intellectuals, see Casey Nelson Blake, *Beloved Community: The Cultural Criticism of Randolph Bourne, Van Wyck Brooks, Waldo Frank, and Lewis Mumford* (Chapel Hill: University of North Carolina Press, 1990); Casey Blake, "The Young Intellectuals and the Culture of Personality," *American Literary History* 1, no. 3 (Fall 1989): 510–34; Thomas P. Hughes and Agatha C. Hughes, eds., *Lewis Mumford: Public Intellectual* (New York: Oxford University Press, 1990); and John L. Thomas, "The Uses of Catastrophism: Lewis Mumford, Vernon L. Parrington, Van Wyck Brooks, and the End of American Regionalism," *American Quarterly* 42, no. 2 (June 1990): 223–51. More generally, see T. J. Jackson Lears, *No Place of Grace: Antimodernism and the Transformation of American Culture, 1880–1920* (1981; reprint, Chicago: University of Chicago Press, 1994); and Bruce Kuklick, *A History of Philosophy in America, 1700–2000* (Oxford: Oxford University Press, 2001). Daniel H. Borus, *Twentieth-Century Multiplicity: American Thought and Culture, 1900–1920* (Lanham, MD: Rowman & Littlefield, 2009) provides a helpful synthesis.

On the complexities of "culture" in American intellectual life, see Lewis Perry, *Intellectual Life in America: A History* (Chicago: University of Chicago Press, 1989); Joan Shelley Rubin, *The Making of Middlebrow Culture* (Chapel Hill: University of North Carolina Press, 1992); and John S. Gilkeson Jr., "The Domestication of 'Culture' in Interwar America, 1919–1941," in *The Estate of Social Knowledge*, ed. JoAnne Brown and David K. van Keuren (Baltimore: Johns Hopkins University Press, 1991), 153–74. John S. Gilkeson has published a new study, *Anthropologists and the Rediscovery of America, 1886–1965* (Cambridge: Cambridge University Press, 2010). Always helpful is Raymond Williams, *Culture and Society, 1780–1850* (New York: Columbia University Press, 1960).

On the sexual revolution of the time, see John D'Emilio and Estelle B. Freedman, *Intimate Matters: A History of Sexuality in America* (New York: Harper and Row, 1988); Beth Bailey, *From Front Porch to Back Seat: Courtship in Twentieth-Century America* (Baltimore: Johns Hopkins University Press, 1988); George Chauncey, *Gay New York: Gender, Urban Culture, and the Making of the Gay Male World, 1890–1940* (New York: Basic Books, 1994); Christina Simmons, *Making Marriage Modern: Women's Sexuality from the Progressive Era to World War II* (New York: Oxford University Press, 2009); and Paula Fass, *The Damned and the Beautiful: American Youth in the 1920s* (Oxford: Oxford University Press, 1977), which also provides the best treatment of college youth. On psychoanalysis, see Nathan G. Hale Jr., *The Rise and Crisis of Psychoanalysis in the United States: Freud and the Americans, 1917–1985* (New York: Oxford University Press, 1995). For an incisive critique of the emerging cultural norms and battles over censorship, see Rochelle Gurstein, *The Repeal of Reticence: A History of America's Cultural and Legal Struggles over Free Speech, Obscenity, Sexual Liberation, and Modern Art* (New York: Hill and Wang, 1996).

On the social transformations in women's political, social, and cultural life, see, first and foremost, Nancy F. Cott, *The Grounding of Modern Feminism* (New Haven, CT: Yale University Press, 1987) as well as Christine Lunardini, *From Equal Suffrage to Equal Rights: Alice Paul and the National Woman's Party, 1910–1928* (New York: New York University Press, 1986); J. Stanley Lemons, *The Woman Citizen: Social Feminism in the 1920s* (Urbana: University of Illinois Press, 1973); Ann Butler, *Two Paths to Equality: Alice Paul and Ethel M. Smith in the ERA Debate, 1921–1929* (Albany: State University of New York Press, 2002); and Jan Doolittle Wilson, *The Women's Joint Congressional Committee and the Politics of Maternalism, 1920–1930* (Urbana: University of Illinois Press, 2007). For an older but still useful historiographical review, see Estelle B. Freeman, "The New Woman: Changing Views of Women in the 1920s," *Journal of American History* 61, no. 2 (Sept. 1974): 372–93.

On cultural anthropology and the Boasians, I have relied on the following: George W. Stocking Jr., *Race, Culture, and Evolution: Essays in the History of Anthropology* (New York: Free Press, 1968); George W. Stocking Jr., *The Ethnographer's Magic and Other Essays in the History of Anthropology* (Madison: University of Wisconsin Press, 1992); George W. Stocking Jr., *Delimiting Anthropology: Occasional Essays and Reflections* (Madison: University of Wisconsin Press, 2001); Richard Handler, *Critics against Culture: Anthropological Observers of Mass Society* (Madison: University of Wisconsin Press, 2005); Lois W. Banner, *Intertwined Lives: Margaret Mead, Ruth Benedict, and Their Circle* (New York: Knopf, 2003); and Nancy C. Lutkehaus, *Margaret Mead: The Making of an Icon* (Princeton, NJ: Princeton University Press, 2008). On culture, more generally, see Susan Hegeman, *Patterns for America: Modernism and the Concept of Culture* (Princeton, NJ: Princeton University Press, 1999) and Paul R. Gorman, *Left Intellectuals and Popular Culture in Twentieth-Century America* (Chapel Hill: University of North Carolina Press, 1996).

On consumer culture, see William Leach, *Land of Desire: Merchants, Power, and the Rise of a New American Culture* (New York: Pantheon, 1993); Gary S. Cross, *An All-Consuming Century: Why Commercialism Won in Modern America* (New York: Columbia University Press, 2000); and Roland Marchand, *Advertising the American Dream: Making Way for Modernity,*

1920–1940 (Berkeley: University of California Press, 1985). On leisure and recreation in general, see David Nasaw, *Going Out: The Rise and Fall of Public Amusements* (Cambridge, MA: Harvard University Press, 1999) and Lewis A. Erenberg, *Steppin' Out: New York Nightlife and the Transformation of American Culture, 1890–1930* (Chicago: University of Chicago Press, 1984).

For film in the 1920s, see William K. Everson, *American Silent Film* (New York: Oxford University Press, 1978); David Robinson, *Hollywood in the Twenties* (London: A. Zwemmer, 1968); Richard Schickel, *His Picture in the Papers: A Speculation on Celebrity in America Based on the Life of Douglas Fairbanks, Sr.* (New York: Charterhouse, 1973); and Lea Jacobs, *The Decline of Sentiment: American Film in the 1920s* (Berkeley: University of California Press, 2008). On the movie industry and popular reception of film, see Richard Koszarski, *An Evening's Entertainment: The Age of the Silent Feature Picture, 1915–1928* (New York: Charles Scribner's Sons, 1990); Robert Sklar, *Movie-Made America: A Cultural History of American Movies* (New York: Vintage, 1994); Kathryn H. Fuller, *At the Picture Show: Small-Town Audiences and the Creation of Movie Fan Culture* (Washington, DC: Smithsonian Institution Press, 1996); Kathryn H. Fuller-Seeley, ed., *Hollywood in the Neighborhood: Historical Case Studies of Local Moviegoing* (Berkeley: University of California Press, 2008); Lary May, *Screening Out the Past: The Birth of Mass Culture and the Motion Picture Industry* (Chicago: University of Chicago Press, 1983); Samantha Barbas, *Movie Crazy: Fans, Stars, and the Cult of Celebrity* (New York: Palgrave Macmillan, 2001); and Miriam Hansen, *Babel and Babylon: Spectatorship in American Silent Film* (Cambridge, MA: Harvard University Press, 1991). On silent comedians, the classic account is Walter Kerr, *The Silent Clowns* (New York: Knopf, 1975). See also Alan Dale, *Comedy Is a Man in Trouble: Slapstick in American Movies* (Minneapolis: University of Minnesota Press, 2000); Henry Jenkins, *What Made Pistachio Nuts? Early Sound Comedy and the Vaudeville Aesthetic* (New York: Columbia University Press, 1992); and for a seminal review, James Agee, "Comedy's Greatest Era," in *Agee on Film: Reviews and Comments by James Agee* (New York: McDonnell Obolonsky, 1958), 2–19.

Basic works in the history of music from this period include, on jazz and blues, Burton W. Peretti, *The Creation of Jazz: Music, Race, and Culture in Urban America* (Urbana: University of Illinois Press, 1992); William Barlow, *"Looking Up at Down": The Emergence of Blues Culture* (Philadelphia: Temple University Press, 1989); Daphne Duval Harrison, *Black Pearls: Blues Queens of the 1920s* (New Brunswick, NJ: Rutgers University Press, 1990); Hazel V. Carby, "It Jus Be's Dat Way Sometime: The Sexual Politics of Women's Blues," in *The Jazz Cadence of American Culture*, ed. Robert G. O'Meally (New

York: Columbia University Press, 1998), 469–82; Macdonald Smith Moore, *Yankee Blues: Musical Culture and American Identity* (Bloomington: Indiana University Press, 1985); and Kathy J. Ogren, *The Jazz Revolution: Twenties America and the Meaning of Jazz* (New York: Oxford University Press, 1989). On black secular music generally, see Lawrence W. Levine, *Black Culture and Black Consciousness: Afro-American Folk Thought from Slavery to Freedom* (Oxford: Oxford University Press, 1977). For popular commercial music, see Arnold Shaw, *The Jazz Age: Popular Music in the 1920's* (New York: Oxford University Press, 1987). On the origins of country music, see Bill C. Malone, *Country Music, USA*, rev. ed. (Austin: University of Texas Press, 1985); Richard A. Peterson, *Creating Country Music: Fabricating Authenticity* (Chicago: University of Chicago Press, 1997); and Diane Pecknold, *The Selling Sound: The Rise of the Country Music Industry* (Durham, NC: Duke University Press, 2007). Relevant to the cultural background of country music is Anthony Harkins, *Hillbilly: A Cultural History of an American Icon* (New York: Oxford University Press, 2004). For a biography of the chief celebrant of the popular arts, see Michael Kammen, *The Lively Arts: Gilbert Seldes and the Transformation of Cultural Criticism in the United States* (New York: Oxford University Press, 1996). On the development of radio, some general introductions are Susan Smulyan, *Selling Radio: The Commercialization of American Broadcasting, 1920–1934* (Washington, DC: Smithsonian Institution, 1994); Michele Hilmes, *Radio Voices: American Broadcasting, 1922–1952* (Minneapolis: University of Minnesota Press, 1997); Paul Starr, *The Creation of the Media: Political Origins of Modern Communications* (New York: Basic Books, 2004); and Clifford J. Doerksen, *American Babel: Rogue Radio Broadcasters of the Jazz Age* (Philadelphia: University of Temple Press, 2005).

For the general literary history of the era, see the still useful Alfred Kazin, *On Native Grounds: An Interpretation of Modern American Prose Literature* (New York: Harcourt, Brace and World, 1942) and the classics Frederick J. Hoffman, *The Twenties: American Writing in the Postwar Decade*, rev. ed. (New York: Free Press, 1965) and Daniel Aaron, *Writers on the Left: Episodes in American Literary Communism* (New York: Columbia University Press, 1992). Richard H. Pells, *Radical Visions and American Dreams: Culture and Social Thought in the Depression Years* (Middletown, CT: Wesleyan University Press, 1973) contains a substantive introduction dealing with the 1920s. See also Marc Dolan, *Modern Lives: A Cultural Re-Reading of "The Lost Generation"* (West Lafayette, IN: Purdue University Press, 1996); Catherine Turner, *Marketing Modernism: Between the Two World Wars* (Amherst: University of Massachusetts Press, 2003); and Michael Soto, *The Modernist Nation: Generation, Renaissance, and Twentieth-Century American Literature* (Tuscaloosa: University of Alabama Press, 2004). Walter Benn Michaels, *Our America: Nativism, Modernism, and Pluralism* (Durham, NC: Duke University Press, 1995) is a provocative treatment of race and ethnicity in the literature of the period.

Particularly enlightening are four literary figures from the decade: Malcolm Cowley, *Exile's Return: A Literary Odyssey of the 1920s*, rev. ed. (New York: Viking, 1951); Edmund Wilson, *The Shores of Light: A Literary Chronicle of the Twenties and Thirties* (New York: Farrar, Straus and Young, 1952); Edmund Wilson, *The American Earthquake: A Documentary of the Twenties and Thirties* (Garden City, NJ: Anchor, 1964); Matthew Josephson, *Life among the Surrealists* (New York: Holt, Rinehart, and Winston, 1962); and Gorham Munson, *The Awakening Twenties: A Memoir-History of a Literary Period* (Baton Rouge: Louisiana State University Press, 1985). Jack Selzer, *Kenneth Burke in Greenwich Village: Conversing with the Moderns, 1915–1931* (Madison: University of Wisconsin Press, 1996) is useful and detailed. On the art of the period, see Dickran Tashjian, *Skyscraper Primitives: Dada and the American Avant-Garde, 1910–1925* (Middletown: Wesleyan University, 1975); Dickran Tashjian, *A Boatload of Madmen: Surrealism and the American Avant-Garde, 1920–1950* (New York: Thames and Hudson, 1995); and Wanda M. Corn, *The Great American Thing: Modern Art and National Identity, 1915–1935* (Berkeley: University of California Press, 1999). On regionalism, see Robert L. Dorman, *Revolt of the Provinces: The Regionalist Movement in America, 1920–1945* (Chapel Hill: University of North Carolina Press, 1993); Charles C. Alexander, *Here the Country Lies: Nationalism and the Arts in Twentieth-Century America* (Bloomington: Indiana University Press, 1980); and Roy Lubove, *Community Planning in the 1920s: The Contribution of the Regional Planning Association of America* (Pittsburgh: University of Pittsburgh Press, 1964).

For the life of H. L. Mencken, I have relied on Fred Hobson, *Mencken: A Life* (New York: Random House, 1994); and Marion Elizabeth Rodgers, *Mencken: The American Iconoclast* (New York: Oxford University Press, 2005). Another recent biography is Terry Teachout, *The Skeptic: A Life of H. L. Mencken* (New York: Perennial, 2002). Of the innumerable literary biographies, I have consulted Richard Lingeman, *Sinclair Lewis: Rebel from Main Street* (New York: Random House, 2002); Kenneth S. Lynn, *Hemingway* (New York: Simon and Schuster, 1987); Lewis M. Dabney, *Edmund Wilson: A Life in Literature* (New York: Farrar, Straus and Giroux, 2005); Hans Bak, *Malcolm Cowley: The Formative Years* (Athens: University of Georgia Press, 1993); Matthew J. Bruccoli, *Some Sort of Epic Splendor: The Life of F. Scott Fitzgerald* (New York: Harcourt Brace Jovanovich, 1981); John Unterecker, *Voyager: A Life of Hart Crane* (New York: Farrar, Straus, and Giroux, 1969); Clive Fisher, *Hart Crane: A Life* (New Haven, CT: Yale University Press,

2002); Arnold Rampersad, *The Life of Langston Hughes*, vol. 1, *1902–1941, I, Too, Sing America* (New York: Oxford University Press, 1986); George Hutchinson, *In Search of Nella Larsen: A Biography of the Color Line* (Cambridge, MA: Harvard University Press, 2006); Daniel J. Singal, *William Faulkner: The Making of a Modernist* (Chapel Hill: University of North Carolina Press, 1997); and Richard S. Kennedy, *E. E. Cummings Revisited* (New York: Twayne, 1994). I have consulted Sherman Paul, *Hart's Bridge* (Urbana: University of Illinois Press, 1972), on Hart Crane's epic poem.

On social science, see Dorothy Ross, *The Origins of American Social Science* (Cambridge: Cambridge University Press, 1991); Mark C. Smith, *Social Science in the Crucible: The American Debate over Objectivity and Purpose, 1918–1941* (Durham, NC: Duke University Press, 1994); Carl Degler, *In Search of Human Nature: Decline and Revival of Darwinism in American Social Thought* (New York: Oxford University Press, 1991); and Robert C. Bannister, *Sociology and Scientism: The American Quest for Objectivity, 1880–1940* (Chapel Hill: University of North Carolina Press, 1987). On the Chicago school of sociology, see Fred H. Matthews, *Quest for an American Sociology: Robert E. Park and the Chicago School* (Montreal: McGill-Queen's University Press, 1977); Stow Persons, *Ethnic Studies at Chicago, 1905–1945* (Urbana: University of Illinois Press, 1987); Eli Zaretsky, "Editor's Introduction," in William I. Thomas and Florian Znaniecki, *The Polish Peasant in Europe and America*, ed. Eli Zaretsky (Urbana: University of Illinois Press, 1984), 1–46; Henry Yu, *Thinking Orientals: Migration, Contact, and Exoticism in Modern America* (New York: Oxford University Press, 2001); and Kathleen Neils Conzen, "Thomas and Znaniecki and the Historiography of American Immigration," *Journal of American Ethnic Studies* 16, no. 1 (Fall 1996): 16–25. The classic account of nativism is John Higham, *Strangers in the Land: Patterns of American Nativism, 1860–1925*, 2nd ed. (New York: Atheneum, 1965). See also John Higham, *Send These to Me: Jews and Other Immigrants in Urban America* (New York: Atheneum, 1975); David A. Hollinger, *In the American Province: Studies in the History and Historiography of Ideas* (Baltimore: Johns Hopkins University Press, 1985); and Mae M. Ngai, *Impossible Subjects: Illegal Aliens and the Making of Modern America* (Princeton, NJ: Princeton University Press, 2004). For introductions to the new history of the second Ku Klux Klan, see Leonard J. Moore, *Citizen Klansmen: The Ku Klux Klan in Indiana, 1921–1928* (Chapel Hill: University of North Carolina Press, 1991); Nancy MacLean, *Behind the Mask of Chivalry: The Making of the Second Ku Klux Klan* (New York: Oxford University Press, 1994); and Shaw Lay, ed., *The Invisible Empire of the West: Toward a New Historical Appraisal of the Ku Klux Klan of the 1920s* (Urbana: University of Illinois Press, 1992).

Two works in whiteness studies most relevant to this period are Matthew Frye Jacobson, *Whiteness of a Different Color: European Immigrants and the Alchemy of Race* (Cambridge, MA: Harvard University Press, 1998) and Matthew Pratt Guterl, *The Color of Race in America, 1900–1940* (Cambridge, MA: Harvard University Press, 2001). Jonathan Peter Spiro, *Defending the Master Race: Conservation, Eugenics, and the Legacy of Madison Grant* (Burlington: University of Vermont Press, 2009) provides a lively account of pseudoscientific racial theory. On the Rhinelander case, see Earl Lewis and Heidi Ardizzone, *Love on Trial: An American Scandal in Black and White* (New York: Norton, 2001). On Marcus Garvey, see Alphonso Pinckney, *Red, Black, and Green: Black Nationalism in the United States* (Cambridge: Cambridge University Press, 1976); Judith Stein, *The World of Marcus Garvey: Race and Class in Modern Society* (Baton Rouge: Louisiana State University Press, 1986); and Mary G. Rolinson, *Grassroots Garveyism: The Universal Negro Improvement Association in the Rural South, 1920–1927* (Chapel Hill: University of North Carolina Press, 2007). A study of three dissenting black social thinkers is Jonathan Scott Holloway, *Confronting the Veil: Abram Harris, Jr., E. Franklin Frazier, and Ralph Bunche, 1919–1941* (Chapel Hill: University of North Carolina Press, 2002).

For the standard accounts of the Harlem Renaissance, see David Levering Lewis, *When Harlem Was in Vogue* (New York: Penguin, 1997); Nathan Irvin Huggins, *Harlem Renaissance* (London: Oxford University Press, 1971); and George Hutchinson, *The Harlem Renaissance in Black and White* (Cambridge, MA: Harvard University Press, 1995). For an early assessment, see Gilbert Osofsky, "Symbols of the Jazz Age: The New Negro and Harlem Discovered," *American Quarterly* 17, no. 2 (Summer 1965): 229–38. See also Cheryl A. Wall, *Women of the Harlem Renaissance* (Bloomington: Indiana University Press, 1995) and Paul Allen Anderson, *Deep River: Music and Memory in Harlem Renaissance Thought* (Durham, NC: Duke University Press, 2001). Houston A. Baker Jr., *Modernism and the Harlem Renaissance* (Chicago: University of Chicago Press, 1987) provides a critical interpretation. On W. E. B. Du Bois, see David Levering Lewis's monumental two-volume biography: *W. E. B. Du Bois: Biography of a Race, 1868–1919* (New York: Holt, 1993) and *W. E. B. Du Bois: The Fight for Equality and the American Century, 1919–1963* (New York: Holt, 2000) as well as Thomas C. Holt, "The Political Uses of Alienation: W. E. B. DuBois on Politics, Race, and Culture, 1903–1940," *American Quarterly* 42, no. 2 (June 1990): 301–23. On the New Negro, see Barbara Foley, *Spectres of 1919: Class and Nation in the Making of the New Negro* (Urbana: University of Illinois Press, 2003). An excellent introduction to the thought of Alain Locke is Jeffrey C. Stewart, "Introduction," in *Race*

Contacts and Interracial Relations: Lectures on the Theory and Practice of Race, ed. Jeffrey C. Stewart (Washington, DC: Howard University Press, 1992), xxxv–xlii. Leonard Harris and Charles Molesworth have published a full biography, *Alain L. Locke: The Biography of a Philosopher* (Chicago: University of Chicago Press, 2008).

On reform politics, see Clarke A. Chambers, *Seedtime of Reform: American Social Service and Social Action, 1918–1933* (Ann Arbor: University of Michigan Press, 1967); Otis L. Graham Jr., *An Encore for Reform: The Old Progressives and the New Deal* (New York: Oxford University Press, 1967); James Weinstein, *The Decline of Socialism in America: 1912–1925* (1967; reprint, New Brunswick, NJ: Rutgers University Press, 1984); Robert D. Johnston, *The Radical Middle Class: Populist Democracy and the Question of Capitalism in Progressive Era Portland, Oregon* (Princeton, NJ: Princeton University Press, 2003); Nelson Lichtenstein and Howell John Harris, eds., *Industrial Democracy in America: The Ambiguous Promise* (Cambridge: Cambridge University Press, 1993); Liette Gidlow, *The Big Vote: Gender, Consumer Culture, and the Politics of Exclusion, 1890s–1920s* (Baltimore: Johns Hopkins University Press, 2004); Paul W. Glad, "Progressives and the Business Culture of the 1920s," *Journal of American History* 53, no. 1 (June 1966): 75–89; and Richard Schneirov, "The Odyssey of William English Walling: Revisionism, Social Democracy, and Evolutionary Pragmatism," *Journal of the Gilded Age and Progressive Era* 2, no. 4 (Oct. 2003): 403–30. Arthur S. Link, "What Happened to the Progressive Movement in the 1920s?" *American Historical Review* 64, no. 4 (July 1959): 833–51, remains insightful. John P. Diggins, *Mussolini and Fascism: The View from America* (Princeton, NJ: Princeton University Press, 1972) and Benjamin L. Alpers, *Dictators, Democracy, and American Public Culture* (Chapel Hill: University of North Carolina Press, 2003) provide fascinating insights on the allure of authoritarianism. On Herbert Hoover, see Joan Hoff Wilson, *Herbert Hoover: Forgotten Progressive* (Boston: Little Brown, 1975). On Sacco and Vanzetti, see Paul Avrich, *Sacco and Vanzetti: The Anarchist Background* (Princeton, NJ: Princeton University Press, 1991) and Michael M. Topp, *The Sacco and Vanzetti Case: A Brief History with Documents* (New York: Bedford Books, 2005). A recent study is Bruce Watson, *Sacco and Vanzetti: The Men, the Murders, and the Judgment of Mankind* (New York: Viking, 2007).

For the larger political and economic context, including political and social thought in the Progressive Era and beyond, see Michael McGerr, *A Fierce Discontent: The Rise and Fall of the Progressive Movement, 1870–1920* (New York: Oxford University Press, 2003); Daniel T. Rodgers, *Transatlantic Crossings: Social Politics in a Progressive Age* (Cambridge, MA: Harvard University Press, 1998); Lizabeth Cohen, *Making a New Deal: Industrial Workers in Chicago, 1919–1939* (Cambridge: Cambridge University Press,

1990), which also contains an important treatment of consumer culture; Charles Forcey, *The Crossroads of Liberalism: Croly, Weyl, Lippmann, and the Progressive Era, 1900–1925* (London: Oxford University Press, 1961); David Steigerwald, *Wilsonian Idealism in America* (Ithaca, NY: Cornell University Press, 1994); James T. Kloppenberg, *Uncertain Victory: Social Democracy and Progressivism in European and American Thought, 1870–1920* (New York: Oxford University Press, 1986); Edward A. Purcell Jr., *The Crisis of Democratic Theory: Scientific Naturalism and the Problem of Value* (Lexington: University Press of Kentucky, 1973); Howard Brick, *Transcending Capitalism: Visions of a New Society in Modern American Thought* (Ithaca, NY: Cornell University Press, 2006); James Livingston, *Pragmatism and the Political Economy of Cultural Revolution, 1850–1940* (Chapel Hill: University of North Carolina Press, 1997); Colin Gordon, *New Deals: Business, Labor, and Politics in America, 1920–1935* (Cambridge: Cambridge University Press, 1994); and Frank Stricker, "Affluence for Whom?—Another Look at Prosperity and the Working Class in the 1920s," *Labor History* 24, no. 1 (Winter 1983): 5–33.

Important studies of particular thinkers include Ronald Steel, *Walter Lippmann and the American Century* (New York: Vintage, 1980) and Joan C. Tonn, *Mary P. Follett: Creating Democracy, Transforming Management* (New Haven, CT: Yale University Press, 2003). John Dewey was a towering presence in the 1920s and pragmatism was generally influential. See Robert B. Westbrook, *John Dewey and American Democracy* (Ithaca, NY: Cornell University Press, 1991); Alan Ryan, *John Dewey and the High Tide of American Liberalism* (New York: Norton, 1995); Louis Menand, *The Metaphysical Club* (New York: Farrar, Straus and Giroux, 2001); John Patrick Diggins, *The Promise of Pragmatism: Modernism and the Crisis of Knowledge and Authority* (Chicago: University of Chicago Press, 1994); and George Cotkin, "Middle-Ground Pragmatists: The Popularization of Philosophy in American Culture," *Journal of the History of Ideas* 55, no. 2 (April 1994): 283–302. On the origins of industrial psychology and social engineering, see Loren Baritz, *The Servants of Power: A History of the Use of Social Science in American Industry* (1960; reprint, Westport, CT: Greenwood Press, 1974); Richard Gillespie, *Manufacturing Knowledge: A History of the Hawthorne Experiments* (Cambridge: Cambridge University Press, 1991); William Graebner, *The Engineering of Consent: Democracy and Authority in Twentieth-Century America* (Madison: University of Wisconsin Press, 1987); and John M. Jordan, *Machine-Age Ideology: Social Engineering and American Liberalism, 1911–1939* (Chapel Hill: University of North Carolina Press, 1994). See also James Hoopes's lively *False Prophets: The Gurus Who Created Modern Management and Why Their Ideas Are Bad for Business Today* (New York: Basic Books, 2003).

On the Scopes trial, see Edward J. Larson, *Summer for the Gods: The Scopes Trial and America's Continuing Debate over Science and Religion* (New York: Basic Books, 1997); Michael Lienesch, *In the Beginning: Fundamentalism, the Scopes Trial, and the Making of the Antievolution Movement* (Chapel Hill: University of North Carolina Press, 2007); Paul K. Conkin, *When All the Gods Trembled: Darwinism, Scopes, and American Intellectuals* (Lanham, MD: Rowman & Littlefield, 1998); and Willard B. Gatewood Jr., ed., *Controversy in the Twenties: Fundamentalism, Modernism, and Evolution* (Nashville, TN: Vanderbilt University Press, 1969). George M. Marsden, *Fundamentalism and American Culture* (New York: Oxford University Press, 2006) is indispensable on fundamentalism. On liberal Protestantism, see William R. Hutchison, *The Modernist Impulse in American Protestantism* (Cambridge, MA: Harvard University Press, 1976); Gary Dorrien, *The Making of American Liberal Theology: Idealism, Realism, and Modernity, 1900–1950* (Louisville: Westminster John Knox Press, 2003); and Richard Wightman Fox, "The Culture of Liberal Protestantism, 1875–1925," *Journal of Interdisciplinary History* 22, no. 3 (Winter 1993): 639–60. Also consult Richard Wightman Fox, *Reinhold Niebuhr: A Biography* (San Francisco: Harper and Row, 1985). On Catholicism, see William M. Halsey, *The Survival of American Innocence: Catholicism in an Era of Disillusionment, 1920–1940* (Notre Dame, IN: University of Notre Dame Press, 1980); Philip Gleason, *Contending with Modernity: Catholic Higher Education in the Twentieth Century* (New York: Oxford University Press, 1995); and John T. McGreevy, *Catholicism and American Freedom: A History* (New York: Norton, 2003). Eugene McCarraher, *Christian Critics: Religion and the Impasse in Modern American Social Thought* (Ithaca, NY: Cornell University Press, 2000) contains an insightful chapter on the 1920s.

The best study of new humanism is J. David Hoeveler Jr., *The New Humanism: A Critique of Modern America, 1900–1940* (Charlottesville: University Press of Virginia, 1977). On the southern agrarians, see Paul V. Murphy, *The Rebuke of History: The Southern Agrarians and American Conservative Thought* (Chapel Hill: University of North Carolina Press, 2001); Louis D. Rubin Jr., *The Wary Fugitives: Four Poets and the South* (Baton Rouge: Louisiana State University Press, 1978); Mark G. Malvasi, *The Unregenerate South: The Agrarian Thought of John Crowe Ransom, Allen Tate, and Donald Davidson* (Baton Rouge: Louisiana State University Press, 1997); and Paul Conkin, *The Southern Agrarians* (Knoxville: University of Tennessee Press, 1988). On southern intellectual life generally, see Michael O'Brien, *The Idea of the American South, 1920–1941* (Baltimore: Johns Hopkins University Press, 1990); and Daniel Joseph Singal, *The War Within: From Victorian to Modernist Thought in the South, 1919–1945* (Chapel Hill: University of North Carolina Press, 1982).

Index